# New Directions in Congressional Politics

As the U.S. Congress has steadily evolved, so too has our understanding of the institution. *New Directions in Congressional Politics* offers an accessible overview of the current developments in our understanding of America's legislative branch. Jamie L. Carson helps students to bridge the gap between roles, rules, and outcomes by focusing on four themes woven throughout: the importance of *electoral considerations*, legislators' *strategic* behavior to accomplish objectives, the unique challenges of Congress as a *bicameral* institution, and the often-overlooked *policy outputs* of the institution.

This book brings together leading scholars of Congress to provide a general overview of the entire field. Each chapter covers the cutting-edge developments on its respective topic. As the political institution responsible for enacting laws, the American public regularly looks to the U.S. Congress to address the important issues of the day. The contributors in this volume help explain why staying atop the research trends helps us better understand these issues.

**Jamie L. Carson** is Associate Professor of political science at the University of Georgia, where his research is focused on congressional politics and elections, American political development, and separation of powers. He is the recipient of numerous teaching and research awards.

# New Directions in American Politics

The Routledge series *New Directions in American Politics* is composed of contributed volumes covering key areas of study in the field of American politics and government. Each title provides a state-of-the-art overview of current trends in its respective subfield, with an eye toward cutting-edge research accessible to advanced undergraduate and beginning graduate students. While the volumes touch on the main topics of relevant study, they are not meant to cover the "nuts and bolts" of the subject. Rather, they engage readers in the most recent scholarship, real-world controversies, and theoretical debates with the aim of getting students excited about the same issues that animate scholars.

Titles in the Series:

# New Directions in
# Congressional Politics

Edited by
Jamie L. Carson

Routledge
Taylor & Francis Group

NEW YORK AND LONDON

First published 2012
by Routledge
711 Third Avenue, New York, NY 10017

Simultaneously published in the UK
by Routledge
2 Park Square, Milton Park, Abingdon, Oxon OX14 4RN

*Routledge is an imprint of the Taylor & Francis Group, an informa business*

*Library of Congress Cataloging in Publication Data*
New directions in Congressional politics / edited by Jamie L. Carson.
    p. cm.—(New directions in American politics)
    Includes bibliographical references and index.
    1. United States. Congress. 2. United States—
Politics and government—1989- I. Carson, Jamie L.
JK1021.N49 2011
328.73—dc22
2011002629

ISBN13: 978–0–415–88526–3 (hbk)
ISBN13: 978–0–415–88527–0 (pbk)
ISBN13: 978–0–203–83984–3 (ebk)

Typeset in Minion & Gillsans by Swales & Willis Ltd, Exeter, Devon
Printed and bound in the United States of America on acid-free paper by
Edwards Brothers, Inc.

SUSTAINABLE FORESTRY INITIATIVE  Certified Fiber Sourcing  www.sfiprogram.org

# Contents

# Tables

# Figures

# Preface

For those of us who analyze the U.S. Congress, it can be difficult at times to convey our sense of enthusiasm to our students about studying this legislative institution. Much of the day-to-day activity and procedural minutiae that transpires on the floor of the House or Senate might seem like "inside" baseball to the uninitiated. Yet, as the national institution responsible for making our laws, it is important that everyone has a solid understanding of how individual members get elected, the role of committees, leaders, and parties in the lawmaking process, and why legislative outcomes look the way they do. As one of three main branches of government, the U.S. Congress does not function in isolation. Rather, individual members in both chambers attempt to reach legislative compromises with other political actors in order to enact solutions for the issues and problems facing today's citizens. This is especially true in the polarized era of politics that characterizes the contemporary House and Senate.

In the chapters that follow, a number of leading scholarly experts address many of the traditional subjects associated with the study of the U.S. Congress. I want to especially thank the contributors for writing an original set of essays that deal with a variety of interesting and timely issues associated with congressional politics. As someone who has read each of the chapters quite closely, it is no exaggeration to say that I am thoroughly impressed with the overall quality of the individual contributions. Each of the contributors put in a considerable amount of time and effort pulling together their respective chapters. They also graciously dealt with me asking them to make revisions and nudging them gently when it was necessary. Even though it required considerable effort on their part with minimal compensation, all of the authors generously offered to contribute a chapter to the edited volume and for that I am especially grateful.

This book would not exist in its present form if it were not for the encouragement from Michael Kerns, the Acquisitions Editor at Routledge Press. In early 2010, he approached me with the idea of editing a new type of volume on Congress, one that attempted to make cutting-edge scholarly research more accessible to undergraduate and graduate students. After giving the idea of working on an edited volume considerable thought, I decided to pursue the project. Although the entire process involved a fairly substantial amount of work, I am very pleased with the final outcome and I want to thank Michael for his hard work and dedication. I also want to thank editorial assistant Mary Altman and production editor Gail Newton who were extremely helpful along the way. Additionally, I want to thank the Taylor & Francis Project Manager, Colin Morgan, as well as Rachel Hutchings, who copyedited the manuscript. Lastly, I want to thank the scholars who anonymously reviewed the text. Their comments were incredibly helpful and made the book project even better in the end. At the end of the day, I hope you find the book useful in the classroom.

*Athens, Georgia*
*December 2010*

# Contributors

**Jamie L. Carson** is Associate Professor in the Department of Political Science at the University of Georgia. He received his Ph.D. from Michigan State University in 2003 and studies primarily congressional politics and elections. His work has appeared in such journals as the *American Political Science Review*, *American Journal of Political Science*, the *Journal of Politics*, *Legislative Studies Quarterly*, *Political Analysis*, and *Political Research Quarterly*. He is currently revising a book manuscript, co-authored with Jason Roberts (UNC), entitled, *Ambition, Competition, and Electoral Reform: The Politics of Congressional Elections Across Time.*

**Michael H. Crespin** is Assistant Professor of Political Science at the University of Georgia. His research interests include American politics, Congress, and Political Geography. Professor Crespin's work has been published in the *American Journal of Political Science*, the *Journal of Politics*, *Legislative Studies Quarterly*, and other political science journals.

**Erik J. Engstrom** is Associate Professor of Political Science at the University of California, Davis. He received his Ph.D. in 2003 from the University of California, San Diego. His research on congressional elections has appeared in the *American Political Science Review*, the *American Journal of Political Science*, and *Legislative Studies Quarterly*. His current research focuses on congressional elections, electoral laws, and the evolution of American political institutions.

**C. Lawrence Evans** is the Newton Family Professor of Government at the College of William and Mary. His books include *Congress Under Fire* (1997) and *Leadership in Committee* (2001). He has been an APSA Congressional Fellow (1991–92), associate staff to chairman Lee H. Hamilton on the Joint Committee on the Organization of the U.S. Congress (1992–93) and the Joint Economic Committee (1993–94), and co-editor of the *Legislative Studies Quarterly* (2003–07). Evans is the recipient of several awards for research and teaching.

**Charles J. Finocchiaro** is Assistant Professor of Political Science at the University of South Carolina. He specializes in legislative politics with a focus on the role of political parties and committees in the procedural process, the organization and development of American political institutions, and congressional elections. His published work on these topics, as well as earmarks and killer amendments, appears in numerous outlets including *Legislative Studies Quarterly, Political Research Quarterly, American Politics Research*, and various edited volumes.

**Jeffery A. Jenkins** is Associate Professor in the Department of Politics and Faculty Associate in the Miller Center of Public Affairs at the University of Virginia. He received his Ph.D. from the University of Illinois-Urbana in 1999. His work has appeared in such journals as the *American Journal of Political Science*, the *Journal of Politics, Legislative Studies Quarterly, Studies in American Political Development*, and *Perspectives on Politics*. He is currently finishing up a book manuscript, co-authored with Charles Stewart III (MIT), entitled, *Fighting for the Speakership: The House and the Rise of Party Government*, which will be published by Princeton University Press.

**Anthony J. Madonna** is Assistant Professor in the Political Science Department at the University of Georgia. He received his Ph.D. from Washington University in St. Louis in 2008. His work has appeared in such journals as the *American Journal of Political Science, Presidential Studies Quarterly, Political Research Quarterly*, and *Perspectives on Politics*.

**Cherie Maestas**, Associate Professor at Florida State University, studies the linkages between citizens and government. Her research on legislative elections focuses on how lower level political offices foster ambitions for higher offices. She also examines consequences of ambitions for legislative activities and citizen representation. She is one of the principal investigators on the multi-election Candidate Emergence Study and her work has appeared in numerous journals and books in Political Science.

**Bryan W. Marshall** is Associate Professor of Political Science at Miami University. He received his Ph.D. while a fellow with the Political Institutions and Public Choice (PIPC) program at Michigan State University. His areas of specialization include Congress, congressional-executive relations, separation of powers, and quantitative methods. Marshall's research on Congress focuses on how party leaders and procedures affect coalition building and congressional behavior. Bryan's first book, *Rules for War* (2005), looks at the effects of legislative rules on policymaking. Marshall is also keenly interested in questions related to congressional power in relation to the Supreme Court and executive. Bryan's second book with Richard Pacelle and Brett Curry is titled *Decision Making on the Modern Supreme Court: Creating the Living Law and Maintaining the Constitutional Shield* (forthcoming 2011). The book analyzes major theories of judicial decision-making and offers a theory emphasizing conditions in which the president and Congress affect the Court as well as legal precedent, issues, and judicial preferences. Marshall's recent articles appear in *Legislative Studies Quarterly, Journal of Theoretical Politics, American Politics Research, Conflict Management and Peace Science, Presidential Studies Quarterly,* and *Social Science Quarterly.* In addition, Bryan recently served as APSA's Steiger Congressional Fellow (2008–09) working for the House Majority Whip, the Honorable Jim Clyburn.

**Nathan W. Monroe** (Ph.D., UC San Diego, 2004) is Associate Professor of Political Science at UC Merced. He studies American politics with a focus on legislatures, especially the U.S. Congress. He is co-editor of *Why Not Parties? Party Effects in the United States Senate* (2008, University of Chicago Press), and co-author of *Agenda Setting in the U.S. Senate: Costly Consideration and Majority Party Advantage* (forthcoming, Cambridge University Press). His research has also been published in the *Journal of Politics, Legislative Studies Quarterly, Political Research Quarterly,* and *State Politics and Policy Quarterly,* and the *Election Law Journal.* Prior to joining the faculty at UC Merced, Monroe held faculty positions at the University of the Pacific, and at Michigan State University.

**Anthony J. Nownes** is Professor of Political Science at the University of Tennessee. He received his Ph.D. from the University of Kansas. His research on interest groups has appeared in *American Politics Research, British Journal of Political Science,* and *Journal of Politics.* His second book, *Total Lobbying: What Lobbyists Want (and How They Try to Get It)* was published by Cambridge University Press in 2006.

**Jason M. Roberts** is Associate Professor of Political Science at the University of North Carolina. He received his Ph.D. in 2005 from Washington University in St. Louis. Roberts' research focuses on historical institutionalism, congressional procedure, and congressional elections. His work has appeared in such journals as the *American Political Science Review, American Journal of Political Science,* the *Journal of Politics,* and *Legislative Studies Quarterly.* He is currently revising a book manuscript, co-authored with Jamie L. Carson (UGA), entitled, *Ambition, Competition, and Electoral Reform: The Politics of Congressional Elections Across Time.*

**Charles Stewart III** is Kenan Sahin Distinguished Professor of Political Science at the Massachusetts Institute of Technology. He received his Ph.D. from Stanford in 1985 and has been a faculty member at MIT ever since. Professor Stewart has written broadly about congressional politics, election reform, and American political history. He is the author or co-editor of four books and numerous journal articles about Congress and co-author with Jeff Jenkins (Virginia) of the forthcoming *Fighting for the Speakership: The House and the Rise of Party Government.* With Wendy Schiller (Brown), he is beginning a new book manuscript that examines the election of U.S. senators before the passage of the 17th Amendment.

**Melissa Stewart** is Assistant Professor of Political Science at Texas A&M University Corpus Christi. Her research interests include the influence of conference committee appointments on the votes of members of Congress as well as the role of political parties in American politics. Specifically, her current research attempts to answer questions related to the role that political party identification plays in voter response to female candidates as well as negative campaign advertising. Her previous work on Women and politics has been published in *Politics and Policy* as well as *Legislative Women: Getting Elected, Getting Ahead.*

**Andrew J. Taylor** is Professor of Political Science in the School of Public and International Affairs at North Carolina State University. He received his Ph.D. from the University of Connecticut in 1995. His work has appeared in such journals as the *American Journal of Political Science, Legislative Studies Quarterly, American Politics Research*, and *Political Research Quarterly*. He is currently finishing up a book manuscript entitled, *The Floor in Congressional Life* for University of Michigan Press.

**Sarah A. Treul** is Assistant Professor of Political Science at the University of North Carolina at Chapel Hill. She received her Ph.D. from the University of Minnesota in 2009. Treul's research focuses on American political institutions, including the U.S. Congress, Courts and the separation of powers. Her recent work has appeared in the *Journal of Politics* and *American Politics Research.*

# Part I

# Overview

## New Directions in Congressional Politics

# Introduction

*Jamie L. Carson*

Congress is a dynamic institution. Since the country's founding, the U.S. Congress has steadily evolved in response to the changing political landscape. Although certain similarities exist to the early congresses, much has changed across the two legislative chambers over the past 200+ years. In addition to procedural changes, competitive elections regularly bring new members to both the House and Senate. Consider the recent 2010 election, which resulted in the biggest turnover at the midterm for either party since 1938. After four years of Democratic control, the Republicans regained majority status in the House of Representatives and will have to work in the next two years with a Democratic President and Senate. The 112th Congress will also be one of the most polarized in history, harking back to levels of partisan polarization that have not been seen in this country since the Civil War. When one factors in the current budget deficits, debates over taxes, and the lingering economic turmoil in the nation, it is clear that Congress will continue to play a central role in politics in the years to come.

Studies of congressional politics are often at the forefront of research on American politics and political institutions. Given the complexities associated with numerous aspects of congressional politics, we often rely on cutting-edge research to make sense of political changes and new developments in the House and Senate. Unfortunately, much of the most important research on congressional politics is published in academic journals, whose target audience is either professors or advanced graduate students. This research tends to address fairly narrow questions one at a time or in the context of a specialized debate, often without the necessary background to allow those not working within the subfield to fully understand. Moreover, an increasing proportion of this research requires advanced statistical knowledge to evaluate these findings. As a result, many aspects of the study of congressional politics can seem confusing and incoherent to undergraduates. To better engage students in the classroom, we need a new type of textbook that can overcome these specific limitations.

*New Directions in Congressional Politics* offers an accessible and coherent overview of the current state of research on the U.S. Congress. This book brings together leading scholars of congressional politics in one edited volume that deals with myriad important topics. Along the way, a number of important themes in the study of Congress are considered throughout the text: 1) Although representatives have multiple goals in office, their behavior is often motivated by electoral considerations; 2) Legislators often behave strategically in order to accomplish their individual or collective objectives; 3) Congress is a bicameral institution, which often provides a unique set of challenges in the legislative process given the need to reconcile differences in legislation across the two chambers; and 4) An examination of policy outputs and the legislative process is often overlooked in the scholarly research on the institution, but is vitally important.

In terms of specific topics covered in the edited volume, Chapter 1 begins by considering the recent turn to history in the field of congressional studies. The author of this chapter, Jeffery A. Jenkins, argues that scholars have incorporated congressional history in three distinct ways. First, congressional history has been used to test the robustness of existing theories, because certain behavioral conditions or institutional arrangements may have only existed in the past. In other words, history has offered new ways of studying a particular theoretical issue, which has led to the extension or refinement of general theories. Second, congressional history has been used to build new theories. For example, modern theories often take certain institutional features, such as the committee system, rules of procedure, and the party system, as givens, in order to pursue more contemporary theoretical questions. However, these institutional features are *endogenous*, resulting from institutional choices made by members of Congress in bygone eras. This has opened the door for students of Congress to use congressional history to develop new theories of institutional development. Finally, congressional history has been a site for social-scientific investigations. This constitutes a sort of "normal science" approach, which involves a substantive, case-specific inquiry, rather than an attempt at theory building or theory extension/refinement.

The second and third chapters highlight the electoral foundations of Congress, first by examining who runs for Congress. As Cherie Maestas and Melissa Stewart note in Chapter 2, a growing body of legislative scholarship recognizes the role of strong congressional candidates in promoting democratic outcomes. Nevertheless, in order to have competitive elections, you need willing candidates to emerge, something that is often in short supply in modern elections. In an attempt to systematically examine candidate emergence, this chapter draws together important themes in recent scholarship to highlight the individual, contextual, and institutional factors that influence the strategic choices of candidates as they consider running for Congress. Additionally, the chapter highlights several understudied areas, including the role of parties in recruitment and campaigning, the role of electoral institutions in shaping candidacy decisions, and the role of sub-national political institutions in building a broad pool of high-quality potential candidates for Congress.

In Chapter 3, Erik J. Engstrom argues that one can frame the last thirty years of scholarship on congressional election as a quest to explain the relative lack of competition in congressional elections. Most incumbents, most of the time, appear insulated from national political tides. This chapter explores current trends in the study of congressional elections by focusing on the changing dynamics of electoral competition. It first places modern congressional elections in a historical context, showing trends over time in the translation of vote swings into changes in legislative membership. It then examines three areas of current research that attempt to explain changes in electoral competition: district design, the influence of national and local electoral forces, and the incumbency advantage. The chapter concludes by discussing possible future directions in the study of congressional elections.

The next few chapters focus on key institutional features of the modern Congress. In Chapter 4, C. Lawrence Evans reviews scholarship about the roles that party leaders in the two chambers play in the lawmaking process, including formulation of party legislative agendas, the involvement of party leaders during the committee stage of the legislative process, and party leadership tactics on the floor. The emphasis here is on the strengths and weaknesses of existing scholarship about leadership strategies and tactics and the ability of leaders to exert independent impact on legislative outcomes. The core of the chapter is a discussion of how increased levels of polarization have altered the strategies parties and leaders employ to achieve preferred policy outcomes. Like much of the earlier chapters, it closes with a discussion of topics in need of further research, providing concrete approaches for conducting this research, including potential data sources.

The goal of Chapter 5, according to Charles Stewart III, is to discuss the traditional view of congressional committees—one that focuses on their relative autonomy—and then document their gradual evolution across time. Committees have long been considered the lynchpin of congressional activity. They embody the expertise that allows Congress, alone among major world parliaments, to legislate independently of the executive. Committees have also been associated with congressional dysfunctions, such as the fragmentation of policymaking and the persistence of "iron triangles." What few people appreciate, however, is that committees have changed significantly across the past two decades. On the one hand, their operations have become more closely tied to the agendas of the two political parties. On the other hand, party leaders, especially in the House, have increasingly channeled important legislation away from committees. The chapter concludes with suggestions about where scholars should look next in terms of understanding recent developments in committee politics.

In Chapter 6, Jason M. Roberts reviews the historical development and modern uses of House rules and procedures. The chapter starts with the development of the majoritarian House and covers the "Czar" era in the late nineteenth and early twentieth centuries, the conservative coalition era, as well as the recent polarization of the two major parties. The history and development of "special rules" and their innovative uses over time are discussed as well. Special emphasis is given to recent scholarship that highlights the factors that explain formal changes in House rules and the procedural evolution of House rules over time.

To give equal time to procedures in the U.S. Senate, Anthony J. Madonna highlights this topic in Chapter 7. Although the Senate has many distinguishing institutional features, the ability of a minority to defeat legislation by filibustering is unquestionably the most well known. Despite the prominence of the filibuster, political scientists have been unable to come to a consensus on why the institution persists. Scholars on one side argue there have been times when Senate majorities have been blocked from altering the chamber's debate rules by minorities. An alternative account suggests that the Senate's rules reflect the preferences of majorities. The two scholarly camps reach competing conclusions on whether the Senate's rules are harmful to policy output. This chapter speaks to this important debate over Senate procedure in three ways. First, it provides a detailed comparison of both theoretical explanations. Second, it reevaluates the empirical and qualitative evidence cited in support of both. Finally, the chapter identifies several potential research questions that could shed further light on this debate.

In Chapter 8, Andrew J. Taylor begins with a discussion of how congressional scholars have traditionally studied floor voting—by evaluating important individual roll calls or clusters of roll calls on a particular policy issue. He then looks at the many efforts to analyze roll calls in the aggregate that have been used to place legislators in a policy space and explain the importance of party affiliation in congressional politics. In both cases, attention is paid to the many variables congressional scholars believe influence the way members vote— party leadership, ideology, constituent preferences, interest group lobbying, and presidential pressure. Finally, he examines an eclectic array of approaches to the study of floor voting undertaken in recent years. These include, but are not limited to, work on voice voting, super-majority rules, the timing of votes, "vote buying" and coalition building, coalition sizes, sophisticated voting, status quo points, and pivotal members.

How do conference committees affect policy outcomes in Congress? Renewed interest in this question during the last decade has sparked several distinct, but necessarily interrelated, strains of congressional scholarship. Namely, there have been recent surges in research seeking to understand the determinants of who is appointed to serve on conference committees, the bill level changes that occur during the conference process, and the degree to which the Senate and House use conference as a means of either inheriting or forfeiting certain policy provisions. In Chapter 9, Nathan W. Monroe surveys the current state of these research trends, and calls for a theoretical "unification" of these topics, as a means of more fully understanding the benefits and potential pitfalls of this procedural regularity in Congress.

The remaining chapters in the book focus more directly on the policymaking process in Congress. In Chapter 10, Bryan W. Marshall focuses on the relationship between Congress and the executive. By design, the U.S. Constitution invites competition for power between Congress and the president. What are the factors and strategies that affect the ebb-and-flow of this power struggle? Richard Neustadt's framework has profoundly shaped decades of research and established a persistent theme in the literature—one that judges power based on the president's ability to prod Congress through bargaining and persuasion. The study of presidential appeals, veto bargaining, and coalition building in Congress represent just a few of the important strategies useful for understanding this view of congressional-executive interactions. However, recent work on presidential unilateralism—strategies employed to advance presidential goals in the face of a recalcitrant Congress—have offered another important dimension to understanding the power struggle between branches. Indeed, presidents have increasingly relied upon tools such as executive orders, international agreements, recess appointments, and signing statements to achieve their ends. Although these different views are distinct in the literature and seemingly in tension, they are not incompatible. This chapter surveys and compares these areas of research in order to assess the scope of theoretical understanding, highlight contradictions and/or puzzles, and offer some avenues for future research in congressional-executive relations.

Chapter 11 reviews scholarship on the relationship between the courts and Congress. More specifically, Sarah A. Treul investigates the role the Senate plays in the confirmation of Supreme Court justices, justices as policymakers, and the Court's influence on representation through redistricting and campaign finance decisions. The chapter then analyzes legislative responses to Court decisions, specifically focusing on the Court's latest decision in *Citizens United v. Federal Election Commission*. When does Congress choose to respond to the Court? Under what circumstances does the Court invite Congress to respond to its decision? These important questions are carefully considered and the chapter concludes with a discussion of topics in need of further research.

In Chapter 12, Anthony J. Nownes discusses the role of lobbyists and the interest groups they represent in the congressional process. Specifically, he examines who lobbyists represent, what they do, and the extent to which they get what they want in the policymaking process. Additionally, this chapter reviews two competing perspectives on interest group influence in Congress: subgovernment theory and neopluralism. Finally, the chapter examines what is probably the most important role played by interest groups in the legislative process—reducing transaction costs by providing information to individual legislators.

Michael H. Crespin and Charles J. Finocchiaro discuss the topic of congressional spending in Chapter 13. Narrowly targeted projects inserted into congressional spending bills—often referred to as earmarks—have garnered considerable attention from candidates, elected officials, and the media in recent years. A common criticism is that they are politically motivated tools by which members of Congress circumvent the typical budgetary process for self-seeking electoral gain. In this chapter, the authors trace the evolution and current practices surrounding earmarks. After describing the trends and scope of earmarking in Congress, they examine one of the most heavily criticized aspects of the process—when "pork" is added at the end of the legislative process, in the fairly obscure conference committee process—to determine the relative winners and losers. The authors conclude with a discussion of recent efforts at reform and the underlying challenges to altering the institutional landscape in Congress.

# Part II

# Historical and Electoral Foundations

# Chapter 1

# Studying Congress Historically[1]

*Jeffery A. Jenkins*

In recent years, an increasing number of political scientists have set their Way-back Machines[2] for travel to earlier eras in order to study various aspects of congressional history. This trend is remarkable in that, not long ago, most students of Congress focused almost exclusively on contemporaneous events and behaviors, to the point where (testing the boundaries of hyperbole) a casual observer of the literature might think that the institution did not exist prior to World War II. This propensity to ignore the past can be explained in part by data constraints, as systematic member, constituency, and electoral data for the pre-1940s period had, until only recently, been in short supply. Yet, this did not prevent such luminaries as Joseph Cooper (1970), Nelson Polsby (1968; 1969, with coauthors), David Brady (1973, 1991), Samuel Kernell (1977a), and Charles Stewart III (1989) from carrying out their masterful studies.[3] Moreover, the necessity of collecting data has never prevented scholars from exploring new or understudied questions relating to the *contemporary* Congress. Another explanation, therefore, must be in order. I posit that congressional scholars typically have not considered the net benefit of studying congressional history to be sufficiently high. Why has this been the case?

Certainly, doing congressional history has never been an especially "sexy" endeavor. Flipping through dusty old journals, digging around in poorly organized archives, and growing dizzy scrolling through old newspapers on microfiche has left a lot to be desired. Nor has congressional history traditionally been considered cutting edge. In fact, it has not been unusual for some political scientists to question the worth of doing historical research at all, suggesting that little can be learned from events and interactions that took place 100, 150, or 200 years ago. To understand why members of Congress vote, interact with constituents, and pursue reelection as they do, scholars have generally immersed themselves in the changing dynamics of the contemporary legislative and electoral environments.

This tendency to focus almost exclusively on the contemporary Congress is understandable. Most theories of congressional behavior and organization in recent decades, after all, have been designed in the "here and now," and it is only natural that most empirically driven political scientists have concentrated on deriving and testing hypotheses from those countervailing theories. Yet, beginning a little more than a decade ago, more and more political scientists began directing their energies toward the study of congressional history. This was due partly to new data gathering efforts that had begun to emerge—such efforts would eventually produce complete voting histories and preference (or "ideological") measures for all members (Poole and Rosenthal 1997), as well as fuller constituency snapshots (Parsons, Beach, and Dubin 1986; Parsons, Dubin, and Toombs Parsons 1990), cleaner partisan codings (Martis 1989), and more complete electoral data (Dubin 1998). Moreover, technological advances have made finding congressional voting records and biographical information, debates and proceedings, and election results—as well as newspaper stories on Congress—back to the late eighteenth century a trivial matter, requiring only a computer, an internet connection, and a couple of key strokes.[4] Thus, for scholars of Congress, the cost of studying congressional history has decreased considerably in recent years.

This data "windfall" and accompanying electronic availability, however, is only part of the story. Another explanation is based on a change in the way Congress has been studied by legislative scholars. As rational-choice theorists in the 1970s began to realize the importance of studying legislative rules, processes, and structures, the view of Congress as a venue for sociological-based analysis of elite behavior, typified by Truman (1959) and Matthews (1960), gradually gave way to one that emphasized the study of legislative behaviors and outcomes through the lens of institutions. This movement, termed "The New Institutionalism," traces its origins to research by Rohde and Shepsle (1978) and Shepsle (1979) and often required a "before and after" analysis, along the lines of: how did legislative voting and/or outcomes change after an institutional innovation? The first generation of such before-and-after analyses focused on post-World War II institutional innovations; eventually, scholars turned their attention to innovations from earlier eras to conduct lengthier comparative (across-time) analyses. Such analyses allowed for more and different institutional variation. History thus provided for the natural evolution in institutional analyses.

Thanks to greater data availability, technological advances, and new theoretical directions, then, students of Congress began to realize that congressional history was a lush, untapped resource that could be used to advance a number of intellectual agendas. With that realization came a rush of interesting and creative studies in the mid-to-late 1990s, and an even greater expansion in the first decade of the twenty-first century.

The use and application of congressional history has taken three general forms: (1) testing the robustness of existing theories; (2) building new theories; and (3) explaining historical events. These three forms are not mutually exclusive, as scholars have sometimes traversed their boundaries in pursuit of scientific inquiry. Nevertheless, for simplicity, I treat them as separate for this discussion.

## Testing the Robustness of Existing Theories

Congressional history can be used to test the robustness of existing theories, because certain behavioral conditions or institutional arrangements that offer different perspectives on theoretical questions may have only existed in the past. In other words, history can offer "new" ways of studying a particular theoretical issue, which might lead to the extension or refinement of the general theory.

One example is the notion of the "electoral connection," which holds that members of Congress are held accountable for their actions and behaviors by their constituents through the electoral process. Until recently, the electoral connection had always been considered a relatively contemporary phenomenon, the assumption being that electoral accountability required constituents to possess the ability to punish candidates *selectively*, a scenario only in place since the rise of the Australian (secret) ballot in the 1890s. Prior to the Australian-ballot movement, constituents were forced to vote by party ballot, which made it difficult to punish a given candidate without voting against an entire party. Moreover, Mayhew (1974a) has argued that the electoral connection has grown appreciably stronger in recent decades, as parties-in-elections have grown weaker and candidate-centered campaigns have grown in prominence.

Research by Bianco, Spence, and Wilkerson (1996), Carson et al. (2001), and Carson and Engstrom (2005), however, suggests that an electoral connection was present much earlier during the nineteenth century, when party ballots were the norm and congressional parties controlled campaigns with an iron fist. In all three cases, congressional incumbents were punished by their constituents for their policy choices—which ranged from voting for a congressional pay-raise in 1816 (Bianco et al.), to support for the ineffective Republican-led war effort during the Civil War (Carson et al.), to voting for John Quincy Adams in the 1825 House election for president when constituents voted for Andrew Jackson in the popular election (Carson and Engstrom). These cases suggest that the electoral connection is more robust than was originally thought, and might simply require the existence of regular, district-level elections without the additional assumptions of a secret ballot and candidate-centered campaigns. Recently, Carson and Jenkins (2011) have investigated the temporality of the electoral connection in much greater depth—in effect, unpacking the electoral connection into its component parts of ambition, autonomy, responsiveness, and accountability—and argue that most aspects of the contemporary electoral connection existed in some form (perhaps weaker and/or less formalized) as early as the late eighteenth or early nineteenth century.

Another example is the degree to which parties influence member behavior in Congress, which stems from a lively debate that has raged in the congressional literature over the past two decades regarding whether partisan or majoritarian influences more strongly shape the institution. At the heart of this debate is the question of whether parties exert an independent influence on members' vote choices or members simply vote their preferences absent any party influence (for the beginnings of this debate, see Krehbiel (1991, 1993), Rohde (1991, 1994), and Cox and McCubbins (1993)). While most participants in the debate have used contemporary (post-World War II) data to make their respective cases, some scholars have recently turned to congressional history for a fresher angle. Perhaps not surprisingly, historical research has not converged on a definitive conclusion in the partisan–majoritarian debate.[5]

Jenkins (1999), in a comparative analysis of the partisan U.S. Congress and non-partisan Confederate Congress during the Civil War, finds evidence of significant party effects. Snyder and Groseclose (2000) leverage "close" votes in the House between 1871 and 1988 and uncover evidence of significant party pressure on a range of votes, especially procedural votes. Schickler (2000), in an investigation of the determinants of institutional change in Congress between 1867 and 1998, finds stronger evidence for majoritarian influences than partisan influences. Schickler (2001), in a detailed and mainly qualitative analysis of four periods in congressional history beginning in the late nineteenth century, argues that party is sometimes influential and sometimes is trumped by other factors. Cox and Poole (2002) use the Rice index of party dissimilarity and find strong evidence of party influence in the House back to 1877, influence that (consistent with Snyder and Groseclose) is strongest on procedural votes. Finally, Binder (2006), in a critique of Schickler (2000), extends the institutional-change data series back to 1789 and discovers that partisan influences were stronger than Schickler had claimed, especially during the antebellum period.

Students of legislative politics have also examined how well various theories of congressional elections hold up across time. For example, Carson and Roberts (2005), in their analysis of strategic politicians during the late nineteenth and early twentieth centuries, find that experienced candidates exhibit behavior that is remarkably similar to candidates in the contemporary era. Building on their results in conjunction with Engstrom's (2006) work on nineteenth-century redistricting, Carson, Engstrom, and Roberts (2006) find that candidates are more likely to emerge in House races when their congressional districts are drawn in a favorable, partisan manner. On a related point, Engstrom and Kernell (2005) find that ballot structure and redistricting efforts played an important and significant role in influencing electoral outcomes in House races. Lastly, Carson, Engstrom, and Roberts (2007) uncover strong evidence of an incumbency effect in late nineteenth-century House elections, casting doubt on contemporary explanations for the emergence and growth of the incumbency advantage over time.[6]

## Building New Theories

Congressional history can also be used to build new theories. For example, modern theories of Congress often take certain institutional features, such as the committee system, rules of procedure, and the party system, as givens, in order to pursue more contemporary theoretical questions. Yet, these institutional features are *endogenous*, resulting from institutional choices made by members of Congress in bygone eras. This has opened the door for students of Congress to use congressional history to develop new theories of institutional development.

The development of the standing committee system was an obvious candidate for an extended theoretical examination. Cooper (1970) first tackled the subject with regard to the House in a rigorous way using an organizational theory approach, but little additional work followed over the next two decades. In time, Gamm and Shepsle (1989) and Jenkins (1998) revisited Cooper's work, using a rational choice (more specifically, a New Institutionalist) approach. They argue that standing committees became predominant in chamber politics not so much because of increased external demands as Cooper (1970) had argued, but because a stronger standing committee system corresponded to the mutual interests of both Henry Clay, the House Speaker, and the general membership.[7] Jenkins and Stewart (1997, 2002) build on the Gamm–Shepsle–Jenkins approach, but in a more nuanced fashion, arguing that standing committee emergence occurred in stages over time for a variety of reasons, such as efficiency and oversight, in addition to self-interest. Finally, Canon and Stewart (2001, 2002) have moved beyond the House to study the development of the Senate committee system, finding that the Senate initially lagged behind the House in shifting to standing committees but made the *complete* transition to a standing committee system a decade earlier than the House.

The development of congressional rules of procedure was a woefully understudied topic for nearly a century. Scholars interested in the subject were left to consult Harlow (1917), a historical treatment hopelessly out of date. Finally, several studies emerged to fill this gaping hole in the literature, all of which focus on the role of the majority party in instituting change. Binder (1995) examines the adoption of the "previous question" rule in the House, and finds that it was a calculated move by the Jeffersonian majority to control floor debate by suppressing the procedural rights of the Federalist minority. Binder (1997) and Dion (1997), in separate analyses of rules changes during the first part of the nineteenth century, argue that the governing party in Congress (regardless of whether it was the Jeffersonians, Democrats, or Whigs) routinely used its majority status to restrict the procedural rights of the minority party. Fink (2000), in an analysis of rules changes during the first twenty-eight Congresses, finds that the majority party mainly initiated restrictions when it either viewed itself as growing weaker or perceived the minority party as growing stronger.

The origin and development of the political party system in Congress was another subject begging for a more thorough examination. Aside from two works by Hoadley (1980, 1986), students of Congress who were interested in the genesis of congressional parties had to rely largely on sketchy historical accounts, many of which were biographies only tangentially interested in the topic. However, Aldrich (1995) emerged to tackle the subject in force, and has provided a definitive account of the early development of parties in Congress. Relying largely on theories of social and collective choice, Aldrich argues persuasively that members of Congress established parties as "organizational devices" that would allow them to win more often, in both the policy and electoral arenas. Aldrich examines roll-call voting over the first several Congresses and shows how first the Federalists, then, in response, the Democratic-Republicans, became much more cohesive in their collective behaviors.

More recently, others have contributed to the question of party development in Congress. Kolodny (1998) documents the rise of Congressional Campaign Committees (CCCs) after the Civil War, which were created to direct and fund their respective parties' efforts to achieve or maintain majority-party status in the House. Cox and McCubbins (2005) examine how parties became procedurally powerful in the House—or developed into "cartels"—around the turn of the twentieth century. They find evidence that the adoption of the Reed Rules, procedural innovations attributed to House Speaker Thomas Reed (R-ME) in the early-1890s, led to the development of negative agenda (or blocking) power for the majority party—power that the majority has retained, despite a number of internal and external changes, ever since. Roberts and Smith (2007) discuss reasons for the difference in party leadership development in the House and Senate, respectively. They argue that the Senate's lack of both a previous question rule and a presiding officer elected by its membership restricted the majority's ability to control the legislative agenda, relative to that of the House. Finally, Roberts (2010) builds on Roberts and Smith (2007) by focusing specifically on the House, finding that the chamber's decision to grant agenda power to the Rules Committee increased legislative efficiency significantly and allowed the majority party (via special rules) to maintain control over the legislative agenda.

## Explaining Historical Events

Congressional history is also ripe for social-scientific investigations. This constitutes a sort of "normal science" approach, which involves a substantive, case-specific inquiry, rather than an attempt at theory building or theory extension/refinement. In short, historical events have often been documented and interpreted by historians, who perform admirably in the areas of fact-gathering and story-building, but often are not trained in methods for determining causal inference. Political scientists, on the other hand, possess the background to apply statistical techniques to historical questions, to determine if social-scientific findings correspond with historical explanations. As such, modern political science can shed light on the often-murky historical world.

A number of these normal science investigations have appeared in recent years. I mention just a few below.

- Fink (1995) examines the development of the Bill of Rights, and finds that its creation was due to political rather than democratic considerations; that is, the Bill of Rights was less a simple popular initiative than a strategic political concession by the Federalist majority to forestall a growing Anti-Federalist movement.

- Jenkins and Sala (1998) investigate the House election for president in 1825 and find, contrary to the conventional wisdom, little evidence of a "corrupt bargain" between John Quincy Adams and Henry Clay; instead, they discover that House members' votes for president were consistent with their underlying ideological positions.

- Krehbiel and Wiseman (2001) examine the revolt against House Speaker Joseph Cannon in 1910, and find evidence to suggest that Cannon was not a party "czar" or tyrant, as historians generally contend, but rather behaved as a majoritarian, as his committee slates often took on a bipartisan quality. Lawrence, Maltzman, and Wahlbeck (2001) also examine Cannon's behavior as Speaker and tell a more nuanced story, finding that partisanship was one of several factors that help explain Cannon's distribution of committee assignments.

- Theriault (2003) investigates the passage of the Pendleton Act in 1883, and finds that civil-service reform was driven as much by public pressure as by the self-interested machinations of members of Congress. Theriault's argument builds on Johnson and Libecap (1994), who argue that members of Congress passed civil-service reform as a strategic initiative to facilitate their reelection efforts—with more skilled politicians in the civil service, members could better manage their remaining political appointees.

- Jenkins and Stewart (2003) find that the adoption of *viva voce* (or public) balloting for House officers in the late 1830s was not due to a desire to firm up the representative-constituency linkage, but because majority-party leaders sought to eliminate partisan defections and cross-partisan deals that had plagued majority-party governance during the secret-ballot era.

- Clinton and Meirowitz (2004) investigate the Compromise of 1790, and find little evidence of a logroll or "vote trade" between Southern and Northern representatives, as the standard historical account contends; instead, their results suggest that the issues in question (the permanent location of the nation's capitol and assumption of state debt) were dealt with independently.

- Binder (2007) uncovers little evidence that the senatorial practice of issuing holds on judicial nominees (via "blue slips"), which emerged in the early twentieth century, was intentionally designed to undermine the president's ability to influence the makeup of the federal bench; rather, it appears to have been an unintended consequence of an effort to reduce uncertainty in the confirmation process.

## What's Next? Opportunities and Challenges for Historical Congressional Scholars

In covering the major developments in historical congressional research over the past decade and a half, I have no doubt failed to mention some important and influential studies and, for that, I apologize. Nonetheless, I believe my point is clear: congressional history has emerged from the dark recesses of the discipline and vaulted into the mainstream. Doubts about the benefits of historical research have vanished, to the point where congressional history is now viewed as an "exciting" area within congressional studies more generally. The transformation, which has occurred over a fairly short time period, has indeed been remarkable.

This leads to the question: What's next? What opportunities and challenges await young congressional scholars who want to have a go at historical congressional research? I offer some of my thoughts below. While the topics I note do not represent an exhaustive list, they strike me as some obvious ones that can (and likely will) be addressed in the near future.

### Greater Focus on the Senate

The Senate has always been the ugly duckling of congressional research, as scholars have focused a disproportionate amount of attention on the House. In recent years, however, scholars of Congress have been more inclined to focus attention on the Senate and have discovered a range of interesting questions to examine. For example, Schiller and Stewart (2004, 2006, 2008) have investigated how Senate elections were organized and conducted prior to the Seventeenth Amendment (and direct election); Bernhard and Sala (2006), Meinke (2008b), and Gailmard and Jenkins (2009) have examined how senators' behavior has changed after the move from indirect to direct election; and Binder and Smith (1997) and Wawro and Schickler (2006) have participated in a spirited debate on how Senate proceedings were determined—on a majoritarian basis or by unanimity?—before the adoption of Rule XXII (a formal cloture rule).[8]

These research inquiries aside, the Senate remains a fertile venue for interesting and creative research, as many important questions remain largely unexplored. I discuss a range of these potential questions in more detail elsewhere (see Jenkins 2011); here, I offer a quick summary.

Perhaps the biggest question is: How did party leadership in the Senate develop, and how did it affect Senate decision-making across the nineteenth century? For example, the historical role of the Senate majority leader—and how the position evolved from a more informal "floor leader" position—begs for greater explanation. While Smith (2007: 68) notes that the majority leader achieved the "full range of modern leadership responsibilities," including the right of first recognition, in the 1930s, we (as a scholarly community) know very little about even these relatively recent developments.

The general issue of party power in the Senate—and whether it in fact exists on a meaningful level—has generated increased attention in recent years (see Monroe, Roberts, and Rohde 2008). But almost all of that attention has been focused on the modern era, specifically the post-1970s era. Yet, there is evidence that strong parties in the Senate could have been present in earlier eras as well. For example, roll-call data suggest that partisan unity was strong in the Senate between 1890 and 1910—the heyday of party power in the House, when Speakers Reed and Cannon ruled with an iron fist. Historical accounts contend that a group of four Republican senators controlled the Senate agenda at this time (see, e.g., Gould 2005). If so, how was such control accomplished? What mechanisms did these Senate leaders have to maintain partisan unity and prevent defection? Investigating these questions is important, as the literature has relied upon "institutional structure" to explain leadership power in the House (and to posit why such leadership power may not exist—or is weaker—in the Senate).

Another interesting avenue for study involves cross-institutional analyses. One example would be to investigate the timing of institutional adoption across chambers. For example, the House and Senate adopted standing committees (1810s) and caucuses (1840s) around the same time. In each case, it appears that the Senate followed the House. This begs the question: does cross-chamber "learning" go on? Do party leaders in one chamber analyze what institutional choices work (or not) in the other chamber, and copy (or not) accordingly? And are there other examples of institutional copying beyond standing committees and caucuses? Relatedly, the increasing size gap between the House and Senate through the early twentieth century is an institutional (structural) factor that deserves greater attention in future explanations of cross-chamber leadership development. That is, while other (different) cross-chamber choices early in congressional history have been stressed—on presiding-officer capabilities and previous question rule decisions—to explain how party leadership in the two chambers has evolved over time, the differing membership sizes of the House and Senate over time might have also had a significant impact.

### Data and Methodological Issues

As scholars continue to tread into the field of congressional history, lingering data and methodological issues remain to be solved. I note two particular issues, which I think are the most important to address in the near future.

The first issue is mostly data-related. More and more, an increasing number of studies attempt to study congressional behavior across time, leveraging changes in the constituency–representative linkage that underlies the electoral connection. More specifically, scholars seek to establish a link between House members and senators and their geographic constituents, using a variety of demographic and economic data, usually drawn from the decennial U.S. census. Data issues generally do not hamper Senate-based studies in this regard, but House-based studies are another matter. That is, assembling district-level measures is sometimes difficult. In the post-1940s era, such district-based data have been organized by Scott Adler[9]; for the pre-1910s era, such district-based data are typically drawn from the Parsons et al. (1986, 1990) volumes.

Apart from the noticeable gap in available data for the 1910s, 1920s, and 1930s, another problem exists: the mapping between counties (the geographic unit in which most census-based information is organized) and districts is not always one-to-one. Specifically, there are, census to census, a number of cases of multi-district counties—or large counties that are divided into multiple congressional districts. These counties typically fall within large urban areas.

The issue, then, is what to do with these multi-district counties? Or, alternatively, what can be done about districts that are carved out of *parts* of counties? If systematic analysis across time is the goal, these districts cannot be dropped, otherwise important contextual variation is lost (and any effects attributed to urban or rural districts will be lost). One option would be to just assume uniformity across all districts carved out of a single county: for unit-based variables, divide the total by the number of districts; for percentage-based variables, assume that percentage is distributed equally across all districts. This is the decision rule followed by both Adler (2002) and Parsons et al. (1986, 1990).

The problem is that district characteristics are not uniform, and often are *far* from uniform. A case in point is the distribution of racial groups within counties—such groups are often geographically concentrated, which creates significant measurement error in any uniform-based coding scheme. While a multi-district county might only be 20 percent black, for example, those citizens will often live in adjoining neighborhoods and thus reside mainly in one or two districts. But a uniform-based allocation would assign 20 percent black to *every* district carved out of that county, leading to overrepresentation in some districts and significant underrepresentation in others. This is clearly a problem for any study that hinges on race as a major component of representation.

Unfortunately, a simple fix to this problem does not exist. This is because multi-district counties cannot always be reconstructed using ward or precinct data (geographic units that would allow for census-based data collection). Many of these districts are constructed in a much more fine-grained way, often based on street-level data which do not correspond to any census-based data categories. An example of the contours of such a district—the 22nd district in early-1920s New York state, which was carved out of New York City—appears below:

> New York City (beginning at the Harlem River and E. 117th St., and thence westerly along E. 117th St. to 2nd Ave., along 2nd Ave. to E. 118th St., along E. 118th St. to Park Ave., along Park Ave. to E. Morris Park and along 5th Ave. to the Harlem River, and along the Harlem River to W. 145th St., along W. 145 St. to 8th Ave., along 8th Ave. to the Harlem River, thence along the Harlem River to E. 117th St., the point or place of beginning); Bronx (beginning at Jerome Ave. and the Harlem River, thence along

Jerome Ave. to E. 161st St. to Melrose Ave., along Melrose Ave. to E. 157th
St., along E. 157th St. to 3rd Ave., along 3rd Ave. to E 156th St., along E.
156th St. to St. Ann's Ave., along St. Ann's Ave. to E. 149th St., along E.
149th St. to the East River, thence along the East River, Bronx Kills and the
Harlem River to Jerome Ave., to the point or place of beginning; North
Brother's, South Brother's, and Riker's Island).[10]

Perhaps technological advances, like Geographic Information Systems (GIS),
might prove to be a solution to these types of problems. Until then, though,
this problem in geographic mapping will continue to be a hindrance to scholars
interested in conducting systematic studies of representation across time.

The second issue, while related to the first, is more methodological in nature.
Many historical congressional studies that focus on representation incorporate
presidential-vote share, whether at the district or state level, as a proxy for the
general partisanship or ideological leanings of the geographic unit in question.
Without survey-based data, which only become readily available after World
War II, presidential-vote share is often the best measure that is systematically
available across both geographic units (states/districts) and time (congresses).

The problem with using a measure like presidential-vote share in across-
time studies is determining whether it remains explanatorily reliable—is there
temporal consistency? Focusing on the state level, does a 55 percent vote share
for the Democratic presidential candidate (Grover Cleveland) in Georgia in
1884 mean the same thing as a 55 percent vote share for the Democratic presidential candidate (Walter Mondale) in Georgia in 1984? If we (as a scholarly
community) believe that vote share in 1884 and 1984 are *not* tapping the same
underlying phenomenon (in this case, "ideological liberalness"), the question
then is: what are the inferential consequences for creating such an across-time
measure? Aside from measurement error, do other problems also result?

This is an issue, I believe, with which congressional scholars need to struggle
further. Too often we seek data that can be collected across wide spans of time,
without taking care that such data are in fact comparable—or measuring the
same thing—across the period in question. Perhaps a conservative answer to
the general question is that data should only be used within "normal" periods
of politics, when we have a solid grasp of the regularity of the political phenomena underlying our measures. Of course, such a conservative approach would
eliminate lengthy—more than a century, perhaps more than a half-century in
some cases—across-time analyses. There is almost certainly no perfect answer;
nevertheless, engaging the question is a healthy and useful endeavor.

### Congressional History and American Political Development (APD)

A final topic deals with the connection between congressional history and
"traditional" American Political Development (APD). Traditional APD traces

its modern origins as a subfield within American Politics to Skowronek's (1982) masterpiece on state formation in the U.S. The subfield emerged in response to behavioralism's dominant position in the American Politics field and its lack of attention paid to the role of institutions in political life.[11] APD scholarship is largely sociological in nature (and sometimes has a distinctive normative flavor) and thus falls within the larger genre of Historical Institutionalism. APD scholars, at their core, are interested in topics like the development of the state, temporality in decision-making, liberalism, policy feedback, and the interplay of multiple institutions at the national level (see, e.g., Orren and Skowronek 2004).

Despite the theoretical focus of the enterprise, scholars of APD have not made Congress a pivotal player in their research. Rather, the focus has been on the "state of courts and parties" in the nineteenth century and the turn toward bureaucratic development, administrative capacity, and presidential power in the twentieth century. Katznelson and Lapinski (2006) note the glaring absence of Congress in APD accounts and build an entire essay around developing stronger ties between the APD and Congress subfields.[12] In their minds, the issue of lawmaking, which is Congress's main role, is central to the focus of APD; thus, developing stronger ties between the subfields is entirely possible.

From the point of view of APD scholars, several barriers exist that make a broader union between APD and Congress scholarship more difficult. One is methodological—Congress scholars are typically rational-choice "normal scientists" and thus approach questions from an individual-level basis and with critical tests in mind, whereas APD scholars (as noted before) are sociological, more "big picture" in orientation, and less inclined to seek causal relationship via critical tests. Another barrier is scope—Congress scholars are often focused on contemporary legislative phenomena within fairly fixed time intervals, while APD scholars ascribe great importance to temporal factors, which persist and evolve across long swaths of time, to explain events. Yet another barrier is substantive—Congress scholars typically downplay (or ignore) the role of policymaking, and how it shapes and affects broader concepts such as representation, while APD scholars put a premium on policymaking and its relationship to American society at large.

The barriers noted above are non-trivial. Still, Katznelson and Lapinski (2006) are optimistic that stronger ties between the Congress and APD subfields can be made. Scholars of congressional history might prove to be the key in this endeavor. Typically, historical Congress scholars are sensitive to issues of temporality and often engage with the broader concept of policymaking. Methodological issues still exist, of course, as congressional scholarship—even that which is historical in nature—tends to be premised on individual models of behavior and often incorporates standard (large- or small-$N$) tests of causality. That said, an increasing number of historical congressional studies that take matters of APD seriously—such as Schiller (2006), James (2007), Jenkins and Nokken (2008), Jenkins, Peck, and Weaver (2010), and Ansolabehere, Hansen,

Hirano, and Snyder (2010)—have appeared in the flagship journal for APD research, *Studies in American Political Development*—in the years since Katznelson and Lapinski's essay was published. Congressional historical scholarship that has focused on temporality, policymaking, and representation—like Lapinski (2008) and Gailmard and Jenkins (2009)—has also appeared in mainstream political science journals in recent years.

Thus, closing the gap between the Congress and APD subfields is gradually occurring, and is being led by scholars of congressional history. I anticipate this trend to persist into the future, as scholars in the different subfields maintain their dialogue and continue to engage each other's work. Efforts that continue these trends will most likely characterize historical research on Congress for many years to come.

## Notes

1  This is a revised and significantly expanded version of an earlier essay, "Doing Congressional History," which appeared in *Extensions of Remarks, APSA Legislative Studies Section Newsletter* 24 (July 2001).

2  Fans of *Peabody's Improbable History* will immediately recognize this reference. For those who are unaware of Mr. Peabody and his pet boy Sherman, see: http://www.toonopedia.com/peabody.htm.

3  In truth, several of these early historical studies—and others like them—were helped along by early efforts to gather and publish Congress-related data, such as the *Biographical Directory of the United States Congress* (first published in 1961) and the *Congressional Quarterly Guide to U.S. Elections* (first published in 1975).

4  For example, various congressional roll-call voting records, scores, and data, back to the First Federal Congress, are provided by Keith Poole (http://voteview.com/); congressional biographical information, back to the First Federal Congress, are provided as PDF documents by the Government Printing Office (http://www.gpoaccess.gov/serialset/cdocuments/hd108-222/index.html) and electronically, via a search engine, by the Library of Congress (http://bioguide.congress.gov/biosearch/biosearch.asp); congressional debates and proceedings through the 1870s are provided by the Library of Congress (http://memory.loc.gov/ammem/amlaw/lawhome.html); congressional election data, back to 1896, are provided by Andrew Gelman (http://www.stat.columbia.edu/~gelman/book/data/incumbency/); and a search engine for historical newspapers between 1860 and 1922 is provided by the Library of Congress (http://chroniclingamerica.loc.gov/). Other congressional datasets and research materials require a university affiliation. Such restricted-access resources, which include a lengthier series of congressional election data, all congressional proceedings and debate, and a range of historical newspapers and periodicals, are provided by the ICPSR (http://www.icpsr.umich.edu/icpsrweb/ICPSR/), HeinOnline (http://heinonline.org/HOL/Welcome), and ProQuest (http://www.proquest.com/en-US/), respectively.

5  Nonetheless, I think it is fair to say that most research finds *some* evidence of significant party influence in Congress, especially in the House.

6  See also Carson and Roberts (n.d.) for an extensive discussion of the politics underlying congressional elections during the late nineteenth and early twentieth centuries.

7  In this respect, they built on earlier work by Young (1966).

8  For other entries in this debate, see Binder (1997), Binder, Madonna, and Smith (2007), Koger (2010), and Madonna (2011).

9   http://socsci.colorado.edu/~esadler/Congressional_District_Data.html. For a related publication using these data, see Adler (2002).
10  Taken from Martis (1982: 251). The district in question corresponds to the 66th (1919–21) and 67th (1921–23) Congresses.
11  Behavioralism was predicated on understanding "empirical regularities by appealing to the properties and behaviors of individuals. According to the behavioral persuasion, individuals constituted the fundamental building blocks and political results were simply the aggregation of individual actions" (Shepsle 1989: 133). In this regard, historically based institutional work and rational-choice-based institutional work both emerged in response to the hegemony of behavioralism.
12  Katznelson and Lapinski are quite explicit in their belief that APD scholarship has ignored Congress almost entirely. The exceptions, from their perspective, would be Bensel (1984, 1990, 2000), Sanders (1999), Schickler (2001), and Swift (1996).

# Chapter 2

# Recruitment and Candidacy
## Ambition, Strategy, and the Choice to Run for Congress

*Cherie Maestas and Melissa Stewart*

Candidates for office are a fundamental building block of legislative politics because the nature of the candidate pool defines the characteristics of the members who serve in the U.S. House and Senate. A candidate's background, political ideology, and prior work experience shape not only his or her political ambitions and chances of election, but also the skills and political perspectives he or she brings to the job as a representative. For example, state legislators who win a seat in the U.S. House are more adept at securing plum committee positions to pursue their policy agendas from the outset compared to amateurs who lack legislative experience (Berkman 1993) and they are more likely than amateurs to become legislative leaders (Canon 1990). Similarly, the demographics of the candidate pool, such as race and gender, shape the boundaries of descriptive representation in Congress and the diversity of voices engaging in legislative debates. Thus, understanding why specific candidates run for Congress is an important step toward understanding who makes legislative decisions and why.

Second, understanding candidacies in congressional elections is important because candidates provide a mechanism of accountability in American politics. Strong candidates are necessary for competitive elections, which, in turn, engage the interest of citizens, inform them of key political debates, and mobilize public participation (Jackson 1996; Coleman and Manna 2000). A robust pool of strong potential candidates means that incumbents are more likely to be challenged if they perform poorly as representatives or step out of line with constituent preferences (Canes-Wrone, Brady, and Cogan 2002; Stone, Maisel, and Maestas 2004). In fact, at the aggregate level, one way that legislative policy shifts in response to changes in public preferences is through the "replacement mechanism" where members who are less aligned with public preferences are replaced by new, more "compatible" members (Stimson, MacKuen and Erikson 1995). However, this replacement mechanism only works if new candidates are willing to step into the electoral ring to challenge those who are out of sync with constituents.

This chapter draws together important themes in recent scholarship to highlight the individual, contextual, and institutional factors that influence the strategic choices of candidates as they consider running for Congress. As part of this, we draw on empirical evidence from the Candidate Emergence Study (CES), which conducted surveys of potential candidates for the U.S. House during 1997–98 and 2001–02 in a random sample of House districts.[1] Potential candidates received the survey prior to the filing deadlines in each state, at a time when they might be actively considering entering a race. The survey respondents came from two sources, state legislators whose districts overlapped with the U.S. House districts in the study, and a list of candidates suggested by local party leaders and political activists. Their responses reveal important strategic and personal considerations that shape the pool of candidates for office. The chapter concludes with a look at understudied areas that warrant greater attention: the role of sub-national political offices in building a broad pool of high-quality potential candidates for Congress and the role of state-level electoral institutions—specifically, primary election institutions—that potentially shape incentives for candidacies.

## Congressional Candidates and Candidate Quality

Generally, when scholars characterize candidates for congressional office, they classify them in terms of their "quality," meaning their ability to run a visible and credible campaign for office. Although candidate quality conceptually encompasses many different characteristics such as fundraising ability, name recognition, integrity, dedication to public service, and knowledge about public policy, by far the most common measure of classifying candidates is based simply on their prior political experience (Jacobson 2009; Stone, Maisel, and Maestas 2004). Most studies use a two-category indicator of whether the candidate held any previous office (Jacobson 1989; Box-Steffensmeier 1996; Carson 2005; Lazarus 2006, 2008), but several scholars have developed more elaborate measures of prior experience that take into account the characteristics of lower office and the size of their constituencies (see, e.g., Bond, Covington, and Fleisher 1985; Krasno and Green 1988; Squire 1989; Lublin 1994; Maestas and Rugeley 2008). In many ways, prior experience makes sense as a measure of quality because individuals who have previously run for and won office are judged to have the experience and skills necessary for voters to take them seriously as contenders for a congressional seat. Moreover, their prior experience of winning office suggests that they have the skills and expertise to mount a complex and expensive campaign.

At the top end of the scale of candidate quality we typically find *incumbents* who already hold a U.S. House or Senate seat. By definition, they possess the skills to run an effective campaign since that is how they attained office! They generally have high name recognition among their constituents, and they have strong fundraising and campaign skills (Zaller 1998; Jacobson 2009). Moreover, voters have a basis for judging their quality as representatives. As candidates, most bring to the race a tangible record of legislative activities as well as more personal qualities associated with quality representation. These dimensions of quality can be thought of as *performance* quality and *personal* quality, and the two are strongly correlated with one another (Stone, Maisel, and Maestas 2004; Stone et al. 2010). Taken together, the strategic, personal, and performance qualities of an incumbent make them formidable candidates for reelection. As a result, many eligible potential candidates are unwilling to step into the ring as challengers (Cox and Katz 1996; Gordon, Huber, and Landa 2007; Lazarus 2008; Stone et al. 2010). Instead, non-incumbent candidates tend to wait for opportunities where at least one of these dimensions in incumbent quality has decreased (Carson 2005; Gordon and Landa 2009; Stone et al. 2010).

Non-incumbent candidates bring the same types of strategic, personal, and performance qualities to campaigns, but their degree of quality depends heavily on their background prior to running. At a basic level, an indicator of whether a candidate is *experienced* or *amateur* picks up the three types of qualities outlined above. Experienced office holders have honed their strategic skills through seeking and winning lower office and they have demonstrated their performance and personal qualities through prior service. In contrast, the qualities of amateurs might be less apparent to voters and more variable. Some amateurs come from high-visibility professions such as law, business, or careers as civic leaders, but most amateurs are relatively unknown to constituents prior to entering a race. Some high-profile amateurs are self-funded, wealthy candidates or celebrity candidates, but most are from more modest backgrounds (Canon 1990; Steen 2006). A key quality amateurs lack compared to experienced candidates is a record of representing a constituency, so amateurs must highlight their personal characteristics, their non-political career experience, or their "outsider" status to appeal to voters.

On average, candidates with prior political experience tend to perform better at the polls in general elections than those who are inexperienced (Jacobson 1989; Squire 1989). Likewise, in primary elections, experienced candidates fare much better than amateurs (Lazarus 2008). This success is attributed to resource biases such as name recognition or fundraising connections gained in lower office (Squire 1992; Berkman and Eisenstein 1999; Jacobson 2009), and to experienced candidates' strategic entry into winnable races (Jacobson and Kernell 1983; Banks and Kiewiet 1989; Lazarus 2008).

Notably, this simple classification of candidates into "experienced" and "amateur" misses some important nuances within each group. For example, not all elective offices provide the same quality of prior experience in campaigning and fundraising. Those with large constituencies and high visibility are advantaged in running the type of campaign required to win a high-dollar House or Senate campaign compared to local or non-professionalized lower offices (Lublin 1994; Squire and Wright 1990; Berkman and Eisenstein 1999; Maestas and Rugeley 2008). However, candidates from local office or non-professional legislatures have no advantage in fundraising compared to serious amateur candidates (Maestas and Rugeley 2008).

Differences in the quality of amateurs can be especially stark. Canon (1990, 1993) argues there are several different types of amateurs—ambitious office-seekers who behave much like experienced candidates, "hopeless" amateurs with no chance of winning or "policy" amateurs who run to gain visibility for a policy issue or cause. *Ambitious amateurs* are serious candidates who have much in common with experienced office holders. Often, they have high name recognition because they are local celebrities or civic leaders, or they are successful in business and law. They do well at fundraising, many on par with experienced office holders (Maestas and Rugeley 2008) and those who beat experienced candidates in the primary go on to fare as well as experienced candidates in the general election (Lazarus 2008).

### Gender and Racial Biases in Candidacies

It is important to note that there are key gender and racial biases in candidacies and that these biases have consequences for who holds office. Even a casual glance at the racial and gender makeup of Congress reveals that its membership is not reflective of the racial and gender makeup of the population. Although nearly 13 percent of the population is black, only 42 (9.6 percent) black representatives serve in the U.S. House, and none currently serve in the U.S. Senate.[2] Latinos make up nearly 16 percent of the population, but less than 5.2 percent of the House and Senate. Likewise, the proportion of women in the population is 50.7 percent while the proportion of women in both the House and Senate is only 17 percent. What produces patterns of bias in descriptive representation? A large part of the answer is that it stems from biases in the candidate pool and the willingness of individuals to run for office.

Researchers over the last few decades have clearly documented the paucity of ethnic minority and female candidates for the House and Senate (Burns, Schlozman, and Verba 2001; Moncrief, Squire, and Jewell 2001; Fox and Lawless 2004, 2005; Lawless and Fox 2005, 2010; Branton 2009). This is true in 2010 as well. As of August 10, 2010, there were only sixty-two African-American candidates and forty-five Hispanic candidates slated to run in the general election for the House and Senate and a total of 152 women. Scholars have identified a number of reasons why women and ethnic minority candidates run less frequently than white males. For minority potential candidates, district composition plays a large role (Branton 2009). For women, a number of personal and contextual factors depress the odds of entering a race. Female potential candidates differ from men in how they value holding national-level office compared to state and local offices (Fox and Lawless 2005; Fulton et al. 2006), they differ in their views of their capability of running for office (Lawless and Fox 2010), they differ in how they respond to the competitive electoral environment (Fulton et al. 2006), and they are recruited less often than men by political elite (Sanbonmatsu 2002; Fox and Lawless 2010).

## Candidates: Strategic Self-starters

Constitutionally, the eligible pool of candidates for the House includes everyone over the age of twenty-five who has been a U.S. citizen for at least seven years. Eligibility for the Senate is only slightly more restrictive, with an age limit of thirty and a citizenship requirement of nine years. However, most citizens never seriously consider a run for office, and only a small portion of those who seriously consider running actually enter a race. Who runs and why?

Notice in Figure 2.1 that by far the most common type of general election challenger to incumbents in U.S. House elections is the amateur candidate.[3] Experienced candidates challenge only a fraction of incumbents who run each year. Instead, it is much more common to find experienced challengers in open-seat races—races with no incumbent running. On average, between 1970 and 2008, 84 percent of open seat races per year have at least one experienced challenger, compared to only 18 percent per year for incumbent-held seats.

This pattern of challenge highlights the *strategic* nature of candidate entry—the best candidates tend to wait for races with the highest chances of winning. In the United States the party system is relatively weak and the requirements for getting onto the ballot are largely set by state laws rather than party elites. As a result, most candidates are "self-starters," meaning that they make very personal decisions about whether to subject themselves and their families to the rigors of political life (Kazee 1980; Kazee and Thornberry 1990). In contrast to nineteenth-century races where party leaders controlled almost every aspect of the nomination process, today's elections are candidate-centered rather than

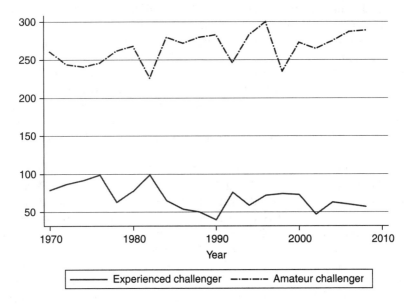

*Figure 2.1* Number of Experienced and Amateur Challengers to Incumbents

party-centered, meaning the pool of candidates that emerges depends more upon individual strategic decision-making than party coordinated recruitment (Carson, Engstrom, and Roberts 2007). Thus, it is more common for scholars to talk about the "emergence" of candidates for office rather than the "recruitment" of candidates for office (Kazee and Thornberry 1990; Maisel and Stone 1997; Moncrief 1999).

Scholars who study the emergence of candidates often take a "rational choice" approach in which they hone in on several key influences on candidates' decisions, including the prospects of winning office, the costs of running, and the intrinsic value of holding a congressional seat. The decision to run for office is one in which potential candidates weigh the expected benefits of winning office against the costs of running for and holding office (Black 1972; Rohde 1979; Jacobson and Kernell 1983; Jacobson 1989). Even those already elected to office are potential candidates in the sense that they can freely choose to retire or move to another office rather than seek again their current office.

Equation 1 is a simplified view of this calculation, but it is a helpful tool for organizing how we think about factors that shape the strategic decision.[4]

$$E(U) = p(B) - C \tag{1}$$

In this equation, $E(U)$ is the potential candidate's *expected utility* of running for office, or the net expected gain from running. The term $p$ is the probability of winning the seat, and $B$ is the benefit of holding office, should the candidate win. Notably, one cannot enjoy the benefits of office unless one wins, so the expected gains from holding office are "discounted" by the chances of winning. The term $C$ captures the tangible and intangible costs of running, thus including the monetary costs of campaigning as well as opportunity costs derived from the time spent campaigning that could have been spent on alternative activities. If the expected benefits exceed the costs of running, the potential candidate enters the race. A potential candidate who is highly likely to win but sees no benefit to holding a House or Senate seat will not emerge to run because the expected gains would not outweigh the costs. Likewise, a potential candidate who highly values service in Congress would not emerge if they deem their chances as zero.

This model, although quite simple, offers a rich launching point for thinking about the many factors that influence each of its components. Over the years, scholars have elaborated or extended this basic model to explain the decisions of lower office holders to seek higher office (i.e., Rohde 1979; Brace 1984; Maestas et al. 2006), the willingness of amateurs to enter a race (i.e., Canon 1993; Lazarus 2008), and the choice of incumbents to run for reelection or retire (i.e., Hall and Van Houweling 1994; Kiewiet and Zeng 1993; Carson 2005). This model also illustrates the strategic interaction between potential candidates for office, as incumbents and potential challengers try to anticipate and incorporate their expectations about opponents' choices to enter or sit out a race (Banks and Kiewiet 1989; Carson 2005). Although there is some debate whether the strategic model applies equally well to the emergence of Senate candidates, recent research supports the idea that they also make rational and strategic entry decisions (Lazarus 2008).

## Factors that Influence p, the Probability of Winning

The probability of winning is determined by several factors including the competitiveness of the district, the qualities of the incumbent, the strength of potential candidates, and year-to-year shifts in political tides (Jacobson and Kernell 1983; Banks and Kiewiet 1989; Carson 2005; Carson, Engstrom, and Roberts, 2007; Stone et al. 2010). For example, since district boundaries determine the socio-economic and partisan composition of the district, they factor heavily into electoral competitiveness, which defines the baseline chances that a potential candidate might win. High-quality challengers appear to be more willing to enter a race in a redistricting year and in districts in which the demographics have been altered as a result of changes to district boundaries (Hetherington, Larson, and Globetti 2003; Carson and Crespin 2004; Carson, Engstrom, and Roberts 2006; Murphy and Yoshinaka 2009). There are other structural factors that are related to general election competitiveness and are likely to also influence a potential candidate's perceptions of his or her chances. These include congruence of media markets and district boundaries (Levy and Squire 2000) and primary election rules that shape candidate entry (Kanthak and Morton 2001).

Potential challengers also factor into their chances of winning the relative quality and ability of the incumbent, and they are deterred from running when a high-quality incumbent is seeking reelection (Jacobson 1980; Jacobson and Kernell 1983; Mondak 1995; Cox and Katz 1996; Stone et al. 2004; Gordon et al. 2007). The strategic qualities of incumbents, such as their fundraising ability or use of perquisites of office, certainly influence an incumbent's chances of winning, but lapses in integrity or representation also weaken the prospects of incumbents (Mondak 1995; Welch and Hibbing 1997; Canes-Wrone et al. 2002; Stone et al. 2004; Carson 2005).

For non-incumbent candidates, the greatest chances of winning office typically occur when incumbents step aside, leaving an open seat. As a result, strategic challengers frequently wait on the sidelines for an open seat to maximize their chances of winning (Banks and Kiewiet 1989; Gaddie and Bullock 2000; Carson 2003, 2005). In contrast, Banks and Kiewiet (1989) demonstrate that weak candidates can increase their chances of winning by actually running against incumbents. Since most strong challengers prefer to wait for an open seat race rather than run against an incumbent, they do not enter primary elections when the incumbent is running. As a result, a weak out-party candidate has a better chance of securing the nomination when the incumbent is running and, therefore, maximizes his or her chances of making it to the general election. Assuming a weak challenger progresses to the general election, other factors such as national-level political shifts favoring the challenger's party, or late breaking scandals and missteps by the incumbent, sometimes propel the weak challenger to an unexpected victory.

Although counter-intuitive, this argument highlights the importance of considering the probability of winning the seat as a product of winning each stage, the nomination *and* the general election. In fact, few studies explicitly incorporate the two-stage probability, but surveys of potential candidates for office reveal that the chances of winning the nomination might even dominate their decision-making (Maisel and Stone 1997; Stone and Maisel 2003). At minimum, the chances of obtaining a seat in Congress hinge on winning both elections, thus consideration of how primary rules and election processes shape the chances of winning, independently, is a much needed area of study in this field.

## Ambition and the Understudied "B" Term

The probability of winning is only part of the story of candidate emergence. A potential candidate's chances are meaningless if he or she does not value holding a seat in the U.S. House or Senate. In fact, among the potential candidates surveyed prior to the 1998 elections, only 56 percent of respondents identified themselves as having any attraction at all to a seat in the U.S. House.[5] Among the same respondents, only 50 percent felt attracted to a seat in the Senate. Thus, for many, the basic ingredient of ambition for a seat in Congress seems to be lacking. Why?

It is certainly easy to speculate about the reasons. In recent years, service in Congress is typically portrayed as overly partisan, unpleasant, or unproductive and this contributes to the public's chronic sense of dislike for Congress and the job they do (Ramirez 2009). The polarized political climate might contribute to incumbent decisions to retire since there is evidence that retirements are higher when the public is more disapproving of Congress (Wolak 2007). In addition, increased cynicism depresses non-incumbent potential candidates' interests in holding office (Fox and Lawless 2010).

Despite the centrality of ambition to candidate's strategic calculus, few studies have examined what influences general political ambitions (but see Fox and Lawless 2011; Gaddie 2004), or specific ambitions for a U.S. House seat (Fulton et al. 2006; Maestas et al. 2006). Due to an absence of data on ambition for office, most studies simply assume that national office is attractive enough to draw candidates into the ring and focus instead on the chances of winning or the costs of running. Yet, evidence from survey research suggests that this is not the case (Maestas et al. 2006). Making this assumption leads scholars to overlook important questions about whether and how the mechanisms of accountability work. As mentioned earlier, a pool of *willing* potential candidates is necessary to provide an alternative to incumbents in office.

Many of the individuals we typically think of as best qualified to run for Congress are not interested in holding any political office or have no interest in serving specifically in Congress. In the parlance of the rational-choice model outlined earlier, the B term is 0, rendering judgments about p moot. Instead, ambitions to hold political office, particularly national-level political office, vary systematically over time and across individuals. Ambitions are shaped by individual characteristics such as gender or family background, early socialization to politics, beliefs about one's abilities as a candidate, and perceptions of political offices (Fox and Lawless 2010, 2011; Fulton et al. 2006; Gaddie 2004; Maestas et al. 2006). Life cycle changes related to marriage, children, and aging factors also alter ambitions (Fox and Lawless 2011). Likewise, national political shifts such as changes in party control make the work environment in Congress seem more or less attractive, leading to shifts in the aggregate pool of potential candidates willing to consider a run for office.

## Perceptions of National Office and National Government

The first, and perhaps most important factor that affects congressional ambition is the potential candidate's perceptions of national offices and national government. We know, for example, that cynicism about political office dampens ambitions to hold office (Fox and Lawless 2011). Thus, we expect that perceptions of Congress, as an institution, influences ambition as well. The 1997–98 CES survey asked potential candidates to rate the U.S. House and Senate's effectiveness of passing public policy on a seven-point scale ranging from *extremely low* (−3) to *extremely high* (+3) with 0 as a neutral category. It also asked them to rate the public prestige of the House and Senate on the same scale. Table 2.1 shows that, on average, potential candidates rated the Senate

*Table 2.1* Potential Candidates' Ratings of Effectiveness and Prestige of Congressional Seats

| | *Effectiveness* House | Senate | *Prestige* House | Senate | *Smallest* N |
|---|---|---|---|---|---|
| All potential candidates | 0.41 | 0.82 | 0.57 | 0.99 | 1158 |
| Democrat | 0.10 | 0.68 | 0.35 | 0.88 | 514 |
| Republican | 0.81 | 1.00 | 0.84 | 1.13 | 640 |
| State legislator | 0.59 | 0.95 | 0.63 | 1.04 | 845 |
| Other political office holder | 0.02 | 0.60 | 0.60 | 0.98 | 119 |
| No political office | −0.12 | 0.40 | 0.31 | 0.83 | 200 |

Source: 1997–98 Candidate Emergence Study

Note
All variables are scaled from (−3) extremely low to (+3) extremely high.

as both more prestigious and effective than the House ($p<.05$). However, the mean rating placed both just slightly above the neutral category, suggesting that on at least two dimensions that might influence the $B$ term in the strategic entry equation, the value of a House or Senate seat might be lower than typically assumed. In fact, fully 27 percent rated the policy effectiveness in the House as low, as did 18 percent of those rating the Senate. Likewise, 25 percent rated the prestige of the House as low, compared with 16 percent for the Senate. To the extent that effectiveness and prestige are benefits that potential candidates consider important in fulfilling career goals, these low ratings suggest a deterrent that is unrelated to the chances of winning.

The subgroup differences in evaluations are also quite interesting because they hint at important dynamics that might underlie the candidate pool. Partisan control of Congress, for example, could alter how Democrats and Republicans perceive national institutions and, as a result, alter the willingness of partisans to seek office. Recall that Republicans controlled both chambers in 1997. Accordingly, we find that Democrats viewed the effectiveness of both chambers as lower than Republicans ($p<.05$). This suggests that the $B$ term in the strategic decision equation depends in part on whether one is a member of the "in-party" or "out-party."

Interestingly, perceptions of the House and Senate also vary by position of the potential candidate. In general, state legislators are more likely to see Congress as effective compared to other office holders or amateurs. Office holders see the prestige of both the House and Senate similarly, but non-office holders see Congress as slightly lower. However, the fact that office holders view House and Senate seats as more prestigious than non-office holders does not really tell us whether they are likely to emerge as candidates. Instead, those in public office are likely to consider the *relative* prestige and effectiveness of higher office.

Table 2.2 shows that most office holders view their current office as *more* effective and prestigious than either the House or Senate. This is very different from early studies of ambition that assumed that national-level offices were at the top of the office hierarchy and considered to be superior positions (Schlesinger 1966). The relative evaluation measures are constructed by subtracting the office holder's evaluation of their own office on the dimensions of prestige and effectiveness from the House and Senate ratings. Negative values indicate that office holders rate their own office higher than the congressional office. For example, 58 percent of all office holders viewed their own office as more effective than the U.S. House at passing policy, while only 20 percent rate the House as higher. Likewise, 43 percent viewed their own office as more prestigious than the House. There are significant ($p<.05$) differences between state legislators' and other office holders' views of the relative effectiveness, but not their views of the relative prestige.

Table 2.3 shows that relative effectiveness evaluations of state legislators depend partly on party and position of the member in their current office. Majority-party members generally enjoy procedural advantages in passing

Table 2.2 Office Holders' Evaluations of Relative Effectiveness and Prestige of the U.S. House and Senate

| | Effectiveness | | | Prestige | | | Smallest |
| | % less | % more | Mean | % less | % more | Mean | N |
|---|---|---|---|---|---|---|---|
| *House* | | | | | | | |
| All office | | | | | | | |
| holders | 58 | 20 | −1.04 | 43 | 30 | −0.48 | 916 |
| State legislators | 57 | 20 | −0.98** | 42 | 29 | −0.46 | 805 |
| Other office | | | | | | | |
| holders | 70 | 20 | −1.57** | 50 | 29 | −0.63 | 111 |
| *Senate* | | | | | | | |
| All office | | | | | | | |
| holders | 51 | 25 | −0.68 | 35 | 38 | −0.09 | 915 |
| State legislators | 50 | 25 | −0.62* | 34 | 38 | −0.07 | 804 |
| Other office | | | | | | | |
| holders | 61 | 24 | −0.96* | 40 | 33 | −0.21 | 111 |

Source: 1997–98 Candidate Emergence Study

Notes
* $p < .05$
** $p < .01$
% less indicates the percent of all respondents rating the U.S. House/Senate as lower than their own office; % more is the percent of all respondents rating the U.S. House/Senate as greater than their own office. The remainder rate them equally.

*Table 2.3* Mean Relative Effectiveness, by Party and Majority Status

| | Relative effectiveness | | Smallest |
| | House | Senate | N |
|---|---|---|---|
| Democrat, majority SL | −1.34[d] | −0.88 | 314 |
| Democrat, minority SL | −1.18[b,d] | −0.67[a] | 173 |
| Republican, majority SL | −0.91[a,b,d] | −0.76 | 105 |
| Republican, minority SL | −0.34[a,b,c] | −0.07[a,b,c] | 201 |

Source: 1997–98 Candidate Emergence Study

Notes
a Difference from mean of Dem. majority, significant at $p < .05$
b Difference from mean of Dem. minority, significant at $p < .05$
c Difference from mean of Rep. majority, significant at $p < .05$
d Difference from mean of Rep. minority, significant at $p < .05$

policies, which suggests that state legislators might view the effectiveness of the policy process as contingent upon the context in which they would legislate. As before, we see there are clear partisan differences between Democrats and Republicans in evaluations of effectiveness. Nevertheless, Republicans currently serving in the minority evaluate the relative effectiveness as significantly greater than those in the majority due to the gain in effectiveness from moving from a minority position at the state level to a majority position in the U.S.

House. These results highlight how the combination of conditions at the state and local levels combine to increase or decrease the relative value of a House seat and suggest that the pool of interested candidates varies based on conditions at both levels.

Prestige and effectiveness are evaluations specific to the offices of interest, but more general views about national government also factor into ambitions. Among the respondents to the CES study, only 44 percent thought the most important policy decisions were made at the national level. The remaining respondents felt the state or local level served as the more important policy venue. Prior research has demonstrated that trust encourages political participation (Bianco 1994), and cynicism about the institutions of government is related to lower levels of ambition (Fox and Lawless 2011). Among potential candidates, trust in the federal government varies considerably, with only 30 percent indicating that the federal government can be trusted to do what is right "most of the time" or "just about always." It is likely that belief in the integrity of the national government serves as another dimension which might shape how a potential candidate values holding a seat in Congress.

### Challenges of Holding Office

Anecdotal accounts of candidacy decisions that regularly appear in news stories often highlight the personal challenges of holding office, such as subjecting one's self or family to constant scrutiny from the press and political opponents, spending large amounts of time away from family and friends, and meeting the heavy demands of the legislative schedule. The CES survey asked potential candidates to indicate how much each of several different cost factors would discourage them from running for a House seat. Fifty-six percent indicated that they would be at least somewhat discouraged by the loss of leisure time; 82 percent thought they would be at least somewhat discouraged by separation from family and friends; and 68 percent would be at least somewhat discouraged by the loss of personal and family privacy. In addition to these personal costs of holding office, there are also opportunity costs of serving—having to give up one's current career, for example. These play an important role in deterring some candidates, but they are not as influential as other costs. Only 39 percent of potential candidates surveyed reported that they would be deterred from running for the House for this reason.

Studies also show that individual characteristics are important predictors of ambition, in part because they reflect different personal costs of holding office. Younger people tend to be more interested in a political career than older people. However, the rigorous schedule of members of Congress and the lack of time they have to spend with their families is a deterrent to those with young children who might otherwise believe they are qualified to run (Fox and Lawless 2003, 2005). This challenging environment is even mentioned by members of Congress who choose not to run for reelection (Theriault 1998).

So, while younger people are more likely than older people to contemplate running for office, they are also more likely to have the challenges of juggling a demanding career, significant amounts of time out of the state, and a young family keeping them from running. Gender also influences ambition, in part because family concerns weigh more heavily on women, but also because they view the costs of campaigning as greater than men (Fulton et al. 2006). There is also a gap between men and women in "candidate efficacy"—the belief that they are qualified to run for office (Lawless and Fox 2005, 2010). But, even among women who do view themselves as highly qualified, very few of them express interest in a high-level position—in fact, "there is a 32% gender gap in eventual interest" level among highly qualified women and men (Lawless and Fox 2005: 654).

Taken together, the costs of holding office are high, and the perceived benefits might be insufficient to offset them. The preceding evidence suggests there is ample reason to question whether there is a sufficiently large pool of individuals who hold ambition for office. The robustness and diversity of the candidate pool is of significant concern because this is the pool of individuals that eventually determine the contours of representation in American government. In terms of the strategic calculation, the value of office ($B$) is part and parcel of the larger concept of ambition. Ambition, in turn, determines whether potential candidates will run, even in the best of electoral circumstances. At the extreme, one could imagine a vicious cycle in which extreme public negativity towards Congress reduces the value of office to potential candidates, which, in turn, reduces the entry of high-quality alternative candidates, thus limiting the public's ability to replace the incumbents that frustrate them.

## Factors that Influence the Costs of Running

The final factor that candidates consider when deciding whether to run is the costs associated with seeking office. We generally think of anything that creates a barrier to entering a congressional race as a "cost" of running. This includes legal hurdles such as the requirements set by the state that define the eligibility criteria for running for office as well as the tangible and intangible costs of running. Tangible costs are things like the financial requirements of running a campaign, including staffing, advertising, travel, campaign materials, and organizational infrastructure. Intangible costs include things such as the psychological costs of campaigning, enduring negative ads, or discomfort with fundraising (Maisel and Stone 1997; Maestas et al. 2006).

The legal barriers to running vary since each state determines the criteria for entering a race. Generally, there are two ways to get on the ballot for a congressional election—paying a filing fee or obtaining and submitting a predetermined number of signatures from registered voters. The former imposes a direct monetary cost, while the latter imposes mostly time costs. Ansolabehere and Gerber (1996) examine the requirements across states and find wide variation in the costs of entering a race, with consequences for candidate entry. At the low end of requirements, Indiana in 1990 "require[d] merely a pledge to the party," but at the high end, Florida required 5 percent of the congressional salary, which amounted to over $6000 at the time. Over half of the states only require filing fees while others require petitions to demonstrate at least minimal voter support for the candidacy (Ansolabehere and Gerber 1996: 251).

Although the costs appear small relative to the costs of running a serious campaign for office, Ansolabehere and Gerber (1996) find that the cost of ballot entry significantly deters candidates. The rate of uncontested races is greater and the number of strategic retirements among incumbents is lower in states that have costly requirements of ballot access compared to those with minimal requirements. While it is likely that those most deterred by costs of entry are probably amateurs, it is also true that when barriers to entry lead to more uncontested races, they eliminate the possibility that unexpected national shifts in mood or major transgressions by incumbents will translate into a change in representatives for races with no challenger.

Other costs of running for office are well known, such as the high cost of running a professional campaign. In 2008, the average House challenger spent just over $424,000, although the median was only a little over $34,000. This means that half of challengers spent less than $34,000—hardly a sufficient sum to run a competitive race against an incumbent.

The difference in campaign costs varies in part by the competitiveness of the campaign. Serious challengers to incumbents or competitive open seat candidates usually raise and spend upwards of one million dollars. In fact, the average spending by challengers in close races (races with 10 percent margin or less) in 2008 was 1.13 million dollars. Not surprisingly, when asked, potential candidates for the U.S. House indicate that fundraising is a deterrent to running. The CES survey indicates that 88 percent of potential candidates were at least somewhat discouraged from running for office, with 38 percent reporting they were *strongly* deterred. Carson (2005) finds that incumbent spending in prior elections is a significant deterrent to candidate emergence as it provides a baseline for potential candidates to estimate the costs needed to run an effective campaign. When incumbents demonstrate their financial prowess through spending, the perception of the "C" term in the strategic decision calculus increases.

Candidates also face possible lost income as they step away from their regular jobs to campaign full time, although this is not a major deterrent. Only 42 percent of CES respondents were discouraged from running by the potential for lost income, and less than 10 percent were strongly discouraged. Other types of costs are less tangible but more significant in the minds of potential candidates, such as the psychological challenges of facing character attacks or other types of negative advertising. Sixty-five percent of CES respondents felt discouraged from running for a House seat due to the possibility of facing negative advertising, although only 12 percent reported feeling strongly discouraged by this factor. Finally, 82 percent of potential candidates indicated that separation from friends and family would discourage them from running.

In general, the tangible and intangible costs of running are understudied relative to the probability of winning, yet they are a considerable deterrent to candidate entry. In fact, studies of gender and candidacy suggest that the tangible and intangible costs of running depress the chances of women running for both Congress and for lower offices (Fox and Lawless 2004, 2005, 2010). It is also likely that the same costs depress ambition for office as well. For example, we created an index that averages each potential candidate's responses to the questions about the costs of running for office. The result ranges from 1 to 4, with scores above 3 indicating that the potential candidate views running as very costly. Sixty-one percent of likely candidates who view running for a seat as very costly had low attraction to a seat in the House, compared with only 27 percent of those who viewed running as not very costly (campaign cost index of 2 or less). When the costs of running for office discourage potential candidates, the accountability mechanism in American democracy is put at risk. The pool of individuals who are responsive to shifts in local or national conditions is smaller and, therefore, entrenched politicians are safer regardless of their actions.

## Some Understudied Areas in Recruitment and Candidacy

There are two broader factors that shape the candidate pool through influencing multiple parts of the equation that have not received sufficient scholarly attention. These are the role of recruitment and the role of lower office conditions in encouraging progressive ambition, or the ambition for higher office. Both serve as mechanisms that link preferences of citizens to the size and quality of the candidate pool in any given year.

### Political Recruitment

Political recruitment occurs when party or community leaders encourage a candidate to run for office. Sometimes this occurs over a long period of time, as parties nurture their activists, first helping them to secure local or state offices, then encouraging them to run for Congress when the time is right. Occasionally, this happens quickly, as parties seek fresh faces to compete in a race. Other groups besides the two major parties can be active in recruitment as well. At the local level, community leaders and interest groups often identify several individuals who would be good public servants for the area, and encourage them to run with promises of support. In the 2001 study of potential candidates, 16 percent were only contacted by community leaders or interest groups about running, not by any party organization. On the other hand, 20 percent were contacted by both, giving reinforcing messages to potential candidates.

Political recruitment is important at two levels. First, it is important because individuals, whether male or female, express "greater levels of political ambition when they perceive that they have been encouraged to run" (Lawless and Fox 2010: 322), and they are more likely to run in a given race (Maestas et al. 2006). Thus, even though U.S. elections are candidate-centered, the political parties do influence which candidates choose to run for Congress. Party leaders do this by identifying and contacting strong candidates and encouraging them to run (Herrnson 1988). Such encouragement from one's political party is valuable to a potential candidate because it helps better determine his or her likelihood of winning (Herrnson 1988; Kazee and Thornberry 1990; Maisel 2001; Maisel, Maestas, and Stone 2002).

Political recruitment is also important in terms of translating public shifts in political preferences into new representation in Congress. Even a casual glance at the political landscape in 2010 suggests that candidate recruitment is one way in which political groups gained voice in the electoral process and influenced the positions of major political parties. The Tea Party, a political faction generally associated with the Republican Party, has actively recruited candidates who align with their political preferences for limited government. Although many are amateur candidates, the Tea Party has been successful in recruiting and supporting experienced candidates in competitive districts.[6] In fact, in the 2010 midterm election, the first election since the movement began, 32 percent of candidates backed by the Tea Party won national office. Five U.S. senators and forty members of Congress who were supported by various Tea Party organizations will make up a portion of the 112th Congress.

Table 2.4 shows that potential candidates who were contacted by political parties or outside groups were much more likely to perceive their chances of winning in 1998 as higher than those not contacted.[7] Potential candidates who had been recruited by national, state or local parties *and* community groups or leaders viewed their chances of winning as .28—just over 1 in 4—compared to those who had no contact. Those that were not contacted rated their chances as merely .10, or 1 in 10. Notably, potential candidates who were contacted only by community leaders or interest groups, but not by their party, rated their chances as lower than those contacted by the party. A limitation with studying contacts, however, is that it is difficult to untangle whether recruitments occur

*Table 2.4* Party Contact and Chance of Winning in the Future

|  | Mean | 95% confidence interval | (N) |
|---|---|---|---|
| No Contact | 0.10 | 0.09–0.12 | (591) |
| Party Only | 0.22 | 0.13–0.30 | (45) |
| Community/Interest Group Only | 0.16 | 0.12–0.19 | (171) |
| Party and Community/Group | 0.28 | 0.24–0.32 | (199) |

Source: 2001–02 Candidate Emergence Study

because the candidate was strong to begin with or whether the candidate boosts his or her beliefs in the chances of winning as a result of contact.

Another common activity of parties is to recruit in order to place names on the ballot in races that are not likely to be competitive. In these cases, recruitment is designed to identify a party standard-bearer, most of whom are amateurs with little or no chance of winning (Lazarus 2008: 839). This is of particular concern in the recruitment of women. Although prior research has shown that men are more likely than women to be recruited by their party leadership (Fox and Lawless 2010), parties are likely to recruit women in select circumstances—particularly when it is difficult to find candidates for particular races. When potential candidates consider the political office very desirable, the parties might be less likely to seek out women candidates because of the long list of potential candidates already at their disposal (Sanbonmatsu 2002).

### Causes and Consequences of Career Ladders in American Politics

In one sense, we can think of American politics as having a career ladder with offices organized by prestige and size of constituency, where office holders generally progress up the rungs over the course of their career (see Schlesinger 1966; Francis and Kenny 2000). Such an image is attractive because each level of office provides training and experience for individuals hoping to move up, thus the pool of candidates for higher office is continually winnowed to those who are the best campaigners and the best representatives in lower offices. In fact, state legislators have often been considered the "farm teams" of Congress (Fiorina 1994). In reality, the notion of a strong, well-defined political career ladder is an overstatement in American politics. The weak party structure, candidate-centered politics, and relative open access to ballots lead to candidates of all types entering at all levels of government. Indeed, the federalist structure of policy makes lower office an attractive policy venue to many individuals, which can often lead to static ambition among office holders. Moreover, state to state variation in the professionalism of state legislative offices and other local offices produce uneven "training" for those with ambitions for higher office. Legislators in non-professional institutions, for example, have no greater advantage over serious amateurs in fundraising for U.S. House races (Maestas and Rugeley 2008) and they can be quite ill equipped to compete against a strong incumbent.

In recent years, even the direction of the loose career ladder that exists has been called into question. With the advent of term limits, state legislators sometimes exit to "lower" local offices rather than "higher" national or statewide ones (Kousser 2005). Historically, service in the state legislature is a frequent precursor to a run for the House, but as Figure 2.2 shows, the number of state legislators who challenge incumbents has declined over time. In recent elections, candidates who have served in state- and local-level offices are more

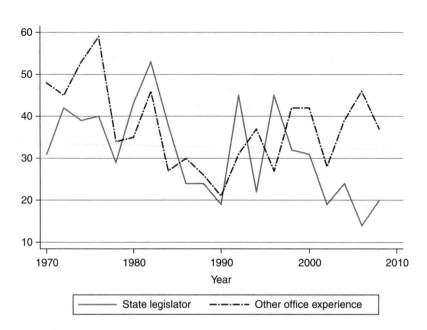

*Figure 2.2* Number of State Legislators versus Other Office Holders who Challenge Incumbents

prevalent. One possibility is that term limits in state legislatures have disrupted this typical career path, but the evidence for the effects of term limits on candidate entry has been mixed (Powell 2000; Kousser 2005; Lazarus 2006). If state legislatures have become an incubator for local office with smaller, narrowly interested constituencies, this has implications for representation at lower levels of office.

Notably, term limits could also have implications for the qualities that potential office holders bring to the table during a campaign. In states without term limits, legislators have ample time to build a network of political and constituent support to leverage when national political shifts open opportunities to run. Term-limited legislators, however, have less time and might feel incapable of building the type of base needed to seek highly competitive House or Senate seats. Thus, it is possible that term limits reduce the chances of winning even among experienced candidates, but this question is largely unexplored in the literature.

In short, understanding how state and local or local elective offices nurture ambitions for national office is important to understanding the size and depth of the potential candidate pool. But, it is also important to understand because career ladders have important implications for representation as office holders with ambitions for higher office tend to shift their positions in anticipation of running (Herrick and Moore 1993; Francis and Kenny 1996). For state legislators, progressive ambition, combined with greater resources, leads to increased attention to constituency interests (Maestas 2003), and at the aggregate level, greater representation of state-level interests (Maestas 2000).

However, the degree to which policy positions moderate toward statewide or extremist interests might depend fundamentally on the primary election structure. Prior research shows that primary election laws influence the ideological positions of candidates (Kanthak and Morton 2001), and that House candidates in partisan primary systems moderate their positions *while in office* to appeal to the party base (Francis 1996). Thus, understanding the representational consequences of institutional career ladders and their effects on ambitions requires an elaboration of the candidate emergence model to account for the primary election context.

## Conclusion

The electoral and representational benefits associated with competitive elections depend upon a pool of willing, high-quality candidates—something that often seems in short supply in congressional elections. In fact, during the last forty years, 16 percent of U.S. House incumbents who ran for reelection ran unopposed by a major party challenger. Of those who faced a challenger, 15 percent won with at least 75 percent of the two-party vote, suggesting a *de facto* lack of challenge. This means that in nearly one third of U.S. House elections, voters had no meaningful choice among candidates. While an absence of challengers in many races is easy to observe, what is less clear is how this absence should be interpreted. On one hand, an absence of candidates might indicate a broken system in which representation is undermined by an absent choice at the ballot box. On the other hand, it might suggest that some incumbents are doing a good job so there is no need for a challenger to channel voter displeasure. This puzzle is of great interest to scholars, but it cannot be fully untangled without knowing something about the size and nature of the pool of potential candidates for Congress, and how they make decisions about running.

## Notes

1 Details about the methodology and survey instruments for the Candidate Emergence Study can be found at http://ces.iga.ucdavis.edu/. The 1997–98 survey garnered responses from 1,190 potential candidates in 192 randomly selected U.S. House districts. The 2001–02 survey drew 1,537 respondents from 242 U.S. House districts.
2 U.S. Census Bureau (http://quickfacts.census.gov/); CQ selection stats.
3 Raw data on the House races and the quality of candidates were generously provided by Gary Jacobson, University of California at San Diego. Any errors in analysis or reporting are the responsibility of the authors.
4 We make the simplifying assumption that the expected benefits from alternative activities is 0 so the more complex equation of $E(U) = p(B_{Cong}) + (1 - p)(B_{Alt}) - C$ simplifies to equation 1.

5 Respondents were asked whether they felt attracted to a career in several different political offices, including House, Senate, State Legislature, and local offices using a 7-point scale ranging from extremely low (–3) to extremely high (+3). Those who score above 0 indicate a positive attraction to the career.

6 http://www.brendan-nyhan.com/blog/2010/10/did-the-tea-party-weaken-gop-candidate-quality.html; http://www.foreignpolicy.com/articles/2010/10/26/the_tea_party_exported.

7 The potential candidate's chances of winning the House seat in 1998 is the product of his or her estimate of chances of winning the primary election and the chances of winning the general election. Potential candidates rated their chances for each on a scale of 1 to 7, highly unlikely to highly likely, with toss-up in the middle. Although we cannot precisely know how categories translate into probabilities, for ease of presentation and discussion, we convert both 7-point variables to a scale in which .01 represents highly unlikely and .99 represents highly likely with .5 indicating the "toss-up" category.

# Chapter 3

# Congressional Elections
## Electoral Structure and Political Representation

*Erik J. Engstrom*

Congressional elections are inherently important. They determine who holds power in Congress and, as a consequence, determine who holds power in the entire government. For this reason alone they would be worth studying. But congressional elections also present a godsend for researchers interested in the study of campaigns and elections. By providing 435 House races every two years with varying political and economic conditions—constituencies, partisan bases, media markets, demographics, economic interests, etc.—congressional elections provide researchers with a series of "mini-laboratories" to study voters, candidates, and campaigns. The presidency, by contrast, offers only one electoral contest every four years, and a unique one at that. Thus it is unsurprising that congressional elections have attracted substantial scholarly attention. And, as a result, students of congressional elections have produced a rich, and well-respected, body of knowledge. The purpose of this chapter is to survey recent developments in the study of congressional elections and to suggest potential new frontiers of exploration.

No single essay, however, can cover the vast literature on the topic.[1] To narrow the focus to a manageable level, the chapter examines the impact of the U.S. electoral structure on the Congress. The first section of the essay examines how changes in electoral rules over time have shaped the behavior and outcomes of congressional elections. The second section examines how the electoral structure shapes voter behavior. The third section turns to the relationships between legislators and constituents. The final section discusses potential new directions in the study of congressional elections. In particular, I discuss how the rise of party polarization has produced a series of new and important questions regarding the conduct of congressional elections.

## The Institutional Foundations of Congressional Elections

One simple, yet powerful, way to classify the world's legislatures is to place them along a spectrum. At one end are strong party systems. At the other end are candidate-centered systems. In a strong party system, voters select candidates based on their party label and the individual attributes of candidates tend to matter less. A Westminster parliamentary system, like Great Britain's, serves as a paradigmatic example (Cox 1987). Voters cast votes based on their feelings towards the political parties, and much less on the personal characteristics of the particular candidates running in their constituency. At the other end of the spectrum are candidate-centered systems. In these systems voters care more about the personal characteristics and issue positions of candidates. Here we might place modern United States congressional elections. This is not to say that party labels are unimportant in candidate-centered elections, or that the personal characteristics of candidates are unimportant in party-centered elections, but that the relative emphasis placed on candidates and party labels differ across the two regime types.

Political scientists have found that, to a great extent, formal institutions undergird these differences. Formal institutions are the rules of the game. Like any game, rules constrain behaviors, by raising the costs of certain actions and providing incentives for other actions. In the context of congressional elections, scholars have emphasized electoral rules as they apply to nominations, the campaign for votes, and how those votes translate into legislative seats. Changes in any one of the various aspects of the game can lead to changes in how elections are conducted. To take one example, letting voters choose party nominees instead of party elites will alter how candidates campaign and how they will behave in the legislature. Thus electoral rules provide incentives for certain types of actions, which in turn shape the behavior of candidates, activists, and voters.

Yet because the rules governing U.S. congressional elections have remained largely constant over the past thirty years, it can be easy to miss their particular, and pervasive, effects. One way scholars have discerned the effects of electoral rules is to compare modern congressional elections to those of the past.[2] Therefore in the rest of this section I examine some of the major historical developments in the conduct of congressional elections. How candidates are nominated, how ballots are cast, and how votes are translated into congressional seats have each changed dramatically throughout American history. Looking backward across time will throw modern elections into sharp relief.

### Nominations

The first step in winning a congressional seat is to gain the nomination of one of the major political parties. Nowadays we take it for granted that voters get to choose their party's nominee in primary elections. But choosing nominees in direct primaries was not the norm throughout the nineteenth century. Instead, congressional nominees were typically chosen in closed party nominating conventions. These conventions were comprised of local party elites who met every two years to select congressional nominees (along with other local offices and delegates to state conventions). These conventions were in some cases  run by party bosses, particularly in urban cities, who held enormous sway over the nomination process (e.g., Yearley 1970; Reynolds 2006).

The image of candidates being selected in smoke-filled backrooms might be exaggerated, but it contains more than a kernel of truth. Nominations were very much an "insider's" game. Party, or factional, loyalty was critical. Running as a maverick who bucked the local party organization was a risky way to build a political career. Rather, the system rewarded loyalty. The nomination system meant that candidates were dependent on local party managers, or party bosses, for their nomination. Even if an incumbent wanted to continue serving in Congress there was no guarantee that he would be re-nominated. Abraham Lincoln, for instance, was one of the casualties of the practice known as "rotation"—where different factions of a party would take turns holding a congressional seat. Elected to the House of Representatives in 1846 as member of the Whig Party, Lincoln served a single term in the U.S. House of Representatives. Although he expressed interest in running for reelection, the Whig organization back in his district chose someone else to be the Whig nominee.[3]

Reforms at the state level during the early twentieth century replaced the convention nomination system with direct primaries. Still used to this day, direct primaries handed the choice of nominees directly to voters. By forcing candidates to make appeals to voters for nomination, the direct primary accelerated the tilt towards a candidate-centered system (Ware 2002). Candidates have to win votes directly from citizens. Primaries are more likely to reward politicians who can develop a personal reputation with voters and away from those whose skills lay in navigating the "back-room" politics of party conventions (Reynolds 2006; Adams and Merrill 2008). A candidate who wants to buck the party organization can still be re-nominated, as long as they win votes in a primary.

Although primaries reduced the influence of party machines, another, perhaps unintended, consequence was to reduce competition for party nominations. Since the initial adoption of direct primaries there has been a steady historical decline in competition within primaries. Incumbents face few serious challengers in primaries and often run uncontested. In a comprehensive study of competition in primaries, Ansolabehere et al. (2006: 78) found that the number of competitive House primaries—where the winner receives 60 percent or less of the vote—was 29 percent between 1910 and 1938. From 1960 to 2000, the number of competitive primaries plummeted to 11 percent. Thus, most incumbents face little serious competition in their primaries, and even fewer lose in primaries.

### Balloting

A second major feature of the electoral system concerns the physical conduct of casting a ballot. Although we may think of the mechanics of casting ballots as a rather mundane aspect of elections, it turns out that the order in which candidate names are arranged on a ballot and how ballots are physically cast can have a huge influence on electoral outcomes. One need only look to the 2000 presidential election to see the potential impact of ballot layouts (e.g., Wand et al. 2001). Today when we vote, we go to a polling station where we receive a ballot containing candidates for every office. These ballots have been compiled and printed out by the state or local government. We then fill out our ballot in secret. Voters are free, if they so choose, to vote for a Democratic nominee for president and a Republican for the House (or vice versa). The ballot is then given to a non-partisan poll worker (or, as is becoming more common, mailed in or recorded on a computer).

Contrast that with voting in the nineteenth century. For most of the nineteenth century, elections were conducted using what is known as the "party strip" ballot. This type of ballot had two distinguishing features. First, the ballot featured the party's nominee for the most important office—such as president or governor—at the top of the ticket and candidates for subordinate offices were listed below it. It did not list candidates for other parties. So, for example, the Democratic ballot would contain only Democratic candidates from president to governor to House candidate and so on. Second, ballots were printed and handed out by the parties (today they are printed by the government). Voters would receive these ballots either in their newspapers or they would get them from party "hawkers" standing outside the polling stations. This turned many polling stations into rough-and-tumble arenas as competing party hawkers tried to force their ballots on prospective voters (Bensel 2004; Summers 2004).

During presidential election years the party's nominees for president and vice-president, and frequently their images, headed the ticket, usually followed by the names of the electors, and then candidates to lower offices in descending order. Thus, candidates for Congress would find their names listed below candidates for more prominent offices (i.e., president, governor). Because the ballot only contained candidates of a single party, voters were faced with a simple choice: vote for all of the Democratic candidates or all of the Republican candidates. The physical format radically curbed split-ticket voting; voting for a Republican nominee for president and a Democrat for Congress was not easy. Although there were some workarounds—such as writing in an alternative name over the name of a listed candidate—these practices were cumbersome. Moreover, voting was public. Voters cast their tickets in full view of anyone who wanted to watch. All of these features reinforced straight-ticket voting (Rusk 1970; Engstrom and Kernell 2005).

Thus, the fates of same-party candidates were thoroughly intertwined. Congressional candidates were dependent on the efforts of local parties to work together to pull them into office (Carson, Engstrom, and Roberts 2007). Congressional candidates were also subject to the popularity of the candidate that headed the ticket. A congressional candidate saddled with an unpopular presidential nominee at the top of the ticket could find the campaign rough-going.

This system fundamentally changed starting in the late 1880s when Massachusetts first adopted what was known as the Australian, or secret, ballot.[4] The reform efforts were pushed by good-government reformers, sometimes in conjunction with politicians, who were fed up with the perceived (and real) corruption of party machines (Ware 2000; Reynolds 2006). The reform quickly spread across the country and by 1920 almost every state had adopted some version of the new ballot format. The new ballot had a number of distinctive features. First, it was printed by the government rather than by the parties. Second, it placed candidates of *all* the parties onto a single, consolidated ballot. Finally, it included provisions for secrecy at the ballot box.

These changes to the electoral system wrought by the Progressive Era helped sweep away the strong party machines and set down the building blocks for the emergence of a candidate-centered system. Candidates began to control their own fates to a much greater degree than they did in the past. They were no longer bound to the fates of the other candidates on the ticket—in particular the presidential nominee at the head of the ticket. They also could no longer rely on the local party organization to pull them to victory by rallying the faithful on Election Day.

Perhaps most important, from the perspective of congressional elections, the individual attributes and campaign talents of candidates began to take on central importance. For instance, Carson and Roberts (n.d.) have shown that the importance of candidates having prior office-holding experience, in terms of electoral success, increased following the passage of the Australian ballot. Candidate quality further spiked-up during the 1960s (Cox and Katz 1996). This is not to imply that partisanship does not matter in terms of voting decisions. It still operates as an informational cue for voters (discussed more below). But it is not the same thing as strong party machines bringing voters to the polls.

In short, changes in the electoral structure over the last 120 years have turned modern congressional elections increasingly into a candidate-centered system. Getting to Capitol Hill takes entrepreneurial self-starters. The next section considers how these changes have influenced the responsiveness and competitiveness of congressional elections.

## Competition and Responsiveness in Congressional Elections

The most powerful tool that voters have, in the aggregate, to influence Congress is changes in the number of seats each party holds. One need only look to the most recent elections to see the dramatic influence congressional elections can have. The 2006 election marked the Democrats' return to the majority for the first time since 1994. Democrats captured control of both the House and Senate by riding a wave of public discontent with both the Iraq War and the Bush administration's handling of Hurricane Katrina. Democrats padded their congressional majorities in the 2008 elections, and, for a brief period, even held a

60-seat filibuster-proof majority in the Senate. In 2010, Republicans retook the House gaining 64 seats from the Democrats.

Though dramatic, the seat swings in recent elections pale in comparison to some of those found in earlier periods of American history. For example, in 1854 the Democrats lost a monumental 74 seats. The House only had 234 members total, so the seat swing accounted for nearly 30 percent of the membership. Similar swings routinely happened throughout the nineteenth century. In 1874 the Republicans were on the losing end of another massive wipeout—surrendering 94 seats. In 1894, the Democrats lost 125 seats (in a chamber of 357). What is fascinating—and telling—about these elections is that the national vote division did not change all that much (Brady 1991). Small vote swings produced outsized seat swings. Political scientists have devised a measure to more precisely capture this connection between vote and seat changes. The measure—known as the swing ratio—calculates the percentage change in legislative seats given a percentage change in the national vote. Higher values of the swing ratio indicate an electoral system where small changes in the vote lead to large changes in seat shares. Lower values indicate a system where large changes in the vote lead to only small changes in seat shares.

Figure 3.1 displays the value of the swing ratio from 1850 through 2008. The figure shows steady erosion in the swing ratio over time. Throughout most of the nineteenth century, the swing ratio was near four. In other words, for every one-point change in the national vote, legislative seats changed by

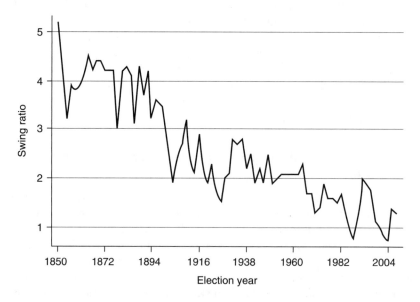

*Figure 3.1* Swing Ratio, United States House Races (1850–2008)

four percent. Compare that to more recent elections. In 2006 the swing ratio was a more modest value of two. Even though that election swept the Democrats into power, the actual swing in seats was modest by historical standards. In short, seat swings in congressional membership have become increasingly less responsive to changes in the vote.

This is not meant to suggest that public opinion does not matter. Macro movements in public opinion certainly influence congressional decision-making (e.g., Erikson, MacKuen, and Stimson 2002). But by looking back across time, we can see that in the modern era it takes a bigger swing in the national vote to alter the seat distribution in the U.S. House. This matters because the seat distribution in Congress shapes the ideological alignment of government. The responsiveness of seat swings to vote swings also matters because it influences how members behave and who they represent. If elections are local affairs, then members of Congress will pay more attention to their local constituency and worry less about their national party label. But if elections are influenced primarily by what the party does on Capitol Hill, then members will gear their actions towards promoting their party label at the expense of local concerns.

Closely tracking the decline in the swing ratio has been a general decline in competitive districts. This is not surprising; the two factors are intimately related. The more districts that are competitive, the more districts that will shift with changes in the national vote (Mayhew 1974b). For instance, a district that is split 52–48 in favor of the Democrats will more likely flip if there is a small shift in the vote to the opposition party. But a district split 70–30 in favor of the Democrats will be much less likely to flip even if there is a major national vote swing to the opposition party. In other words, the more districts that are evenly divided, the more districts that have the potential to change party hands. Thus, as individual districts become less competitive, the responsiveness of congressional membership to changes in the national vote diminishes.

To get a sense of over-time trends in competition, Figure 3.2 plots the number of districts where the victor won by 55 percent or less of the major party vote. The 55 percent threshold is a traditional metric of classifying districts as either competitive or non-competitive (Jacobson 2009; Mayhew 1974b). As with the swing ratio, there has been a steady decline in competitive congressional elections over the last one hundred years. In the late nineteenth century nearly 40 percent of House elections met the competitive threshold. A steep drop-off occurred near the turn of the last century. This was then followed by another drop in the 1960s. The number of competitive races has remained low ever since.

One consequence of low competition is that membership in Congress is relatively stable from one year to the next. Where Congress was once a layover in a longer political career, it is now a destination. For many modern politicians, serving in Congress represents the culmination of a political career. Again, the comparison with the nineteenth century is illuminating. For much of the nineteenth century, serving in Congress was often one stop in an otherwise

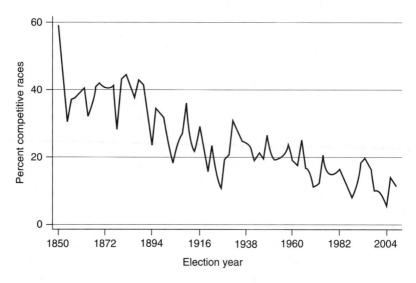

*Figure 3.2* Competitive United States House Races (1850–2008). Winner Wins with 55 Percent of Major-party Vote or Less.

peripatetic career (Brady, Buckley, and Rivers 1999; Kernell 1977a; Polsby 1968). A typical nineteenth-century political career might involve winning a local office, serving in the state legislature, serving a term or two in Congress, and then returning to the state legislature. Nowadays, for many, serving in Congress is a destination office. John Dingell (D-MI) was first elected to the House in 1955 and continues to serve (fifty-five years and counting—he has been reelected twenty-six times). Robert Byrd (D-WV) served in the Senate for a record fifty-one years, by far the longest career to date in the upper chamber.

The search for the cause of declining swing ratios, uncompetitive elections, and decreased turnover has preoccupied students of congressional elections for the past thirty years. Indeed, one can frame the vast modern literature on congressional elections as the search for the reasons contributing to the decline in competition in elections over time. Scholars have looked in a number of places. One suspect that has occurred to many pundits and scholars is redistricting. The suspicion is that incumbents of both parties colluded to draw lines that protect themselves (Tufte 1973). The general consensus, however, among researchers is that redistricting only has a minimal impact on declining competition. Indeed, the general thrust of the literature suggests that while redistricting might depress competition in the short term, it can only account for a small proportion of the overall decline in competition (Friedman and Holden 2009).

Other scholars have argued that voters may be the root cause of "red" and "blue" districts. For example, in an intriguing essay Bruce Oppenheimer (2005) suggested that the residential patterns of voters might be leading to the decline in electoral competition. As the country has become more mobile, citizens have been seeking out places to live that better mesh with their lifestyle. For example, young artisans tend to congregate in urban centers while upper middle class families tend to select upscale suburbs. It so happens that many of these lifestyle choices correlate with partisanship. The result of this lifestyle sorting has also been a political sorting of America into "deep red and blue" districts. Here, according to Oppenheimer, lies the basis of uncompetitive elections. Full empirical documentation of these trends is still lacking, but it is a highly provocative notion.

Finally, some scholars have pointed to the candidates themselves. The single greatest contributor to the decline in competition, according to many researchers, has been the importance of incumbency. To rephrase James Carville's famous mantra from the 1992 presidential election: "It's the candidates, stupid." While issues, party labels, and money all influence elections, the driving determinant of electoral outcomes, according to many scholars, are the particular candidates that run in each district. If you want to predict which candidate will win in a congressional election, you only need to answer one simple question: is an incumbent running for reelection? If so, bet on the incumbent. It is not a foolproof bet, but it is close. When incumbents face political novices, the incumbent almost always wins.

For some scholars, changes in the U.S. electoral structure over the last century have encouraged and accentuated the electoral advantages of incumbency. The story goes something like the following. The demise of strong, local political parties means that representatives had to run on their own (Carson, Engstrom, and Roberts 2007). They could no longer rely on party machines to carry them to victory. As a result members of Congress gradually adapted, developing the skills it takes to win election on their own. As they evolved and adapted they became much better at scaring off challengers, raising financial war chests, performing tasks for their constituents, bringing home pork-barrel projects, etc. The result has been the rise of incumbent victory margins and the decline of competitive congressional elections.

Yet, despite much research into the subject there is still much to learn about the various factors that have contributed to the decline in competitive elections over time. How much weight to put on each of these factors remains an important research task. In addition, another area of potential future research would be to consider in more depth the consequences, if any, of uncompetitive elections. The natural inclination for researchers and the public is to favor more competitive elections. The belief is that uncompetitive elections are somehow a failure of democracy. But it is not entirely obvious that more competition promotes better representation. Indeed, some scholars have recently argued that more competitive districts would in fact make citizens unhappy (Brunell 2008).

For example, Buchler (2005) has argued that thinking of elections as akin to an economic market—where competition is prized—might be the wrong metaphor to apply to elections. Instead, if one thinks about representation as the relationship between an employer and employee (where representatives are the employees) then less competitive districts might ensure better representation. It is easier for the representative (employee) to know what the district (employer) wants if that district is sending a clear signal. Districts that are deep red or deep blue send very clear signals to representatives. Competitive elections, on the other hand, send mixed signals about what the district median wants, making it harder for representatives to cater to the median voter. This is an intriguing perspective, the implications of which might lead to new insights into topics such as redistricting, campaign finance, and negative campaigning.

## Presidents and Midterms

Another major structural feature of congressional elections is the Constitutional staggering of elections. In particular, the division of congressional elections into "presidential" and "midterm" elections creates one of the fundamental dynamics of congressional elections. The division between presidential and midterm years affects who shows up to vote and how they vote. In presidential election years the party winning the presidency usually gains seats in Congress. For instance, in 2008, Democrats captured the White House while at the same time picking up 22 House seats. Since 1940 the party winning the presidency has gained seats in the House in thirteen out of the eighteen elections. This correlation between presidential and congressional success suggests the possibility of a presidential coattail effect, where triumphant presidential candidates pull fellow congressional candidates into office. In the nineteenth century the party ticket ballot induced long coattails. In those states that held congressional elections in November, the fates of congressional candidates were physically linked with the presidential candidate at the top of the ticket. In the modern era, with ballots that allow split-ticket voting, the mechanism underlying "coattail" voting remains unclear. Thus, although there does appear to be a "presidential pulse" to congressional elections (Campbell 1997) the mechanism underlying this relationship is not clearly understood.

On the flip-side are midterm elections. One of the regularities of U.S. politics is that the president's party will lose seats in a midterm election. Only four times since 1826 has the president's party gained seats in midterm elections. A number of different explanations have been offered for this pattern. One of the earliest explanations for this phenomenon was "surge and decline" (Campbell 1960). Popular presidential candidates motivate marginal voters to turn out and vote. And they support congressional candidates of the victorious presidential candidate—the surge. Two years later the absence of a galvanizing presidential race leaves these marginal voters sitting at home. As a result the congressional candidates of the president's party suffer—the decline. The idea of surge and decline fell out of scholarly favor for a number of years but has recently been partially rehabilitated by James Campbell (1997).

Other scholars have argued that voters use the midterm election as a referendum on the performance of the president and his party. Kernell (1977b), for example, argued that voters who are upset or dissatisfied with the president's performance are more likely to turn out to vote. Thus, the preponderance of "negative voters" at the midterm causes the president's party to lose seats. Another variant of the referendum argument is that voters behave strategically. In particular, they use their votes to ideologically balance the government. Voters, in the aggregate, tend to be moderate. Thus if government becomes too liberal (or too conservative) voters can pull the ideological balance of government back towards the center by voting for candidates opposite of the president's party (Fiorina 1992).

Finally, Erikson (1988) has argued that voters simply penalize the party of the president no matter his performance. Whether the economy is up or down, whether there is peace or not, the president's party suffers at the polls. The presidential penalty argument can be supplemented by considering the argument put forth by Oppenheimer, Stimson, and Waterman (1986). They found that the size of the presidential penalty depends on how many congressional seats the president's party holds going into a midterm election. The more seats the president's party holds the more they lose. Here, then, could be one reason why the Democrats lost so many seats—64—in the 2010 election. By gaining a number of House seats in the 2008 election, Democrats entered the 2010 elections "overexposed." They had 255 seats to defend which was well above their historical average. By this logic, Democratic losses in 2010 were large primarily because there was a Democrat in the White House *and* they had a historically large number of seats to defend.

Again, research in this area has pushed forward our understanding of congressional elections. But a number of important and tantalizing research questions remain. What exactly is the psychological basis, if any, of coattail voting? Or is coattail voting an artifact of other factors that simultaneously drive both presidential and congressional voting, such as the state of the economy (Fair 2009)? Why does a presidential penalty exist? Why do some voters punish their House members for what the president has, or has not, done? Who are the voters who engage in "penalizing" behavior? At the heart of these questions lie questions about what motivates voters in congressional elections.

## Congressional Voters

Most of what scholars know about voter behavior comes from research into U.S. presidential elections. Relatively less is known about voting in congressional elections. This imbalance reflects the comparative paucity of reliable survey data at the level of congressional districts. The difficulty of creating large enough statistical samples in each of 435 districts has long served as a barrier for the study of congressional voters. This lacuna, however, is currently being filled by the magnificent new Cooperative Congressional Election Study (CCES). By surveying over 30,000 people, the CCES provides for sufficient sample sizes to make inferences about what is happening within and across individual congressional districts. This will allow scholars to probe district-level opinion in a way that has not been possible previously. The first CCES study was conducted in 2006 and scholars have already begun to produce new insights into congressional elections (e.g., Ansolabehere and Jones 2010; Stone and Simas 2010).

This is not to say, however, that we previously knew nothing about congressional voters. Indeed, scholars have uncovered a number of common facts about congressional voters. In particular, the overriding theme of the study of congressional voters is that voters tend to know few of the policy details about the candidates running in their district. And in many cases, voters are unable to recall the names of the candidates running (Miller and Stokes 1963; Mann and Wolfinger 1980). At first glance, this information deficit might seem troublesome. However, a compelling logic resides behind this "ignorance." The logic was most forcefully laid out by Anthony Downs in his influential book, *An Economic Theory of Democracy* (1957). Whether an individual votes or not has almost no impact on the outcome of an election. In other words, in a large-scale election your vote will have no impact on whether your preferred candidate wins or loses. Thus the instrumental benefits to casting a "well-informed" vote are essentially zero, according to Downs' logic. Yet the cost of becoming informed about the details of candidates running in a House election is not trivial. One has to pay attention to the election, the campaign promises and, in the case of the incumbent, their past record. These are all "costs" (time and effort that could be spent on something else). Thus for most people, according to this logic, the costs of gathering detailed knowledge about politics outweigh the benefits.

Instead, voters rely on simple mental shortcuts. In the context of congressional elections the two primary mental shortcuts voters use are party labels and incumbency. Indeed, research into congressional voters finds that partisanship and incumbency are the two most powerful correlates of the vote. Consider partisanship first. If you only know whether a candidate is a Republican or Democrat, you already know a fair amount of information about those candidates. For instance, one can be almost certain that a Democrat is to the left of a Republican on the ideological spectrum (Ansolabehere, Snyder, and Stewart 2001; Lee, Moretti, and Butler 2004). You might not know precisely where on the spectrum each candidate resides, but you can reliably guess which candidate is on the left and which is on the right.

Thus, the party label provides a simple, yet powerful piece of information. It is therefore not surprising that voters lean on it heavily in making their vote choice. This correlation between party identification and vote choice, however, has fluctuated over time. Reliable survey evidence only dates back to the 1950s but the nadir of party voting appears to be the early 1970s (Bartels 2000; Jacobson 2009). Since the mid-1970s there has been a steady uptick in the association between party identification and vote choice—that is, self-identified

Democrats voting for Democratic candidates, and self-identified Republicans voting for Republican candidates. These changes among the electorate are critical for understanding changes in congressional politics more broadly. The more weight that voters place on the party label will have substantial consequences for both how campaigns are waged, how Congress is organized, and the kinds of legislation that are crafted.

The other major correlate of vote choice is whether a candidate is an incumbent. All else being equal, voters are more likely to select an incumbent than a challenger. The simple fact of putting "incumbent" next to a name on the ballot, however, is not what attracts voters. Instead incumbency acts as a surrogate for the likes and dislikes that voters have about candidates. Gary Jacobson (2009) has shown, for example, that members of Congress, through their various constituency and campaign activities, acquire favorable images among the public. These favorable images then give them a leg-up over challengers (who tend to be less well known). Jacobson found that voters generally report knowing more about the incumbent than the challenger, and that voters are much more willing to report something they "like" about an incumbent than a challenger. It is this disparity in public images that translates into voters being more willing to vote for incumbents. In other words, voters find many things to like about their incumbent.

This underlying basis of incumbent-driven voting has been reinforced in recent work conducted by Stone, Maisel, and Maestes (2004). They discovered that while voters certainly care about partisanship and a candidate's issue positions, they also care about the competence of candidates. All else being equal, voters prefer candidates who demonstrate integrity and a commitment to public service. Again, this makes logical sense from the standpoint of a "low-information" voter. Voters cannot anticipate the panoply of issues that a representative will have to deal with. Nor do most voters have the time to track what a representative is doing in Washington. Instead it may be more rational to choose someone they trust to act in the best interests of the constituency, even if that constituency does not have well-informed views about what it wants (Fenno 1978). Thus, relying on simple pieces of information that signal whether a candidate is trustworthy and will act in the best interests of constituents is more efficient than gathering detailed policy information about candidates.

## Legislators and Constituents

The nature of the electoral system, and the information voters rely on, ultimately matters because it pervades politics in Washington, D.C. In the case of congressional elections, representatives, to a large extent, win election to Congress based on their own entrepreneurial efforts. They cannot depend on a party machine or presidential coattails to pull them through on Election Day. They must work hard for their own reelection. The primacy of reelection in shaping congressional behavior was most famously propounded in David Mayhew's influential book, *Congress: The Electoral Connection* (Mayhew 1974a). While representatives have many goals—securing favorable legislation, capturing positions of power within the legislature, attracting media attention, etc.—one must actually serve in Congress to achieve any of those goals. Thus, Mayhew argued that members could be treated "as if" they were single-minded seekers of reelection. The primal pursuit of reelection influences, to a profound degree, their priorities on Capitol Hill.

Notably the drive for reelection creates an incentive for members of Congress to promote localism and particularistic policymaking. Because the electoral system rewards self-reliant politicians, there is a strong incentive to pursue concentrated benefits for their district while diffusing the costs to the other 434 districts. They can then claim credit for bringing jobs and federal money back to their district. This encourages a policymaking system that divides public benefits into 435 district-sized morsels.

It would be an overstatement, however, to argue that particularistic policy runs unchecked, or that politicians spend all day at the pork-barrel trough. As we saw above, voters also rely on a candidate's party label. The party label conveys information to voters even if voters remain unaware of the arcane details of public policy. But unlike the personal reputation that a member has—which is primarily under their individual control—the reputation of the party as a whole is dependent on the actions of the other politicians who share that label. Developing a reputation as a party that can solve national problems—such as fostering economic growth, peace, or clean air—spills over to all members of that party. The label is therefore a collective good shared by all members of a party. Indeed, the importance of the party label as an informational cue provides one of the chief rationales for creating party leaders. Party leaders are given the task of coordinating the diverse needs of members who share the party label. They also are tasked with preventing actions, or legislation, that might tarnish the party label (Cox and McCubbins 1993; Aldrich 1995). If members go their own way and tailor their campaigns solely to their district median, they run the risk collectively of diluting the informational value of the party label. On the other hand, members who become too tied to their party's ideology, especially where it differs from the local median voter, can face electoral punishment (Canes-Wrone, Brady, and Cogan 2002; Carson et al. 2010). The need to appeal to local, diverse constituencies while at the same time remaining members of a national party creates one of the fundamental and intriguing issues in the study of Congress. The study of this dilemma has long been of interest to legislative scholars (e.g., Stokes 1967; Cain, Ferejohn, and Fiorina 1987). But there is still much to learn. In the conclusion to this essay I discuss how recent changes in the relationship between parties and candidates are leading to new developments in congressional elections.

## A Word about the Senate

Most of this essay has emphasized House elections. This reflects a balance of research between House and Senate elections that favors the former. Though much of what I have discussed also applies to Senate elections, there are some important distinctions worthy of attention. Senate elections themselves have undergone a number of fundamental, and fascinating, changes over time. Indeed, senators were not formally chosen by voters until the 1914 elections following passage of the Seventeenth Amendment. The job of choosing senators instead resided with state legislatures. The framers sought to insulate the Senate from public fads and temporary passions. Indirect elections, coupled with a staggered electoral cycle, were the solution. Perhaps even more so than House elections, nineteenth-century Senate elections were party-dominated affairs. Senators owed their election to fellow partisans in the state legislature (Engstrom and Kernell 2007). And by all accounts the state legislative selections of senators were bitter partisan affairs (Schiller and Stewart 2004).

In an ironic twist, however, opening up Senate elections to public participation, beginning in 1914, has made Senate elections more responsive and competitive than the House elections.

Senate elections tend to be more competitive and the swings in the partisan distribution of seats in the Senate tend to be higher. Figure 3.3 presents the number of competitive Senate races (using the 55 percent threshold) from 1952 to 2008. Overall, Senate elections are more competitive than House elections. The reasons why Senate elections remain more competitive than the House are fairly straightforward. States tend to be more heterogeneous than the average House district. The prestige of a Senate seat entices more competitive

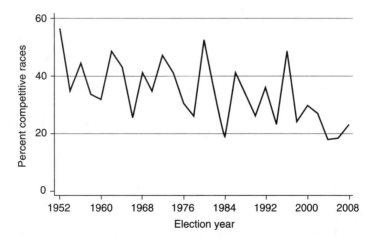

*Figure 3.3* Competitive United States Senate Races (1952–2008). Winner Wins with 55% of Major-Party Vote or Less.

challengers to run against incumbents. Senate races also tend to feature better financed campaigns on both sides. But even here Senate elections do indicate a general downward trend regarding competition. Given the close partisan seat balance in the Senate, the decline in state-level competition has meant an ever-increasing focus on just a handful of Senate races; those that can tip the balance between majority and minority status.

## New Directions: Congressional Elections in an Age of Party Polarization

One reason why the U.S. Congress remains a lively, and fascinating, area of scholarly research is because the institution frequently changes. This essay has examined the recent evolution of congressional elections. But congressional elections, along with the institution itself, continue to evolve. Looking forward, one question scholars have begun to ask is whether we are returning to a party-centered system. Although the strong party machines and bosses of the nineteenth century may have vanished, other partisan actors might be filling the void. The influence of ideological activists, national party committees, partisan news outlets (e.g., Fox and MSNBC), and partisan financial donors (McCarty, Poole, and Rosenthal 2006) could be pushing congressional elections away from candidate-centered politics. What is interesting, from a historical perspective, is that we appear to be in an era of partisan polarization yet without the strong party organizations of the nineteenth century.

By most metrics, congressional parties are as polarized as at any time since World War II (McCarty et al. 2006). The result has been a growing reluctance by either side in Congress to compromise and a rise in obstructionist legislative tactics, especially in the Senate. As Morris Fiorina has eloquently put it: "The political class today allows national problems to fester because its members insist on having the entire loaf, not just a portion, and/or because they would rather have an election issue than incremental progress" (Fiorina 2005: 176).

While the rise of partisan polarization could be troublesome for those concerned about congressional performance, for students of congressional elections it presents a number of fascinating research questions that scholars are just now beginning to explore. To take one example, consider the current configuration of electoral and legislative politics. We live in an era of low intra-district competition *but* high levels of legislative polarization. At first glance, these two trends might seem to naturally follow from each other. Where district-level competition is low, members can take more polarized ideological positions without fear of losing. Deep red, or deep blue, districts should cause little penalty for a member of Congress who stakes out a strident roll-call record (assuming the representative is on the "correct" side of the district).

Yet looking back in history suggests that the two trends need not coincide. The nineteenth century featured high legislative polarization *and* fever-pitch competition at the district level. Legislative polarization for most of the nineteenth century was very high, mirroring the levels that we see now in Congress. This provides scholars with something akin to a laboratory experiment to study the causes and consequences of legislative polarization. How do members behave when competition is high and polarization is high (as in the nineteenth century) compared to a period of low competition and high polarization (as in the twenty-first century)? How does Congress fashion legislation when only a minority of districts are in-play? How does Congress fashion public policy when a bevy of districts are in-play? Does Congress eschew programmatic policy in favor of targeting distributive benefits, or vice-versa?[5]

Questions such as these suggest that there is much still to learn about congressional elections. The importance of congressional elections is hard to overstate. As the other essays in this volume attest, the politics of congressional elections pervade almost everything Congress does. The drive by representatives to get to Washington, and then stay there, casts a long shadow over Capitol Hill. Thus, understanding Congress, and by implication national politics, necessitates understanding the electoral system and its impact on congressional politics.

## Notes

1  For the student interested in a more comprehensive treatment, one can do no better than reading Gary Jacobson's magisterial book, *The Politics of Congressional Elections* (2009).
2  Another approach would be to compare United States congressional elections with other electoral systems around the world (Cain, Ferejohn, and Fiorina 1987).
3  One can engage in a bit of historical fancy wondering what would have happened had Lincoln stayed in the House of Representatives rather than returning to Illinois where he bided his time as a lawyer before reentering national politics in 1858.
4  The ballot was so-named because it was first developed in Australia during the 1850s.
5  For an early example of the kind of research I have in mind, see Brady (1973).

# Part III

# Congressional Institutions

# Chapter 4

# Parties and Leaders
## Polarization and Power in the U.S. House and Senate

*C. Lawrence Evans*

By most accounts, two of the most significant congressional enactments since World War II were both attempts to guarantee that Americans would have adequate access to quality health care—the 1965 legislation that established the Medicare and Medicaid programs and passage in 2010 of comprehensive health care reform. Superficially, there are certain similarities across the two legislative episodes. For one, both measures were championed by newly elected Democratic Presidents—Lyndon Johnson and Barack Obama—who were deeply committed to making major changes in the health care systems of their day. In 1965 and again in 2010, Democrats were able to rely on huge partisan majorities in the House and Senate to help them achieve victory on the floor. And in keeping with the enduring importance of the political parties in American electoral and legislative politics, both enactments were characterized by major ideological and political differences between Democrats and Republicans.

Yet, upon closer examination, the processes through which these two measures were considered and eventually enacted were remarkably different, reflecting the profound changes that have occurred from the 1960s to the 2000s in the roles played by parties and leaders on Capitol Hill. The 1965 legislation that established Medicare and Medicaid, for instance, was largely crafted within the committees of jurisdiction in the House and Senate, especially the House Committee on Ways and Means.[1] The Ways and Means bill, in turn, was the product of a political bargain struck between the Democratic chair at the time, Wilbur Mills (AR), and the Republican ranking minority member, John Byrnes (WI). As a legislative leader, Mills was highly responsive to the mood of the full chamber and he usually sought to minimize conflict in committee and on the floor. In 1965 he wanted to report health care legislation that could pass the House with broad support from members of both political parties, and in his view the version of the bill originally backed by the Johnson administration would have created excessive partisan conflict on the floor. So, early in that year, he proposed to Byrnes that the Johnson bill be merged with an alternative measure that Byrnes himself had introduced. The Republican accepted Mills' offer, the two measures were combined, and after the adoption of scores of modifications proposed by Democrats and Republicans alike, the compromise bill passed the House and Senate by wide margins of 307–116 and 70–24, respectively.

As mentioned, partisan differences were apparent in both chambers during the creation of Medicare and Medicaid in 1965. In the House, for example, the Republican motion to recommit the Mills–Byrnes bill back to committee failed along party lines. Overall, however, congressional action on the measure had all the hallmarks of bipartisan legislating. The basic structure of the legislation was determined in committee, with ample participation by members from both sides of the partisan aisle and only limited guidance from party leaders. Although opposition to the bill came disproportionately from the GOP side of the aisle, there also was substantial bipartisan support for final passage in both chambers.

In sharp contrast, House and Senate action on comprehensive health care reform during 2009–10 was anything but bipartisan, and party leaders played significant parts at all stages of the legislative game.[2] Under the leadership of Majority Leader Harry Reid (D-NV), in April 2009 the Senate adopted a budget resolution on a party-line vote that would allow the chamber to pass health care reform as a budget reconciliation bill. Since reconciliation measures cannot be filibustered and require only a simple majority for passage, the move provided Reid and his fellow Democrats with a vehicle for circumventing the minority party in the Senate. For most of 2009, there were sixty Democrats in the Senate, nominally a filibuster-proof majority. But Reid was concerned that one or two Democratic moderates might vote with the GOP against the package, which made reconciliation a potentially useful backup strategy. In the end, this partisan procedural move was critical to the outcome.

A few months later, in the House, initial legislative action on health care reform took place within three panels with jurisdiction—Ways and Means, Energy and Commerce, and Education and Labor—but the draft legislation considered by these committees had been structured beforehand by Democratic leaders. On the Senate side, Reid at first deferred to the two committees with jurisdiction, Finance and HELP (short for Heath, Education, Labor, and Pensions). But following the breakdown of negotiations between Democrats and Republicans on the Finance panel in August 2009, serious attempts at striking a bipartisan accord on health care reform all but ended in the Senate as well.

As floor action neared in Fall 2009, House Speaker Nancy Pelosi was the central player among House Democrats in forging the compromises necessary to secure passage, including the critical decision to scale back plans for a public health care option managed by the Federal government. Not surprisingly, initial House passage on November 7 was near party line, with only one GOP member voting aye. In the Senate, Reid also structured the version of the bill that was adopted by that chamber in late December 2009. Although there were sporadic attempts to secure the support of Olympia Snowe, a moderate Republican from Maine, who previously had voted in favor of health care reform in the Finance Committee, in the end the Senate measure also was entirely the product of bargaining among the majority Democrats, under the direction of the majority leadership.

This highly partisan, leadership-driven process continued for the next two months as Democratic leaders forged a bicameral package capable of passing both the House and Senate, once again without Republican support. Although the January 2010 election of Scott Brown (R-MA) to replace the late Edward Kennedy meant that Senate Democrats no longer had a filibuster-proof majority, Reid and Pelosi were able to use their procedural prerogatives to structure floor action in both chambers to enable their party to prevail. Relying on a process that was both convoluted and effective, in March 2010 the House first adopted the version of the legislation previously passed by the Senate in December 2009, and then used reconciliation to pass a compromise, "side-car" package that included the modifications necessary to win majority support in both chambers. The Senate then adopted the "side-car" compromise with only fifty-six members, all Democrats, voting in favor. As a reconciliation bill, only a simple majority was required for passage.[3] In both chambers, but especially the House, the last days and hours before the dramatic final roll calls featured intensive efforts by Democratic leaders to whip their party rank and file into line.

The striking differences between congressional action on Medicare and Medicaid in 1965 and the passage of comprehensive health care reform in 2010, we shall see, are far from idiosyncratic. Instead, they reflect broader transformations that have occurred in congressional coalition building over the past half-century, especially in the roles played by parties and leaders. Not surprisingly, much of the best recent scholarship about Congress has been devoted to identifying and explaining these changes. This chapter reviews recent scholarly research about parties and leaders in both chambers of Congress. The goal is to highlight precisely what we know about the remarkable shift from the bipartisan, committee-dominated processes of the 1960s' Congress to the highly partisan, leadership-driven patterns that are apparent in the contemporary House and Senate. To what extent and under what conditions do parties and leaders have an independent and significant impact over legislative outcomes in Congress, and how has this impact changed over time? Only by understanding the causes and consequences of heightened party polarization and strong party leaders can we evaluate whether these features of the contemporary lawmaking process will endure.

## Party Polarization

Perhaps the most striking trend in recent congressional politics has been the significant increase in partisan polarization in the lawmaking process. Intense partisanship is now apparent at all stages of the process, but especially on the House and Senate floor when members cast roll-call votes on major legislation. Scholars use a variety of techniques to gauge the level of roll-call partisanship and for the most part these measures produce the same basic results. For one, consider the index of *party difference*, which is simply the absolute value of the difference between the percentage of Democrats and Republicans voting yes on a roll call. If all Democrats vote yes and all Republicans vote no (or if all Democrats vote no and all Republicans vote yes), then the parties are completely polarized and the party difference index takes on the value of 100. On the other hand, if an equal proportion of members within each party vote yes, then partisan polarization is absent and the party difference index is zero. The July 1965 votes on final passage of the legislation that created Medicare and Medicaid, for example, produced party difference scores of 32.4 for the House and 45.7 for the Senate. In contrast, the party difference values for House and Senate passage of health care reform in 2009–10 were 86.6 and 100, respectively, reflecting the intense partisan polarization that existed within both chambers on the measure.[4]

Figure 4.1 portrays the average level of party difference per Congress on the roll calls cast within the House and Senate from the 83rd Congress (1953–54) through the 110th Congress (2007–08).[5] As you can see, within both chambers the level of party difference, and thus the degree of partisan polarization, was fairly modest throughout the 1950s and early 1960s, reaching minimum levels during the 91st Congress (1971–72) for the House and the 90th Congress (1969–70) for the Senate. The difference index then climbed sharply over the next two decades in both chambers, reaching very high levels by the mid-1990s.

Underlying this striking increase in roll-call polarization was a burgeoning ideological split between the two party caucuses in the House and Senate. Among congressional scholars, the most commonly used indicators of the ideological "preferences" of legislators are the DW-NOMINATE scores developed by Keith Poole and Howard Rosenthal.[6] Poole and Rosenthal used a dimensional

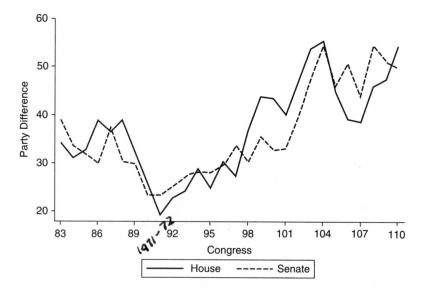

Figure 4.1   Average Party Difference on House and Senate Roll Calls, 83rd–110th Congresses

unfolding technique to assign to each member an ideological score for each Congress in which they served and cast a requisite number of votes, ranging from –1 (very liberal) to +1 (very conservative). During 1965–66, the Congress in which Medicare and Medicaid were established, most Democrats had DW-NOMINATE scores less than zero and most Republican members had scores that took on positive values. But there also was a substantial overlap in the ideological distributions of the two political parties. And more than 100 House members and dozens of senators from both parties had DW-NOMINATE scores located near the center of the ideological distribution in the relevant chamber. Based on the roll-call record, then, there was a sizable ideological middle in the Houses and Senates of the 1960s and early 1970s.

The pattern for more recent Congresses is dramatically different. Figure 4.2 shows the distribution of DW-NOMINATE values for the House and Senate

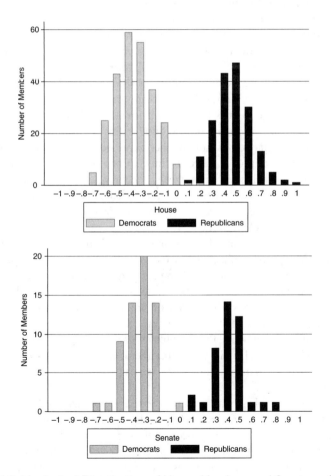

*Figure 4.2* Ideological Distribution of House Members and Senators, 2009

of 2009, the year when the first important votes on comprehensive health care reform occurred. Clearly, the ideological overlap that characterized the Congresses of the 1960s had completely disappeared. In both chambers, the most conservative Democrat was more liberal than the most left-leaning Republican. Moreover, the number of members with DW-NOMINATE values near zero had plummeted to just a few dozen in the House and a mere handful in the Senate.

Over the years, a large scholarly literature has emerged that attempts to identify the causes and consequences of this heightened partisan polarization in Congress. Many pundits and some scholars, for example, argue that the redistricting that occurs after each decennial census (and occasionally during the intervening years because of Court orders or political intrigue) has resulted in a larger proportion of House districts that are gerrymandered to tilt strongly toward one party or the other, which in turn could lead to the election of more party loyalists to Congress (Mann and Ornstein 2006; Carson, Crespin, Finocchiaro, and Rohde 2007). Although there is some evidence that redistricting has increased the number of strongly Democratic and Republican districts in the House, the size of the effect is relatively small. Moreover, as Figures 4.1 and 4.2 show, the rise in roll-call polarization is very similar in the House and Senate, and the Senate of course is not subject to reapportionment.

An alternative argument is that congressional constituencies have become more homogeneous internally, not because of reapportionment, but because of changes in the behavior of individual citizens. According to this view, ordinary Americans have grown more inclined to base their partisan affiliations and their votes on their ideological views, and they also are increasingly likely to live around other people who share their ideological and partisan attachments (Bishop 2008; Levendusky 2009). This political "sorting out" at the mass level is especially prevalent in the South, where the enfranchisement of African Americans following passage of the Voting Rights Act of 1965 led conservatives to transfer their partisan allegiances from the Democrats to the Republicans. The strongly ideological policies of the Reagan administration in the 1980s also appear to have strengthened the connections between personal ideology, partisan affiliation, and voting behavior among ordinary citizens (Sinclair 2006). As a result, the Democratic Party (especially in the South) became more homogeneously liberal, while the Republican Party grew more homogeneously conservative. Not surprisingly, the House members and senators representing these more strongly partisan constituencies have been more likely to toe the partisan line.

Still another possible explanation for the rise of polarization is that changes in the way candidates are selected (especially the shift to mass participation primaries) and in the campaign process itself (for example, the growing importance of money and interest groups) has enhanced the electoral influence of party activists on both sides of the aisle (Fiorina 2009). Activists tend to have more ideologically extreme views than the typical voter, and their heightened role in fundraising and campaigns might create incentives for House members and senators to likewise move toward the ideological left (for Democrats) or right (for Republicans), increasing partisan polarization in Congress.[7]

Scholars disagree about the relative importance of these factors for explaining the polarization of the congressional parties. Still, the most comprehensive analysis (Theriault 2008) suggests that only about a third of the increase in party polarization that took place in the House from the 1970s to the 2000s resulted from some combination of redistricting, the partisan sorting of voters, and the ideological extremism of party activists. For the Senate, increased homogeneity at the constituency level and the role of party activists is probably responsible for about 15 percent of the heightened roll-call polarization that took place within that chamber. In short, the lion's share of the increase in partisan polarization on Capitol Hill does not appear to derive directly from constituency-level factors, including the growing clout of party activists. What, then, is the main culprit?

The answer appears to be the important institutional changes that have occurred within the House and Senate since the 1960s, especially the empowerment of party leaders. Indeed, most of the remarkable increase in party voting in the House and Senate captured in Figure 4.1 occurred on roll calls dealing with procedural matters, rather than on amendments or the passage of legislation (Theriault 2008). These procedural votes, in turn, often concerned attempts by majority-party leaders to maintain their grasp over the legislative agenda, or attempts by minority-party members to undermine the majority's procedural control. The critical importance of procedural votes as a source of the increase in roll-call polarization, in other words, suggests that party leaders and other institutional features within the House and Senate are at the heart of the intense partisan infighting that exists in the contemporary Congress.

## Party Theories

To understand how rules and other structural arrangements within the legislative branch might lead to party polarization and party power, we first need to consider the causal theories that have been developed to explain the lawmaking process. Among scholars, the main conceptual tool for understanding the impact of parties and the other internal features of Congress is called the spatial model of legislative choice.[8] Spatial models make good intuitive sense and generally share three main ingredients. The first assumption is that the policy views of legislators can be captured as points along one or more underlying dimensions of evaluation, such as the liberal–conservative ideological spectrum. Second, spatial models usually posit that the legislative alternatives over which members cast their votes also can be represented as points along the underlying dimension. And third, confronted with two competing proposals, legislators will vote for the alternative that is located nearest their preference on the relevant ideological line.

For purposes of illustration, consider again the distribution of ideological views portrayed in Figure 4.2, which summarizes the DW-NOMINATE scores of House members and senators during 2009. Here, the horizontal axis functions as the underlying dimension of evaluation, in this case the liberal–conservative continuum. The preferences, or "ideal points," of individual lawmakers are located at their most preferred policy outcome on that line. In Figure 4.2, member preferences are captured by their DW-NOMINATE values, which in turn reflect their ideological placement on the liberal–conservative spectrum. In the House, for example, Majority Leader Steny Hoyer (D-MD), had a DW-NOMINATE value of −.362, so that point on the horizontal axis of the figure would represent his "preferences." Minority Leader John Boehner (R-OH), in contrast, had a DW-NOMINATE score of .535, so his ideal point, as captured in the figure, would be right of center and near the middle of the distribution for Republican House members that year.

For obvious reasons, it is not straightforward to summarize a complex piece of legislation like comprehensive health care reform with a DW-NOMINATE value. Still, most observers would agree that the final passage vote on health care reform in March 2010 confronted House members with two main alternatives—a bill that was located in the center-left portions of the ideological spectrum and a status quo (existing law, or the policy that would obtain if the bill failed) located toward the more conservative end of the horizontal axis of Figure 4.2. Thus, for Hoyer, his preference, or ideal point, was closer to the bill than to the status quo and he voted yes. Boehner's ideal point, in contrast, was spatially more proximate to the status quo, so he voted no.

Simple enough. However, spatial models of Congress become more complicated when we start integrating into them important institutional features of the House and Senate. Moreover, the implications of spatial theories for the power of parties and leaders depend in large part on precisely how the various institutional features are incorporated. To see why internal structures matter and might, indeed, be responsible for the lion's share of party polarization in Congress, let's begin by considering the implications of the basic spatial logic, but *without* including these features of the real lawmaking process.

In the House, if party leaders, the committees of jurisdiction, or some other subset of the full membership is not advantaged in some way, then policy outcomes should tend to be located near the preferences, or ideal point, of the median legislator in the full chamber (Black 1958). In the top panel of Figure 4.2, the median House member would be the lawmaker with an equal number of colleagues located to her ideological left and to her ideological right. Or, in the language of DW-NOMINATE values, the median would be the legislator for whom an equal number of colleagues had scores higher than her own score and lower than her own score. In Figure 4.2, that would be a House member with a DW-NOMINATE value of about −.18—in this case a moderate Democrat. Any amendments that would move the legislative outcome to the left of the median position on the ideological line would be defeated by a coalition of the median member and all lawmakers to her right, while more conservative amendments would be voted down by the median member and all legislators to her left. In the House, then, absent empowered leaders, the basic spatial logic implies that the middle rules.

Now consider a spatial model of the Senate that likewise does not include strong party leaders. Here, a simple majority often is insufficient to pass a proposal in the full chamber because of the filibuster. As a result, proponents of a bill might need sixty votes to invoke cloture and pass their measure on the floor. The legislator with preferences located at the median position, in other words, might not be able to provide the pivotal vote. Instead, for proposals such as health care reform in 2009–10, which would move policy to the left, the pivotal vote might be the member with the 60th ideal point, counting from the left toward the right.[9] Prior to the death of Edward Kennedy, the 60th most liberal senator was Ben Nelson of Nebraska, who also was the most conservative Democrat in the chamber based on the DW-NOMINATE index. After Scott Brown replaced Kennedy in January 2007, the 60th most liberal senator was Olympia Snowe (ME), a moderate Republican, which is precisely why Majority Leader Reid needed to use reconciliation (which cannot be filibustered) as the vehicle for passing the side-car portion of comprehensive health care reform without any GOP votes. When filibustering is threatened or employed, supermajorities are required for passage in the Senate and outcomes shift somewhat from the chamber median position in the direction of the minority party.

The implications of spatial theory for lawmaking change significantly, however, as we begin to layer on further institutional details, especially the procedural prerogatives and other resources of party leaders. One theory, called the "Party Cartel Model," posits that, especially in the House, the majority leadership has control over which bills are considered on the floor and which bills never see the light of day (Cox and McCubbins 1993, 2005). This assumption about the leadership's agenda-setting powers is important. Party leaders owe their leadership positions to the relevant partisan rank and file. As a result, majority-party leaders should be disinclined to bring to the floor legislation that on final passage would probably be opposed by most of their fellow partisans. This principle became known as "the Hastert rule" after Speaker Dennis Hastert (R-IL) articulated it during a speech at the U.S. Library of Congress in November 2003. "On occasion, a particular issue might excite a majority made up mostly of the minority [party]," Hastert observed, but "[t]he job of the Speaker is not to expedite legislation that runs counter to the wishes of a majority of his majority."[10]

According to the Hastert rule—and the Cartel Model—if the House majority leadership expects that most majority-party members will support a piece of legislation on final passage, then that bill will be placed on the floor agenda and the outcome within the chamber should be something approximating the preferences of the floor median à la the basic spatial logic without strong parties. However, if the expectation is that most majority-party members will vote no on final passage, then the leadership should use its agenda powers to keep that measure off the floor, avoiding a contentious fight within the majority caucus. Here, the middle only rules when it advantages the partisan majority. Otherwise, the result is inaction and a status quo outcome that also promotes the interests of the majority party.

Another spatial theory, called the "conditional party government" model, layers on still more institutional detail about the role of parties in Congress (Rohde 1991; Aldrich 1995; Aldrich and Rohde 2000a). According to this approach, party leaders can significantly influence the legislative process if the distribution of preferences within the majority party are relatively homogeneous and there is a substantial difference between the policy preferences of the typical Democratic and Republican member. As Figure 4.2 indicates, the House and Senate of 2009 met both of these conditions quite well. The ideal points of most majority-party members, as captured by their DW-NOMINATE scores, were clustered to the left; the policy preferences of most minority-party members were clustered to the right; and there was a noticeable gap located in the middle. According to the conditional party government argument, when these two conditions hold, there are significant incentives for rank-and-file members of the majority party to delegate authority to their leaders, providing them with the resources necessary to control the agenda. This, in turn, could move policy outcomes systematically away from the preferences of the floor median and toward the policy program of the majority party.

The party theories help explain how the institutional features of the House and Senate could have fueled the rampant partisan polarization of the contemporary Congress, and also how leaders can have an independent impact on lawmaking. If the logic of the Cartel Model holds, then legislation that might divide the majority party, and thus dampen party polarization, is systematically blocked from the floor agenda by the majority leadership, and instead the leadership advances measures that divide the chamber cleanly along party lines, enabling the majority party to prevail because of its larger membership. Indeed, the fact that most of the increase in roll-call polarization that has occurred since the 1970s was on procedural votes resonates strongly with the Cartel Model.

The basic logic of conditional party government may also exacerbate congressional partisanship. As member constituencies have become more politically homogeneous since the 1960s, the kinds of Democrats elected to Congress have become more similar ideologically, as have the Republicans who prevailed in their electoral contests. The two party caucuses in both chambers, but especially the House, became more cohesive internally and the ideological gap between the two party memberships grew. As a result, rank-and-file members enhanced the procedural powers and other resources available to their party leaders, enabling them to minimize defections from the party line on major roll calls, which in turn resulted in increased polarization. To what extent does the available evidence back up one or both theories and what are the implications for our understanding of parties and leaders?

# The Case for Party Power

Scores of scholarly studies have explored the role of parties and leaders in the lawmaking process and thus shed light on the explanatory power of the cartel and conditional party government theories. A full review of this scholarship is beyond the scope of a single chapter.[11] But many of the most significant contributions touch on changes over time in chamber rules, the selection of party leaders, the level of participation by the leadership on major legislation, the ability of the majority party to win on final passage votes, and the leadership's use of its procedural prerogatives on the floor. In this section, I summarize key contributions in each area, primarily focusing on the House, and then consider some recent empirical scholarship about party power in the Senate.

## Institutional Development

Let's begin with the evolution of congressional procedure over time. Is it consistent with party influence? The internal procedures and structures of the two chambers are determined by the members themselves and have been altered throughout congressional history. Certain enduring features of congressional procedure clearly advantage the majority party and its leaders. Since the early 1890s, for example, the House has granted the Speaker the power to circumvent obstructionist tactics by the minority party, and has enabled the Rules Committee—which at important junctures has functioned as an arm of the majority leadership—to facilitate the consideration of legislation on the floor. Moreover, the two political parties have played critical organizational roles throughout most of congressional history, determining the committee assignments of their members and effectively selecting chamber leaders.

The relative strengths of the majority and minority parties also help explain the timing of important changes in House and Senate rules. Binder (1997, 2006) demonstrates that decisions to expand or restrict the parliamentary rights of the House minority party are strongly affected by the majority party's size and cohesion relative to the minority. Binder's finding has been challenged by Schickler (2000), who presents evidence that the timing of these rule changes can be explained by the ideological distance of the median voter on the floor relative to the majority party. Overall, it appears that partisan strength is an important determinant of congressional rules affecting the relative parliamentary powers of the two parties during the nineteenth century, and that during the twentieth century such rules changes primarily are sensitive to movements in the floor median. Still, shifts of the floor median obviously are related to changes in the relative cohesion of the majority party. As a result, the conditions in conditional party government are associated with important alterations in House procedure throughout congressional history.

The partisan roots of congressional rules and structures are especially apparent in the House since the 1960s. Consistent with the conditional party government argument, as the two congressional parties became more unified internally and more differentiated from one another in the 1970s, rank-and-file members of the Democratic majority took important steps to strengthen their leaders (Rohde 1991). In 1973, the Democratic Caucus adopted the "subcommittee bill of rights," which significantly curtailed the ability of full committee chairs to delay or derail the majority party's legislative agenda. In 1974, the Speaker was given the authority to select Democratic members of the Rules Committee, which had operated with considerable autonomy since at least the 1920s. The 1974 change gave the majority-party leadership effective control over the procedures that structure floor action on legislation.

Following the Republicans' takeover of the House after the landmark midterm elections of 1994, the new GOP majority was especially unified on the major issues of the day. And once again, a highly unified congressional majority strengthened its leadership (Evans and Oleszek 1997; Aldrich and Rohde 2000b). For example, incoming Speaker Newt Gingrich (R-GA) was granted the authority to select committee chairs and they were limited to six-year terms. These changes enabled Gingrich and his successor as Speaker, Dennis Hastert, to harness the House committee system behind the Republican policy agenda. In short, the broad contours of House procedure, including the timing of important rules changes and reforms, is consistent with party theories of Congress and suggestive of majority-party power in the legislative process.

### Leadership Selection

Second, consider the kinds of individuals that the parties select as their leaders. Over time, the congressional parties have developed fairly elaborate leadership organizations in both chambers. The House Speaker is the most visible and influential leader on Capitol Hill. Although a constitutional officer nominally elected by the full chamber, the Speaker is usually selected by party-line votes, so the position is effectively the top leader for the House majority party. The House majority leader is formally chosen by the majority caucus and is responsible for managing day-to-day operations on the floor. The House majority whip runs the party whip system, which now includes from seventy to 100 members (depending on which party is in control), and is used to track the evolving preferences of members on upcoming floor votes important to the party.[12] On the other side of the aisle, the House minority leader and minority whip are selected by rank-and-file members from that party and have responsibilities that resemble their majority counterparts, albeit with the purpose of undermining the majority coalition on the floor and setting the stage for a change in partisan control after the next election. In the Senate, the two parties each select from among their members a floor leader and whip. And in both chambers, the parties elect members to fulfill a host of secondary leadership positions, such as chair of the relevant party caucus, policy committee chair, or campaign committee chair.

The selection of party leaders is generally by private ballot within the relevant caucus, and perceptions about the skills of individual leadership candidates and personal friendships and relationships can be pivotal to the outcomes of these contests. But one question that has sparked considerable scholarly attention concerns the ideological preferences of party leaders relative to other members of their party in that chamber.[13] One argument, called the middle person hypothesis, is that the members selected as party leaders will tend to have policy views located near the middle of the ideological distribution for their party within the chamber. If the Cartel Model is correct, members might believe that leaders at the median ideological position for their party will be most likely to use their agenda-setting powers to keep bills opposed by most party members off the floor.

An alternative hypothesis is that leaders tend to be selected from the ideological extremes of the relevant party caucus, rather than the middle. It might be that extremist leaders make better negotiators with the other party, chamber, and the White House. The ideological distributions for each party in the House and Senate also tend to be skewed to the left (for the Democrats) or the right (for the Republicans). Perhaps the clusters of ideological extremists within each party caucus attempt to coalesce behind like-minded candidates for their respective party leaderships, increasing the likelihood these individuals will prevail in leadership contests. And, of course, still another possibility is that the role played by party leaders is really not all that important in Congress, in which case the ideological preferences of the legislators elected to the leadership might be a random draw from the relevant party caucus.

The most authoritative study of the selection of party leaders in Congress is Jessee and Malhotra (2010). For the House, they consider elections for Speakers, majority leaders, and whips during 1899–2009 and for other party leadership offices for 1975–2009. For the Senate, their evidence spans the floor leader and whip selections made between 1919 and 2009 and other, secondary, leadership positions for 1975–2009. They find that leaders tend to have ideological preferences located near the median for their party in the relevant chamber. But they also demonstrate that Democratic congressional leaders in both chambers tend to be located just to the left of the ideological median within their caucus, while the members selected to GOP leadership positions tend to have ideological views located just to the right of the median within their party. In other words, some combination of the middle person and extremist hypotheses best fits the available evidence. Rank-and-file members are careful to select as their party leaders legislators who will most effectively manage the agenda and negotiate on their behalf, which is yet another indicator of the vital importance of party leaders in Congress.

### Leadership Activism

Third, if party theories of Congress have explanatory power, then we would also expect that the degree to which party leaders are actively engaged in the lawmaking process should have ramped up markedly after the 1960s. During the middle years of the twentieth century, when the congressional parties were often internally divided on many issues, committees and their chairs should have dominated the legislative process and the role of party leaders should have been limited. Following the 1960s, as the party caucuses became more internally unified and differentiated from one another, the autonomy of the committees should have declined and the legislative activity of party leaders should have grown. Are such trends discernable in the best available evidence?

For the most part, the answer to the question is "yes." In a series of important studies, Sinclair (1995, 2007) demonstrated that the legislative activism of majority-party leaders in the House did grow substantially after the 1960s. Relying on a large sample of major bills, Sinclair showed that the House majority leadership stepped up its involvement in setting the floor agenda, mobilizing the support of rank-and-file members, rewriting committee bills prior to floor action, and structuring the legislative choices confronting members on the floor.

Perhaps a more direct indicator of the level of leadership involvement in the House legislative process is the number of "whip counts" conducted by the majority leadership over time. Prior to major floor votes important to the party, the leadership might poll its members, asking them if they support the party position on the matter. Parties in both chambers have their own internal whip operations. Typically, members are categorized during these counts as yes (supporting the party), leaning yes, undecided, leaning no, or no (opposing the party). Whip counts usually are only conducted when there is some possibility of a unified party position on the underlying issue and the outcome is in doubt. These counts are part of the vote mobilization, or "whipping" efforts that the leadership uses to advance the party agenda through Congress. As a result, the number of whip counts conducted by the majority party is an indicator of leadership activism when it matters the most.

Interestingly, the level of party whipping did rise as the degree of partisan polarization in the House increased over time.[14] The available evidence about majority-party whip activity must be drawn from the archived personal papers of former congressional leaders and thus there are some years for which systematic evidence is unattainable. Still, nearly comprehensive data are available for the House majority party from the 1950s to the 2000s and the results are instructive. During 1955–72, with Democrats in majority control of the chamber, the average number of counts per two-year Congress was about eighteen. In the 1970s, the average number of Democratic whip counts rose to about fifty per Congress, and increased still further during 1982–94. With the Republican takeover of the House in 1995, the average number of majority-party whip counts per Congress jumped to over 100. Clearly, there are strong linkages between the degree of party polarization within the House and the incidence of majority-party whipping over time.

However, there was a significant spike in majority-party whip counts in the late 1970s, prior to the sharp turn toward polarization in Congress (Evans and

Grandy 2009). In 1977–78, for example, the Democratic leadership whipped its members on over 100 issues, which is a significant increase from prior periods. What does this spike indicate about the causes and consequences of party leadership activity in the chamber? Prior to the 1970s, roll-call votes did not generally occur during the floor amendment process in the House. However, as a result of a 1970s' rule change and the establishment of electronic voting in 1973, roll calls on amendments became both permissible and easy to administer. In the mid-1970s, the number of amendments and amendment votes skyrocketed, creating a daunting challenge for majority-party leaders. Much of the increase resulted from the minority's attempts to use the amendment process to force Democratic members to cast politically difficult votes, potentially helping the Republicans win more seats. Not surprisingly, the Democratic leadership had to step up its whipping in the late 1970s in order to maintain control over the floor agenda. However, as the Democrats made increased use of highly restrictive amendment procedures in the 1980s, the number of floor amendments dropped and majority whip activity likewise declined, before rising again at the end of the decade because of burgeoning partisan polarization within the chamber.

In short, the level of majority-party whipping over time is yet another indicator of the importance of parties and leaders in the legislative process. And the level of whip activity is associated with the degree of partisan polarization within the chamber, mediated by the strategic behavior of the minority party and the magnitude of the legislative challenge confronting the majority caucus.

### Roll Rates and Rules

Now consider the extent to which party leaders, especially leaders of the majority party in the House, are able to successfully carry the day on the floor of the chamber. That is, how often is the House majority party "rolled" on final passage votes, where a "roll" is said to occur when a majority of the majority party fails to prevail? Recall that the Cartel Model predicts that the majority leadership will use its agenda prerogatives to block from the floor bills that are not supported by a majority of the majority party within the chamber. If so, then the majority party should almost never get rolled on final passage votes.

Indeed, Cox and McCubbins (2005) demonstrate that bills seldom pass on the House floor without the support of most members of the majority party. Not surprisingly, roll rates for the minority party are much higher and also vary systematically over time, depending on the ideological distance between the typical member of the minority party and the preferences of the median voter in the chamber. The greater (smaller) the ideological distance between the minority-party median and the ideological center of the chamber as a whole, the more (less) often the minority party will be rolled on the floor. Although the evidence that Cox and McCubbins and others have marshaled about majority- versus minority-party success on final passage votes is not definitive (e.g.,

Krehbiel 2006), it still is highly suggestive of effective agenda control by the partisan majority in the House.

Lastly, the rules that the House leadership uses to structure floor debate in the chamber are another potentially important source of majority-party power. Since the mid-1970s, the Speaker has been responsible for appointing all major-ity-party members to the Rules Committee and the minority leader has had that prerogative for the minority party. There are two motions on the floor that must pass before the "rule" reported by the Rules Committee has force. First, the majority must win the vote on the motion on the previous question on the rule. If this motion fails, under House rules the minority party is able to offer a substitute rule for the bill, effectively circumventing the majority party's control over the agenda. And after the previous question motion is adopted (by voice vote or roll call), there typically is a vote on the rule itself, which likewise must pass the full chamber. Finocchiaro and Rohde (2008) demonstrate that since 1975, the majority party has rarely lost on rule votes and almost never on previous question motions. The roll calls that have occurred on previous ques-tion motions and on rules votes have become increasingly partisan, so that near party-line votes are now the norm. Moreover, the likelihood the majority party will prevail on these votes is strongly associated with intra-party homogeneity and polarization between the parties, which is fully consistent with partisan theories of Congress.

Beginning in the 1980s, the House majority leadership also made increased use of highly restrictive amendment procedures that constrain the ability of individual lawmakers, especially members of the minority party, to offer amend-ments on the floor (Marshall 2005; Sinclair 2007). If the majority leadership can limit the choices of members so that votes are cast between the majority party's most preferred policy and a fairly extreme alternative offered by the minority, then centrist legislators could be left with no other choice than to support the majority's proposal. Indeed, scholars have marshaled intriguing evidence that the majority leadership does use amendment rules in this way to tilt the proce-dural playing field in its favor, shifting policy outcomes toward the majority's most preferred outcome (e.g., Monroe and Robinson 2008).[15]

### The Senate

The best available evidence about the timing of procedural changes, leadership selection, leadership activity levels, roll rates, and the use of special amendment rules is highly suggestive of influential parties and leaders in the House. But what about the U.S. Senate? The Senate, of course, differs procedurally from the House in significant ways. The Senate majority leader is unable to rely on special rules from a leadership-controlled Rules Committee to structure floor action on legislation. Unlike the House, there also is no general germaneness requirement in Senate rules, which means that rank-and-file members of both parties have ample opportunity to bring their legislative proposals before the full body. The ability of senators to filibuster and engage in other obstructionist tactics also limits the majority leadership's effectiveness at managing the floor agenda (Koger 2010). And since it is rare for the Senate majority party to have sixty or more members, the Senate majority leadership often is unable to pass legislation without a degree of support from across the partisan aisle. For these reasons, the majority party and its leaders are not as formally empowered in the Senate as they are in the House.

Still, Majority Leader Reid clearly played a significant role in the passage of comprehensive health care reform in 2009–10, and the best scholarship indicates that Reid's clout during that legislative episode was not all that exceptional. For instance, majority-party roll rates are not significantly higher in the Senate than they are in the House, suggesting that the Senate majority leadership also exercises a significant degree of agenda control, blocking initiatives from the floor that are opposed by a majority of the majority party (Gailmard and Jenkins 2007). However, if the Senate majority leadership lacks the formal powers and other procedural advantages exercised by the House leadership, what precisely is the source of its influence?

Existing scholarship suggests two potential answers to the question. First, Den Hartog and Monroe (2011) point out that the majority leadership in the Senate, although less empowered than the House leadership, is not completely lacking in parliamentary privileges and other political resources. For example, the majority leader has the right of priority recognition on the Senate floor, conveying procedural "first mover" advantages to the majority party. The Senate leadership also has disproportionate staff help, which provides certain informational advantages in the legislative process. Rather than attempt to defeat a minority-party amendment outright, the majority leader can instead move to table the proposal. Party loyalty tends to be higher on procedural motions such as the motion to table, which can give the majority leader enhanced leverage on the Senate floor. These and other prerogatives, resources, and tactics apparently aggregate into a degree of agenda control and power for the Senate majority party.

Perhaps most important, public perceptions about the competence of a Senate party and the quality of its policy program can influence whether voters support the candidates of that party at the polls (Jones and McDermott 2009). To some extent, even senators share a common electoral fate with colleagues from their party, which creates incentives for them to support the leadership on roll calls important to the party agenda and reputation. Moreover, the electoral importance of the legislative agenda creates incentives for the leaders of the two parties to transform potentially nonpartisan matters, such as budget process reform, procedures for conducting the U.S. Census, and other "good government" measures, into party-line issues and votes. Lee (2009) demonstrates that much of the increased partisan polarization that has occurred in the Senate (and presumably the House), results from the efforts of party leaders to create "wedge" issues, with an eye toward dramatizing differences between the party programs and advantaging their party in campaigns. In the contemporary House and Senate, then, any distinctions between party campaigning and lawmaking have all but disappeared, which has fueled both polarization and leadership influence in Congress.

## Conclusion

The striking differences between the relatively bipartisan enactment of Medicare and Medicaid in 1965 and the intense partisan infighting apparent during congressional action on comprehensive health care reform during 2009–10, reflect a broader transformation in the role of parties and leaders on Capitol Hill. Scholars have documented with precision the remarkable increase that has occurred in partisan polarization within the House and Senate from the 1960s to the 2000s. A portion of the intense party polarization that defines the contemporary House and Senate is rooted in the growing ideological and partisan homogeneity of the constituencies of individual members, including the enhanced electoral role of party activists. But the weight of scholarly evidence suggests that most of the rise in partisan polarization is caused by institutional features and strategic decisions that are internal to the House and Senate.

The leading theories that scholars have developed to understand the lawmaking process provide ample guidance about the institutional sources of polarization and strong party leaders. The Cartel Model emphasizes agenda control, while the conditional party government theory also integrates the procedures and tactics that leaders can use to keep potential defectors on the party reservation on major roll-call votes. Diverse empirical studies marshal considerable evidence in support of these theories, which scholars for the most part treat as complementary to one another. Research about the temporal development of congressional procedure, leadership selection, the legislative involvement of party leaders, party success or failure on final passage votes, and the strategic use of floor rules is suggestive of consequential parties and leaders.

As is the case with any body of research, however, there are important gaps in existing scholarship about the congressional parties.[16] For example, the finding that the rise in roll-call polarization mostly occurred on procedural votes is somewhat puzzling. The party cartel and conditional party government arguments imply that the majority leadership will use procedure to stack the deck in favor of its legislative program. If so, then shouldn't one consequence be a noticeable increase in partisan conflict on amendments and final passage votes, as well as procedural motions? The strategic linkages between the procedural tactics employed by House and Senate leaders, the content of legislative alternatives, and the composition of the coalitions supporting and opposing majority-party initiatives need further clarification.

More generally, the leading party models need to be extended to better integrate the full range of coalition-building tactics that are available to congressional party leaders. There is some evidence that leaders use agenda setting, the provision of information, promises of sanctions or rewards to fellow members, substantive changes in the relevant legislation, careful bargaining, the mobilization of public and interest group pressure, and a host of other tactics to advance their legislative and political agendas. Unfortunately, existing scholarly research provides only fragmentary guidance about how often these tactics are employed and under what conditions.

Along those lines, scholarship about parties and leaders in Congress needs to pay more attention to the role of the president. During congressional consideration of Medicare and Medicaid in 1965 and the fight over comprehensive health care reform in 2009–10, the White House was highly involved in mobilizing support for passage among the public and within the House and Senate. Yet, the president is largely absent from leading party theories of Congress. Clearly, the policy priorities, tactics, and political clout of the White House have consequences for the fate of legislation, especially items on the programmatic agendas of the two parties. Lee (2009), for instance, shows that presidential priorities are particularly likely to produce party-line votes within Congress. Party theories and research about congressional leadership need to better incorporate the role of the president.

Existing scholarship on parties and leaders takes us a long way toward understanding coalition building in the contemporary Congress. The implications should be troubling to many citizens. Public opinion polls routinely show that ordinary Americans are deeply dissatisfied with Congress, in part because of the level of partisan conflict that they perceive on major issues. Why, Americans ask, cannot Democrats and Republicans in Congress simply get along and confront the major issues of the day in a constructive, bipartisan fashion? The best scholarship, however, indicates that the root causes of the intense partisan polarization that concerns so many Americans are longstanding and deep and unlikely to change anytime soon. Like it or not, the era of polarized congressional parties and strong party leaders will probably continue for the foreseeable future.

## Notes

1  For an insightful description of Congressional action on Medicare and Medicaid in the mid-1960s, see the relevant portions of Manley (1970).
2  The best scholarly review of coalition building on comprehensive health care reform in 2009–10 is Jacobs and Skocpol (2010).
3  The Senate slightly modified the House-passed version of the reconciliation measure, which necessitated a final, anticlimactic roll call on the measure in the House, also along party lines, 220–207.
4  These difference scores are for the Senate-passed version of the main legislation. For the reconciliation "side-car" portions, the party difference scores were 87.0 for the House and 94.9 for the Senate.
5  The party difference scores are adapted from the party "likeness" scores compiled by Joseph Cooper and Garry Young and downloaded from https://jshare.johnshopkins.edu/jcooper6/web/research.htm.

6  For an in-depth explanation of the DW-NOMINATE scaling technique, see http://
   voteview.com. In Figure 4.2, the common-space versions of the scores are used to
   facilitate bicameral comparisons. See also Poole and Rosenthal (1997), which is the
   landmark study of the congressional roll-call record.
7  See also McCarty, Poole, and Rosenthal (2006) for evidence linking partisan polarization to the growing income inequality between the rich and poor.
8  For an overview, see Krehbiel (1988).
9  For proposals that, in contrast, would move policy from the left to the right, the filibuster pivot is the 60th position counting in from the conservative end of the ideological spectrum. Krehbiel (1998) shows precisely how the location of the pivotal
   voter in legislatures such as the U.S. House and Senate depends on both the distribution of preferences and on chamber rules. His model also integrates the presidential
   veto and override procedures, but these aspects of the analysis are excluded from the
   discussion here for reasons of expositional parsimony.
10 The Hon. Dennis Hastert (R-IL) "The Cannon Centenary Conference," U.S. Library
   of Congress, page 62: http://www.gpoaccess.gov/serialset/cdocuments/hd108-204/
   pdf/reflections.pdf.
11 See Smith (2007) for a book-length treatment of the literature about parties and their
   leaders in Congress.
12 In the House, the Democratic whip operations of the 1990s and 2000s generally
   included around 100 members, while the Republican networks were somewhat
   smaller, usually 60–70 members (Evans 2010).
13 Noteworthy scholarship about the ideological positions of party leaders includes
   Peabody (1976), Clausen and Wilcox (1987), and Grofman, Koetzle, and McGann
   (2002). But see especially Jessee and Malhotra (2010) for a review of the competing
   hypotheses about leadership ideology as well as the most systematic and comprehensive analysis of the alternative arguments.
14 For a full discussion of whip activity over time, including the specific archival sources
   from which the relevant evidence is drawn, consult Evans and Grandy (2009) and
   Evans (2010).
15 For more details on the development of House procedures over time, see
   Chapter 6.
16 See Smith (2007), Chapter 8, for a thorough discussion of the strengths and weaknesses of scholarship about the congressional parties.

# Chapter 5

# Congressional Committees in a Partisan Era

## The End of Institutionalization as We Know It?

*Charles Stewart III*

Ever since Woodrow Wilson first wrote about congressional government (1885), students of Congress have agreed that committees are where the action is. What they have done with this fact is something else. Wilson's identification of committees as the effective power centers of Congress began a complicated relationship between scholars and the institution they study. The purpose of this chapter is to put the long sweep of this scholarship into perspective, to assess the current role of congressional committees in the American political system. The conclusion of this assessment is that congressional committees have fully emerged from the post-war congressional system that obscured party differences, highlighted the particular goals of legislators, and was studied through a series of theoretical lenses that treated committees as autonomous actors on the legislative stage. In the new era, which is still in its infancy, party differences are sharp, party goals dominate, and committees are no longer as autonomous as they once were.

In the words of Polsby and Schickler (2002: 26–7) the study of Congress is driven by events and literature. Events and scholarly literature have intersected in recent years, as approaches to Congress that highlight the role of congressional parties have been applied to an institution that is increasingly polarized ideologically, and guided by party agendas. The rise in prominence of the congressional parties raises the question of what good are committees. This shift in policymaking focus should cause us to question whether Congress (or more precisely, the House of Representatives), which Polsby (1968) used to illustrate what an "institutionalized" political body looked like, hasn't begun a process of *de*institutionalizing.

The degree to which partisan polarization now pervades lawmaking is unprecedented in the period during which political scientists have chronicled and explained congressional committee dynamics. This polarization rivals that of the late nineteenth century, which many regard as the high-water mark of partisanship in Congress. Because the influence of parties and committees is often viewed as inversely correlated, it is natural to suppose that we are witnessing a diminution of committee influence. If we rely on a half-century of congressional scholarship, it is hard to believe otherwise. However, before we march off into a new world that simply assumes that committees are unimportant and peripheral to lawmaking, it is necessary to take stock of the accumulated knowledge about congressional committees, and to assess the degree to which that knowledge is helpful in charting our understanding of modern committees.

To provide perspective on the current role of committees in Congress, this essay takes a dynamic approach to the historical development of congressional committees and the scholarship that has sought to digest this development. We start with events. Congress is a dynamic institution, driven by the exigencies of the age and the link of its members to voters through elections. The institution of Congress is a major player on the national stage; the big events that serve as benchmarks in American history—wars, recessions, crises, scandals, and the like—have profound effects on what it is that members of Congress (MCs) do and how they do it. Congress is also a social system, buffeted by the outside to be sure, but also developing in its own distinctive way, due to the legacies of past decisions, strategic calculations of leaders, and the serendipity of elections that select some in and others out.

The dynamics of congressional development travel along two great rivers of events—macro-historical forces and middle-level institutional dynamics—that are related, but distinct enough to warrant considering separately. The top part of Figure 5.1 makes note of these two major event-driven streams. The first is an ideological sorting of the electoral bases of the parties, catalyzed by the 1965 Voting Rights Act, which has resulted in greater clarity of policy direction among national parties and is reflected in the rising prominence of congressional party leaders over the past half-century. The events illustrated below are the more Congress-centered set of events that produce struggles within the institution over the distribution of power and policy agenda setting. Two significant inflection points, in the mid-1970s and mid-1990s, punctuate this stream. As a result, the stylized facts about congressional committees that might have been true in 1960 are much less likely to be true today, and in some cases, outright false.

The bottom part of Figure 5.1 summarizes the appearance of six different scholarly approaches to the study of Congress that have molded our understanding of congressional committees over the same period. Each strand begins with a small number of seminal works that have been incorporated into subsequent scholarship, coloring how scholars, and eventually the public, understand committees. These strands, along with their (approximate) beginning dates, are the following:

- Committees as groups (1962)
- Committees as election vehicles (1974)
- Committees as stability inducers (1979)
- Committees as rent seekers (1988)
- Committees as party agents (1991)
- Committees as information providers (1992)

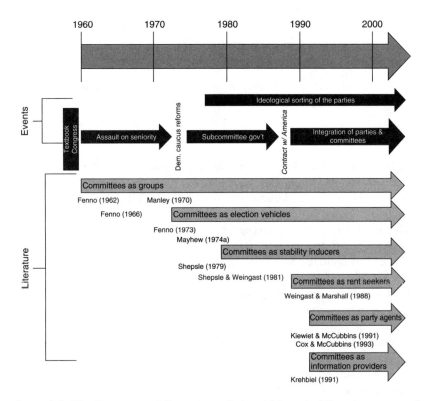

*Figure 5.1* The Dynamics of Committee-Related Historical Development and the Scholarly Literature: Schematic of Argument

The arrows in the figure indicating the intellectual streams have clear beginnings, but no clear ends. This illustrates the fact that, unlike many areas of scientific endeavor, new theoretical perspectives in the study of Congress tend not to supplant the old, but build on them. Some of these intellectual currents are focused primarily, or even exclusively, on the committees of Congress as the primary subject of study. This is particularly true of "committees as groups," "committees as rent seekers," and "committees as information providers." For the other three currents, committees are part of the complex of institutions, rules, and norms that allow members to pursue reelection, achieve decision-making stability, and prosecute policy partisanship.

One final word of introduction: like most essays on the role of committees in Congress, the bulk of the material here will be drawn from committee politics in the House. As much as one tries to give equal billing to the upper chamber, the well-known realities of that body conspire to shift lawmaking attention away from committees and toward the members themselves. If Senate committees are given short shrift in this essay, it is merely a reflection of the reality we are presented with.

## The Events in More Detail

In this section, I lay out in more detail the unfolding of significant political events that have animated attention on the committee system of Congress.

### Congressional Evolution as seen on Capitol Hill

The first, Congress-centered historical strand begins with what Shepsle (1989) called the "textbook Congress," which formed the basis of scholarly and public understanding of the institution after World War II. In the post-war Congress, members held deep cultural ties to their constituents, which gave MCs considerable autonomy in their day-to-day Washington work.[1] That work was divided between a relatively small personal staff, which focused on casework, and the member's committees, which were better resourced, but under the control of autocratic chairs. MCs were counseled that "if you want to get along, go along." The congressional career stretched out over many years, in which rookies served an apprenticeship, worked hard, and kept out of the public eye (Matthews 1959, 1960). Committee service was a significant part of the congressional career, particularly in the House. Members who were serious about making a name for themselves specialized; committees were the channel of that specialization. If members demonstrated seriousness and competence, they could be assured better subcommittee assignments or plum assignments on better committees down the road (Masters 1961). Long recesses allowed members to travel home a couple of times a year, to make speeches to community groups, attend to office hours, and gather political intelligence from local elites.

Two related sets of developments helped to undermine this textbook Congress and the role of committees in it. The first was the struggle between different wings of the two parties over fundamental questions like the role of government in the economy and the power of the federal government to end segregation. The variant of this struggle that occupied the Democratic Party was more consequential for committee development, since they had a majority of members of the two chambers from 1955 to 1980, with the House continuing to hold a Democratic majority until 1994.

At the risk of over-simplifying, the Democratic party was divided between a Southern wing, of mostly conservative members from safe seats, and a Northern wing, of more liberal members who had to face fiercer electoral competition in constituencies whose voters were more favorably inclined toward an activist role for the federal government. An important complication to this generalization is that Northerners were divided as well, between members who came from traditional, party machine-based areas that were almost as uncompetitive as Southern districts, and those who came from suburban, faster-growing areas that were electorally competitive. These facts led to a generational divide in the Democratic Party, between younger, liberal, and electorally vulnerable members, on the one hand, and older, conservative, and electorally safe members, on the other.

The fact that electoral vulnerability and ideology were so highly correlated was critical for the work of Congress, since seniority was inexorable in granting greater influence over lawmaking (Polsby, Gallaher, and Rundquist 1969). The Legislative Reorganization Act (LRA) of 1946 had consolidated the committee system significantly, creating a narrow hierarchy through which aspirants to chairmanships had to navigate. The LRA was coincidentally passed on the eve of one of the most significant two-election turnover sequences in the history of congressional elections (Hinckley 1971). The result of this sequence was to purge Northern Democrats from the top of the committee rosters in 1946, install the invulnerable Southern Democrats as chairs of these committees after 1948, and then re-stock the rosters with liberal Democrats at the bottom rungs of the committee hierarchies. Although generational replacement would eventually turn the tables in favor of the liberal wing of the party, time marched too slowly for some, which led to calls for the Democratic caucus to become more assertive in overcoming the conservative bias of the committee system.

The first salvo in the war to align the committee system more closely with the mainstream of the Democratic caucus was the expansion of the House Rules Committee in 1961 (made permanent in 1963), to ease the way for legislation that had cleared more liberal-leaning legislative committees to the House floor (Peabody 1963; Robinson 1963). These attacks reached their apotheosis between 1970 and 1973 through a series of reforms, mostly accomplished by changing Democratic caucus rules, which delivered a blow to the practice of deciding who would chair committees strictly by seniority and, in general, shifted power within committees from chairs to subcommittees and to the Democratic caucuses within each committee (Rohde 1974; Ornstein 1975; Dodd and Oppenheimer 1977).

These changes had two major practical effects on the institution of Congress, particularly the House, where committees organized the bulk of legislative business. The first was that members learned that if they wanted to rise to the leadership of a committee or subcommittee chair, they had to pay closer attention to the aspirations of the Democratic party caucus. Democrats did not go so far as to institute a litmus test for committee leadership and, indeed, used their new authority over choosing committee chairs to depose a few who were doddering, rather than disloyal (Hinckley 1976; Crook and Hibbing 1985). The first exercise of accountability to the caucus occurred in 1975, when Wright Patman (D-TX), F. Edward Hebert (D-LA), and W. R. Poage (D-TX) were defeated for reelection as chairs of the Banking, Armed Services, and Agriculture Committees, respectively.[2]

A cautionary tale involved the deposition of Melvin Price (D-IL) as chair of Armed Services and subsequent election of Les Aspin (D-WI) to take his place.[3]

Price, who had replaced Hebert in the previous committee chair controversy ten years earlier, was said by some to be too ill to lead the committee at a time when the majority Democrats wished to challenge the Republican administration on military priorities. This led to Aspin successfully running against Price in 1985 and winning. When Aspin himself disappointed a coalition of liberals and conservatives over his leadership of the committee, his reelection two years later as chair of Armed Services was initially denied, forcing a *mea culpa* from Aspin before he could be granted another term as chair by his colleagues.[4]

The operation of "subcommittee government" (Rohde 1974; Haeberle 1978; Davidson 1981; Dodd and Oppenheimer 1985; Hall and Evans 1990) in the immediate post-Watergate era coincided with a period of "stagflation" and general political malaise that roiled the political landscape for the next decade. Whether the ailments that afflicted the political economy in the late 1980s/ early 1990s were caused by the unbridled committee system, the Republican Party effectively linked maladies such as deficit spending and over-regulation of the economy to the committee system, which they viewed as facilitating the reelection of Democrats at the expense of taxpayers. The *Contract with America*, which was the manifesto on which House Republicans ran in the 1994 congressional election, promised a series of reforms to streamline the committee system and make it more accountable to the majority-party leadership.[5] Among these changes were: (1) cutting the number of House committees, (2) cutting the number of committee staff by one-third, (3) limiting the terms of all committee chairs, (4) banning proxy votes[6] in committees, and (5) requiring that all committee meetings be public.

In the process of implementing these promises, the new Republican leadership abolished three committees—District of Columbia; Merchant Marine and Fisheries; and Post Office and Civil Service—that were regarded as vehicles for benefits to Democratic constituencies. To drive home the fact that committee leaders had to be team players, Speaker Newt Gingrich (R-GA) insisted that the chairs of the subcommittees of the House Appropriations Committee sign a loyalty pledge to the *Contract* (Aldrich and Rohde 1997, 2009; Owens 1997).

Finally, in the move that probably had the greatest long-term impact on the life of the House, Republican Party leaders demoted seniority as a factor in choosing committee chairs, elevating party loyalty and fundraising acumen (Smith and Lawrence 1997). Although the sea change in leadership criteria had an immediate practical effect on committee leadership, when Gingrich skipped over the most senior Republicans to name three committee chairs in late 1994, he also spared some heterodox members, such as Gerald Solomon (R-NY), who moved up to chair Rules, honoring the seniority norm. Its most significant effects would come later.

When the "Newt time bomb" of the six-year term limit on committee chairs went off in 2001, seniority was significantly subordinated to the needs of the party in selecting new chairs (Brewer and Deering 2005; Heberlig and Larson 2007). Aspirants for committee chairs had to apply and interview with the

Republican committee on committees. Only seven of the thirteen new chairmanships went to the most senior members of the relevant committees. In general since 1994, only about half of the Republican committee leaders, committee chairs, and ranking minority members have been the most senior member of the committee.

As they were serving their time in the minority, Democrats continued to live by the rule that their ranking members were subject to confirmation by the caucus, but in practice, seniority was the norm for electing committee leaders. However, views were evolving. One sign that the thinking about committee leadership posts had changed came after the 2006 election, when Democrats regained control of the House. Without pre-clearing her decision with senior Democratic leaders, Speaker-elect Nancy Pelosi (D-CA) announced at the start of the 110th Congress that she would support a continuation of the six-year term limit for committee chairs, meaning that Democrats would be faced with policy- and campaign-related tests if they wanted to lead important committees.

Pelosi backed down on this decision at the start of the 111th Congress, but a bigger assault on the seniority system came anyway, when Henry Waxman (D-CA) challenged John Dingell (D-MI) for the chair of the House Commerce Committee, over Dingell's recalcitrance on environmental legislation. The resulting struggle and close (137–122) caucus vote in Waxman's favor revealed that Democrats, unlike Republicans, were still divided over whether party loyalty or seniority should rule in doling out leadership positions. Nonetheless, unlike the three cases in 1975, when three senior Democrats were toppled from their chairs, or Aspin's victory over Price in 1985, Waxman's defeat of Dingell was entirely motivated by policy, not capability. This signals that the Democratic caucus has moved much closer to the Republican caucus in how its members regard what it takes to assume the chair of an important committee.

Standing in 2011 and looking back more than a half-century to 1950, the overall congressional landscape, of which the committee system is a major feature, is quite different. As this brief overview of the internal developments has made clear, committee autonomy is largely a thing of the past. Polsby's "universalistic criteria" for the choice of committee leaders no longer rule, especially for Republicans, and increasingly for Democrats.[7] Congress is less "bureaucratic," in the sense of being hierarchical and predictable, and more "entrepreneurial" and "mission-driven," in the sense that committees are now instruments of party government.

This tour of events has emphasized internal developments that have marked an evolution of congressional committees from being member-centric to being party-centric. Focusing on internal dynamics involving the committee system can leave one with the impression that these struggles are unrelated to the larger political currents of the nation. However, the urgency around the evolution of committee politics has been driven by electoral dynamics, and in particular, a sea change in the electoral landscape that landed MCs in the institution in the first place. This leads us to the second major stream of events indicated on Figure 5.1, electoral dynamics.

### The Changing Electoral Environment and Committee Politics

Even though both parties have always had recognizable and distinct policy tendencies, from the mid-1930s to well into the 1970s the electoral bases of both parties were ideologically heterogeneous. Democratic voters included Southern whites, who were anxious about granting African Americans full political rights and desirous to maintain business-friendly labor laws, and urban Northerners, who were more racially tolerant and diverse, and who often favored active government management of the economy. Republicans appealed to captains of industry and suburban white collar professionals in the north, and to participants in the farm economy and small-business owners throughout the north and west.

The 1965 Voting Rights Act (VRA) helped change all that (Black and Black 1987). Its immediate effect was to drive a wedge between white voters and the Democratic Party in the South.[8] Democrats had an overwhelming vote advantage in the South in the 1950s, which steadily eroded through the 1980s. The election of 1994 shifted support among Southern Democrats dramatically, so that what was once a thirty-point Democratic advantage in the region switched almost overnight to a ten-to-twenty point Republican advantage, where it has stayed ever since. In the rest of the nation, Democrats have held a slight advantage over Republicans, although there were signs in the federal elections from 2002 to 2006 that Democrats were beginning to develop an advantage in the non-South that rivaled the Republican advantage in the South—a trend that may or may not have survived the Democratic shellacking of 2010.

Related to the dramatic regional turn in 1994 was a similar shift in racial patterns of support for the parties. African-American support for Democratic congressional candidates has remained at a steady 90 percent rate for over half a century. The average Democratic–Republican split among white voters was 55/45 for the same period. Black voting patterns did not shift in 1994, but white patterns did; whites now support Republican candidates for Congress, on average, by a 60/40 margin. Most, but not all of this shift has come from white voters in the South.

As a result, the few Democrats who now hale from the South tend to come from constituencies that are like traditional Northern Democratic districts— disproportionately urban, low-income, and minority. If we factor in the subtle ideological shift of white voters between the parties because of "cultural issues" such as abortion and gay marriage, the net result is a realignment that has produced greater ideological distinctiveness between the parties, and greater policy cohesion among identifiers with each party. If we reexamine the effects of the 1994 election in ideological terms, we see that liberals have increasingly identified as Democrats, and conservatives as Republicans. The intraparty cohesiveness of rank-and-file Democrats and Republicans has increased for each party, as inter-party distinctiveness has also grown.

This macro-historical trend toward greater ideological distinctiveness of the two parties' electoral bases is obviously related to the more Congress-specific events discussed earlier. As the electoral bases become more distinct and internally cohesive, the parties within Congress become more distinct and internally cohesive (Rohde 1991; McCarty, Poole, and Rosenthal 2006; Theriault 2006). This, in turn, makes MCs more likely to delegate authority to party leaders and committees, so that they can coordinate the work of committees to better meet the electoral and ideological needs of the parties. An idea very close to this one has motivated Rohde (1991) to develop his theory of *conditional party government*. However, it is important to remember that the effort to bring committee behavior into line with the mainstream of the parties—to make them more like agents of the parties and less like the "disintegrate ministries" that Wilson complained about—began *before* the passage of the VRA, met with initial success *before* the VRA was passed, and probably would have continued, albeit at a more glacial pace, had the electoral effects of the VRA not been so powerful.

It would be incorrect to assert that the efforts to bring committees and parties closer into alignment during the 1950s and 1960s caused the ideological sorting of the parties that we have witnessed in recent years, but the two *are* related. Efforts to give party leaders and caucuses some parliamentary steel to pass important liberal legislation like the VRA, demonstrated what could be accomplished if the efforts of parties and committees were more closely aligned. The liberal achievements of the Great Society caused elements of the electorate to reevaluate their past support for the parties, causing growing polarization in the electorate, which in turn emboldened party activists to bring parties and committees into even greater alignment. In this sense, committee dynamics and electoral dynamics have been symbiotic systems.

## The Literature in More Detail

In this section, we review some of the same chronology we have just encountered, but with an eye toward understanding how political scientists have used events to develop general explanations for committee dynamics. What follows is a very high-level tour of how political scientists have approached committees. It is like a national roadmap, which shows the Interstate highways, but not the state highways or local streets. If such a roadmap had all the side streets along the way, it would be a multi-volume encyclopedia, not a single foldout map. In a similar vein, the purpose here is not to help the reader understand the politics of a particular committee at a particular point in time, but to instruct about where important scholarly strands began and how they intersected with intellectual currents that came before. To do otherwise would similarly result in the production of a multi-volume work.[9]

It is possible to identify six major, successive strands of scholarship that have focused on the work of congressional committees since 1960. In the introduction, I put labels on these strands and noted where they began. Here, we explore the substance behind these labels.

### Committees as Groups

When viewed from the perspective of congressional committees, the inauguration of political science as a profession began inauspiciously. As Richard Fenno notes in the introduction to his classic *Power of the Purse* (1966), when Woodrow Wilson wrote, "Congress in session is Congress on public exhibition, whilst Congress in its committee-rooms is Congress at work" (Wilson 1936 [1885]: 69), he was not blazing an empirical trail, but rather describing a deplorable condition that needed to be reformed. Wilson's disciples read his book "as a call for congressional reform and not as a call for empirical research" (p. xvii).

*Power of the Purse* helped move our approach to committees from "problems to be solved" to "institutions to be understood." It draws directly from sociology, a well that the other great works about Congress written at midcentury drank from, such as Donald Matthews's *U.S. Senators and Their World* (1960). Fenno's magisterial study of the House Appropriations Committee is a model of how the sociological approach to studying congressional committees was carried out. (See also Fenno 1962.) The following paragraph summarizes as well as anything the overall approach to the study of committees from this perspective:

> The necessity for integration in any social system arises from the differentiation among its various elements. Most importantly there is a differentiation among subgroups and among individual positions, together with the roles that flow therefrom. A committee faces the problem, how shall these diverse elements be made to mesh together or function in support of one another? No political system (or subsystem) is perfectly integrated; yet no political system can survive without some minimum degree of integration among its differentiated parts. *Committee integration is defined as the degree to which there is a working together or a meshing together or mutual support among its roles and subgroups.* Conversely, it is also defined as the degree to which a committee is able to minimize conflict among its roles and its subgroups, by heading off or resolving the conflicts that arise. A concomitant of integration is the existence of a fairly consistent set of norms, widely agreed upon and widely followed by the members. Another concomitant of integration is the existence of control mechanisms (i.e., socialization and sanctioning mechanisms) capable of maintaining reasonable conformity to norms. In other words, the more highly integrated a committee, the smaller will be the gap between expected and actual behavior.
>
> (Fenno 1962, emphasis added).

In the case of the House Appropriations Committee, integration was facilitated by: (1) a consensus about the nature of the committee's task, which was rooted in constitution, (2) the nature of the subject matter, which allowed members to focus on the relatively bloodless task of cutting spending requests that were always assumed to be padded, rather than spend too much time in partisan battles over spending priorities, (3) a pattern of committee appointments that emphasized assigning members who worked well with others and were comfortable with legislative give-and-take, (4) the attractiveness of the assignment to members and aspiring non-members, and (5) membership stability across time.

Complementary to Fenno's analysis of the appropriations committees of the House (and somewhat the Senate), was John Manley's study of the House Ways and Means Committee (Manley 1965, 1969, 1970). Like Fenno, Manley's analysis was deeply rooted in the sociological theory of small groups propounded by writers such as Homans (1950) and Parsons (Parsons and Shils 1951). In explaining the integration of the Ways and Means Committee, Manley was drawn to the activity of its long-time chair, Wilbur Mills (D-AR), who was the key agent responsible for the socialization of members to the committee's work and for guiding the committee's relationship with the rest of the House. Mills was so effective that even though Ways and Means was responsible for the tax code, the core of legislative power, its bills were almost always considered under a "closed rule"—that is, under a procedure that made them impossible to amend, subjecting them simply to an up-or-down vote.

Consistent with the Fenno/Manley approach to committees was Polsby's more macro-level approach to congressional institutional development, describing its "institutionalization" over time (Polsby 1968; Polsby et al. 1969). Whereas Fenno and Manley had been interested in integration as a strategy that facilitated the working of the committees, Polsby was interested in how large institutions in society functioned so as to avoid being "unstable, weak, and incapable of servicing the demands or protecting the interests of its constituent groups" (Polsby 1968).[10]

In Polsby's view, the committee system provided evidence of the institutionalization of the House and an explanation for how it had developed into a strong institution capable of writing complex legislation and governing a modern, complex society. Two of the features were: (1) the presence of the committee system itself and (2) the use of universalistic and automatic criteria, such as seniority, for the allocation of committee leadership positions on committees, rather than discretionary criteria, such as allegiances to particular factions or political leaders.

### Committees as Election Vehicles

The early research into congressional committees that was inspired by Fenno opened up the institution to scientific study. It used theory to discipline the method of elite interviewing. It also provided a way to compare behavior in Congress to other institutions, including legislatures across the United States and around the world (Squire 1992; Epstein et al. 1997). However, as Fenno notes in *Congressmen in Committees*, committees differ, and those differences are driven by the goals of the members who populate them (Fenno 1973).

This insight was consistent with the parallel breakthrough at the time that attempted to explain all of congressional behavior, not just its committees—Mayhew's (1974a) *Congress: The Electoral Connection*. Mayhew proposed looking at the behavior of members of Congress through the lens of their election-seeking behavior—assuming they were "single-minded seekers of reelection" and then asking what this assumption implied for individual member behavior and internal organization. Mayhew posited that MCs pursued three types of behavior in the pursuit of reelection—advertising, position taking, and credit claiming. Committees were key in this world. Party leaders assigned members to committees to help them gain reelection on their own terms. The priority in staffing the committees was not to serve the interests of party, except to the degree that each member could build his or her own unique portfolio of advertising, position-taking, and credit-claiming activities.[11]

Committees differ in how well they help members pursue these three activities. For instance, service on the House Education and Labor Committee might not be so useful for getting things done (credit claiming), but it is a great place to be if one wants to stake out a clear position on ideological issues (position taking). On the other hand, members in dire need of gaining a reputation of bringing home the bacon (credit claiming) might gravitate toward the Public Works (now Transportation and Infrastructure) committee.

Mayhew recognized that negative externalities would arise in a chamber that was organized entirely with the narrow reelection interests of members in mind, blind to negative consequences of the "tragedy of the commons" (Harding 1968). For example, letting members who wished to take credit for bringing home the bacon without fiscal discipline would undermine the common good embodied in balanced budgets and rational fiscal policy. An important response to this problem, in Mayhew's view, was to maintain "control committees," such as Rules, Ways and Means, and Appropriations, that were given the job of making sure that the individual goals of members did not undermine the collective interest. Nevertheless, these committees are the exception, not the rule, in the organization of the House.

Whichever way we choose to highlight the goal-seeking behavior of members of Congress—Mayhew's pared-down formulation that posited one goal or Fenno's slightly less elegant formulation with three—the intellectual consequences were the same. The shift from the sociological approach of the 1960s to the economics-inflected approach of the 1970s marked a shift in perspective. Scholars began to worry less about how the institution shaped members, and more about how members shaped the institution so that it could help them achieve their own private political goals.

## Committees as Stability Inducers

Mayhew's book was a clarion call for the mutual exploration of Congress and its committees by both political scientists and economists. Its central analytical lens was borrowed by analogy from economics. Although this point of view had an economist's perspective, Mayhew himself admitted to "no economics expertise to display" (Mayhew 1974a: 6). When scholars with "economics expertise to display" took on Mayhew's challenge, they began by skipping over the electoral connection, looking instead at how the committee system helped the most important legislature in the world avoid perpetual indecision.

The problem for students of majority-rule decision-making was crystallized by Gordon Tullock (1981) in a famous essay in which he posed the question "why is there so much stability" in majority rule settings? Theorists of decision-making had long understood that if you allow a group of people to vote on policy proposals that are complicated, allowing members of the group to make amendments and then resolve differences using majority rule, some amendment could always attract a majority to beat any other proposal. Yet, when we observe actual decision-making institutions in the world, such as Congress, voting does not go on forever. Policy choices seem to be quite stable, even under majority rule. Thus, Tullock's question, why so much stability?

To explain the problem with a little more specificity, it is important to know that Tullock was following through on the implications of Kenneth's Arrow's (1950) very influential "impossibility theorem." Arrow's theoretical work demonstrated that if we allow citizens (or legislators) to have any preferences about public policy they wish, and they resolve differences over policy through "nice" democratic procedures such as majority rule, then we can never identify a single policy outcome that is unambiguously "better" than all others. Subsequent theorists translated Arrow's ideas into the spatial voting context, examining the behavior of "pure majority rule" in settings involving numerous decision-makers trying to agree to policy whose salient features exist along more than one dimension.

Figure 5.2 illustrates how this works in the spatial context, and what the puzzle is. Imagine a legislature debating how much to spend on food assistance for the poor and on medical care for the indigent. To simplify things significantly, imagine the legislature has three members, $A$, $B$, and $C$. Their "ideal points"—the amounts of spending each would enact if he or she were a dictator—are indicated on the graph. Again, to simplify so that we can focus on the logic of the problem, suppose that when motions are made about how much to spend, each legislator will vote in favor of the proposal that is closest to him or her, using a simple distance rule. For instance, if the policy labeled $w$ on the figure were the bill and someone moved to amend the bill to $x$ (a lot more spending on food assistance and a little more spending on medical assistance), $A$ and $B$ would favor $x$ over $w$, because it is clearly closer to their ideal points, and $C$ would oppose the amendment, for the opposite reason.

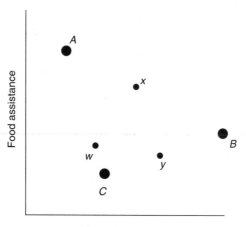

*Figure 5.2* Simple Example of Three-Person Legislature Voting Using Majority Rule

Notice in this example, that a majority of the legislature favors *x* over *w* (as just mentioned), a majority favors *y* over *x* (*B* and *C* voting for the former and *A* favoring the latter), but that a majority favors *w* over *y* (*A* and *C* vs. *B*). If these three options are the policy alternatives voted on through simple majority rule, there is no "equilibrium" of tastes; voting goes on forever. This instability is not simply due to the alternatives *w*, *x*, and *y* being unusual. For *every* policy alternative that could be proposed in Figure 5.2, there is *always* at least one alternative in the issue space that will beat it in a majority vote.

Kenneth Shepsle and Barry Weingast (1981) noted that real-world legislatures had an arsenal of organizational tricks that limited the likelihood that the type of majority rule instability illustrated in Figure 5.2 would appear in practice. Some of these rules, such as requiring the status quo (that is, the current policy, in the absence of new legislation) to be voted on last, do not directly affect committees.[12] But some do. Two in particular are: (1) the *gatekeeping* power of committees and (2) the distribution of policy dimensions to committees through a *jurisdictional system*.

To return to the example in Figure 5.2, imagine there is a jurisdictional system that assigns oversight of medical assistance policy to one committee and oversight of food assistance programs to another committee. The medical committee cannot recommend changes in food assistance policy, and vice versa. Furthermore, imagine that this assignment of jurisdictions to committees is reinforced through a *germaneness* rule, such that when the food assistance bill is brought to the floor, it cannot be amended to change medical assistance, and vice versa. With these rules in place, the proposal to amend *w* by adopting *x* instead that is shown in Figure 5.2 could not be offered, because it changes food and medical assistance policy *simultaneously*, in violation of the jurisdictional and germaneness rules.

With these common legislative rules that are usually associated with committees, policy alternatives can only be considered "one dimension at a time," such as illustrated in Figure 5.3. Here, we have the same three-person legislature as in Figure 5.2 and the same starting point, *w*. Now, to preserve the jurisdictional/germaneness rules, any proposal to change policy can only move in one direction or the other. Suppose, for instance, that a proposal is made to increase medical assistance spending to point *v*. Members *B* and *C* support this; *A* is opposed. Now, suppose a proposal is made to increase food spending to point *t*. It is supported by members *A* and *B*, opposed by *C*, and it, too, passes. *Any* proposal to change policy in a vertical or horizontal direction from point *t* will be opposed by a majority of this legislature. Thus, stability has been induced by the rules of the legislature. There *are* policy proposals that would pass this legislature to change *t*, if they were allowed to be offered, such as something that proposed increasing medical assistance and cutting food assistance, such as policy *y* in Figure 5.2. However, the jurisdictional and/or germaneness rules preclude such a proposal from being made.[13]

The outcome labeled *t* in Figure 5.3 is what Shepsle and Weingast termed a "structure-induced equilibrium." It is an equilibrium because the rules do not allow any further motions to be made that could change the outcome through a majority-rule vote. It is "structure-induced" because *only* the rules, not the preferences of the legislators alone, produce the equilibrium.

Thus, common rules that are associated with congressional committees are responsible for producing a desirable result in a democracy: stability. Beyond

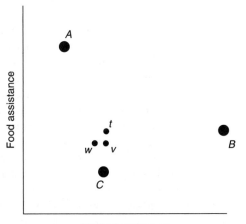

*Figure 5.3* Example of Legislative Decision-Making if Motions can be Made "One Dimension at a Time"

stability, are these rules policy-neutral in practice? Not necessarily. If we graft onto the structure-induced equilibrium system some old congressional norms, such as assigning "interested" members to committees that would facilitate reelection, the results could actually be perverse. This is precisely the insight exploited in the approach that followed next.

### Committees as Rent Seekers

To what end could structure-induced stability be put? A direct implication is that this stability could be put to the narrow ends of committee members, who were said to be effectively self-selected on committees. The problem of the self-selection of committee members had previously been identified by William Niskanen in his book, *Bureaucracy and Representative Government* (1971). Niskanen noted that committees tended to be populated by "high-demand" legislators—an excess of farmers on agriculture committees, lawyers on judiciary committees, representatives of military bases on the armed services committees, etc.—who tended to be sympathetic to the policy proposals made to them by the bureaucrats in the executive branch agencies they regularly monitored. This insight was naturally wedded to the structure-induced equilibrium idea to yield an explanation for why government might be "too big" if a legislature like Congress created a committee system that was deferential toward its committees.

To see how this result might come about, revisit the examples from Figures 5.2 and 5.3, with an additional twist. Let us suppose that member *B* is the "Medical Committee" and *A* is the "Food Committee." These two members have been chosen because they have the highest demand for spending along these two dimensions. The rules endow the committees with *gatekeeping* and *agenda-setting* powers. The gatekeeping power means that the Medical Assistance Committee, and only that committee, can decide whether to bring a bill to the whole legislature changing policy along that dimension, and therefore whether the chamber gets to vote on that policy. The agenda-setting power means that the committee gets to determine which exact policy the chamber gets to consider.

Figure 5.4 illustrates what happens in our idealized legislature with two "high-demand" committees that have gatekeeping and agenda-setting power. Start with the status quo at *k*. *A* can propose a significant increase in food assistance spending, moving policy to point *m*, which passes on a vote pitting *A* and *B* against *C*. Then, *B* could propose an increase in medical assistance spending, moving policy to point *n*, drawing support from members *B* and *C*, with opposition from *A*. Note, yet again, that it is easy to find policies that a majority would support, compared to *n*. Indeed, point *q* would beat point *n* in a *unanimous* vote. However, the rules preclude such a motion—it would violate the gatekeeping rule, because *A* would oppose the reduction in food assistance and *B* would oppose reducing medical assistance. The jurisdictional and germaneness rules would also be violated, because moving from *n* to *q* would involve changing policy in two dimensions, not one.

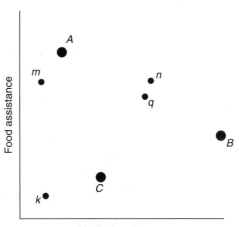

*Figure 5.4* Example of Legislative Decision-Making with a Simple Committee System that Embodies Agenda-Setting and Gatekeeping Powers

I have termed this variant of the structure-induced equilibrium model the view of committees as rent seekers, because "rent" is the term that economists use to describe the excess distribution of resources to an agent in the economy, beyond what is necessary to keep that agent participating in the economy. In the simple example we just worked through, the allocations to food assistance and medical assistance that are shown in Figure 5.4 give more to those programs than a majority would normally support, absent rules that stacked the decks in favor of these interests. Seen another way, medical and food interests are able to extract government spending on their favored programs above-and-beyond what the legislature prefers on aggregate, because of the special powers committees have to protect the interests they oversee.

The rent-seeking view proved to be a powerful way of thinking about committees theoretically while also being consistent with critiques of congressional decision-making from both the left and the right in the 1970s. For the right, which believed the federal government spent too much, this sort of analysis identified the mechanism that led government spending to balloon. For the left, this line of thinking helped explain why "interest group liberalism" (Lowi 1969) had robbed liberal Democratic presidents of their ability to enact redistributive social policies or smash the last vestiges of racist practices in the South.

The rent-seeking perspective was subject to considerable criticism, however. For the moment, consider two lines of investigation, both associated with Krehbiel (1991, 1998). The first line is theoretical, and can be seen by returning to the outcome illustrated in Figure 5.4. Remember that this legislature would *unanimously* vote to reduce spending on both policies, but cannot do so because of the germaneness, agenda-setting, and gatekeeping rules. This only raises questions like, "why would a legislature that can set its rules through majority vote, agree to rules that would make *everyone* worse off in policy terms?" The rules themselves would seem not to be in equilibrium, if they can produce such perverse results (Riker 1980).

The second line of criticism is empirical—although one can find examples of committees being composed of high-demand outliers, this appears to be the exception, not the rule, when considered across-the-board. For instance, Krehbiel (1990) examined whether House standing committee members were extreme, measured in terms of interest group scores that might gauge demand for federal activity in specific policy areas associated with those committees. With only a couple of exceptions, House committees seemed to be composed of members who were a lot like the rest of the chamber. The exceptions, such as Education and Labor and Armed Services, were substantively significant, but the important thing was these were not the rule.

## Committees as Party Agents

These two literatures together, the structure-induced equilibrium and the "rent-seeking" views, helped to provide theoretical guidance for the understanding of how Congress might systematically favor special interests. However, almost as soon as this literature had gained momentum, another one emerged that focused on another set of outliers—the political parties (Kiewiet and McCubbins 1991; Cox and McCubbins 1993, 2005). The distinctiveness of this perspective is perhaps best seen in Kiewiet and McCubbins (1991), which focused on the politics of appropriations. Remember that by 1990, the general view of the appropriations committee was influenced by the earlier work of Fenno, who had described a pair of appropriations committees that leaned against the partisan winds, particularly the big-spending tendencies of the majority Democrats. The House Appropriations Committee, in particular, had been said to achieve power in the chamber by pursuing a set of tactics that were described as "'cut,' 'carve,' 'slice,' 'prune,' 'whittle,' 'squeeze,' 'wring,' 'trim,' 'lop off,' 'chop,' 'slash,' 'pare,' 'shave,' 'fry,' and 'whack.'" (Fenno 1965: 312)

Looking back over the same history as Fenno, McCubbins and Kiewiet found something quite different. First, they discovered a pattern of committee assignments that rewarded party loyalists. Second, they discovered that although Appropriations Committee leaders would argue they were simple non-partisan guardians of the Treasury, whenever interviewed by political scientists, the policy consequences of their *actions* were decidedly partisan. If one is interested in policy outputs, rather than the trappings of power, then it is necessary to judge the system by those outputs, and not by the often self-serving claims by politicians.

This viewpoint was taken to a more general level in two subsequent books by Cox and McCubbins (1993, 2005). The organizing principle here is the *legislative cartel,* which is based on four key claims: (1) legislative parties arise to deal with the need to manage elections for their members, (2) members of legislative parties can be divided into junior and senior partners, much like law and accounting firms, (3) legislative parties specialize in controlling the agenda, not the votes of their members, and (4) the majority party in a legislature primarily achieves its goals by allocating procedural rights of both a negative and positive sort (Cox and McCubbins 2005).

Many of these features have direct implications for committees. For instance, the senior members of the legislative cartels certainly include committee leaders and members of committees that are directly implicated in the electoral brand name of the parties. The bulk of negative agenda-setting power is situated in committees who can refuse to report out legislation that harms the party's interest. When party leaders deem it important to skirt legislative committees, the House, at least, still relies on the work of the Rules Committee to pave the way for consideration of legislation on the floor.

### Committees as Information Providers

In parallel with the development of party cartel theory, Krehbiel proposed an alternative, based on the informative role played by committees in legislatures (Krehbiel 1991). Central to Krehbiel's argument is the fact that it is rarely precisely clear how a policy under consideration by Congress will work in practice. This uncertainty is most clearly on display when Congress considers historic legislation, such as health care reform, but it is constantly on display when less momentous issues are considered, such as whether the labeling of "organic" foods should be regulated, whether the FCC should be required to adopt "net neutrality" as Internet policy, or whether more money should be invested in understanding the mathematics behind origami.

Regardless of their ideological predispositions, it benefits all members of Congress if uncertainty about proposed legislation can be reduced. The hard question is how to acquire and disseminate the knowledge necessary to reduce this uncertainty for the *typical* MC—not the atypical high-demanders, but the low-demand skeptic. A logical organizational strategy is for both chambers of Congress to create a division-of-labor system dedicated to information specialization. Call it a committee system.

However, there is no guarantee that a committee system will acquire the information needed by the median member of Congress to make an informed choice or, if acquired, to disseminate it. First, a committee's members might just shirk, relying uncritically on information provided by executive agencies and interest groups. This is the dynamic that gave rise to the idea that policy-making was dominated by "iron triangles." Second, if they do work to acquire independent information, committees might not share it with the rest of the chamber, choosing instead to obfuscate legislative language so that the benefits of the proposed legislation will disproportionately benefit members of the committee, not the typical legislator. Finally, if they do share the information with the legislature, a majority on the floor may use it to undo the careful drafting and political compromises the committee worked hard to achieve.

There are solutions available to legislatures to meet these challenges. For instance, to induce committees to do the hard work to investigate policy and write legislation that reflects the information they have gathered, Congress has been known to grant greater latitude in bill drafting to committees that acquire reputations as being expert and responsive to the chamber. A good example of this was the Ways and Means Committee under Wilbur Mills, whose committee enjoyed the privilege of reporting its bills under a closed rule, a privilege Mills worked tenaciously to maintain. Committees can also be populated with a heterogeneous collection of members, not just high-demanders, so that if the legislation does not reflect the best information or the political desires of a majority of the chamber, committee members who are predisposed to skepticism can serve as legislative "canaries in the coal mine" (Calvert 1985).

There is evidence that committees in Congress, especially the House, are constructed according to this logic. As mentioned above, only a few committees are regularly dominated by members who are obvious policy outliers, and when they are, their legislation is subjected to greater skepticism, and possibility of defeat, on the floor.

\* \* \*

This literature presents a synthetic view of congressional committees that is a useful starting point to understand them, regardless of the particular era we are studying. The view of political scientists emphasizes how committees operate within social and political systems; there are numerous dynamics that act on them, through their members, to keep committee behavior in equilibrium with these systems. Members are selfishly motivated. The consequences of that motivation cause the committee system to tend toward favoring private goods and rent seeking, but there is enough of an acknowledgment within Congress of the "tragedy of the commons" that the committee system is also constructed to rein-in the most extreme of self-seeking behavior, channeling it toward a public good. This is not to say that behavior is channeled toward *the* public good. Rather, there are practices in place that help the system achieve collective benefits for members, such as national party goals, as well as provide more particular benefits to members and their separate constituents.

## Committees in a Partisan Era, Or Committees and the Deinstitutionalization of Congress

With this background, it is now possible to step back and assess the nexus between events and literatures pertaining to congressional committees, to gain some perspective on where they are now, and where committees are going in the contemporary Congress.

The "big bang" of scholarship about committees in the 1960s happened at a very unusual moment in American political history. The division within the Democratic Party over race obscured the existence of the poles around which the parties organized—around the issue of central governmental power in managing the economy and the role of government in helping the working classes. Southern Democrats, for whom the most salient issue was the role of the central government in bringing political equality to African Americans, were able to introduce a second dimension into American politics, allowing them to play Northern Democrats and Republicans against each other.

Being from an economically under-developed region, Southern Democrats were delighted to bring home as much bacon as possible and to litter the region with military installations. In this endeavor, they found many points of agreement with their Northern co-partisans, and could act without much friction as part of a unified national party coalition. On the other hand, by coalescing with Republicans over questions of the general capacity of the federal government, and in particular over the regulation of labor markets, they could maintain many of the essentials of a regional economy based on low pay and few prospects for mobility, re-tooled for a post-13th Amendment world, including so-called right-to-work laws.[14]

This tricky coalitional reality had its most obvious manifestation in committees, which were divided by the same coalitional challenges that beset the larger body. Because the committees were much smaller in size, they were amenable to the one-on-one leadership tactics that were necessary to hold together highly unstable coalitions of legislators. Thus, it is unsurprising that political scientists first encountering congressional politics and its committees would draw on social scientific theories that focused on the behavior of small groups, nor that they would focus on the contributions played by individual leadership and social expectations in keeping decision-making from devolving into chaos—this is Fenno's "integration."

However, the seeds of the demise of this system were already planted, even though contemporary political science seems to have missed them. Kiewiet and McCubbins (1991) show that even when Fenno was doing field work, the parties were constructing the Appropriations Committees in a partisan fashion, as they were constructing committees more generally. The parties used the committees to exercise agenda control in Congress throughout the twentieth century.

As the coalitions comprising the two parties have become more clearly ideological, the types of activities necessary to hold them together have shifted. While one always prefers a committee chair with deft interpersonal skills, there has nonetheless been a marked shift in the optimal skill set of committee leaders in Congress. They have moved away from a more "Johnsonian" attention to the individual quirks of committee members toward qualities such as party loyalty, fundraising success for party candidates, and strategic intelligence in doing battle with the opposition.

The shift in expectations about what it takes to lead committees has occurred during a time when the capacity of committees to legislate in the face of an antagonistic executive branch and ravenous interest groups has diminished. Prior to 1994, when parties were ascendant but committees were still in a position to roll party leaders, committees had staffs and budgets to assert their influence. On the eve of the 1994 election, the congressional standing committee system possessed 2,050 staff members in the House and 950 in the Senate. Two years later, those numbers had shrunk to 1,200 in the House and 800 in the Senate; they have not grown significantly since (Ornstein, Mann, and Malbin 2008). Budgets have also been slashed proportionately.[15] Thus, with a reduction in institutional capacity in the committee system—a reduction that has hit the committee-centric House much harder than the more individualist Senate—it is not at all surprising that influence over the making of policy would shift elsewhere.

If the skills most valued on committees now are less relevant today, what is the role of committees in the contemporary Congress? This question would seem to be the next major puzzle for students of Congress, especially for the generations of scholars who were schooled in the notion that it was a prime example of an "institutionalized" legislature. The new reality seems to be one of deinstitutionalization.

Recent legislative developments, culminating in the 111th Congress (2009–10) provide evidence that committees are no longer the place to be, if one is interested in legislation. The most subtle indicator of the waning role of committees in legislating is the demise of the conference committee, which was the lynchpin of committee power in the structure-induced equilibrium literature (Krehbiel, Shepsle, and Weingast 1987; Shepsle and Weingast 1987). In particular, as Shepsle and Weingast point out in the mid-1980s, the common practice was to reconcile House–Senate differences by resorting to conference committees. An important feature of conference committees, from the perspective of the various "committee dominance" approaches, is they are usually composed of members drawn from the committee that reported the legislation in the first place. The House and Senate might amend bills on the floor, but the legislative committees would get one last chance to defend their handiwork, by producing a conference report that would be subjected to a take-it-or-leave vote.

However, the percentage of public laws that have gone through the conference process has declined over the past decade. Differences are more often resolved through a less public process, in which revised versions of the bill are passed back-and-forth between chambers, a practice sometimes referred to as the "ping-pong approach" to ironing out differences. While committee leaders are usually involved in this process, they merely share the stage with party leaders, cutting out much of the committee rank and file and, most importantly, members of the minority party. Many reasons explain this shift, but the most important seem to be party polarization and the resulting difficulty of getting the Senate to agree to conference committees, given the filibuster barrier. Consequences of the demise of the conference are a decline of deliberation, a lack of transparency, and a decline in the testing of new ideas against harsh criticism (Oleszek 2008).

It is impossible to read Oleszek's analysis of the conference committee's decline and not recognize how the shift from relying on the committees to broker complex deals over important legislation to relying on an ad hoc collection of majority-party leaders, executive branch officials, and lobbyists, would ultimately undermine the legitimacy of landmark legislation. Indeed, this could be an important source of some of the vitriolic rhetoric attacking the Health Care Reform Act of 2010, denying the legitimacy of the act because of how its details were finally constructed and the bill passed.

Reinforcing the decline of committees as the arbiters of what goes into the important laws is the decline of committees as the originators of important bills in the first place. A good example of this was the "first hundred hour" plan, in which Nancy Pelosi pledged immediate action on Democratic-priority legislation in the opening days of the 110th Congress (Aldrich and Rohde 2009). Across a six-day period in early 2007, the House passed six bills, numbered symbolically H.R. 1 to H.R. 6, representing a significant range of policy activity. These bills proposed to enact the recommendations of the 9/11 commission, raise the federal minimum wage, grant funding to stem cell research, allow the government to negotiate lower prescription drug prices under Medicare, cut interest rates on student loans, and reduce tax subsidies for oil companies. These were all significant bills, none of which saw committee action before coming to the House floor.

A similar, though perhaps anticlimactic, story began the 111th Congress, when the House passed, without initial committee consideration, H.R. 1 (The American Recovery and Reinvestment Act), H.R. 2 (Children's Health Insurance Program Reauthorization Act), and H.R. 11 (Lily Ledbetter Fair Pay Act). But the serious attention was focused elsewhere, on health care reform. The monumental Health Care Reform bill that was finally signed into law in the spring of 2010 (H.R. 3962, PL 111–192) illustrates the new interplay between committees and party leadership in important legislation, and the degree to which party leaders play high-profile roles, even when committees are deeply involved in hammering out the details of legislation. Originally constituted as H.R. 3200 in the House, the health care bill was cleared by three committees in July 2009, after a series of highly partisan proceedings over the structure of the plan. After being cleared by the committees, and facing further controversy within the Democratic caucus, negotiations shifted to a party-led process which eventually yielded a party plan, unveiled by Speaker Pelosi at the end of October. Committees got the ball rolling, but the Speaker led the bargaining over its details, ultimately determining the fate of the bill's most controversial provisions.

When it comes to policy matters that define the parties, the committees are now on a short leash. If important legislation is referred to committees at all, it is with a requirement that the committee report back by a certain date. If the Speaker is unhappy with the bill, she or he will call the committee chair on the carpet to get it changed to her or his liking. The time given to committees to report important legislation is often too short for deep policy expertise to be applied to the drafting of the bill, or for the committees to hatch the political deals necessary to pass complicated legislation. Thus, important decisions made about legislation are shifted back to party leaders, who preside over an ad hoc, deinstitutionalized lawmaking process.

In this environment, why the two chambers have committees at all, why they equip them so lavishly, and why interest groups target campaign contributions to members as a function of their committee membership is a major puzzle. It might very well be that the committee system now exists as part of a two-tier legislative process. Tier I consists of legislation that the parties put their brand on. In this tier, committees lend a patina of legitimacy to the process, but the parties rule on the big questions. Tier II consists of legislation that keeps bureaucracies functioning and earmarks delivered back to one's district. Here, committees make a difference, but in a manner that escapes serious public review.

As Congress enters the thicket of a new partisan age, a number of questions remain for the future of the committee system. Do committees remain the central font of expertise in crafting important national legislation? Have they ceded more of the detailed work to the executive branch and lobbyists, much as has happened in state legislatures, where term limits have robbed those institutions of members with a deep understanding of the details of public policy? Will the House eventually become more like the Senate, in terms of shifting resources to member offices, away from committees, with members shifting their attention away from legislating? In a sense, the world described here is one of all "show horses" and few "work horses." This is not a sign that Congress will proceed into the partisan era with the capacity in its committee system to meet the challenges that stand before it.

## Notes

1 The representational basis of this autonomy rested on the assumption that by virtue of this cultural tie, the representative had a very good idea about how his constituents thought about issues already, and therefore could act on their behalf without much second thought. In fact, the research of Miller and Stokes (1963) suggested that except for civil rights, House members were not especially good at knowing their constituents' opinions about important national issues.
2 "Congressional Reforms Made In 1975." CQ Press Electronic Library, CQ Almanac Online Edition, cqal75–1210820. Originally published in *CQ Almanac 1975* (Washington: Congressional Quarterly, 1976). http://library.cqpress.com/cqalmanac/cqal75-1210820 (accessed November 4, 2010).
3 "Major Leadership Changes as 99th Convenes." CQ Press Electronic Library, CQ Almanac Online Edition, cqal85–1146594. Originally published in *CQ Almanac 1985*

(Washington: Congressional Quarterly, 1986). http://library.cqpress.com/cqalma-nac/cqal85-1146594 (accessed November 4, 2010).

4 "100th Congress: Democrats at the Helm Again." CQ Press Electronic Library, CQ Almanac Online Edition, cqal87-1143660. Originally published in *CQ Almanac 1987* (Washington: Congressional Quarterly, 1988). http://library.cqpress.com/cqalma-nac/cqal87-1143660 (accessed November 4, 2010).

5 The text of the *Contract* can be found at the following URL: http://www.house.gov/house/Contract/CONTRACT.html.

6 A *proxy vote* is when a member of a committee gives someone else on the commit-tee, usually the chair, the right to cast his or her vote on the absent member's behalf. This was seen as a way of both giving rank-and-file members greater flexibility with their time while at the same time centralizing even greater power in the hands of the chair.

7 Emblematic of the decline of seniority as an automatic criterion for the selection of the top Democratic member of committees, the post-election struggle for the posi-tion of ranking minority leader began immediately upon the outcome of the 2010 midterm congressional elections. For instance, three sitting committee chairs were defeated for reelection in 2010—Ike Skelton (D-MO, Armed Services), John Spratt (D-SC, Budget), and James Oberstar (D-MN, Transportation and Infrastructure). Dennis (2010) was able to identify four representatives potentially vying to serve as ranking member of Armed Services and three for Transportation. In addition, well before the election season was under way, a contest had broken out between Sander Levin (MI) and Richard Neal (MA) to take over the top Democratic position on Ways and Means (Palmer and Newmyer 2010; Palmer 2010). But perhaps the most telling sign that Democrats can no longer count on seniority to automatically identify new ranking members of committees, the presumptive ranking member of Appropriations, Norm Dicks (WA) was slated to receive a challenge from the 21st ranking Democrat on the committee, Chaka Fattah (PA) (Dennis 2010; Palmer 2010).

8 Analysis in these two paragraphs is based on data taken from the American National Election Studies, http://www.electionstudies.org/nesguide/nesguide.htm.

9 To give a sense about how voluminous the literature on congressional committees is, Nelson and Stewart (2010) contains a bibliographic essay about current House and Senate standing committees. The total number of works cited in these essays is 102—and these are simply the most prominent works out of a much larger corpus of scholarship.

10 An even broader variant of this argument, in a comparative context, is contained in Polsby's now-neglected essay on legislatures in the *Handbook of Political Science* (see Polsby 1975).

11 Of party, Mayhew (1974a) wrote "no theoretical treatment of the United States Con-gress that posits parties as analytic units will go very far" (p. 27). Mayhew later noted that if he were to write the book in the early twenty-first century, he would back off this statement.

12 Proposal *w* is the status quo in Figure 5.2.

13 More technically, *t* is an equilibrium because, when we investigate the location of the policy along a single dimension, it is located at the median. For instance, the median member of the legislature on the medical assistance dimension is *C*, because one member (*A*) wants less spending and one member (*B*) wants more spending. Similarly, *B* is the median member along the food assistance dimension. As a general matter, the median voter is the equilibrium outcome under pure majority rule and voting along one dimension. See Black (1958) for more details.

14 The struggle over the future of the Southern economy following the Civil War is one of the great issues of Southern political development, epitomized by leaders such as

Henry Grady, who articulated a vision of a "New South" that was industrialized and integrated more thoroughly into the rest of the American economy. As Key's classic *Southern Politics* (1949) makes clear, by the mid-twentieth century, evidence of Grady's vision within Southern politics was thin, seen in a few industrial/financial centers dotted around the region, and perhaps in many of the policy choices made in North Carolina early in the twentieth century.

15 Evidence about post-2007 support of committees is based on examination of recent releases of the Statement of Disbursements by the House and the Report of the Secretary of the Senate.

# Chapter 6

# House Rules and Procedure

## A Procedural Arms Race

*Jason M. Roberts*

On November 7, 2009, the U.S. House adopted H.R. 3962—the Affordable Health Care for America Act—also known as the health care reform bill. Passage of this bill was a major achievement for President Obama, Speaker Nancy Pelosi (D-CA) and many members of the Democratic Party. Though the bill faced strident opposition from House Republicans and some segments of the American public, House floor action on the bill was largely anticlimactic. Before taking the bill to the floor, Speaker Pelosi and the House Rules Committee had carefully scripted a special rule for consideration of the bill.[1] The rule specified the time allowed for debate, which of the scores of proposed amendments would be voted on, and in what order they would be considered. The rule also allowed the Speaker to halt proceedings at any time if she saw fit. The special rule cemented many of the agreements that had been struck off the floor, including a compromise on an abortion-related amendment offered by Bart Stupak (D-MI) that had threatened to scuttle the entire bill. In the end, though the debate was fierce and some of the votes were close, the outcome followed the script laid out by Pelosi and the Rules Committee (Hulse and Pear 2009).

As the health care bill example demonstrates, the modern day U.S. House of Representatives often functions as an efficient legislative machine. In contrast to the more individualist U.S. Senate, House majorities can and do quickly dispose of even the most controversial pieces of legislation without extensive debate, amending, or procedural chaos. Voting on amendments and on the passage of bills takes place in an orderly manner and on a predictable schedule. Over the course of its history, the U.S. House has developed a number of procedural tools that facilitate smooth operations in the chamber. Many of these tools have been created at the impetus of the majority party in the House and, as a result, many of the key features of House procedure can be used to further the partisan goals of chamber majorities. The purpose of this chapter is to highlight both the historical development of many of the key procedural tools that allow the House to function efficiently and the role of political parties in creating and using the procedures for partisan gain.

## Procedural Choice and the Motion on the Previous Question

Article I of the U.S. Constitution sets out a broad and detailed set of powers for the U.S. Congress, ranging from coining money, to collecting taxes, to declaring war on foreign countries. However, the document provides little guidance in terms of how each chamber should go about actually using the broad powers given. Beyond quorum requirements and the identification of presiding officers, Article I, section 5 of the Constitution leaves to each chamber the power to "determine the Rules of its Proceedings." As such, each chamber of the U.S. Congress has adopted and changed its rules repeatedly over the course of history. These changes have typically been a function of partisan conflict in the chamber and the rules changes themselves have often served to further enhance conflict between majority and minority parties. Arguably, no rule choice has affected the development of the two chambers more than their differing practices with regard to the motion on the previous question.

In its current form, the motion on the previous question ends debate on the issue under consideration in the U.S. House. If a majority of the House votes to enact the previous question, the chamber then moves to a vote on passage of the underlying question. As Binder (1997: 49–50) describes, the original previous question motion did not end debate. The motion took the form of "Shall the main question be now put?" If the motion failed, the chamber moved away from the bill under consideration to other measures; if it passed, the chamber would continue considering the item on the floor. Through the first 10 Congresses, the House operated under this interpretation of the rule and without a direct means to end legislative debate. This changed in late 1811 as the majority party in the House voted to interpret the previous question motion so that a majority in favor of it would end debate on the measure (Binder 1997). This interpretation of the previous question motion has persisted since that time and has provided a means for House majorities to end debate. The U.S. Senate, for its part, inadvertently dropped the motion on the previous question during a rules revision in 1806 and has never reinstated it (Binder and Smith 1997). Eliminating the motion proved to be quite consequential, as without it the Senate lacks a means to allow a majority to end debate on a measure. This lack of a previous question motion in the Senate is the procedural foundation for the most widely known procedural tactic in the Senate—the filibuster (Binder and Smith 1997).[2]

## Obstruction in the Nineteenth-Century U.S. House

As Koger (2010) notes, adoption of the revised motion on the previous question did not end all obstruction in the U.S. House. Determined House minorities still had myriad ways available to obstruct and prevent the passage of legislation. One such tactic was through the use of "dilatory motions." These are motions that are proposed simply to waste plenary time and prevent action on the underlying bill or item of business. Examples of motions that were often used to waste time include: a motion to adjourn, motion to recess, motion to table a bill, and motions to set time to meet after adjournments and recesses (Binder 1997; Koger 2010). These motions were effective because due to existing House rules, they took procedural precedence over the current business on the floor and it took a considerable amount of time to cast votes on these motions even if they were ultimately defeated. Koger (2010) finds that there were over 2,000 dilatory motions offered in the House between 1789 and 1901, with sharp spikes associated with controversial, partisan legislation.

In addition to dilatory motions, House minorities could also employ a delaying tactic known as the "disappearing quorum." As noted above, the Constitution requires that a majority of House members constitute a quorum—if less than a majority are present then the House cannot conduct official business.[3] The Constitution does not clearly specify how one determines if a quorum is in fact present, but the House interpreted votes in which less than a majority of the membership voted as null due to the quorum requirement. This created an opening for obstructionists, as absenteeism was quite high in the nineteenth-century House due to illnesses and travel difficulties. This meant that the majority party often did not have enough of its own members present to meet the quorum requirement. Minorities could choose to simply not attend the House session to prevent a quorum, but the most common tactic was refusing to answer the roll call on a vote.[4] If enough members who were physically present chose not to vote, the House would be unable to conduct official business. Koger (2010) counts more than 900 instances of disappearing quorums in the House between 1789 and 1901.

Even with the strengthened motion on the previous question, nineteenth-century House majority parties often found that the combination of dilatory motions and disappearing quorums made it very difficult to enact legislation without cooperation from the minority party. In effect, the majority and minority parties had mutual vetoes over each other's legislative proposals.

### Thomas Brackett Reed and Majority Rule in the U.S. House

Thomas Brackett Reed (R-ME) is one of the most significant figures in the storied history of the U.S. House. His tenure in the U.S. House (1877–1900) coincides with the most significant procedural developments in the chamber's history. Reed himself was a staunch believer in the power of the majority to rule even if he found himself on the losing side. Reed summed up his view of party government best, "The best system is to have one party govern and the other party watch; and on general principles I think it would be better for us to govern and for the Democrats to watch" (Cox and McCubbins 2005: 56). While he is best known for his role in instituting the "Reed Rules" (see below), he also played a role in the development of one of the most flexible procedural tools available to House majorities—the special rule.

The standing rules of the House declare that when a bill is reported from a committee it is placed on one of five House calendars.[5] The rules also state that bills are to be taken off the calendars in the order in which they went on the calendar. This is an inflexible rule that can make it difficult for the House to reach important legislation in a timely manner. As the number of bills introduced and the role of the federal government grew in the latter half of the nineteenth century, the House struggled to reach some important agenda items prior to the end of the legislative session. Though the House experimented with a number of mechanisms to expedite legislation, the one with the most amount of promise was the special order. A bill that was made a special order could be taken off the calendar out of order and immediately put before the House, after which it was considered under the chamber's standing rules. Special orders were effective as long as both parties cooperated in their use. Early special orders required consent of two-thirds of the chamber and could also be used as dilatory motions (Bach 1990). The major procedural problem plaguing the House was that there was far more legislation than time to consider it, and much of the available floor time was consumed by a combination of obstruction and infighting over which bills to consider.

As Roberts (2010) reports, the House majority began to develop more effective agenda control tools in 1883 during the consideration of the Tariff Act of 1883. During consideration of the bill, Thomas Brackett Reed wrote what would come to be known as the first "special rule" in the U.S. House. The rule allowed the House to supplant or supplement the standing rules by a simple majority rather than a two-thirds majority in order to pass the tariff bill (Hinds 1907: §1932).[6] As noted above, special orders such as the one used for the tariff bill were not new features of House procedures, but the ability to adopt one with a majority vote was a new innovation. In fact, Hinds (1907) notes that during early uses of special rules by majority vote, many members questioned the validity of the new tactic, while Reed himself—the author of the first special rule—said that, "unless there was a great emergency, I should not be in favor of its passage" (Alexander 1916: 216).

While the advent of the special rule gave House majorities the ability to determine which bills they would consider, the special rule had no immediate effect on the ability of minorities to obstruct legislation through the use of dilatory motions and the disappearing quorum. Legislative minorities still had the ability to cause chaos in the chamber and effectively force the majority party to negotiate with them over the content of the agenda. The ability of legislative minorities to obstruct ended abruptly in 1890, through the implementation of what came to be known as the Reed Rules.

As Binder (1997) notes, the Reed Rules were implemented in two steps. First, during consideration of a contested election case in January 1890, House Democrats attempted to obstruct a vote on the seating of a member through the use of a disappearing quorum. On a roll-call vote on the question of consideration, 165 Democrats did not register a vote, enough to prevent the House from having a quorum. Rather than accept the defeat, Speaker Reed ordered the clerk to record the names of members who were present in the chamber, but not voting. Upon recording the names of those present, but not voting, Reed declared that a quorum existed. Needless to say this ruling did not go over well with the House Democrats. The pages in the *Congressional Record* containing the debate that ensued are voluminous and highly entertaining. Many Democrats shouted to appeal the ruling of Speaker Reed, with William Breckinridge of Kentucky denouncing it as "revolutionary." James McCreary (KY) exclaimed that he denied the right of the Speaker to count him as present, to which Reed cleverly retorted, "The Chair is making a statement of fact that the gentleman is present. Does he deny it?" After four days of what Binder (1997) calls "pandemonium" on the House floor, Reed and the Republicans rounded up enough votes to uphold Reed's quorum counting ruling. After winning the quorum fight, House Republicans proceeded to enact a complete package of reforms that came to be known as the Reed Rules.

The major provisions of the Reed Rules included: allowing the Speaker to refuse to recognize members seeking to offer a dilatory motion, allowing the Speaker to count all members present but not voting as part of a quorum, lowering of the quorum requirement in the committee of the whole,[7] and allowing the Speaker to refer bills to committee without debate (Binder 1997; Cox and McCubbins 2005). The Reed Rules fundamentally changed the balance of power between House majorities and minorities. No longer could minorities obstruct legislation through the use of dilatory motions or the disappearing quorum. Combined with the powerful new tool—the special rule—House majorities permanently gained the power to legislate efficiently without minority obstruction.

### *"Czar Rule" and the Revolt against Speaker Cannon*

In the aftermath of the implementation of the Reed Rules, the power of the House Speaker reached its apex.[8] Republican Speakers Reed, David Henderson (IA), and Joseph Cannon (IL) chaired the three-person Committee on Rules that was charged with writing special rules for pieces of legislation, they had the sole power to recognize members to speak and offer motions, assigned bills to committees, and they alone were responsible for determining the committee assignments given to other majority-party members. Reed and Cannon were dubbed "czars" due to their penchant for ruling the House with an iron fist (Alexander 1916). Cannon in particular was considered to be especially overbearing in terms of using his considerable powers to further his personal and political goals. While recent academic literature has found Cannon's reputation is lacking in empirical support (Lawrence, Maltzman, and Wahlbeck 2001; Krehbiel and Wiseman 2001), a cross-party coalition of Democrats and

Progressive Republicans united to strip the Speaker of some of his key powers in March of 1910.

This "revolt" against Cannon shifted power from the Speaker to the majority party by removing the Speaker from the powerful Committee on Rules, enlarging the committee from three to ten members, and allowing the caucus to vote on committee assignments. As Cox and McCubbins (2005) note, the revolt against Cannon did not so much weaken the powers of the majority party as it simply shifted power from the Speaker to the party caucus itself. Roberts (2010) finds support for that argument, noting that the majority party increased their usage of special rules after the revolt against Cannon and increasingly turned to restrictive or "closed" rules to insure the efficient passage of legislation through the beginning of the New Deal.

### Conservative Coalition Era

The New Deal era that began in the 1930s saw fewer innovations in House rules and procedures and fewer instances of closed or restrictive rules. Democrats held incredibly large majorities in both chambers during the early years of Franklin Roosevelt's presidency. A large contingent of Northern Democrats combined with Democrats elected from the one-party South held a firm majority in the House for all but two of the thirty congresses that first met between 1933 and 1993. Though Democrats dominated the House in terms of pure numbers, they often faced serious obstacles in terms of enacting major legislation due to fragmentation between the Northern and Southern members. Many Southern Democrats held conservative policy positions that were more consistent with the typical Republican than the typical Democrat on major left–right issues. Southern Democrats also were in disagreement with their Northern colleagues on issues of civil rights and race relations in the South. On occasion, these Southern Democrats would ally with Republicans in a "conservative coalition" on roll-call votes (Rohde 1991).

The split in the Democratic party coincided with the rise of the seniority system in the chamber with regards to committee assignments (Deering and Smith 1997). Committee assignments, transfers, and committee leadership positions were doled out not in terms of which members would best represent the caucus, but based on how long a particular member had served in the committee in question and/or the chamber. Given the lack of two-party competition in the South, many Southern members acquired seniority rights and emerged to lead key committees. In terms of rules and procedures, this meant that the Democratic delegation on the Committee on Rules often had a Southern tilt (Rohde 1991; Schickler and Pearson 2009). With a divided Committee on Rules and a divided caucus, majority-party Democrats were typically unable to use House rules and procedures to secure legislation consistent with the goals of more liberal Democrats (Rohde 1991). In fact, under the chairmanship of Howard "Judge" Smith of Virginia, the Committee on Rules often acted as an independent agenda-setting body rather than as an agent of the majority-party Democrats (Schickler and Pearson 2009). Aside from tax bills reported from the Ways and Means committee, most special rules in this era were primarily open rules that did not restrict the amending activity of rank-and-file members.

## The Reform Era and the Rise of Restrictive Rules

The 1970s saw a series of changes to House and Democratic Caucus rules that facilitated the more aggressive use of House rules and procedures to secure outcomes more in line with the policy preferences of Northern Democrats (Rohde 1991). These rules changes combined with the strategies pursued by the leadership of both parties in the House set off a procedural "arms race" that continues unabated in the House today (Rohde 1991; Roberts and Smith 2003; Marshall 2005; Sinclair 2006).

At the outset of the 92nd Congress (1971–73), House rules were changed to allow recorded voting in the Committee of the Whole (COW)[9] for the first time. The COW is simply a committee comprised of all members of the House. It has less stringent quorum requirements (100 rather than a majority of members) and more flexible debate rules. The COW is employed by the House for many aspects of bill consideration—most notable of which is the consideration of amendments to legislation.

Prior to the 1971 rules change, votes on amendments were tabulated either through a standing division vote, where members for or against an amendment would stand to be counted, or through a "teller vote." A teller vote was conducted by having members pass by an individual designated to count "aye" and "nay" votes. Critically, in neither case were the votes of individual members recorded or reported publicly (Smith 1989).[10] This rules change, combined with the adoption of an electronic voting machine in the 93rd Congress (1973–75), led to a rapid increase in the number of recorded votes on amendments to legislation. As Smith (1989) reports, in the five congresses preceding the rules change, amendments made up approximately 10 percent of the roll-call record. In the five congresses after the rules change, amendments votes constituted approximately one-third of the roll-call record.

These amendment votes often sharply divided Democrats from Republicans, leading to an increase in the number of votes that were considered "party votes"[11] along with other measures of party cohesion (Roberts and Smith 2003). The evidence suggests that minority-party Republicans saw potential electoral advantages in forcing recorded votes on amendments. As Smith (1989) notes, House Republicans actively courted amendment proposals from Republicans who were running against Democratic incumbents. The Republican strategy only intensified as Newt Gingrich (GA) assumed a more prominent role in the Republican caucus. He co-founded the Conservative Opportunity Society (COS) in 1983 and spearheaded a more aggressive legislative strategy by minority-party Republicans (Roberts and Smith 2003).

Gingrich argued that Republicans were doomed to minority status forever if they continued to be accommodative with the House Democrats. As Roberts and Smith (2003: 307) note, Gingrich and the COS:

> insisted that their party stop working with majority Democrats to make small contributions to policy and instead should oppose the Democrats at every step in the legislative process, avoid accommodation, draw clear ideological distinctions between the parties, and go on the attack with national themes in more aggressive attempts to unseat Democratic incumbents. Vote no and sharpen the criticism was the theme—a "rule or ruin" strategy it was dubbed by one House Republican.

Gingrich's strategies were initially not popular with some Republican leaders such as Bob Michel (IL) who complained that he was "personally uncomfortable being a perpetual antagonist or having to get on the floor every day bitching and griping about being run over by the majority" (Roberts and Smith 2003: 307). However, Gingrich was elected Republican whip in 1989 and, by this point, was in a position to fully enact his legislative strategy.

House Democrats were also changing caucus rules and strategies throughout the 1970s and 1980s. As Rohde (1991) and Sinclair (1995) detail, a group of liberal Democrats known as the Democratic Study Group (DSG) began to propose changes in caucus rules and strategies that would insure that policies in line with the preferences of a majority of House Democrats would be more likely to be enacted. Some of the key changes included having regular caucus meetings, allowing the caucus to vote on committee chairs, enhanced rights for subcommittees, and an understanding that members in leadership positions such as chairs of committees would be expected to vote with the party position on key issues or risk losing their leadership position (see Rohde (1991) for more details on the reforms). Before these changes, conservative Democratic committee chairs from the South could vote against the wishes of the party without fear of retribution; after the reforms, these chairs had to vote more consistently or risk losing their positions. In terms of rules and procedure, the 1970s' reforms allowed the Speaker (with Democratic caucus approval) to appoint all Democratic members of the Committee on Rules and to decide who would be the chair of the committee. This reform effectively ended the Southern Democrats' dominance of the committee and reenergized it as the procedural "arm" of the majority party (Rohde 1991).

By the early 1980s all the pieces were in place for partisan warfare. The Democratic caucus had become more homogeneous in its policy preferences as the proportion of Southern Democrats in the House continued to decline. The DSG had succeeded in enacting a series of caucus reforms that empowered the party leadership to use the procedural tools at their disposal to try to enact policies more consistent with policy views of Northern Democrats (Rohde 1991). On the Republican side, Gingrich and his fellow COS members were increasingly committed to actively trying to undermine the Democratic majority through the use of guerrilla legislative tactics (Roberts and Smith 2003).

Procedurally, something had to give. House Democrats were increasingly attempting to insure that the policies they enacted reflected the majority viewpoint in their caucus. At the same time, they were facing a largely united and increasingly aggressive minority party that was seeking to either obstruct passage of Democratic policy initiatives or force electorally vulnerable Democrats from moderate districts to compile a voting record that would make them ripe for electoral challenge (Marshall 2002, 2005). Democrats responded to the Republican tactics by turning to restrictive and innovative special rules (Bach and Smith 1988). As Figure 6.1 demonstrates, the percentage of rules that heavily restricted or prevented floor amendments increased throughout the 1980s and 1990s, while fewer rules that provided for a more open amending environment were adopted.[12]

For their part, House Republicans strenuously objected to the increase in restrictive rules enacted by House Democrats and began to intensify the strategy of voting "no" *en banc* against Democratic initiatives. As Finocchiaro and Rohde (2008) report, this entailed increasing the number of party-line votes both on adopting special rules and on enacting the previous question on the special rule. As Figure 6.2 demonstrates, the average party difference[13] on special rules grew from approximately 20 percent in the 1970s to more than 80 per-

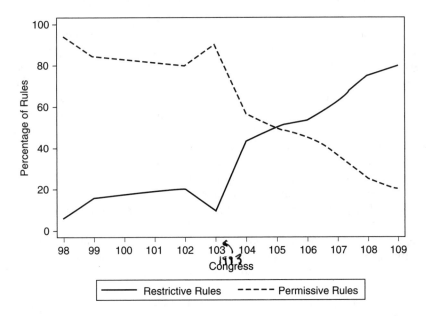

*Figure 6.1* Percentage of Restrictive or Permissive Special Rules in the House, 98th–109th Congresses

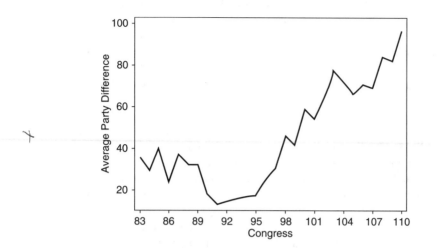

*Figure 6.2* Average Party Differences on Special Rules in the House, 83rd–110th Congresses

cent in the 1990s. This strategy forced Democrats to present a near united front on these votes, lest they lose complete control over House floor proceedings.

House Republicans initially pledged to use fewer restrictive rules upon gaining majority status in the 104th Congress (1995–97). However, as the data in Figure 6.1 reveal, they did not keep this pledge. The data in fact show a sharp increase in the use of restrictive legislative procedures after the Republicans assumed majority control, due largely to concerted efforts by the new Democratic minority to introduce large numbers of amendments to delay the legislative process in the House. Republican Committee on Rules chairperson David Dreier later admitted that it was wrong of House Republicans to commit to more open legislative procedures. He argued that the demands of governing with small majorities facing cohesive legislative minorities required the use of restrictive rules (Davis 2003). Not surprisingly, House Democrats complained vociferously about the use of restrictive rules by the majority-party Republicans. Many Democratic members had never served in the House minority and appeared surprised to find out how unpleasant minority status could be. Despite their complaints about Republican rule, Democrats have not scaled back their usage of restrictive legislative procedures since recapturing the majority in the 110th and 111th Congresses. In the wake of capturing a majority of seats in the 2010 midterm elections, House Republicans claim that they will use less restrictive legislative procedures in the upcoming 112th Congress. It is certainly possible that this might come to pass, but history teaches us that this is highly unlikely to occur, as majority parties rarely, if ever, choose to unilaterally disarm in the procedural arms race.

## The Motion to Recommit

One of the most intense procedural battles between House Democrats and Republicans in recent decades centered on a seemingly obscure procedure known as the motion to recommit. The motion to recommit can take three forms: (1) a straight motion to recommit which, if successful, sends a bill back to its committee of origin and essentially kills the bill; (2) a motion to recommit with instructions to report promptly, which also serves to send a bill back to its committee of origin, but with some vague instructions; and (3) a motion to recommit with instructions to report "forthwith," which if successful requires the chair of the committee of origin to report the amendment to the bill at that time without the bill ever leaving the chamber floor (Roberts 2005).[14] To simplify, one could think of the first two options as tools to kill or delay passage of a bill, while the third option is akin to a substantive amendment to the bill.

The motion to recommit is strategically important for two reasons: (1) it is the last motion in order before a bill's final disposition—that is, it is the last possible chance to change a bill before a vote of passage; and (2) House rules provide that the motion to recommit can only be offered by a member who is opposed to the bill in its current form, which has traditionally been interpreted to mean a member of the minority party in the House (Krehbiel and Meirowitz 2002). So, in effect, the motion to recommit gives the minority party in the House the ability to offer a motion to either delay or amend a bill just prior to it moving to final passage.

The 1980s' controversy over the motion to recommit dealt with the motion to recommit with instructions to report forthwith. A controversial 1934 precedent was interpreted as allowing the motion to recommit with instructions to report forthwith to be disallowed via a special rule (Wolfensberger 2007). As House Democrats began to enact more restrictive special rules on legislation in the 1980s, House Republicans began offering more motions to recommit with instructions to report forthwith as it was often their only option available to offer substantive amendments to legislation. As Democrats tired of the political difficulty inherent in these votes, they began to rely on the Rules Committee to enact special rules that would prevent these motions from being offered (Roberts 2005; Wolfensberger 2007). Not surprisingly, Republicans were incensed by this strategy. They insisted that what the Democrats were doing was both unfair, and an incorrect interpretation of House precedents.

House Republicans felt so strongly about the motion to recommit that they changed the rules of the House at the outset of the 104th Congress to disallow special rules that banned the motion to recommit with instructions to report forthwith. This, of course, ended the practice of special rules prohibiting this motion. Democrats kept this rule upon regaining the majority at the outset of the 110th Congress; they did, however, enact rules that prevent motions to recommit with instructions to report promptly, in response to losing a large number of these votes at the outset of the 110th Congress (O'Connor 2009).

## Innovation in Special Rules

In addition to enacting more restrictive rules over the past two decades, both Democrats and Republicans have created new procedural tools to help them secure their preferred policies outcomes and have found more creative uses for existing procedural tools. Two of the more interesting innovations have been in what could be called the "royalty rules"—King of the Hill and Queen of the Hill rules. Both versions of royalty rules typically deal with complex policies such as budget resolutions or major reforms of existing laws. Both also serve the twin purposes of allowing rank-and-file members to cast votes for politically popular legislative alternatives, while also voting for the alternative preferred by their party's leadership.

Majority-Party Democrats were the first to employ the King of the Hill rule. A King of the Hill rule specifies that several versions of a particular bill or budget resolution—known as complex substitutes—will be voted on sequentially. The rule specifies both the versions of the bill that will be voted on and, most importantly, in what order they will be voted upon. King of the Hill rules typically specify that the last version of a bill to gain a majority vote will be the version that moves to final passage (Sinclair 1995). This is important, as the majority leadership will place its preferred version of the bill last in the sequence. Queen of the Hill rules, which were first used by House Republicans, are very similar in structure to King of the Hill rules. The key difference being that under a Queen of the Hill rule the alternative gaining the *most* votes wins, assuming that it gets at least a majority of those present and voting.

Royalty rules are a win-win for both the party leadership and the rank-and-file members. Rank-and-file members get to vote for as many versions of a bill as they like and hence can be on the "correct" side of the issue with their constituents (Mayhew 1974a). This can help them keep their constituents happy and stave off potential challengers. Likewise, the leadership gets their version of the bill enacted without having to force rank-and-file members to choose between party and their own personal or electorally induced preferences (Carson et al. 2010). In this way, royalty rules convert a zero-sum legislative bargaining situation into a positive-sum situation.

In addition to royalty rules, recent years have seen an increase in what are known as "self-executing" rules. When a self-executing rule is enacted, it specifies that a bill under consideration is automatically amended in some way without the chamber having to take a separate vote on the underlying measure as the new language is "deemed" to have passed. This type of rule is beneficial in at least two ways. First, it can increase legislative efficiency by allowing last minute corrections or additions to a bill that are minor in nature to be incorporated into the legislation. Second, it can be used for strategic reasons to either avoid a vote on a controversial provision of a bill or to secure support for the underlying rule due to the provision in question (Sinclair 1995).

The use of waivers in special rules has also increased in recent Congresses. Waivers are needed when a bill violates one or more standing rules of the House. Without a waiver, any member could raise a point of order against the offending provision and have it stricken from the bill. Often these involve what are known as "unauthorized appropriations," whereby a bill appropriates money for a program or position that has seen its authorization expire or fail to be passed yet. Standing rules require all appropriations to first be authorized, so a waiver is often needed. Typically we think of special rules as limiting the options available to members, yet a waiver can often expand the scope of things that can be accomplished in one bill. These can have partisan consequences, however, as raising points of order can often be a successful strategy for minority-party members. As the procedural arms race in the House has escalated, we have seen more so-called "blanket waivers" enacted via special rule that waive all or most standing rules and prevent members from raising points of order (Hixon and Marshall 2002).

## Summary and Future Directions for Research

This chapter has presented a brief history of procedural reforms in the House of Representatives and attempted to demonstrate how and why the various procedural tools used today came to be adopted and utilized. Legislative majorities and minorities have contested both the procedure and substance of policy from the beginning days of the U.S. Congress. In terms of the evolution of procedure, it is clear that the House can be characterized by a gradual ratcheting up in the restrictiveness of procedures over the course of history. The House majority party has a full arsenal of tools to deploy in order to gain passage of preferred legislation. Unlike the U.S. Senate (see Chapter 7), legislative minorities in the House do not have the ability to obstruct the will of a legislative majority. As the divisions between the parties and the internal homogeneity within the two parties have grown in recent decades, we have seen an increase in the rate at which the House majority is willing and able to use parliamentary procedure in order to pursue party preferred policies (Rohde 1991).

Party leaders as well as rank-and-file members face numerous demands on their time as well as pressure from diverse electoral constituencies. Members and leaders must find ways to balance the policy preferences of their partisan supporters along with the electoral pressures from more moderate members of their constituencies (Smith 2007). Complex and restrictive legislative procedures can serve an important role in helping the party leadership as well as assisting rank-and-file members to negotiate these and other competing demands.

I think there are numerous avenues for exploration in future research. Roberts (2010) and Schickler and Pearson (2009) have both highlighted some patterns in the historical development of special rules from the late 1800s through the 1960s, but they only scratched the surface in terms of exploring how rules shaped legislative outcomes in this era. We also know relatively little about how the Rules Committee decides which amendments they will allow to be voted on. Recent work by Lynch, Madonna, and Roberts (2010) has begun to explore this, but more work is needed. If the past is any guide, we are also likely to see new innovations in House procedures over time. The sharp partisan battles we see in contemporary politics are likely to produce new problems and new procedural solutions as House majorities attempt to enact controversial legislation. These developments will no doubt capture the attention of congressional scholars.

The intricacies of congressional procedure and legislative "minutiae" are often viewed as boring, insignificant, and of little interest to all but a few academics and legislative staffers. This is, unfortunately, a rather narrow view of the legislative process. Indeed, I hope this chapter has highlighted the importance of procedures in determining legislative outcomes and who wins and loses in many key legislative battles. As Michigan Democrat John Dingell once remarked, "I'll let you write the substance ... you let me write the procedure, and I'll screw you every time" (Smith, Roberts, and Vander Wielen 2009: 210).

## Notes

1  As will be described more fully below, special rules are House resolutions that set the terms of debate for a particular bill.
2  See Chapter 7 for a more extended discussion about the filibuster and obstruction in the Senate.
3  This quorum requirement delayed the opening of the 1st House in 1789 from March 4 to April 1 because a majority of elected members were not present.
4  The Constitution allows the chambers to "compel the attendance of absent members," but is silent on whether the chambers could force a member to cast a ballot. Each chamber can choose to expel members, but this would be of little use in terms of garnering a quorum.
5  Today's House has five calendars; during the time of Reed the House had only three, one for public bills, one for revenue bills, and one for private bills.
6  An 1882 rules change preventing dilatory motions on reports from the Committee on Rules made this possible. The rule did have to survive an attempted disappearing quorum prior to passage. A quorum was not present on the first vote, as numerous Democrats abstained, but the next day more Democrats voted and the rule passed by a vote of 125 to 15, with 132 Democrats still abstaining (see Roberts (2010) and Roberts and Smith (2007) for more details on this rule).
7  The committee of the whole or COW is simply a committee made up of all members of the U.S. House. The House typically dissolves into the COW in order to consider amendments to legislation. Quorum requirements are reduced in the COW and other formal rules are relaxed. When the House is meeting as the COW, the ceremonial mace is removed from the rostrum and the Speaker does not preside over the COW.
8  The Democratic party controlled the House during the 52nd and 53rd Congresses (1891–94), with Charles Crisp (GA) serving as Speaker. After initially repealing some of the Reed Rules, they later reinstituted many of them before losing their majority at the start of the 54th Congress.
9  The full name is the Committee on the Whole House for the State of the Union.

10 Members could request and receive a recorded vote in the House on any amendment adopted in the COW.

11 A party vote is one in which a majority of the members of one party opposes a majority of the other party's members.

12 Data made available by Jed Stiglitz. All closed rules, modified closed rules, and "structured" rules are counted as restrictive, while open and modified open rules are coded as permissive.

13 Party difference is the absolute value of the difference in the proportion of each party voting for a measure.

14 Currently House Rules do not allow option two.

# Chapter 7

# Senate Rules and Procedure

## Revisiting the Bank Bill of 1841 and the Development of Senate Obstruction

*Anthony J. Madonna*

The United States Senate is a legislative body that features a wide assortment of unique procedures. In recent years, political scientists have taken a detailed look at many of these. For example, scholars have examined the majority party's usage of the motion to table (Den Hartog and Monroe 2008), the blocking of judicial nominations via the "blue-slip" procedure (Binder and Maltzman 2004; Binder 2007) and the formation of unanimous consent agreements (Smith and Flathman 1989; Ainsworth and Flathman 1995). While the effects these procedures have on policy outcomes differ, the development of each of them stems from the Senate's most distinguishing feature: *the right of a minority to obstruct or filibuster chamber business.* Despite the seemingly prominent role the filibuster plays in the United States Senate, political scientists have been unable to come to a consensus over why the institution persists.

The literature on this issue is largely divided into two camps. Some scholars stress the constraining influence inherited chamber rules have on procedural choice (Binder 1997; Binder and Smith 1997; Binder, Madonna, and Smith 2007; Lynch and Madonna 2009). They argue that there have been times when Senate majorities have been blocked from altering the chamber's debate rules by minorities. An alternative account suggests that the Senate's rules reflect the preferences of majorities (Gold and Gupta 2005; Wawro and Schickler 2004, 2006, 2010; Koger 2010). These theories largely emphasize the importance of reciprocity norms, as well as the applicability of nuclear option-type procedures.[1]

The issue of why Senate obstruction persists is important because it bears directly on the broader, normative issue of whether the chamber's rules are harmful to policy output. Those articulating the view that rules adopted by previous Senates—as well as the United States Constitution—have left the filibuster largely immune to chamber majorities argue further that this has had a substantial limiting effect on the lawmaking process (Binder and Smith 1997). These scholars stress the need for procedural reform. Scholars arguing that the modern Senate reflects the will of chamber majorities suggest that the filibuster fosters compromise and that, "this need to compromise may, in practice, enhance the extent to which Senate outcomes reflect the public's views"

(Wawro and Schickler 2006: 280). Accordingly, these scholars suggest that procedural reforms may be unnecessary.

The evidence presented by both theoretical perspectives has relied primarily on individual case studies of historical episodes of obstruction. Many of the same cases are cited by both theories and, often, the amount of detail given is brief and restricted only to the Senate. In this chapter I provide a detailed discussion of the literature on the filibuster. I then reevaluate one of the most prominently cited case studies in the debate over the filibuster—that of the passage of the Bank Bill of 1841. A more detailed account of the Bank Bill's consideration yields three primary conclusions. First, by employing a strictly unicameral case study, scholars are unable to offer a complete assessment of senators' decision-making. Second, both camps' accounts of the episode were biased by the omission of key issues. Finally, when these issues and the broader separation of powers context are considered, I believe the inherited rules theory offers a more satisfying explanation for how obstruction affected the bill's consideration. I conclude by offering suggestions for future examinations of Senate procedure.

## Inherited Rules and Procedural Choice

In their 1997 book, Sarah Binder and Steven S. Smith put forth the claim that the rules of the modern Senate have been preserved in spite of occasional opposition from chamber majorities. They argue that minorities have taken advantage of inherited chamber rules to thwart potential reforms supported by simple majorities. In later work, they re-specified this theory, arguing that these inherited chamber rules systematically altered the cost–benefit analysis of members in a way that inoculated the chamber from reform (Binder et al. 2007).

There are three primary inherited institutions that have served to constrain member decision-making. The first of these stemmed from an 1806 decision to eliminate the previous question motion from the Senate's standing rules (Binder 1997; Binder and Smith 1997). This rule previously allowed a simple majority of senators to bring debate to an end. The decision to drop the rule was not made in a conscious effort to promote unlimited debate. At the time, the rule had seen limited usage and its removal amounted to little more than parliamentary house-keeping (Binder 1997). Since that decision was made, no formal method of ending debate by a simple majority has existed and any attempt to institute one has been subject to obstruction.

Second, the Constitution specifies staggered terms for senators. This provision was included to provide stability within the chamber during periods of electoral turnover (Story 1833). The clause also created a system where older senators would be able to mentor incoming members (Amar 1988). Accordingly, the Senate never officially ends; rather it operates as a "continuing body." One consequence of this decision is that—unlike the House—the chamber does not adopt new rules at the start of each Congress (Binder 1997). Instead, the new Senate must operate under the rules of its predecessor. Thus, once the only formal method for ending debate by a simple majority was dropped, it could not apply in any future Senates.

Finally, the constitutional designation of the vice president as the president of the Senate has further served to constrain majorities from ending the filibuster (Gamm and Smith 2000; Lynch and Madonna 2009). Debate records from the Constitutional Convention indicate this provision was granted to the vice president for two reasons. First, without the power to serve in this capacity, the officer would essentially have nothing to do. Second, supporters of the provision argued that it would constitute the fairest way to break a tie vote in the Senate (Hatfield 1997). This decision means that the Senate is presided over by a member not elected by that body. As such, Senate majorities have been hesitant to centralize chamber power. This contrasts sharply with the House of Representatives, where members had far less trouble delegating power to the Speaker—a member proscribed by the Constitution to be directly elected by that body.

Thus, inherited rules served to insulate the filibuster from reform by altering each member's cost–benefit calculus. The remaining factors that influence this calculus can be classified into two groups: environmental and political. In order to prevent a final vote, senators must be prepared to hold the floor for hours on end by speaking. Because of this, environmental factors have historically played a major role in limiting the success of obstruction. These include the number of other senators that will support a filibuster on the floor, the quality of the air conditions within the chamber, and total time spent in Washington. When environmental factors are considerable, there should be less obstruction.

Additionally, members must also consider the underlying political context. The most primal of these variables is the member's attitude with respect to the underlying legislation. However, electoral factors are also important, as is the potential impact obstruction might have on the future legislative agenda.[2] As the legislative agenda is typically set by the majority party, minority-party obstructionists typically have less to sacrifice by a manifest filibuster.[3] Thus, scholars in the inherited rules camp argue that "the threat of minority retaliation is sufficient to derail majority efforts to significantly curtail the filibuster" (Binder et al. 2007).

Figure 7.1 outlines how inherited rules impact procedural choice. Environmental and political factors combine to influence the decision to obstruct. When these variables suppress obstruction, reform efforts are unlikely to be entertained because of the perceived lack of necessity. When they facilitate more filibusters, reform should be more desirable. However, in order to alter inherited chamber rules, members must either fight lengthy battles on the chamber floor or be prepared to centralize power under a vice president who is not chosen by the party. This forces senators seeking political reform to sacrifice their short-term legislative goals for an increase in long-term chamber efficiency. As each individual member makes this decision independently, creating

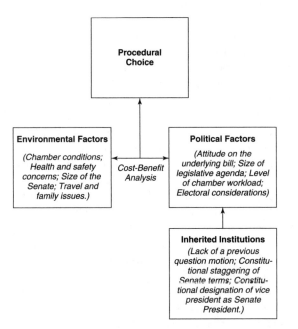

*Figure 7.1* Inherited Institutions and Procedural Reform

and maintaining a coalition in favor of amending the rules becomes extremely difficult. Thus, while changes in environmental factors might facilitate more obstruction, increasing the desire for procedural change, this effect is mitigated by the depressing influence inherited institutions have on the political benefits for reformers. According to scholars in the inherited rules camp, this has essentially insulated the Senate's debate rules from any meaningful alterations.

## Remote Majoritarianism in the Senate

Recent theoretical work has argued that inherited institutions have not left the chamber's rules immune to reform efforts. Instead, the Senate's procedures have always been subjected to majority approval due to the presence of unorthodox rules changes—such as that of the "nuclear option." While Senate observers had long acknowledged the technical feasibility of unorthodox rules changes, Gregory Wawro and Eric Schickler (2006) were the first to claim that the procedure has had a substantial effect on chamber development.[4] The authors argue that majorities have not been thwarted from changing chamber rules by threats of minority obstruction. Rather, majority threats of "going nuclear"—as well as norms of restraint—have reined in the minority's usage of obstruction. They suggest that because majorities could always change the rules, the Senate has operated under a form of "remote majoritarianism" (Wawro and Schickler 2006).

Like the inherited institutions theory presented in Figure 7.1, Wawro and Schickler's thesis emphasizes a strong connection between procedural choice and a cost–benefit analysis. The factors that go into an individual's cost–benefit calculus under the remote majoritarianism theory are fairly similar to those discussed by scholars in the inherited institutions camp. Again, these factors can be best thought of as being either political or environmental. The authors discuss many of the same concepts, such as time spent away from families, the physical costs obstructionist senators need to pay by speaking at length on the Senate floor, electoral concerns, and the sacrifice of future legislative goals.

However, Wawro and Schickler's cost–benefit analysis does depart in two notable ways from the process detailed by Binder and Smith. First, they emphasize the connection between procedural choice and levels of resolve. Once the other environmental and political factors are controlled for, the success of obstruction is determined by the amount of resolve the minority has relative to the majority. The authors analogize this concept to a "war of attrition." The second point of departure is closely related. The remote majoritarianism theory predicts that manifest filibusters should only occur if there is incomplete information about the cost–benefit calculi. Otherwise, one side would recognize the futility of acting on their procedural preferences and abandon their position. Doing so would save them from having to bear the physical and political costs associated with holding the floor during a filibuster, or forcing the other side to actually hold the floor during a filibuster.

Wawro and Schickler (2006) argue that this informational component is beneficial to the chamber for two reasons. First, it increases Senate effectiveness by blocking "inefficient policies"—or policies favored by a less intense majority over a more intense minority. Second, when a member observes an opponent displaying a high level of resolve, it serves as a cue to the attitudes of their home state constituencies. The authors conclude by warning that this informational component is only useful if environmental factors force obstructionists to bear high physical costs. If not, the filibuster is costless for the minority and the majority gains nothing while being forced to pay higher political costs by sacrificing items from their future legislative agenda. This can lead to an increased desire for reform.

Under this theory, the informational benefits for the majority are dependent on obstructionists bearing high physical costs. However, those physical costs are negatively related to the time left before the mandatory adjournment date. Without another credible constraint upon the minority's procedural choice, end-of-the-session filibusters would be innumerable. The existence of Senate norms against obstruction serves as that additional theoretical constraint. The evolution and maintenance of these norms was closely tied to the size of the chamber. In the early era, the small size of the Senate allowed senators to develop close relationships with colleagues. The concern over maintaining these good relationships operated as a major constraint on obstruction, thus decreasing the overall political benefit majorities would have received by enacting reforms.

When the Senate's membership expanded in the late nineteenth century, the relationships weakened and the norms broke down. This was evident with the defeat of several significant pieces of legislation considered close to the mandatory adjournment deadline. Ultimately, it was this breakdown of chamber norms that led the Senate to formally codify a method for ending debate. Adopted in 1917, cloture (or Rule 22) allowed a supermajority (two-thirds) to set a date for a final passage vote. This meant that large majorities could cut down on uncertainty late in a congressional session. However, the adoption of the rule signaled to minorities that obstruction was acceptable. This ultimately served to "institutionalize" the filibuster.

Threats of unorthodox rules changes supplement relations-based norms and also served to constrain minority obstruction. This procedure necessitates a favorable ruling from the chamber's presiding officer upon a question of order. Once the ruling is made, it sets a precedent that binds future rulings. Moreover, the minority learns that the majority has a particularly high level of resolve on this issue. Accordingly, under the war of attrition framework, they should drop the obstruction.

Figure 7.2 outlines how procedural choice is made under the theory of remote majoritarianism. Like the inherited institutions theory, environmental

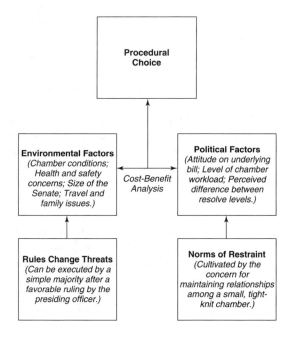

*Figure 7.2* Remote Majoritarianism and Procedural Reform

and political factors are weighed in a cost–benefit analysis. However, in that account, existing chamber rules force majorities into lengthy floor battles. This results in substantial legislative costs for the majority. Under remote majoritarianism, unorthodox rules changes free potential reformers from having to engage in that long floor battle, and thus, they no longer have to sacrifice their future agenda. Additionally, even when environmental factors facilitate obstruction, senators are still conditioned by relations-based norms. This results in few instances of manifest obstruction.

## Testing Theories of Procedural Choice

While these two camps specify largely distinct accounts of procedural choice in the United States Senate, testing these theories has proven difficult for several reasons. First, both theories yield similar predictions for the usage of obstruction in the early Senate. Environmental factors featured high physical costs for senators looking to hold the Senate floor while political factors such as chamber workload and electoral incentives were fairly low. Because of this, Binder and Smith (1997) predict limited success for obstructionists in the nineteenth-century Senate. Similarly, Wawro and Schickler (2006) argue that norms against obstruction were robust and the threats of unorthodox rules changes were consistently high during this era. Thus, they also predict limited success for obstructionists in the early era.

In the modern Senate, the theories should yield differing predictions. Binder and Smith (1997) argue that changes in environmental and political conditions have resulted in more incidents of obstruction. This has resulted in many bills and nominations being killed by minorities. The remote majoritarianism thesis suggests that this should only be true for issues where the majority has less resolve than the minority. This makes any evidence regarding the number of manifest filibusters difficult to interpret.

Such data would be problematic to interpret for several reasons. First, determining whether or not a filibuster has taken place is almost entirely arbitrary. While some scholars define a filibuster as an outright attempt to kill a bill, others will count attempts to delay the vote or extract concessions as filibustering. Both perspectives require some subjective judgment about what constitutes legitimate debate. Second, accurate accounts are far easier to come by in the most modern Congresses, when sources such as *Congressional Quarterly* give detailed summaries of legislation. For the nineteenth and much of the twentieth century, scholars like Burdette (1940) had to rely on less reliable sources. Third, the threat of obstruction often keeps legislation off the floor, and there is no way to accurately account for this phenomenon. Finally, when a successful manifest filibuster occurs, it often kills not only the underlying bill, but also other pieces of legislation that would have been considered later in the session.

Since empirical evidence is particularly challenging to acquire and evaluate in this debate, scholars have focused on interpreting historical incidents involving obstruction. Unfortunately, these case studies are rarely presented with enough detail to adequately separate the effect of inherited rules, relations-based norms, and threats of unorthodox rules changes from other political and environmental factors that make up a senator's cost–benefit analysis. The remainder of this chapter demonstrates this by providing an expanded account of one key episode of obstruction—the Bank Bill of 1841.

## The Bank Bill of 1841

The case of the Bank Bill of 1841 represents the first occasion where chamber obstruction prompted an attempted change in Senate rules. A brief outlining of the facts is as follows. The Bank Bill debate occurred during the 27th Senate, the first controlled by the Whig party. On June 21, 1841, Whig leader Henry Clay reported the Bank Bill out of committee and on to the Senate floor. Three weeks later, with the debate continuing, Clay proposed a rules change to "give to the majority the control of the business of the United States Senate" (*Congressional Globe*, 27 Cong. 1, July 12, 1841, 184). Minority Democrats expressed outrage at the Clay proposal, prompting Senator William Rufus King (D-AL) to reply, "I will tell the Senator [Clay], then that he may make his arrangements at his boarding house for the winter" (*Congressional Globe*, 27 Cong. 1, July 12, 1841, 203). The inference from King's statement, as well as from the comments of other prominent Democrats, is that they intended to prevent a vote on the Clay resolution by obstruction. Clay eventually retreated from his rules change proposal. Then, on July 28th, the Bank Bill passed the Senate on a largely party-line vote.

To bolster their theoretical claims, both the inherited institutions and remote majoritarianism camps draw competing inferences from this episode. Binder and Smith (1997: 75) conclude that "a majority in favor of [Clay's] reform was apparently forced to retreat in face of a determined filibustering minority." This, they imply, is due primarily to the constraining influence of inherited institutions. Wawro and Schickler (2006) disagree, arguing that Clay's rules change proposal actually facilitated the passage of the Bank Bill. Moreover, they argue that rather than kill the Whig agenda, the minority party allowed it to pass in its entirety.

To arbitrate between these two competing interpretations, I take a more comprehensive look at the consideration of the Bank Bill. While it is doubtful that the minority was intent on killing the Bank Bill via filibuster, the evidence suggests that obstruction played an important role in the failure of the bill, and the Whig agenda more broadly. Obstructive Democrats strung out the session and exploited every opportunity to exacerbate internal tension within the Whig Party. My evaluation of the Bank Bill starts with a consideration of the election of 1840 and the cohesiveness of the Whig coalition.

## The Election of 1840

The election of 1840 produced a resounding victory for the Whig Party. Their candidate for President, William Henry Harrison trounced incumbent Democratic President Martin Van Buren in the Electoral College. Both Houses of Congress moved into Whig control as well, with the party holding a seven-seat majority in the Senate. Historians have argued that this contest was one of the first in American history that pitted two political parties with clear, contrasting viewpoints regarding the proper role of government in shaping public policy (Holt 1992). This is evidenced by the sharp increase in partisan voting during this era (Silbey 1985; Binder 1997; Poole and Rosenthal 1997).

The Whigs ran on a platform that called for an increase in government intervention. This included seeking an upward revision of the tariff, distribution of land revenues to the states, federal- and state-financed internal improvements, and an increased federal role in banking and currency. The Democrats, following the positions taken during the Jackson presidency, rejected an active role for the government (Holt 1992). Harrison's election represented an opportunity for the Whig Party to strengthen its ideological association with the voters. Clay and other Whig legislators felt the party needed to act quickly to capitalize on their momentum. Moreover, Treasury Secretary Thomas Ewing reported that the government needed to raise revenue quickly to cover an exorbitant national debt. In response, Harrison summoned the emergency session on March 17, 1841. Eighteen days later, he died of pneumonia, elevating the relatively unknown Vice President John Tyler to the presidency.

## The Whig Congressional Agenda

On May 31, 1841, the emergency session of the 27th Congress convened. After quickly electing John White (W-KY)—a Clay ally—Speaker of the House, sectional cracks in the Whig party began to emerge. Henry A. Wise (W-VA) moved that the party adopt the previous rules of the House, which included a previous question motion for ending debate. John Quincy Adams then offered an amendment rescinding the rule prohibiting the reception of abolition petitions. This sparked a prolonged debate in the chamber, which Democrats happily sought to enable.[5] Adding to this was President Tyler's continued association with a group of states' rights Virginians. Clay was acutely aware of this, writing in mid-June that there was a concern that Tyler would fall in with this crowd, and that it would jeopardize the Whig agenda (Coleman 1871: 157).

This appears to have reinforced Clay's belief that the Whig agenda must be passed quickly. On June 7th, the Kentucky senator outlined the goals of the session. The Whigs sought a repeal of the sub-treasury system, the distribution of land revenues to the states, a new loan to pay for governmental business until revenues were increased, an upward revision of the tariff, a national bankruptcy law to relieve debtors, and the incorporation of a new national bank (Holt 1999:

129). Further, they hoped to complete all this within the emergency session. The consensus of modern historians and contemporary legislators was that the incorporation of a new national bank was the centerpiece of this agenda. Senator John C. Calhoun argued that defeating the bank would "defeat all the other measures and terminate the session" (Jameson 1900: 481). Holt (1999: 129) put it bluntly, "on that rock (the Bank Bill) the Whig program would flounder and the Whig party splinter."

Further evidence of internal problems with the Whig Party was given by President Tyler's statement to Congress. Tyler indicated support for the repeal of the sub-treasury system. However, his support for distribution and the loan were conditional on the upward revision of the tariff being less than 20 percent. This was not likely to be feasible. Furthermore, he indicated his opposition to the incorporation of a new national bank he deemed to be unconstitutional. In summary, as the emergency session began, the Whigs were set to implement an ambitious agenda with internal sectional tension and a president that shared their party name, but expressed—at best—tepid support for their legislative goals.

### Unlimited Debate in the Senate

Clay believed the key to success was to act quickly. On April 30, 1841, he wrote to Treasury Secretary Ewing and asked him to prepare a copy of an administration-approved Bank Bill before the opening of Congress (Seager 1988: 524). He reiterated this request in writing on June 2nd and then on the floor of the Senate on June 7th. However, sometime during this period Ewing had taken ill and was unable to accomplish this in a timely fashion.[6] This would ultimately prove to be fortuitous for the Democrats. The administration-backed bill was reported to the Senate on June 12, 1841, nearly a month and a half after Clay first requested it.

The Ewing Bill infuriated Clay supporters. Primarily, this was because it allowed the states to tax the bank. Although it also allowed the national bank to establish banks in the states, it made this contingent on the approval of state legislators. The view of many Whigs on this were adequately summarized in a letter by New York Whig Mordecai Noah to Senator Willie Mangum (W-NC), "I believe when I say that of the Whig party in this city, that not one in a hundred approve of Mr. Ewing's plan I am short of the truth" (Shanks 1953: 167). Over the next five days, the Whig caucus convened to design a substitute.

Democrats sought to seize on the apparent unrest within the Whig Party. In mid-June, Silas Wright (D-NY) gave a three-hour speech against the Bank Bill, which was not under consideration. This led to Clay's taking up his first rules change resolution.[7] It provided that the chamber, after any adjournment of the Senate during consideration of a given subject, resume consideration of that subject during the next meeting of the Senate. Presumably, this would facilitate quicker passage for the caucus bill, which had not yet been reported. The

Democrats strongly objected to Clay's resolution. Thomas Hart Benton declared "it showed a determination to dictate to the Senate its order of business and the duration of the session" (*Congressional Globe*, 27 Cong. 1, June 12, 1841, 45). Calhoun declared that this "attempt thus to cut off debate was a thing unprecedented in the Senate" (*Congressional Globe*, 27 Cong. 1, June 12, 1841, 46).

In spite of the Democrats' objections, a united Whig Party then rejected a Calhoun proposal to table the resolution by 27 to 19. During the debate, Clay chided the minority by asking, "Did the gentlemen really imagine, that because as a minority they possessed certain rights, they had the right of controlling the business of Congress?" (*Congressional Globe*, 27 Cong. 1, June 12, 1841, 47). However, the tabling motion could not end debate, forcing Clay to placate the minority by offering a modification to the rule, allowing for one hour of discussion of other subjects. The rule then passed by a voice vote. Notably, this rule was not a mere compromise for the minority, but a complete capitulation by Clay. Senator Ambrose Sevier (D-AR) asked Clay, "is this resolution not nearly word for word with the long standing rules of the Senate?" (*Congressional Globe*, 27 Cong. 1, June 12, 1841, 48). To his credit, Clay acknowledged that it was.

Unable to secure a favorable rules change, Clay and the Whig leadership went ahead with the caucus-backed Bank Bill. They kept the pressure on the Democrats by keeping the chamber in session eight hours a day, six days a week. Calhoun described the harshness of the situation: "our sittings are exceedingly laborious, averaging about six hours in the day and thirty six in the week. This, at this warm season, combined with a heavy correspondence, reading of documents and preparation for discussion is heavy and exhausting work" (Jameson 1900: 481). Moreover, the Whigs united behind the caucus bill and agreed to vote down all Democratic amendments during the caucus (Shanks 1953: 182).

On June 21, 1841, Clay reported the Bank Bill out of committee. The chamber then commenced debate on a bill appropriating 25,000 dollars for the relief of President Harrison's widow. Consideration of this bill consumed a full two legislative days, largely attributed to lengthy speeches offered by Senate Democrats. The relief bill passed near the end of the day on June 25th, by 28 to 16, with all Whigs and two Democrats voting in support. The Bank Bill was then taken up, and Whig amendments were considered.

Throughout this period, cracks in the Whig coalition began to worsen. Secretary of State Daniel Webster began lobbying Senate Whigs to oppose Clay's caucus bill and support the Ewing Bill. His reasons for doing so were three-fold. First, he believed it would provoke an executive veto, resulting in the dissolution of the cabinet and eventual expulsion of Tyler from the party. Second, Webster believed that a Bank Bill was better than no bill at all. On the same lines, he argued that the provisions of the Ewing Bill were strong enough and that the omission of the branching power is not a "surrender of a great principle" (Wiltse and Moser 1982: 135). Third, there was clearly an electoral benefit for Webster to be seen as the power broker between Tyler and Congressional Whigs.

His lobbying, combined with Democratic obstruction, facilitated the defection of at least four Southern swing votes: William C. Rives (W-VA), William S. Archer (W-VA), William C. Preston (W-SC), and John Henderson (W-MS). Later, the administration would allocate favorable patronage appointments to garner the support of William Merrick (D-MD) and Alexander Barrow (D-LA) (Shanks 1953: 182; Holt 1999: 132).

By late June it was clear that Clay's caucus bill was in trouble. Calhoun, expressing confidence, noted that "we have, I think, gained on them since the beginning of the [s]ession. They are now dispirited and distracted" (Jameson 1900: 479). The minority continued to operate under a strategy of obstructing consideration of the caucus bill, while seeming supportive of Tyler's objectives. On this point, a Benton biographer notes that the Democratic objective was, "delay and an appeal to public opinion through the [Globe] and other Democratic organs" (Chambers 1956: 252). Holt (1999: 132) argues that "minority Democrats played a brilliant hand, offering little opposition to those measures Tyler agreed with but strenuously objecting to the measures that offended the president's constitutional sensibilities."

Appearing amiable to Tyler did not, however, dwarf the minority's larger strategy of driving a wedge in the majority party. When Rives (W-VA) offered a compromise amendment on July 1, 1841, restoring the Ewing Bill, the Democrats joined with Clay's supporters to overwhelmingly defeat it. The minority, wrote Poage (1936: 57) was "delighted at the quandary of the Whigs, and, as was manifestly their policy, resolved to vote en masse against the Rives Amendment in order to increase the confusion of the Whigs." Further, the nature of the debate between Clay and the Whigs backing the Ewing Bill indicated to Senate Democrats that Tyler intended to veto the caucus bill. Democrats were eager to see this happen.

After defeating the Rives amendment, Clay himself began expressing doubts about his ability to pass the caucus bill. Adams chronicled in his journal dated July 7th, that Clay "thinks the passage of the Bank bill in the Senate doubtful" (Adams 1876: 498). However, on July 12th and 13th, the Whig leadership again held a caucus to work out a compromise to ensure the passage of the caucus bill (Remini 1991: 589). On those days, they voted down five straight Democratic amendments on party-line votes. It also was during this time of renewed Whig unity that Clay's second rules change threat was made. The proposal came at the heels of a Calhoun speech that lambasted Clay for accusing the minority of offering amendments and speeches for no other purpose than to "embarrass the majority by frivolous and vexatious delay" (*Congressional Globe*, 27 Cong. 1, July 12, 1841, 184).

Calhoun asserted that Clay's proposal called for the Senate to "adopt the same means which had proved so beneficial in the House" (*Congressional Globe*, 27 Cong. 1, July 12, 1841, 203). After a series of long, aggressive speeches by King (D-AL), Calhoun (D-SC), Linn (D-MO), and Benton (D-MO), the proposal was dropped and the chamber went into executive session. On July 23,

1841, after again consulting with the Whig caucus, Clay offered a compromise amendment. The amendment allowed states to accept or reject bank branches. However, Congress could then override the states' decisions. The compromise amendment passed 25 to 24 after Preston (W-SC) voted in support and Henderson (W-MS) abstained. A motion by Thomas Hart Benton (D-MO) to postpone the bill indefinitely was then beaten back 28–21 on a party-line vote. The compromised caucus bill passed the chamber 26–23 with nearly all Whigs voting in favor. The passage of the caucus bill had been in doubt at times, but it was not a mortal blow for Senate Democrats. Indeed, from their unified rejection of the Rives amendment, it was apparent the party preferred to pursue a strategy that would lead to a Tyler veto. Calhoun discussed this in a letter to Thomas Clemson: "I should much rather Clay's bill should pass and be vetoed (than Ewing's bill pass and be signed by the President)" (Jameson 1900: 480).

### The Previous Question Motion in the House

Early in the emergency session, House Whigs appeared to be more divided than their Senate counterparts. On June 7, 1841, the House adopted a set of rules that included both the previous question motion, and Adams' amendment barring the "gag rule" against abolitionist petitions. This was reversed nearly a week later. The new rule deferred consideration of the gag rule one full year. Binder (1997: 102) argues that this compromise was a partisan one, with Southern Whigs largely joining Northerners in support of the measure.

It is within this parliamentary environment that the chamber received the Senate Bank Bill. The presence of the previous question motion virtually ensured quick passage of the bill. Representative Cave Johnson (D-TN), writing to Polk, noted that: "It will pass the House, probably during the ensuing week. With their amended rules, they have the previous question ... [and] use it upon all occasions" (Cutler, Smith, and Parker 1979: 710). On August 3rd, the House voted on the first amendment to the Bank Bill, rejecting a minority proposal to liberalize the chamber's rules with regard to the bill by a vote of 107 to 84. The next day, the chamber passed a resolution setting a date to end debate on the Bank Bill. On August 6, 1841, the House passed the Bank Bill by a vote of 128 to 98. However, and as the Democrats anticipated, the bill was vetoed by President Tyler on August 16th.

## Revisiting the Evidence

The history of the Bank Bill of 1841 demonstrates that there were many important factors that led to the bill's failure, not the least of which was the attitude of the executive branch. Also important was the timing of the bill's consideration, as well as how Clay and the other Whig leaders in the Senate managed the entire chamber agenda, electoral considerations, the composition of the bill itself, and minority obstruction. So how does one interpret the role unlimited debate played in the consideration of the Bank Bill of 1841? To answer this, I reconsider the claims made by both the inherited institutions and remote majoritarianism camps.

Wawro and Schickler (2006: 74–5) argue that "obstruction might have delayed progress, but in the face of a determined majority willing to threaten changes in the rules, the minority relented." To support this claim, they argue that when he proposed the rules change, Clay actually lacked a majority for the Bank Bill. The evidence suggests that this is likely the case. However, the evidence also is clear that Clay had a majority *in favor* of the Bank Bill at several different points during the session. In his letter to Cameron describing the Whig caucus, Mangum makes it clear that a majority supported the caucus bill. This is consistent with Binder's (1997) observation of near-perfect party unity on procedural votes.

Further, Wawro and Schickler claim the Whig majority was only secured after Clay's compromise amendment was adopted. However, that amendment sacrificed virtually nothing of the substance of the caucus bill. Remini (1991: 589) dismisses it as a "wretched compromise," that "hardly deserved the name." The rule, if passed, would have allowed Clay and the Whig leadership to call for a caucus, line up support, and then minimize the possibility of defections by cutting off debate and limiting the amount of time the opposition could influence moderate Whigs. It also would have allowed for earlier passage of the bill, which might have led to Tyler's support. Many congressional Whigs believed that Tyler's support waned over the course of the session. Just as the long debate afforded the minority time to pressure moderate Whig senators, it also allowed them to influence Tyler. Like Wawro and Schickler, scholars in the inherited institutions camp also fail to adequately account for the effect the delay had on President Tyler.

Wawro and Schickler also argue that there was a precedent established earlier in the session where Clay passed a rules change resolution over the minority. The evidence suggests that just the opposite occurred. Clay's rules change resolution was met with determined Democratic resistance. Rather than face a prolonged battle over it, the Kentuckian proposed a face-saving compromise. The compromise resolution was allowed to pass as a voice vote—not because the minority feared the majority—but because it was a "word for word" reiteration of the Senate's current standing rules.

Finally, the remote majoritarianism account posits that "one difficulty with [the inherited institutions] interpretation of the Whigs' troubles in 1841 is that Clay actually succeeded in passing his substantive agenda through the Senate" (Wawro and Schickler 2006: 75). The authors cite the eventual passage of the Bank Bill, the repeal of the sub-treasury plan, the Loan Bill, an enacted tariff and the Land Distribution Bill as evidence. This argument is, at best, overly simplistic. Holt (1999: 123) argues that "almost every one of their [The Whigs] bright expectations went aglimmering." Colton (1904: 375) argues that nearly all the Whig's great measures, "were defeated by the political defection and faithless conduct of the acting chief magistrate." This was certainly not a favorable outcome. The Loan Bill passed in mid-June and was a moderate victory for the Whigs. The Land Distribution Bill also passed—but in a compromised form that rendered it impotent even before the end of the Congress.[8] Of the five planks in their agenda for the 27th Congress, only the Tariff and Loan Bills could be considered successes, and of those two, only the former had any lasting impact. Their legislative failures led to the Whigs losing roughly half of their seats in the House of Representatives during the 1842 election (Holt 1999).

The inherited institutions account argues that "a majority in favor of [Clay's] reform was apparently forced to retreat in face of a determined filibustering minority" (Binder and Smith 1997: 75). The evidence for this contention is suggestive, but ultimately inconclusive. It is true that the Whigs rejected a proposal to table the rules change on a united vote. Further, Benton's discussion indicates that at one point the Whigs likely held a majority in support of the rules change. How long this majority existed, however, is unclear. Once the debate dragged on, Clay and the Whigs essentially backed off the proposal.

Ultimately, it is true that the minority relented and let the majority vote on final passage. However, three factors likely influenced this decision. First, as both camps recognized, the physical costs of delay were taking their toll. This is evident in Calhoun's letter to Thomas Clemson, wherein he complained about the length of the days spent in chamber and the heavy correspondence. Additionally, consistent with a costs–benefits framework, there would likely be some sort of electoral retribution for a manifest Democratic filibuster. The party suffered staggering defeats the previous year, largely due to inaction in the wake of the depression. By failing to allow a vote on the centerpiece of the Whig agenda, Clay and his supporters would have been able to reiterate this accusation. Perhaps most importantly, though, by this point the damage had largely been done. There was an open fissure between Clay's supporters and the Whigs supporting President Tyler. This culminated in an admission by one of the Tyler Whigs that the president planned on vetoing the Clay bill. Contrary to Wawro and Schickler's argument, by the time the bill passed, the veto was fairly evident. Calhoun had predicted it, and Democrats went so far as to reject the more preferable administration bill so as to encourage the Tyler veto.

Two important conclusions can be reached from the Bank Bill episode. Again, unlimited debate does not need to be exploited in a way that prevents a vote on a bill to be effective. The episode demonstrates that majorities are rarely stable and fixed. Had the Bank Bill been considered under modern House rules, there is little doubt the majority would have been able to pass it—and pass it quickly. This would have minimized the strain placed upon the fragile Whig coalition and possibly preserved it throughout the session. It is possible that this might have led to vastly different policy outcomes. In this respect, while unlimited debate did not play the role of the murder weapon in the earlier analogy, it did serve as the dark alley that concealed the crime. Second, while the dispersed physical costs in the House better facilitated obstruction compared to the Senate, this episode reinforces the observation that when House majorities were forced to deal with dissident minorities, they could turn to the inherited previous question motion.

## Discussion

Conducting empirical tests for theories of filibustering in the Senate is difficult due to both the availability of reliable data and the relative observational equivalency of the two leading theories. As such, drawing implications from key historical case studies is a necessary tactic for scholars seeking to bolster their theoretical accounts. Both the inherited institutions and remote majoritarian camps glossed over critical details in their consideration of the Bank Bill of 1841. When those details are included, I believe that, on balance, the inherited institutions account offers a more satisfying explanation for how obstruction affected the bill's consideration.

The broader point, however, concerns how scholars of legislative obstruction utilize historical case studies. The preceding discussion demonstrates that they need to be discussed in greater detail to properly evaluate all possible explanations. Further, by restricting case studies to only the Senate, scholars are unable to capture the full cost–benefit calculation made by members. However, the Bank Bill of 1841 is just one of several cases cited by these two scholarly camps. As such, future work is needed to clarify the role of obstruction in other cases. See, for instance, the Oregon Territory Bill of 1848; the Federal Elections Bill of 1890–91; the Armed Ship Filibuster of 1917; anti-lynching bills in 1922, 1935, and 1938; Rule 22 reform proposals in 1967 and 1969; and the 2003 battle over the nuclear option.

In conjunction with case studies like this, empirical research linking these incidents of obstruction with the success of the majority party's agenda could prove valuable. Specifically, the claim that obstruction forces the majority to sacrifice some of its agenda could be examined in a more rigorous manner. Looking at issues reported by newspapers or stressed in party platforms should serve as a sufficient, exogenous proxy for a party agenda. Then evaluating the success rate on those issues and linking it to the case studies discussed could provide additional evidence for or against the leading theories of procedural choice in the Senate.

## Notes

1 The term "nuclear option" stemmed from a 2003 episode in which majority-party Republicans sought to employ an unorthodox procedural tool in order to overcome Democratic obstruction of several of President George W. Bush's judicial nominees. The proposed procedure was to operate accordingly: A senator favoring the confirmation of the judicial nominee would raise a point of order that the Senate must reach a vote on nominations in order to execute its constitutional "advise and consent" power. The chair would then sustain the point of order, thus establishing a new precedent for

limiting consideration of those matters. An opponent of the ruling could appeal the chair's decision and the appeal would be subject to a filibuster. However, supporters would be able to offer a motion to lay the appeals on the table. The motion to table is not debatable, requires only simple majority approval, and if accepted would uphold the chair's ruling and force all senators to cast up or down votes on the nominations.

2 Since being subjected to direct elections by the Seventeenth Amendment, research has demonstrated that senators have become more responsive to their constituents (Crook and Hibbing 1997).

3 Bills cannot be considered in the Senate without majority approval. Generally this is done by unanimous consent. But if consent is not given, a motion to proceed to consideration is in order and subject to simple majority approval. See Den Hartog and Monroe (2011) and Gailmard and Jenkins (2007) for a more detailed discussion of majority-party control in the Senate.

4 See also Burdette (1940), Binder (1997), and Tiefer (1989) on this point.

5 See Cutler et al. (1979) and Shanks (1953) on this point.

6 See Senator Willie Mangum's (W-NC) letter to Duncan Cameron, dated June 26, 1841 (Shanks 1953: 182).

7 In addition to Wright's speech, Clay also dealt with significant obstruction during a special session of Congress in early March that was to be confined to executive business. The outgoing Democratic majority decided to continue the Senate's association with *Congressional Globe* printers Francis Preston Blair and John Cook Rives. This angered the Whigs, who believed the printers distorted the debates. In the special session, the Whigs went ahead with a resolution removing them. This was met with fierce resistance from the Democrats who did not back down for six days (Burdette 1940).

8 This was due to a provision that land sales would cease if tariff rates were over 20 percent. Consequently, when the Whigs finally passed a tariff in 1842—after being thwarted twice—the party was forced to sacrifice distribution.

# Chapter 8

# Voting on the Floor

## Members' Most Fundamental Right

*Andrew J. Taylor*

No formal action taken by members of Congress is more important than floor voting. The legislative process culminates in a vote of the full House and Senate gathered in their bodies' chambers. All members get one and only one vote per roll call. Without floor votes bills cannot become law, the country cannot legally go to war, programs cannot be funded, presidential vetoes cannot be overridden, and the executive and judicial branches cannot be fully staffed. In short, Congress, and indeed the federal government more generally, cannot act with any real degree of effectiveness.

No behavior is more scrutinized, either. The media report on roll calls regularly. Legislators tout their votes as proof of their importance in Congress, support for popular issues, and partisan and ideological fidelity. Their opponents use them as a main form of attack—to demonstrate the member's connection to an unpopular president, party, or cause. Incumbents' votes on health care reform and the federal stimulus bill became a central part of campaigns in House and Senate races across the country in 2010. Congressional votes also follow members into their presidential races. The Senate vote on the Troubled Asset Relief Program (TARP) at the height of the financial crisis became a focal point of the 2008 presidential campaigns of Senator Barack Obama (D-IL) and John McCain (R-AZ). And who can forget Senator John Kerry's (D-MA) memorable line about his votes on supplemental spending for the Iraq and Afghanistan wars during the 2004 presidential election: "I actually did vote for the $87 billion before I voted against it"?

This chapter provides a broad overview of this most fundamental of congressional activities. I will describe the kinds of votes members take and how these have changed across congressional history. I will also examine in detail the forces that shape legislators' voting decisions. I conclude by describing some new and exciting work on the topic.

## Some Basics about Floor Voting

Members vote on a wide array of matters. Bills, the principal legislative vehicle, may be voted on a number of times. If bills are to become law they must, of course, be passed by the House and Senate after a vote in which a simple majority of those present and voting have supported them—although the House can expedite bills through its suspension of the rules procedure in which case the bill is approved on a two-thirds vote. If House and Senate versions of a bill are not identical, one of the bodies might decide to take a further vote to adopt the iteration passed by the other. The House essentially did this in March 2010 to provide final congressional approval to President Obama's health care reform. Alternatively, if both bodies decide to reconcile their differences in a conference committee, their floors must approve the product without amendment. Congress enacted the roughly $800 billion stimulus package in January 2009 and financial regulation overhaul in the summer of 2010 this way. If the president vetoes the bill, there can be yet another floor vote. Then two-thirds of members from both chambers must vote to override the veto if the bill is to become law.

Three other legislative vehicles are voted upon. Concurrent resolutions must be passed by both bodies but do not go to the president. The resolution that forms the first part of Congress's annual budget process is probably the most important example. Joint resolutions are exactly like bills, although the most important, declarations of war and constitutional amendments, do not go to the president. Resolutions are single-house vehicles that alter chamber rules, express the sentiment of the institution, or embody some kind of procedural matter, such as a special rule from the House Rules Committee.

Bills can be amended by floor vote. There are several types of amendments, although in the House they must be germane to the underlying bill. Members might offer "sweeteners" to generate support or "poisoned-pill" amendments that, if approved, are likely to make the underlying bill unpopular (Wilkerson 1999; Jenkins and Munger 2003; Finocchiaro and Jenkins 2008). Many believed the "Stupak amendment" to health care reform legislation offered in the House during 2009 was such a ploy. Named for sponsor Rep. Bart Stupak (D-MI), it barred health care exchanges created by the bill from covering abortion.

A variety of procedural motions are voted on. The very first House vote in a Congress determines who the Speaker shall be. The House votes to approve its journal (Patty 2010) and on motions to discharge a committee of a bill (Miller and Overby 2010). In both chambers, members can approve a motion to reconsider a vote. The House minority has the right to offer, and have voted on, a motion to recommit a just-passed bill to committee (Krehbiel and Meirowitz 2002; Roberts 2005). Matters on the Senate's Executive Calendar are subject to floor votes. The Constitution grants the Senate sole responsibility for the confirmation of a majority of presidential appointments. Executive nominations must be confirmed by floor votes, either individually or *en bloc*. Treaties must be approved by two-thirds of members present and voting.

Votes can be recorded or unrecorded. House rules dictate votes on general appropriations bills, tax increases, and the annual budget resolution must be for the record. Article I Section 7 of the Constitution compels both bodies to report votes on attempts to override presidential vetoes in their journals. But other than that members must formally ask for a recorded vote. Under Article I Section 5 of the Constitution at least one-fifth of a quorum is needed for the request to be granted. In the House this is forty-four (20 percent of a simple-majority of 218 members), in the Senate it is eleven (20 percent of 51). House rules make it easier for the body to record votes in its Committee of the Whole. Here twenty-five members must support the request (the quorum is 100, but 25 percent of members are needed).

Votes are recorded in three ways. In the Senate, a clerk reads members' names alphabetically and senators respond with their vote. This "roll-call" method can be used in the House as well, although it was traditional to employ teller votes. Under teller voting, members handed colored cards—green for "Yea," red for "No," and orange for "Present"—to a clerk. Since January 1973, the House has used an electronic device to record votes. Members vote by inserting a plastic identification card into terminals located on the backs of benches on the floor. The member presses a red button to vote "No," a green button to vote "Yea," and a yellow button to vote "Present." Running totals and members' individual votes are displayed in the chamber.

By far the most commonly used unrecorded vote is by voice. The presiding officer asks for the "yeas" and "nays" and estimates whether the question has passed or not. Neither the overall result nor individual members' votes are recorded and the result cannot be appealed. Voice votes are typically employed on uncontroversial matters such as bills passed under the suspension of the rules procedure in the House (Lynch and Madonna 2008).[1]

When a recorded vote is called for, members not on the floor generally have fifteen minutes to get there. A series of bells across the House-side of the Capitol alert that body's members. Often votes, particularly on amendments, will be "stacked" so members can take care of more than one at a time. In such cases the initial vote will be open for fifteen minutes and subsequent ones for as little as two. In all cases, and in both chambers, the vote is not final until the presiding officer declares it to be. The majority party will, therefore, sometimes keep votes open until it secures a favorable outcome. The House vote on the conference report establishing a prescription drug benefit for Medicare in November 2003 was extended for three hours as the Republican leadership attempted—successfully in the end—to twist enough arms so the measure could pass. Rep. Nick Smith (R-MI) claimed Majority Leader Tom DeLay (R-TX) and colleague Candice Miller (R-MI) had offered to direct $100,000 to his son's campaign for his seat—Smith was retiring from Congress—if he switched to vote for the report. DeLay and Miller were eventually admonished by the House's ethics committee for their role in the matter.[2] In February 2009 Senate Democrats kept open the vote on the stimulus bill for over five hours so Sen. Sherrod Brown (D-OH) could participate upon returning from his mother's wake.

Members take lots of recorded votes, or at least they do these days. Figure 8.1 shows the number of recorded votes taken in the House and Senate from the 1st Congress (1789–91) through the 110th Congress (2007–09). There are some noticeable features. First, the number of these votes has risen dramatically since the mid-1960s. There were 180 recorded votes in the House during the 86th Congress (1959–61), just eighteen years later the 95th Congress (1977–79) had 1,540 of them. Much of the initial acceleration is attributable to a dramatic increase in the number of amendments offered on the House and Senate floors (Smith 1989). In more recent years, observers suspect many votes—particularly in the House—allow members to take symbolic positions on issues for the purposes of furthering their electoral prospects (Mayhew 1974a).

Second, the number of votes plateaus in the roughly sixty years between 1830 and 1890 before falling rather precipitously. Much of this is explained by procedural innovations in both chambers. New House standing rules restricted dilatory motions and reduced the incentive to call for quorum votes (Schickler 2001: 32–43). The House Rules Committee issued restrictive special rules to limit floor amendments (Roberts 2010) and senators crafted unanimous consent agreements (UCAs) to do the same on their side of the Capitol (Evans and Oleszek 2000: 86; Roberts and Smith 2007: 193–4). In 1917 the Senate established the cloture procedure that enabled two-thirds of members to cut off debate on a bill. This discouraged obstructionists from deploying procedural votes as a delaying tactic, although today the Senate's cloture rule seems to generate more roll calls than it prevents.

There are more votes in the House during some Congresses, in others more in the Senate. There are, however, clearly greater numbers in the Senate for

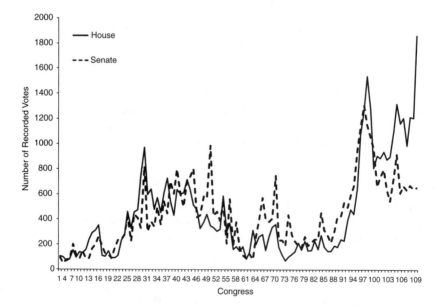

*Figure 8.1* The Number of Recorded Votes in the House and Senate, 1789–2009

most of the post-Civil War period. Again the reason is procedural. The House majority generally exerts tighter control of the floor's agenda and proceedings (Cox and McCubbins 2002, 2005). Since the mid-1980s it is the House that has had more recorded votes. Much of this seems explained by the majority leadership's response to obstructionist tactics in what has become a polarized and partisan Senate. In reply to the proliferation of holds and other clear intentions of minority-party members to filibuster, the majority-party leadership has either pulled bills from the floor or used parliamentary strategies—such as filing preemptively for cloture and offering amendments so others cannot (a practice called "filling the amendment tree"). These reduce the number of floor votes.

After accounting for basic trends, the variation in the number of votes across Congresses is explained largely by bursts of legislative activity. There were spikes in the Senates of the 27th (1841–43), 35th (1857–59), 47th (1881–83), 51st (1889–91), and 67th (1921–23) Congresses—at least partially because all witnessed lengthy debates on comprehensive and controversial trade legislation prone to amendment by senators protecting parochial economic interests. There was a steady increase in the number of votes during the 1960s and 1970s. This was not only a period of procedural innovation but a highly productive one as Congress passed many bills expanding social welfare programs and extending the federal government's regulatory reach (Mayhew 2005). The jumps in the 104th (1995–97) and 110th Congresses are attributable to new majorities—Republicans in the case of the former, Democrats the latter—interested in changing the ideological direction of public policy.

All one hundred senators have a vote. The Vice-President of the United States, in his role as President of the Senate, has no vote unless, as Article I Section 3 of the Constitution allows, the Senate is "equally divided." On occasions this can be crucial. President Bill Clinton's first budget in 1993 passed only because Vice-President Al Gore broke a tie in the Senate. At the beginning of the 107th Congress (2001–03) the Senate was split with fifty Republicans and fifty Democrats. Knowing that Vice-President Dick Cheney could break ties in favor of the Republicans, the Democrats agreed to allow Sen. Trent Lott (R-MS) to become Majority Leader and Republican senators to chair standing committees.[3]

In the House, four delegates and the resident commissioner—from American Samoa, the District of Columbia, U.S. Virgin Islands, Guam, and Puerto Rico—were able to vote in the Committee of the Whole during the 103rd Congress (1993–95) so long as their votes did not affect the outcome. This right was removed by the new Republican majority at the start of the 104th Congress (1995–97). Now only the 435 "regular" members can vote on the floor.

Attendance at votes fluctuates across time and members; today it is generally around 95 percent. It is traditional for the Speaker not to vote on the floor of the House, although it remains a personal choice. Speaker Nancy Pelosi (D-CA) cast a vote on less than 10 percent of roll calls in the 110th Congress.

Once in a while, as was the case on an adjournment motion towards the end of the 111th Congress, the Speaker must vote to ensure the passage of a measure.

Other members may abstain strategically. Some do so for policy and electoral reasons—they are indifferent about a bill or feel any vote on it is likely to alienate supporters. Those whose district or state is far from the Capitol often abstain because they cannot get back to Washington in time for a vote (Rothenberg and Sanders 1999). Members who miss more than the average share of votes tend to be sick or actively campaigning for higher office. In the 110th Congress, for instance, Sen. John McCain (R-AZ) missed 64 percent of Senate votes and Sen. Barack Obama (D-IL) 46 percent. This is consistent with Jones's (2003) argument that senators seeking higher office are keen not to take formal positions on controversial issues, but is also a product of the punishing travel schedule presidential candidates put themselves through these days. In fact, six of the seven most absent senators in that Congress were, at one stage or another, in the 2008 presidential race. The exception was Sen. Tim Johnson (D-SD) who had suffered a brain hemorrhage in December 2006.

## The Analysis of Votes

### Why Do Members Vote the Way They Do?

There has been a tremendous amount of research on the recorded or roll-call votes of members of Congress. The determinants of members' votes constitute an important focus. Recently political scientists have examined roll calls on race (Hero and Preuhs 2010), national security (Fordham 2008), the minimum wage (Meinke 2005), and, it seems particularly, trade (Kahane 1996; Bailey and Brady 1998; Uslaner 1998; Conley 1999; Biglaiser, Jackson, and Peake 2004; Boehmke 2006; Xie 2006). Several scholars have taken to analyzing procedural votes across congressional history (Binder 1997; Schickler 2001; Schickler, Sides, and McGhee 2003; Meinke 2007). These studies have significantly enhanced our understanding of the pressures that are exerted on legislators as they cast their votes on the House and Senate floors.

Several important influences have been identified (Kingdon 1989). The views of constituents are crucial, especially since members are generally concerned with reelection. Established thinking suggests members should be most responsive to the preference of the district or state median when they vote (Black 1948; Downs 1957). Interestingly, recent research emphasizes the importance of "sub-constituencies" or selective groups of citizens to whom legislators are most responsive. Clinton (2006) finds, for example, that the votes of House members, particularly Republicans, tend to reflect the preferences of partisans more than the district median. Bishin (2000) argues members vote with one eye on the electoral coalition they need to put together to win the next election—a coalition that is made up of individuals who identify with their party and independents. An influential literature proposes legislators' roll calls are more consistent with the interests of their most affluent and politically active constituents (Bartels 2008).

Interest groups might be considered an organized sub-constituency. They frequently have chapters or regional and state associations in the constituencies of legislators whose votes they wish to affect. Research has shown their influence to be important. It is exerted in several ways. The first is by mobilizing voters. Many interest groups have thousands of members who heed their endorsements and can be employed to assist with campaigns (Skinner 2007: 101–22). Second, groups provide valuable information to lawmakers (Carpenter, Esterling, and Lazar 2004; Boehmke, Gailmard, and Patty 2006). Members of Congress, particularly on the House side, have small staffs and must frequently rely on other sources for expertise about policy. Third, interest groups donate to campaigns. Because the vast majority of interest groups' Political Action Committee (PAC) contributions go to incumbents—about 82.3 percent of them in the 2008 cycle according to Center for Responsive Politics—and incumbents generally win reelection—in 2008 at rates of 94 percent in the House and 83 percent in the Senate—financial donations seem more a strategy to access the policy process than an effort to affect election outcomes. Still it should be noted that a great deal of the research suggests PAC contributions are a reward for votes previously taken and that they follow rather than influence them (McCarty and Rothenberg 1996; Gordon and Hafer 2007).[4]

Interest groups have also taken to "rating" members. For each Congress many groups identify the votes that are most important to them. Unsurprisingly, bills such as the federal stimulus, health care reform, and financial regulation overhaul were all "scored" by the AFL-CIO and the U.S. Chamber of Commerce in the 111th Congress (2009–11). This meant the groups took positions on the votes and gave points to members who voted "with them." Groups then publicize the scores to signal how supportive members are of their goals. Groups will also tell legislators in advance which measures will be scored in hopes of influencing their vote (Roberts and Bell 2008). It is important to some members that they have high scores from groups that are popular among their constituents.

Political parties are, of course, believed to shape their members' votes. They can do this because they have significant resources members need. The national committees and congressional campaign committees, as well as the leadership PACs of high-profile legislators in the party, can provide critical money for general election campaigns. The party can also work to secure a member's renomination. We saw this to mixed effect in Senate primaries during 2010—the national parties were unable to save incumbents in Alaska (Republican Lisa Murkowski), Pennsylvania (Democrat Arlen Specter), and Utah (Republican Bob Bennett).[5]

In the House, leaders also have considerable institutional and procedural resources at their disposal. The majority-party leadership effectively determines what bills will come to the floor (Cox and McCubbins 2002, 2005; Finocchiaro and Rohde 2008) and whether or not they can be amended (Monroe and Robinson 2008). Party leaders are responsible for making committee appointments and loyalty to the party agenda can be used as a metric by which assignments to popular committees are made (Leighton and Lopez 2002; Frisch and Kelly 2006).

Considerable debate continues to surround the question of the congressional parties' capacity to structure members' floor votes, however. Some scholars suggest a recent increase in partisanship is exaggerated (McCarty, Poole, and Rosenthal 2001) or is a function of an electorate polarized along partisan lines rather than any concerted effort by congressional leaders to direct the votes of their rank and file (Krehbiel 1993, 2000; Volden and Bergman 2006). This, in turn, is caused by the gerrymandering of congressional districts (Carson, Crespin, Finocchiaro, and Rohde 2007; Theriault 2006) and a concerted strategy of party elites (Levendusky 2009). Skeptics of vigorous congressional parties can also point to continued bipartisanship in floor voting. There are still a large number of votes on which nearly all members are on one side—a phenomenon called universalism (Collie 1988). This kind of voting is particularly prevalent on ceremonial legislation such as the naming of post offices, resolutions of support for popular causes, and bills that contain spending for programs across a wide number of states and congressional districts (Balla et al. 2002; Evans 2004).

Others say party leaders do much to structure the floor votes of rank-and-file members. Cox and McCubbins (2002, 2005) have shown the House majority party controls the flow of legislation to the floor tightly so that it is rolled—that is a majority of its members are on the losing side of a vote—very infrequently. Results like these hold in the Senate (Gailmard and Jenkins 2007). Congressional majority parties are therefore said to have significant negative agenda power—they can prevent bills from coming to the floor. Largely through their influence over what happens in committee, majority-party leaders can also shape the content of measures that are debated on the floor—that is, they have positive agenda power as well.

Once bills are on the floor parties have the ability, particularly the House majority, to utilize the resources described above to twist arms or, in the words of some congressional scholars, "buy" votes (Snyder and Groseclose 2000; Wiseman 2004).[6] King and Zeckhauser (2003) posit the party leadership exercises options on members' votes, and "pay"—in the sense they provide important institutional and electoral resources—for the votes of those needed to ensure the bill passes. Leaders release those from supporting the party if the bill can be approved without their support. This produces many narrow victories on significant legislation. For instance, in the House of the 111th Congress the hugely important health care reform and cap-and-trade energy/environment bills passed by a combined twelve votes on original passage. There was a great deal of talk in the media that the Democratic leadership "allowed" some members to vote against the bills if there was a need to demonstrate opposition or a willingness to buck the party to constituents.

Scholars have explored other dimensions of the party–vote linkage. For-gette (2004) shows scheduling a caucus meeting prior to a vote brings about greater party unity on the floor. Burden and Frisby (2004) and Meinke (2008a) illustrate the importance of the whipping mechanisms—essentially a group of members assigned to persuade rank-and-file members to support the party position—in shaping legislators' votes. Recent research reveals party leaders reward rank-and-file members uncomfortable with supporting the party on procedural matters with pork-barrel spending to secure their votes (Carroll and Kim 2010). Lawrence, Maltzman, and Smith (2006) argue party influence is felt more through agenda control than loyalty inducement on the floor. Regard-less of its source, it is fair to say many scholars now believe parties do much to shape roll-call behavior. Cox and Poole (2002) show this has become stronger over time too.[7]

Figure 8.2 helps illuminate the debate about the role of party in floor voting. It shows the parties in both chambers have become more unified on roll-call votes over the past thirty years, therefore providing some evidence they are increasingly capable of molding member decisions. The figure reveals the per-centage of party unity votes in each chamber or the proportion of all roll calls on which a majority of Democrats opposed a majority of Republicans. The data series is from the 40th Congress (1867–69) to the 110th.[8] Two observations are particularly important. In many Congresses party voting is higher in the

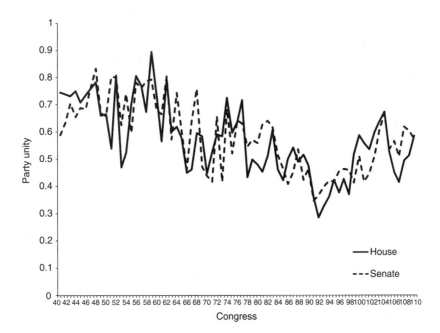

*Figure 8.2* Party Unity Votes in Congress, 1869–2009

Senate than the House. This is despite the Senate majority lacking the procedural advantages of its House counterpart. Second, there was a marked decline in party voting between about 1950 and 1980. This is attributed to the heterogeneity of preferences within both parties in the Congresses of the time reflected by a "conservative coalition" of Southern Democrats and right-of-center Republicans that blocked a more liberal agenda championed most aggressively by Northern Democrats (Schickler, Pearson, and Feinstein 2010). The 1970s saw the beginning of a process in which Southern white conservative Democrats were largely replaced by liberal African-American Democrats or conservative white Republicans and the moderate Republicans of New England and states like New York and Illinois were switched out for energetic liberal Democrats. Party voting began to climb. Still, although it continues to accelerate, the current partisanship is not excessively strong by historical standards.

Presidents also exert pressure on members as they vote. Like the congressional majority-party leadership, they do this in two ways: by pushing to have proposals placed onto the floor and by influencing members' votes on those that get there (Beckmann 2008). Presidents tend to be particularly successful when they use their considerable resources—their access to the public, their significant patronage powers, and their large staff—to exert pressure on members of their own party to vote for items on their personal legislative agenda (Edwards and Barrett 2000; Rudalevige 2002; Barrett and Eshbaugh-Soha 2007). President George W. Bush leaned extremely hard on wavering Republicans, especially those with struggling manufacturing plants in their constituencies, to pass the Trade Promotion Authority necessary for him to negotiate free-trade agreements in 2002. He even hiked tariffs on steel to assuage the concerns of Republican members in states like Ohio and Pennsylvania. President Obama worked assiduously with the House and Senate leadership to get his signature legislative achievement, health care reform, passed in 2009–10. Members of the White House staff closely coordinated their lobbying strategy with House Speaker Nancy Pelosi and Senate Majority Leader Harry Reid (D-NV).

Like party pressures, the success of presidential influence fluctuates markedly over time. Figure 8.3 shows the average of House and Senate presidential support scores on an annual basis since 1953. The figures are calculated by *Congressional Quarterly*, which takes the proportion of measures on which the president has made a position known that pass. Note presidents tend to get what they ask for—or perhaps ask for what they can get. Two trends in the data are particularly striking. With the possible exceptions of Kennedy, Ford, and Carter, there is a discernible decrease in support over a president's time in office. Some political scientists attribute this to an initial honeymoon with Congress and the American public and the general erosion of popular support for the president across his terms in office (Marshall and Prins 2007). Others have revealed a more nuanced relationship between public approval and presidential success on floor votes—including those who argue popular presidents only do better on salient legislation (Canes-Wrone and De Marchi 2002) and enjoy greater success on

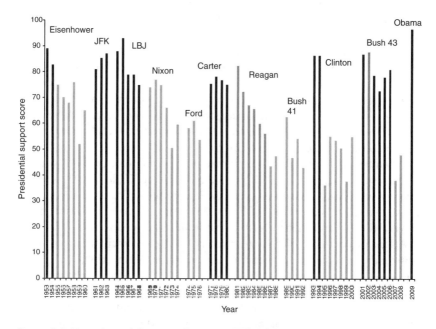

*Figure 8.3* Presidential Support Scores, 1953–2009

foreign policy than domestic policy, a phenomenon sometimes called the "two-presidencies thesis" (Canes-Wrone, Howell, and Lewis 2008).

The second pronounced trend reveals presidential agendas enjoy greater success under unified government—the years of which are denoted by black columns. The Clinton and George W. Bush presidencies provide spectacular illustrations of this. Notice the significant drop-off in the congressional support of their proposals following the 1994 and 2006 elections, midterms after which the opposition party took control of both chambers of Congress.

A final influence on a member's votes worth some discussion here is personal values. Of these perhaps ideology is the most significant. Ideology usually means a coherent set of positions on separate issues that allow us to place a member on the typical liberal-to-conservative dimension familiar to anyone with more than a perfunctory understanding of American politics. Scholars face considerable difficulties when trying to gauge the effect ideology has on floor votes, however (Levitt 1996). This is largely because voters tend to send like-minded candidates to represent them in Congress. It is also because ideology is not directly observable, except perhaps in the roll-call record itself (Ansolabehere, Snyder, and Stewart 2001).

But there are pertinent personal attributes beyond political ideology we can analyze more easily. Smith, Olson, and Fine (2010) demonstrate the personal religion of senators helps explain a propensity to vote with issues important to the Family Research Council. Burden (2007) has shown a member's background can influence how she votes. Legislators who smoke tend to oppose intensified regulation of tobacco and those who send their kids to public schools vote against the use of vouchers. Sometimes these relationships are better illustrated by floor-speech or sponsorship activity, but roll-call behavior is generally consistent with them as well.

The pressures members feel as they vote are conditioned in some way. I have already discussed the temporal variability in the effects of party and the president. Constituency pressures also seem to fluctuate in their capacity to explain roll-call behavior. Ladewig (2010) explains how large electoral mandates permit members to have voting records that are more extreme than the district's politics would suggest. Canes-Wrone, Rabinovich, and Volden (2007) show the safer a seat the more distant its occupant is from the policy preferences of her constituents. In their analysis of how redistricting influences electoral safety, Hayes, Hibbing, and Sulkin (2010) detect similar, if muted, effects.

At least in the context of the contemporary Congress, perhaps the most important condition is the type of measure being voted on. Members will be tremendously sensitive to constituency opinion on votes that attract public attention. Party pressure also varies across vote type. Because securing loyalty on amendments is very difficult for leaders, they compel the rank and file to support proposals that restrict floor procedures. As a result, party-line voting is higher on procedural matters (Snyder and Groseclose 2000; Cox and Poole 2002; Young and Wilkins 2007; Theriault 2008). It has also traditionally been greater on policy of national concern than on issue areas susceptible to pork-barrel politics like agriculture and transportation (Snyder and Groseclose 2000; Evans 2004).

### Ideal Point Estimation

However they might be derived, congressional scholars have worked assiduously to understand legislators' ideal points in the policy space. Most of this work is designed to locate positions on the conventional liberal-to-conservative dimension and is undertaken using floor votes. Probably the best-known and widely utilized instrument comes from the work of Poole, Rosenthal, and McCarty (McCarty et al. 2001; Poole and Rosenthal 1997). Using a computer algorithm that digests all roll calls on which at least 2.5 percent of members were on either side, these scholars have constructed NOMINATE scores for both the House and Senate in every Congress. The scores place legislators on a liberal-to-conservative continuum with −1 essentially the liberal pole and +1 the conservative pole. The DW-NOMINATE version of these scores allows for temporal comparisons, the life-time Common Space score meaningful intercameral analyses because it treats all 535 members of a Congress as if they served in a single body. Each contains coordinates for two dimensions; a scale that is based upon economic issues and one that detects members' positions on racial issues. The first dimension explains over 85 percent of the actual classification of members. The second dimension was particularly important in the thirty years before the Civil War and during the middle third of the twentieth century but today adds only marginally to the explanatory power of the first.

Political scientists have put these scores to tremendous use.[9] They are generally used as a succinct and clean indicator of members' policy preferences or revealed ideology. Here, I just want to present House and Senate party medians and standard deviations since the 80th Congress. The results, shown in Figure 8.4 for the House and Figure 8.5 for the Senate, tell a very interesting story about modern congressional politics. The solid lines reveal the median first-dimension DW-NOMINATE score for each party, the space between the dotted lines the size of one standard deviation of all member scores for each party. Notice two things. First, the parties in both bodies have moved apart perceptibly since World War II. Roll-call voting reveals the Democrats to have become more liberal and the Republicans—especially—more conservative. This is particularly the case since about the 100th Congress (1987–89). Second, the parties have become more cohesive. The standard deviations of the scores for both parties in both bodies have shrunk, although the finding is more marked for Democrats. Scholars have labeled this inter-party polarization and intra-party homogeneity "conditional party government" (Rohde 1991; Aldrich 1995; Aldrich, Berger, and Rohde 2002).[10]

Other measures of ideal points aggregate roll calls. Heckman and Snyder (1997) use factor analysis and an approach simpler than NOMINATE-related measures. Clinton, Jackman, and Rivers (2004) and Martin and Quinn (2002) use a Bayesian technique to estimate ideal points.[11] Scholars have used the vote

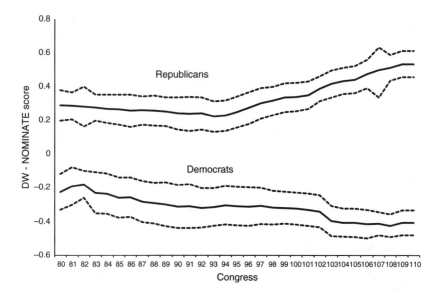

*Figure 8.4* House Party DW-NOMINATE Scores, 1947–2009

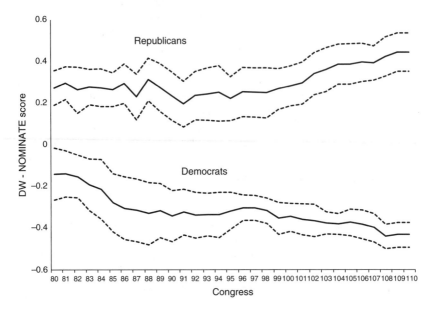

*Figure 8.5* Senate Party DW-NOMINATE Scores, 1947–2009

scores of explicitly ideological interest groups, such as the liberal Americans for Democratic Action (ADA) and American Conservative Union (ACU), to approximate members' positions on the liberal-to-conservative continuum (Groseclose, Levitt, and Snyder 1999; Brady and Volden 2006). Some have used groups that focus on a narrower set but still multiple roll calls, like the AFL-CIO or Family Research Council (Grofman, Griffin, and Berry 1995; Hayes et al. 2010).

## New Directions in the Research on Floor Voting

Floor voting remains a focus of congressional research. Much current work on the topic has built on the foundation of knowledge we have about partisan, ideological, and other cleavages and the pressures that are exerted on members as they cast their votes on the floor. Below, I identify eight clusters of new research on floor voting that I feel are especially interesting, innovative, and important. It is likely work will continue in these areas, with good prospects for significant advances in our understanding of congressional life.

### The Problem of Using Roll Calls to Estimate Ideal Points

Despite their widespread use, recent research has suggested measures of preferences derived from roll calls should be used with caution. It is problematic, for example, to use only roll call-based indicators to gauge the extent by which various actors—the president, interest groups, and party leaders—manipulate the votes of members. This is because the roll call comes after any structuring of the voting decision has taken place (Roberts 2007). A different indicator of a member's preferences prior to her exposure to external pressures is therefore required. With this in mind, researchers have taken to using measures of members' policy preferences based on their activities prior to election—such as Project Vote Smart's National Political Awareness Test (NPAT) (Ansolabehere et al. 2001) and campaign pledges made in commercials (Sulkin 2009). Griffin (2008) has employed an exogenous measure of legislator ideology that captures members' views after they have left office. Computing power is now so great and simulation techniques so advanced, that a Bayesian approach permits analyses of the influences exerted on the voting decision using measures of ideal points derived directly from roll calls (Clinton et al. 2004).

But there are additional problems. The floor agenda changes greatly from Congress to Congress so as to inhibit temporal comparisons. Moreover, innovative research reveals existing roll call-based measures are ignorant of institutional nuances. For instance, Roberts (2007) examines roll-call voting in the House's Committee of the Whole, which was established during the 92nd Congress (1971–73). Because votes in this forum are almost entirely on amendments and these are generally divisive, he shows estimates of ideal points based on roll calls from the period before the 92nd Congress are very different from those since then.

Voice votes are particularly challenging in this regard. Many important amendments and bills, including landmark legislation, are approved by voice vote (Lynch and Madonna 2008). The number of public laws that receive final passage roll calls varies considerably across Congresses (Smith 2007; Clinton and Lapinski 2008). Analyses of bills passed in one body but that receive a recorded vote in the other also suggest voice votes are not necessarily unanimous ones (Lynch and Madonna 2008). The considerable presence of voice votes casts additional doubt on the capacity of roll-call analyses to provide a reliably robust indicator of member ideal points.

### Status Quo Points

To understand how members vote on measures, we need to locate not just their ideal points but where in the policy space the legislation and its status quo equivalent are. Members' votes are essentially a choice between supporting a measure and maintaining the current state of affairs. Even though a legislator's ideal point might be distant from a bill, she will vote for it if the status quo is even further away.

Placing a bill in the policy space is fairly easy—particularly since we know who the sponsor is. Estimating status quo points is much trickier. Still, this has not delayed work on the issue. Cox and McCubbins (2005) argue lagged indicators of the preferences of the body's median or what they consider to be a constitutionally weight average of House, Senate, and presidential preferences make good approximations of status quo points. Brady and Volden's (2006) and Krehbiel's (1998) pivotal politics models suggest status quo points converge to the center of the basic liberal-to-conservative spectrum and policy breakthrough will only occur when the ideal points of "pivotal" players, such as the president and the last senator to break a filibuster fall on the same side of, but external to, a kind of gridlock "interval" or "region" formed by them.[12]

The job is far from done. As Smith (2007: 167–75) has written, a bill's status quo need not be the existing policy. In the case of appropriations, for example, the reversion point is not the current funding level but zero. On other bills, the result of rejection is to allow an executive branch or court decision to stand. Here, the status quo will be moved even without congressional action. The politics of the military's "don't ask, don't tell" policy furnish a nice example of this. In September 2010, Senate Republicans successfully blocked a defense authorization bill that contained an amendment designed to discontinue the policy. This all happened despite a U.S. District judge declaring don't ask, don't tell unconstitutional just over a week earlier. It was obvious to senators the court decision would be appealed and not take effect for some time. But the episode illustrates how unclear the policy consequences of members' no votes can be.

### Dimensionality

Recent scholarship has challenged the simplistic assumption—generated largely from the influential NOMINATE measure—that most congressional voting in the modern era can be explained by a single liberal-to-conservative dimension. Roberts, Smith and Haptonstahl (2008) use optimal classification to reveal more dimensions in congressional voting once it is disaggregated into issue types. That there exist relatively large numbers of dimensions is revealed by an analysis of different votes on the same bill. In an evaluation of appropriations legislation, Crespin and Rohde (2010) confirm the existence of multiple dimensions. This is perhaps not surprising since we should expect numerous dimensions on measures where members essentially divvy up federal spending. Still, this work further erodes our confidence in any parsimonious indicator of member policy preferences based upon analyses of the aggregate roll-call record.

### Roll Calls as an Independent Variable

To this point, I have emphasized the work undertaken to explain members' votes. But roll calls, given their importance and visibility, explain behavior as well. A burgeoning literature is devoted to understanding the impact they have on the public and election outcomes.

In a normative sense, most of its findings are encouraging. The work of Jones and McDermott (Jones and McDermott 2004, 2009; McDermott and Jones 2005) reveal the electorate to hold members at least indirectly accountable for their roll-call record. Voters are sophisticated enough to understand the basic direction of congressional policymaking, decide whether or not they feel this is a good thing, and then cast their ballot in a manner consistent with this basic evaluation. Using survey data from the mid-part of this decade, Ansolabehere and Jones (2010) confirm a similar model—here that most of the public has preferences on measures put in front of members, correctly identify how their members vote on them, and then hold their members accountable for the votes.

Perhaps the most interesting contribution describes how party connects roll-call vote and constituent response. Jones and McDermott (2009) show the majority party is punished at times when the electorate is dissatisfied with congressional action. This was the case in the 2006 election when the public turned on Republicans who had voted to authorize President George W. Bush to use force against Iraq. Voters in districts with relatively large numbers of casualties in the conflict were especially hard on Republican incumbents (Grose and Oppenheimer 2007). Other scholars explain how members are held accountable by the public for their party-line votes (Canes-Wrone, Brady, and Cogan 2002; Carson et al. 2010). On the whole, party unity is found to erode electoral security. Members would be advised to demonstrate their independence, particularly on controversial issues (Carson et al. 2010).

### Roll Calls and Substantive Representation

There is more to democratic theory than the median voter. Substantive representation—the promotion of the interests of all groups of constituents—is thought to be an important part of a member's responsibilities (Pitkin 1967). In Sidney Verba's (2003: 663) words, "The equal consideration of the preferences and interests of all citizens" is "one of the bedrock principles in a democracy."

The consensus of recent literature is that collectively members of Congress do not do this very well. The work of Bartels (2008), Gilens (2009), and McCarty, Poole and Rosenthal (2006) particularly highlight how floor voting and the policy outputs it produces have been increasingly synchronized with the interests of wealthier Americans. There are a number of reasons for this, including the propensity for more affluent citizens to vote and contribute to campaigns and middle class voters to eschew redistributive policies in an era of enhanced inequality.

Others have found members neglect the concerns of racial and ethnic minorities. Griffin and Newman (2007) demonstrate legislators' voting records are much more aligned with the interests of their white constituents than their Latino ones. Scholars have suggested a solution to this particular problem. Grose (2005) shows African-American House members vote more consistently with African-American interests, even when the racial composition of the district is accounted for. Cameron, Epstein, and O'Halloran (1996) argue minorities should be distributed fairly evenly across districts if they are to shape congressional floor votes in a meaningful way.

### Sophisticated Voting

Sophisticated voting is a type of insincere behavior—members do not reveal their true preference when they do it. Although infrequent, it tends to occur particularly on amendments designed to make bills unpalatable to a floor majority (Denzau, Riker, and Shepsle 1985; Jenkins and Munger 2003).[13] Sophisticated voting also poses significant measurement problems for scholars. That has not, however, stopped an innovative and evolving research agenda.

Groseclose and Milyo (2010) have produced probably the most interesting piece of recent work done on sophisticated voting in Congress. Their formal model explains why members vote in a sophisticated fashion only very rarely. This is not because agenda setters prevent them from doing so. Floor votes, as we noted earlier, take place over roughly a fifteen-minute period. Members can see totals and alter their choice during the voting window. Groseclose and Milyo (2010) claim it is prohibitively difficult to vote sophisticatedly when decisions are transparent and mutable.

### The Timing and Sequencing of Votes

The Speaker and Senate majority leader schedule bills for debate. The final vote on a bill will follow shortly after, unless in the Senate cloture cannot be invoked against a filibuster. One question that researchers have not investigated fully is: How do leaders decide when a bill should be voted on?

I have taken a stab at this over the past couple of years. In one paper, I explain the leadership of the majority that is more extreme relative to the president will schedule a vote first when the House and Senate are controlled by the same party (Taylor 2008). The model I present explains this is the result of an intercameral strategy to maximize the probability that the final bill will be somewhere close to a mid-point between the House and Senate majorities' ideal points. Congressional leaders orchestrate bill passage sequence to compel the president to accept an outcome that is closer to their collective preference than one they could expect from a purely haphazard bicameral legislative process.

### Quasi-Experimental Designs in the Study of Congressional Voting

Finally, it is interesting that congressional scholars have begun using quasi-experimental designs to get at the question of what makes members vote the way they do. The complexity of House and Senate rules provides ample opportunities to construct this kind of research design. I note above that researchers have separated votes on procedural and substantive measures to gauge the impact of party pressures (Snyder and Groseclose 2000; Young and Wilkins 2007; Theriault 2008). Party pressures can also be examined if we look at the pre- and post-defection voting records of members who switch parties (Hager and Talbert 2000; Nokken 2000).

There are other ingenious examples of this methodology. Electoral pressures can literally be switched on and off by comparing defeated members' voting records in regular and lame-duck sessions (Goodman and Nokken 2004; Jenkins and Nokken 2008). Espino and Canon (2009) use the unusually large number of re-votes in the House's Committee of the Whole during the 103rd Congress (1993–95) to test theories of vote switching. Meinke (2005) looks at voting on the minimum wage across a member's career to examine the same puzzle.

## Conclusion

Congressional scholars have noted for some time the considerable command the House majority party has over the body's floor agenda. Many are now suggesting the Senate majority exercises similar control over the upper chamber's floor agenda (see, e.g., Monroe, Roberts, and Rohde 2008). Party leaders in both bodies are capable of "twisting arms" quite violently. With increasingly strong parties that can do much to influence members' decisions, you might think floor voting has never been less interesting or important.

A central goal of this chapter has been to disprove any such idea. Floor voting is transparent and frequent. As such, it has attracted congressional scholars interested in large data sets with great variation and testing hypotheses about individual and collective behavior under diverse conditions. These qualities allow for studies on many distinct policy issues using many different methods. As I noted, scholars continue to find new questions to ask about floor voting and new ways to answer them.

Floor voting is consequential too, and in a normative sense to boot. As a public statement of a member's position on an issue, it allows voters to hold their congressional representation accountable. As a collective decision, it constitutes the approval or rejection of important policy options. Not only will political scientists continue to scrutinize it then, the public would be wise to as well.

## Notes

1 Members can also "pair" their votes. The only type of paired voting that exists in the House today is the "live pair." In this case, a member who is present withdraws his vote after an agreement with a colleague who cannot be in the House and who would have voted on the opposite side of the question had she been present. Pairs are not reported in the final vote but are printed in the *Congressional Record*. The Senate still allows "dead pairs." On these occasions, both members are absent.
2 Mann and Ornstein (2006: 1–7) provide a detailed account of this episode.

3  The Democrats captured the majority in June 2001 after Sen. James Jeffords of Vermont quit the Republican Party to become an independent. Jeffords supported the Democrats on organizational matters.

4  It should be noted federal campaign finance laws allow interest groups and individuals to give to candidates running in districts and states where they are not resident. Large PACs and wealthy people direct money across the country. Among individual donors, strong partisans in New York, southern California, and Washington, D.C. give the most (Gimpel, Lee, and Kaminski 2006; Gimpel, Lee, and Pearson-Merkowitz 2008).

5  Murkowski went on to win the general election as a write-in candidate.

6  The language is informative, but not entirely accurate. Votes are, of course, not literally bought. It is illegal to offer money for a legislator's vote. It was suspicions of vote buying that got Reps. DeLay and Miller in trouble during the Medicare vote discussed above.

7  For a thorough treatment of the influence party has on floor voting in Congress, see Smith (2007).

8  Other measures of party unity have been used in the past. Of these, perhaps Rice's (1928) cohesion scores are the best known. Rice calculated the mean absolute difference in the percentage of party members voting yea and the percentage voting nay for all roll calls in a Congress.

9  There are literally too many to mention. Poole and Rosenthal's work on NOMINATE surely constitutes one of the biggest contributions to congressional scholarship over the past thirty years.

10 To those who have written about the phenomenon, the existence of conditional party government allows the majority party to skew policy outcomes towards the ideal point of its median member. It does this because rank-and-file members provide resources and amenable rules to leaders who, in turn, are expected to deploy them so as to secure party unity.

11 The Clinton, Jackman, and Rivers (2004) approach uses simulations to generate probabilistic understandings of how members' ideal points are arrayed along a single dimension. Martin and Quinn (2002) first used their technique in an analysis of Supreme Court justices.

12 For applications, see Chiou and Rothenberg (2003, 2009).

13 Groseclose and Milyo (2010) find only ten roll calls in congressional history on which researchers claim the existence of sophisticated voting.

# Chapter 9

# Bicameral Resolution

## The Politics and Policy Implications of Creating Identical Bills

*Nathan W. Monroe*[1]

In the spring of 2003, with Republicans in control of both the House and Senate, Congress began to consider highly contentious legislation to overhaul U.S. energy policy.[2] With the weight of the Republican White House behind them, Republican proposals in both chambers included wide ranging tax subsidies for energy producers and aimed to overhaul electricity laws to encourage private investment in energy infrastructure such as power plants and transmission lines. The House acted swiftly in adopting a bill based largely on recommendations from an energy task force led by Vice President Dick Cheney, but similar proposals met strong resistance from Senate Democrats. For several months, the bill languished on the floor, with Senate Majority Leader Bill Frist unable to get the sixty votes needed to end debate and move to a final vote. Finally, a breakthrough came when Minority Leader Tom Daschle suggested that they could simply replace the full language of the current bill with that of the Democratic-sponsored energy bill that had passed the Senate during the previous year (but never became law). Frist agreed, and the bill quickly and overwhelmingly passed the Senate.

Given the partisan stakes, this would seem a very odd concession from Frist, if not for one thing: "Republicans made no secret that the move was simply the fastest way to get to conference, where they planned to completely rewrite the bill" (CQ Almanac Online 2003). Because the House and Senate bills were not identical, Republicans knew that the final version of the bill would be formulated in a conference between the two chambers. The Republican chairs of the conference—Senator Pete Domenici and Congressman Billy Tauzin (both of whom were the Chairs of the standing committees in their respective chambers that produced the original legislation)—infuriated Democrats by negotiating and writing the conference report in private, and releasing the bill section by section to the other conferees. Moreover, Domenici made clear from the outset that he planned to use the original Republican bill—not the Democratic bill passed by the Senate—as the starting point for negotiating the Senate's position in conference.

Even with this streamlined negotiation process, however, competing House and Senate preferences over key provisions led to weeks of intense negotiations and major changes to the legislation; in the end, the completed bill reported from conference looked significantly different from both the House and Senate legislation. Needing only a simple majority, the conference report was quickly adopted in the House. However, leadership in the Senate again failed to draw enough support to end debate. Ironically, though they won over the support of thirteen Democratic senators, mostly from oil-producing or farm-belt states,[3] the bill was thwarted by a band of six Republicans who objected to the billions of dollars in tax subsidies for energy producers.

In a sense, this anecdote stands in stark contrast to the impression left by the "presentment clause" of the U.S. Constitution (Article I, Section 7, Clauses 2 and 3), which offers the guidelines by which bills become laws and begins with a seemingly incidental, innocuous requirement: "Every Bill which shall have passed the House of Representatives and the Senate. ... " The fact that bills must be passed *in identical form* by the two chambers was so trivial in the framers' minds that it is passed over without even an explicit acknowledgment. Nevertheless, as demonstrated by the opening anecdote, and more broadly by the history of U.S. policymaking, bicameral resolution of differences in the "same" bill as initially passed by each chamber is often anything but trivial.

For significant legislation, the predominant form of bicameral resolution in modern Congresses has been the use of conference committees. Once the House and Senate agree to disagree, each chamber appoints a set of delegates to serve as their chamber's representatives in conference. After negotiating a version of the bill acceptable to a majority of each chamber's delegates, the conference committee sends the revised bill—or "conference report"—back to the House and Senate for a final, unamendable, up-or-down vote.[4] Because so many bills—especially complex and "important" bills—go through the conference process (Rybicki 2003), and because conferences often make substantial changes to legislation, the conference committee process is an integral factor in the shaping of policy outcomes.

Yet, just as the requirement of "identical bills" seems an afterthought of the presentment clause, the history of scholarship on conference committees is one of incidental interest.

Literature on conference committees emerged in the 1960s and 1970s. These initial works focused on the production of spending and taxation legislation and found the conference committee was an important step in the production of this legislation; the realization that bicameral competition and resolution were essential to the outcomes of these types of bills drew the attention of scholars to bicameral resolution.

The revival of conference committee research in the late 1980s and early 1990s was again motivated by their relevance to a more central theme in the congressional literature: the dominance of standing committees. Conference committees were seen as germane due to the "ex post veto" power they afforded the appointees, most of whom came from the standing committee(s) of origin. After yet another hiatus, much of the recent literature has sprung up as an extension of the "do parties matter?" debate, which has become the central focus of the congressional literature over the past two decades. In that context, conference committees fit as a part of the quest to understand how parties affect outcomes, especially inasmuch as they do so by influencing the legislative agenda and legislative outcomes.

In this chapter, I begin by describing the basic logistics of bicameral resolution, and then proceed to detail the "three waves" of research on bicameral resolution just mentioned. Following my discussion of the most recent research, I offer some suggestions as to both how and why conference committee scholarship should move forward in new directions. Specifically, I argue that (1) the means and outcomes of bicameral resolution are sufficiently important, in terms of determining the ultimate state of public policy, to occupy a more central place in the congressional literature, but (2) that in moving forward scholars should continue to try to integrate the "cutting-edge" research topics (i.e., appointment, outcomes, choice resolution method) into a more unified framework. I conclude by posing several as yet unanswered questions about bicameral resolution that deserve further attention.

## The Logistics of Bicameral Resolution

As noted above, by constitutional mandate, before legislation can be signed into law, the House and Senate must pass a bill in identical form. In many cases, on non-controversial or relatively simple policy issues, the same bill passes each chamber the first time through, and no further congressional action is required. But, when the chambers pass legislation on the same issue, but the bills are even slightly different—as is often the case with the most controversial and complex issues—some method of bicameral resolution is required. There are two primary means for achieving this resolution: amendment trading (or "shuttling") and conference committee.[5] In some cases, the two methods will be used in conjunction, but typically one or the other is used in isolation.

The intuition of the amendment trading method is very straightforward, though the procedures and logistics can become very complicated.[6] When one chamber passes a bill, it then sends the bill on to the other chamber for action. If the second chamber passes the bill without amendment, then no further resolution is needed. However, if any amendments are adopted prior to passage by the second chamber, then those amendments constitute the substance of disagreement between the chambers.[7] In that case, the bill will be passed back to the first chamber, where for each amendment adopted by the second chamber, the first chamber can either "concur" in the amendment or amend the amendment and send the bill back to the other chamber. If they concur in all amendments, then the process is complete and the bill can be sent to the president. However, if they amend the other chamber's amendment—in other words, offer the other chamber a new proposal—then the process continues as described. This is where the process can become procedurally complex; how many amendments to amendments are in order, and how those are considered by each chamber, can be procedurally messy. The basic substantive idea, however, is simple: amendment trading equates to the chambers making proposals back and forth until some agreement is reached.

Conference committees are sometimes formed when amendment trading fails but, more often, both chambers anticipate the need for a conference in advance and go directly to this process after the bill is passed. For major legislation, conference committees have historically been the preferred method, but overall amendment trading is actually more common. Figure 9.1 shows the percentage of all public laws, for each of the 95th through 110th Congresses (1977–2008), that went through each method of bicameral resolution.[8] For each Congress, the left-hand bar represents the percentage of bills that were reconciled using conference committees, and the right-hand bar represents the percentage resolved using amendment trading. In each Congress except the 104th, amendment trading outpaces conference use, in many instances by more than double. Note also that the need for bicameral resolution in general seems to be on the decline. In the early Congress in our time series, 55–60 percent of bills required bicameral resolution, where the most recent Congresses have seen resolution less than 25 percent of the time.

To get to conference, once the chambers have reached the "stage of disagreement" by stating formal disagreement on a bill, one chamber will request a

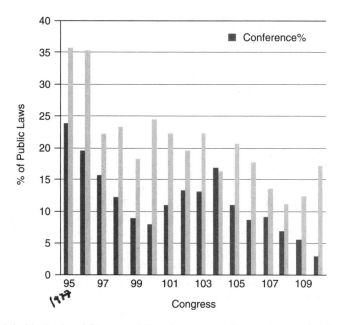

*Figure 9.1* Methods of Bicameral Resolution as a Percentage of Public Laws, 95th–110th Congresses

conference and the other then has the option to agree to the conference or not. Once one chamber has made a request and the other has agreed, each chamber chooses a slate of conference delegates—also called "conferees" or "managers"—from its membership. This process is similar across the two chambers, though it varies in some procedural specifics. Informally, the chairs and ranking members from the standing committees that considered the bill in each chamber have proposal power over the initial slate of majority and minority conferees. In the House, the proposed slate goes to the Speaker, who has final discretion over the makeup of the conference delegation. In the Senate, the conference slate is technically determined by a floor vote, though in effect discretion is almost always granted to the presiding officer and is effectively exercised by the majority and minority leaders.[9]

The size of conference delegations has been relatively stable in recent Congresses, but varies considerably across chambers. Figure 9.2 shows the average size of House (the left-hand bar) and Senate (the right-hand bar) conference delegations for each Congress from the 95th to the 110th (1977–2008). House delegations have a considerably larger range than the Senate, from eleven conferees up to thirty. The Senate's average size, in contrast, is much more stable, hovering between nine and seventeen members for the entire time series. However, given the different sizes of the parent chambers—the House having more than four times as many members as the Senate—the larger House delegations are unsurprising. Indeed, the fact that the averages are as similar as they are implies that the Senate is stretching itself to keep pace with the House.

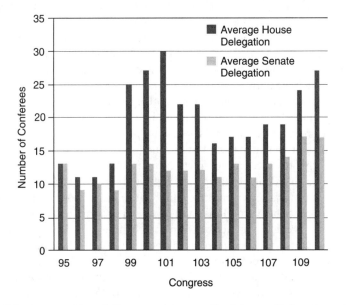

*Figure 9.2* Average Size of House and Senate Conference Delegations, 95th–110th Congresses

Once conferees are appointed, a conference is convened. While there are numerous well-defined procedures for handling conference-related business *in each chamber*, there are virtually no set rules governing what actually happens in conference. In essence, each conference delegation can decide what, if any, formal procedures they wish to adopt. The only rules required by each chamber mandate that a majority of each chamber's delegation vote to approve the conference report, and that meetings be open to all conferees and to the public.

Once the bill is reported back to the chambers, typically the bill is not amendable and is subject to an up-or-down vote on adoption. However, in the Senate, the report can be filibustered and is subject to the same sixty-vote cloture requirement as bills earlier in the process. In practice, conference reports are rarely filibustered, though in some cases where significant changes are made at the conference stage, such as the opening example of the 2003 energy bill, conference reports provoke renewed resistance from opponents of the legislation.

## Bicameral Resolution Research: Wave I

Recall from the opening anecdote that even with Republicans from both chambers firmly in control of the energy bill conference negotiations, House–Senate differences ultimately stalled the legislation for months. The first wave of literature over bicameral resolution focused almost exclusively on this horse-race aspect of modern politics—i.e., which chamber won as opposed to what was decided in conference. Each author begins with the question of whether the House or the Senate "wins" in conference committee negotiations, with winning being defined as a simple measurement of which side got more policy movement their way. The authors offer various explanations as to why a particular chamber won and the strategies that each side implements, but generally limit the application of their analysis to the determination of an intercameral victor. Though the narrow focus of scholarship on bicameral interactions is the by-product of a more focused interest in other aspects of congressional politics, it is this period which marks the foundation of a more systematic interest in the role of bicameral resolution in the legislative process.

The works of Pressman (1966) and Fenno (1966) are implicated as the initial source of scholarly focus on conference committees, though in both cases their role is seen as incidental to the primary question of which chamber wins with regard to appropriation committee bills.[10] Pressman (1966) begins his writing with the conflict between House and Senate appropriations committees but expands it to general conflict between the chambers. He employs studies of bargaining strategies and references other literature on tactics employed by the opposing chambers, but comes to no specific conclusion as to why they disagree or the general outcomes of their fighting, a result of his work's emphasis on providing a broader overview of congressional conflict. Fenno (1966) studies the results of House and Senate appropriations committees' resolutions, generally finding that the Senate wins more often than the House. To understand why, he uses the framework of the committees existing as entities both separate and composite to their larger chambers; to survive, the committees must please their broader constituencies while minimizing conflict with their opponents. He finds the Senate suffers less in trying to reconcile these two goals, which explains their disproportionate success in conference.

Manley (1970), in a similar manner to the preceding literature, addresses the role of conference committees only as they affect the resolution of disputes between the chambers on the particular policies on which he focuses. In Manley's work, he analyzes bills coming from the House Ways and Means Committee in terms of whether they affect taxation, social security, or trade legislation. In determining whether there are systematic differences between House and Senate committee victories, he finds that the House wins on bills dealing with social security while the Senate wins over trade and taxation. His theory is that the difference lies in interest group support differentials between the House and Senate, and that this, more than intrachamber support, helps account for legislative outcomes.

Vogler (1970) is the first author to begin to emphasize the importance of conference committees among a broader range of policies and legislation, though again their import is a function of how they influence which chamber wins the post-passage resolution process. In his article, he essentially replicates Fenno's (1966) findings that the Senate tends to win more than the House in conference committee bargaining. His important contribution is to analyze a greater variety of committees, dealing with more than merely appropriations bills. He suggests that different trends in outcomes among different committees would be a fruitful area for study. Vogler (1971) expands this analysis to a book-length treatment, which provides support for his earlier work, serving primarily to expand upon his prior findings.

Ferejohn's (1975) work serves as a counterpoint to the initial forays into the field by Pressman and Fenno; where their work on conference committees was incidental to a more specific emphasis on appropriations bills, Ferejohn's focus on a narrow subset of legislation is incidental to his work on the role of conference committees. Ferejohn examines appropriations bills for the army corps of engineers and finds that final passage from conference committee favors the Senate position two-thirds of the time. This support echoes most other literature on the subject; nevertheless, Ferejohn's key contribution is his theory that it is the sequence of steps in the legislative process that results in this outcome bias. By acting first, the House commits to certain goals in the bill; as a result, the Senate can ensure their amendments will survive reconciliation by restraining their recommendations to certain limits.

Strom and Rundquist (1977) serve to expand upon and offer additional support for the initial work by Ferejohn (1975), as their work replicates and expands Ferejohn's findings of a sequence bias in apportioning outcomes. The chamber that made the initial proposal "loses" more than two-thirds of conference committee outcomes. Their empirical addition is to examine bills that originate in either chamber rather than only the House of Representatives, but they also offer some additional theoretical clarity: conferences act as bargaining venues, wherein the conferees from the first chamber, by virtue of their "last mover" advantage at the prior stage, are simply in a superior bargaining position.[11]

In sum, this first wave of research broke critical new ground in understanding the theoretical mechanism and uncovering the empirical regularities of bicameral resolution. Boiled down to a single punch line, the scholarship of this era showed us that the Senate tends to win more often at conference. The question begged by this answer, however, is who is "the Senate" (and "the House," for that matter)? Put another way, when we try to assess House and Senate "wins" at conference, whose interests should we be attentive to? As the opening example of 2003 energy policy demonstrated, there are clearly subgroups and actors—such as parties, leaders, and committees—within each chamber that will accrue disproportionate benefits from a given conference outcome. Thus, the critical task of looking inside each chamber to assess the strategies and payoffs surrounding bicameral resolution was left to the next waves of research.

## Bicameral Resolution Research: Wave II

Returning again to the energy bill example, one facet of that conference process that clearly escaped the lens of the first wave revolves around the central role of standing committee actors at the conference stage. On the energy bill, the chairs of the standing committees that originally reported the bill eventually helmed the conference. After the appearance of the initial writings on the role and significance of conference committees in the 1960s and 1970s, there was a decline in scholarly interest on the question, with most congressional scholars turning their attention to the power of standing committees in the legislative process. Thus, conference committee and bicameral bargaining literature of the 1980s and early 1990s was dominated by the concept of the "ex post veto." In particular, the focus was on the power of standing committees to influence legislation at both the first and last stage of the legislative process. Strongly informed by the work of Shepsle and Weingast (1987), the bicameral resolution literature of this period sought to expand upon the initial interest generated by Fenno (1966) and others in post-passage negotiation through a less partisan or intercameral lens. There are also echoes of the work done by Ferejohn on the role of legislative sequencing, with the ex post veto serving as an anchor point in the policymaking process.

In their groundbreaking work on the explicit and exogenous sources of committee power, Shepsle and Weingast (1987) construct a broad theoretical model to explain what methods and tools committees possess that grant them influence. Of particular concern for the literature on conference committees is their reliance on the ex post veto, the fact that conference committees generally contain a large number of legislators from the jurisdictional committees where the bill first originated. This combination of gatekeeping and reconciliatory powers is invested as the predominant source of committee power and is seen as the natural evolution of the question first posed by Fenno (1966) as to who wins in conference committees.

Longley and Oleszek (1989) follow in Shepsle and Weingast's footsteps by dispensing with the question of who wins in conference committees and instead focus on the relationship between individual members of Congress, the standing committees and the parent chambers. Through an exhaustive sampling of the extant literature and several case studies focusing on specific examples, the authors provide an incredibly rich, broad view of bicameral negotiation and post-passage bargaining, though they draw few connections with, or conclusions about, the theoretical literature. Though their writing does touch on the power of the ex post veto and the role of standing committee members in conference committee delegations, the nature of their work—providing a broad array of descriptive examples and explanations—serves as a dramatic contrast to the formal theoretic focus of other literature.

Much of the action in this second wave, however, begins with the exchange in Krehbiel, Shepsle, and Weingast (1987), where Krehbiel and Shepsle–Weingast have a back-and-forth discussion within the article. Somewhat ironically, this coauthored work with Shepsle and Weingast marks the first of several publications by Krehbiel that critique the committee dominance perspective. Krehbiel proposes several limitations and omissions in Shepsle and Weingast's (1987) original work; Shepsle and Weingast respond to Krehbiel's criticisms, and conclude that their work might require revision, but it remains generally sound, and that it is significant for more than its illumination of the dominant role of the ex post veto model on this period's conference committee literature. Krehbiel argues that the parent chambers of each conference committee's delegation are not in fact as constrained by the threat or employment of the ex post veto as previously asserted. Rather he contends that the members of each chamber, who form the majority that vote on floor motions, have at their disposal many powers that they can use to constrain the ostensibly dominant committees. The thrust of his argument is that the assumptions in Shepsle and Weingast's model are unrealistic and that the ex post veto is not as powerful as they contend it to be. In their rebuttal, Shepsle and Weingast concede that Krehbiel has meaningful objections and that their work would certainly be no worse for the addition of some of his critiques, but that the evidence which he asserts as a check on the ex post veto is not as easily or frequently observed as he might assume; while they concede their model would be richer for the inclusion of parent chamber influence on committee power, it is not negated for the lack of it.

From his initial objections to some of the assumptions of the ex post veto model of committee power, Krehbiel proceeds to formulate a challenge to the distributional model of Congress as a whole. Krehbiel's (1991) book-length treatment on the role of informational theory as a paradigm to understand congressional organization and outcomes touches only briefly on the role of conference committees in the legislative process. In his model, it is individual legislative preferences, rather than partisan committee dominance, that truly affect post-passage bargaining. In a follow-up article on the declining evidence of partisanship in the U.S. Congress, however, Krehbiel's (1993) focus on conference committees takes center stage. Krehbiel again objects to the unifying theme of this period's conference committee literature—the role of standing committees with regard to the implementation of the ex post veto. In marshaling his data to disprove anecdotal claims of rising tides of partisanship in Congress through the mid to late 1980s, Krehbiel makes the point that the role of partisanship, for appointments to both standing committees and conference committees, is declining. This attack on the relevance of partisanship for congressional organization and decision-making foreshadows the direction the literature would move over the next two decades.

## Bicameral Resolution Research: Wave III

Perhaps the most glaring, as of yet unaddressed feature of the energy bill example is the party influence exhibited: that conference served as a means of cross-chamber partisan coordination and provided the Senate leadership with an opportunity to advance their agenda further through the process. The third wave takes aim at how parties utilize bicameral resolution for their own benefit.

### Conference Committee Appointments

Of the identifiable categories of modern scholarship on conference committees, those works explicitly focused on the determinants of conference committee appointments are of the oldest origin. The phenomenon of conference committee appointments as a focus of bicameral bargaining is not a new one, but the recent literature is notable for the rigor of the models and the increased emphasis on both partisanship and collective action issues. In the context of principal/agent relationships, it is helpful to view conference committee members as the agents; the subsequent question is, who is/are the principals? The answer to that question is the focus of this section.

Though temporally situated in the second wave, both Nagler (1989) and Ortega and McQuillan (1992) serve as important precursors for work in the most recent wave of bicameral resolution scholarship. Nagler's analysis examines minimum wage legislation negotiation in the House of Representatives from 1972, 1973, and 1977 in the context of a modified form of Shepsle and Weingast's theorem of committee influence as the product of the ex post veto power. Nagler goes into greater depth, treating the selection of committee members as endogenous to the Speaker's preferences rather than exogenously given by committee actors. He contends that the Speaker, whose decisions and preferences are a product of the general attitudes and preferences of the majority party, wields considerable power in the conference committee process. The paper asserts that the ex post veto is not a trump card, and that the parent chamber does influence legislative outcomes in a way not predicted by previous literature on the subject.

Ortega and McQuillan's article forms, alongside Nagler's piece, the historical roots of modern conference appointment scholarship. This paper is a useful empirical extension of Nagler's critique of the ex post veto model. Using a test of preferences as opposed to representation, the authors show that conference committee members, though overwhelmingly selected from the jurisdictional committee from which the bill originates, have preferences distinct from those standing committee members that were not selected. Furthermore, the paper demonstrates that the preferences of the committee delegates are aligned not with the standing committee chair, but with party leaders of the parent chamber, providing substantive empirical support for Krehbiel's (1991) contention that preferences rather than representation is significant.

Carson and Vander Wielen (2002) mark the beginning of the modern period of congressional work on conference committee appointments. Their paper uses data on conference committee delegations from both the House and the Senate between 1979 and 2000, which is significant in part because the preponderance of research on the subject has focused exclusively on the House. The paper analyzes the role that the Speaker of the House and the Senate majority leader play with regard to their appointment power, focusing on strategic and partisan considerations that influence their decisions. An important aspect of this work is its relationship with the previous period's literature on conference committees, specifically its emphasis on explicit and partisan-based models of congressional organization. The significant findings of the paper are that conference delegations are picked to represent the preferred policy outcomes of powerful institutional actors in both chambers, as distinct from committee chairs, and that the frequency and magnitude of the strategic and partisan considerations vary according to the partisanship of each chamber as a whole.

Hines and Civettini (2004) continue the renewed interest in conference committee appointments, analyzing data from the Senate during the 101st through 107th Congresses, complementing a similar study by the authors in the House. They use these data to test the hypotheses first put forth by Krehbiel (1991), and find that seniority has a significant impact with regard to strategic considerations and constraints in conference committee appointments. This finding contradicts prior literature in the Senate, and the whole strain of House appointment literature, which emphasizes the pivotal nature of the Speaker with regard to conference appointments. Their work is, in part, very notable for its suggestions of new strands of research to be conducted and an illumination of the significant differences between the House and the Senate, in regard to involvement in the process and power of conference committee appointments.

Much like Hines and Civettini, Lazarus and Monroe's (2007) article on the role of the Speaker of the House in appointing conferees engages in the "parties versus preferences" debate over congressional organization. Using data from the 97th through 106th Congresses they find support for the contention that the Speaker has significant powers over the outcomes of conference committee legislation through his power of appointment. Specifically, they find strong theoretical evidence for explicit circumstances in which the Speaker has both the motivation and ability to influence post-passage bargaining. The work is notable also for its formal theoretic approach, deriving specific testable hypotheses and marshaling empirical evidence for the propositions of the model. Much of the work that follows is noticeably more formal than most of the prior literature on bicameral resolution.

In Vander Wielen and Smith's (n.d.) work, conference committee delegates are analyzed in light of their similarity to the members of their parent chamber as a whole. This work, following in the direction of most recent scholarship, finds that the majority party dominates conference committees disproportionately to their dominance of the House of Representatives as a whole. Their explanation of this partisan power, over delegates directly and standing committees indirectly, lends support to both prior theories of the role of the ex post veto and modern models of partisan and cartel dominance of the House.

## How Policy Changes in Conference

The second observable category of modern bicameral bargaining scholarship concerns the presence or absence of systematic effects of conference committee bargaining. While the literature of the previous section dealt with the ways in which powerful institutional actors could "stack the deck" of conference committee delegations with the goal of affecting the end result, this section's work focuses on whether those actions are indeed borne out by the evidence.

Brady (2008) compiles data from the 97th as well as 101–110th Congresses in an attempt to illustrate systematic trends in conference committee outcomes. The paper finds that partisanship, as implemented through the ability of the Speaker of the House in particular to appoint delegates, is a critical factor in predicting policy shifts in conference. Other predictive factors include the level of partisanship in the standing committees from which the legislation originates and the level of bipartisanship in the Senate. Using these elements ex ante, Brady finds it possible to predict whether, and in what direction, a bill sent to committee will shift as a result of the committee.

Vander Wielen (2010b) addresses the same question by identifying votes on conference bills that generate strong partisan cleavages. On this set of votes, he tests whether conference committee outcomes are shifted not towards the median voter of the majority coalition but the ideal points of the committee members themselves. The paper provides a modern formation of the argument first originating in the literature of the 1980s, that standing committees have significant influence over policy outcomes through their overwhelming representation as conference delegates. In direct contrast to other modern scholarship in this area, Vander Wielen rests a significant degree of power on the jurisdictional committee members chosen as delegates for conference committee resolution, as opposed to chamber-level institutional actors. Though careful to identify the constraint on delegates to propose a bargain that will pass in both chambers, this work is especially significant for its focus on conferees as independent actors.

### Strategic Bargaining/Alternative Resolution Strategies

The final strand of research on post-passage bargaining emphasizes the role of the conference committee as an ex ante procedure that wields significant influence with regard to the actions of congressional actors during the legislative process. In some sense, this line of research is an analog to Ferejohn's (1975) work on the sequence of the legislative process, in that the modern scholarship is primarily concerned with how members in each chamber act in a strategic manner to manipulate the existence of post-passage procedures for their benefit.

The initial formulation of this area of academic interest might be traced to Levmore (1992), who is primarily concerned with the historical foundations and modern applications of the bicameral system. He postulates that, in a two-chamber system, the necessity of proposing policy that is satisfactory to a majority of each chamber constrains the initial policy proposals of legislative actors, though he does note the power of conference committees to act strategically to achieve profitable outcomes. Levmore's work speaks to the first wave of conference committee literature, in that he relies on disparities between actors in each chamber to pursue their own goals, though he uses a more rigorous theoretical construct.

Ortega and McQuillan's (1996) paper serves as a transition between the modern scholarship on the strategic implications of conference committees and the distributive model critiqued by Krehbiel (1993) during the second wave of research on post-passage bargaining. Their addition to these writings is to define a "bicameral stability" model of conference committees where the goal is to maximize the amount of legislation produced by Congress while minimizing the amount of intercameral conflict. Their explanation for pro-Senate bias in conference outcomes is a result of the relative vulnerability of the Senate with regard to partisan fighting. Their model uses data on conference committees from 1949–91.

A more recent extension of the theme first explicated in Levmore's research is Van Houweling's (2007) argument about the strategic actions of members of Congress prior to a bill being sent to conference. His survey of the 83rd–107th Congresses provides compelling empirical evidence that conference committees are used as a way of separating public and private preferences in terms of senatorial accountability. That is, the lack of a closed discussion rule in the Senate makes discrete actors vulnerable to the consequences of their votes, leading them to use conference committees as a way to achieve their privately preferred outcome without a polarizing floor debate. This work is reminiscent of the initial period of conference committee literature and its emphasis on institutional differences between the chambers as a determinant of post-passage outcomes.

Ragusa's (2009) work in this area focuses on the implications of bicameral reconciliation for the ability of the majority party to exert positive agenda control. He asserts that, given a cartel-based theory of congressional organization, any legislative sequence that results in a reconciliation process, either through intercameral shuttling or conference committee, results in a suboptimal outcome for the majority party. This innovative hypothesis is in clear opposition to the model proposed by Brady (2008) and the assumptions underlying much of the literature with regard to conference committee appointments. Like Levmore's earlier work, a counterintuitive implication of this novel argument is that conference committees can functionally limit the influence of agenda setters.

Looking at the implications of failures in post-passage bargaining, Ryan (2011) provides a crucial commentary of many underlying models of congressional organization (i.e., that legislation is the result of negotiation among rational actors). In a model bounded by the most basic economic assumptions that bargaining failures do not occur, their unmistakable presence in the empirical world serves to question the most common models of bicameral resolution, and fuel further research and theorization. By emphasizing outcomes where neither side wins, Ryan is filling in the other part of the literature staked out in the initial wave of conference committee work. His work is also significant for its utilization of intracameral differences to provide a theoretical framework and testable hypotheses for when such failures will occur, which is a useful and important extension of the current academic writings.

Magleby (2008) poses an interesting challenge to the trends of bicameral negotiation literature that first arose during the second wave, the exogenous nature of the use of conference committees. Magleby assumes that the actors affect whether or not a conference committee is used, and therefore exert some influence over the legislative sequence. Magleby proposes a model to account for this, in which the pivotal legislators in each chamber, rather than institutional or powerful partisan figures, are able to influence the nature of policy change. There are clear parallels to Krehbiel's critique of the work of Shepsle and Weingast; both are proposed models of congressional organization that discount the role of the party and challenge the status quo conception of the role and importance of conference committees.

Finally, Vander Wielen's (2010a) model of strategic decision-making by congressional actors relies on literature discussed in the preceding section about the process of conference committee appointments and the expected policy shifts from post-passage bargaining. He contends that conditional upon certain preferences and information, both chambers can capture gains from policy changes by the strategic appointment of delegates given their individual preferences. This work builds upon Krehbiel's criticisms of the exogenous power of jurisdictional and conference committees, echoing his sentiments about the ability of the parent chambers to utilize mechanisms to limit or manipulate conference outcomes.

## New Directions in Bicameral Resolution Research

A common theme of the preceding three sections is that research on bicameral resolution, though rigorous and fruitful, has historically been viewed as largely tangential to the main body of research on congressional politics. This needs to change; below I will suggest both why and how.

First, the "why." The bicameral characteristic of the U.S. Congress has long been underappreciated. That is, as little attention as bicameral resolution has received relative to other features of congressional politics, the more general implications of Congress's bicameral structure have received even less. The dominant theories of Congress have been almost entirely myopic, focusing only on a single chamber at a time (and, disproportionately, that chamber has been the House).

Recently, however, this myopic tendency has begun to reverse itself. Beyond the research on bicameral resolution, there has been an emerging theoretical and empirical focus on the significance of the dual chamber arrangement (e.g., Lupia and Sin 2007; Gailmard and Hammond n.d.). A move in this direction necessitates the increasing significance of work on bicameral resolution. If the general literature becomes more focused on the interplay and anticipation between the two chambers, bicameral resolution research will, of necessity, be a fixture at its center.

The "how" is twofold. First, scholars in this area simply need to maintain a continued research program. Conference committee research has largely seen scholars moonlight on this topic, but none have sustained an ongoing program of research on bicameral resolution. If the topic is to make headway as a central part of the congressional literature this has to change. Perhaps one justification for this transient scholarly interest, however, is that often the topic has appeared to be quite limited and narrow. This, however, is at least partly a limitation of the single-chamber-centric theories that have historically defined the literature; where a given chamber defines the theoretical universe, interactions between the chambers will always be, at best, a secondary consideration. However, assuming congressional theories continue to broaden in their scope (as I suspect they will) to include both chambers as equally important theoretical components, bicameral resolution research might naturally move to the forefront. Under such circumstances, being a dedicated "bicameral resolution" specialist would become a much more attractive, sustainable option.

The second part of the "how," though, depends much less on the context of the broader congressional literature, but instead is a function of the specific structure of the current bicameral resolution literature. At the moment, unfortunately, most of the work on bicameral resolution is hopelessly fragmented and does not build upon prior research in the same way as other areas of legislative politics research. Scholars have focused on one part of the process—appointments, outcomes, or choice of method—without attempting to integrate those processes into a coherent whole or develop theoretical models to account for individual or collective decisions during legislative reconciliation. This oversight contributes significantly to the perception that this literature is narrow or limited.

Despite this, these processes are almost certainly strategically interrelated. For instance, how does the chambers' selection of delegates influence policy outcomes? How does the pool of available delegates influence the choice of resolution method? Do outcomes vary systematically, based on which method of selection is used? Each of these questions lurks in the most recent literature, but to answer them bridges must be built between the questions being addressed.

Indeed, when one steps back and views it with a slightly larger perspective, a unified theoretical framework not only seems desirable, it is absolutely essential. Simply imagine the vantage point of the Speaker or majority leader who has just seen an important piece of legislation pass their chamber in a form quite different from that of the other chamber. How will the leader decide which direction to steer the resolution process? The simplest sequence seems likely to go something like this. The leader might ask: (1) what is the best possible conference delegation I could plausibly send? (2) what is the likely outcome of the conference under that condition? (3) what is the likely outcome under an amendment trading scenario (or some other method)? and (4) how certain can I be of any of these outcomes? Notice that within that sequence, all of the components of the most recent literature are present: appointments, outcomes, and choice of resolution method. Working towards a theoretical framework that incorporates all these disparate elements into a single theoretical model seems like a useful next step for students of legislative politics.

## Conclusion: Unanswered Questions

Over the last four decades, scholars have begun, in fits and starts, shedding light on a key feature of congressional policymaking: bicameral resolution. However, recent research on the topic has become more sustained, broadening the base and increasing the depth of inquiry. Still, there are many more questions to be answered by scholars who seek to make a name for themselves in the area of post-passage politics. I propose several new directions for legislative scholars here.

First, how does bicameral resolution differ in the Senate? Virtually all of the prior literature focuses on the House, which means there is inevitably some catching up to do in the Senate. Moreover, it seems absolutely essential to understand the strategic context of the Senate, as compared to the House, if we are to better understand the interplay between the two chambers. Moreover, as work on the Senate becomes more theoretically formal (see, e.g., Den Hartog and Monroe 2011), extending those theories to include the conference stage is a natural next step in our understanding of bicameral politics.

Second, what goes on inside of a conference committee? Though scholars have taken a before-and-after approach to figure out what changes are made in conference, there has been very little systematic work on what the bargaining process is within a conference (cf. Hennig 1997). Not only is the question inherently interesting, it has major implications for the strategic processes that lead up to a conference; appointments and "instructions," for example, will almost certainly be shaped in part by what happens within the conference, yet we know virtually nothing about that environment. This gap in our understanding is primarily a result of a lack of sources that systematically report what happens in conference. Yet, with appropriate coding schemes, scholars could use secondary accounts available in Congressional Quarterly Almanac and other sources to capture the process and substance of bargaining inside conference.

Finally, how and how much do extra-legislative actors influence bicameral resolution? The obvious starting point in addressing this question is to better understand how, when, and with what effect the president and other administration actors intervene in conference negotiations. But, the question also implies investigation well beyond the White House. Do interest groups, bureaucrats, or even constituents inform bicameral negotiation, both in terms of the choice of method and the substance of its resolution? Addressing these and other questions has the potential to push congressional scholarship in new and interesting directions and, perhaps more importantly, further illuminate a process that has significant consequences for the formation of public policy.

## Notes

1 The author wishes to thank W. Bryce Underwood and Randall Collett for extremely valuable research assistance, and acknowledge Josh Ryan and Jordan Ragusa for providing data.
2 Most of the details for this anecdote are drawn from CQ Almanac Online (2003).
3 The latter stood to benefit from targeted subsidies for corn-based ethanol.
4 Note, however, that each chamber can send "instructions" to conference, either before the conference report has been received or while it is being negotiated.
5 For an excellent, in-depth discussion of the procedures involved in these two methods, see Rybicki (2008). This section is based heavily on information provided in that report.
6 Note that amendment trading, as discussed here, is *not* meant to refer to the informal process that sometimes occurs *prior* to passage of a bill in one chamber, where interested members of each chamber formulate amendments prior to passage that would make the bills identical and thus avoid the need for a formal bicameral resolution process.

7  In practice, one chamber often works on legislation simultaneous to the other chamber. Once the bill is passed by the first chamber and passed on to the second chamber, the second chamber then will simply amend the bill by striking the entire language and substituting in the language of their own bill.

8  Some of the data for this table was generously provided, separately, by Jordan Ragusa and Josh Ryan.

9  The actual distribution of influence between committee and party leaders over the final makeup of the delegation has been the subject of considerable scholarly debate, as discussed later in the chapter.

10  Earlier work by both McCown (1927) and Steiner (1951) focuses directly on conference committees, though both are largely descriptive accounts.

11  Ortega and McQuillan (1996), though writing in a later period, deserve brief mention here as their work is instructive for its incisive analysis and extension of this first wave of conference committee literature. Their article provides an excellent literature review of the majority of early writing with regard to conference committees, but extends the theme of that period substantively. The latter contribution is discussed in more detail below.

Part IV

# The Policymaking Process

# Chapter 10

# Congress and the Executive
## Unilateralism and Legislative Bargaining

*Bryan W. Marshall*

*Yes we can* was the campaign message Barack Obama rode to electoral victory in 2008. But it could have just as easily served to describe his governing strategy once he took the reins of the presidency. Like his immediate predecessors, President Obama asserted unilateral powers, early and often. In the first week alone, he issued executive orders effecting change to a wide spectrum of domestic and international policies. The new president further cemented his power within the White House by appointing several policy czars who would administer and shape key priorities of his agenda, such as health care, energy and environment, and economic policy. Although the president set out to bring about policy change from the previous administration, he would do so with the same inclination toward unilateralism.[1] It seems that the assertive style of executive unilateralism characteristic of recent presidencies is here to stay (Barilleaux and Kelley 2010).

Obama's historic election also delivered unified control of Congress, with a large and relatively cohesive majority-party coalition, an asset largely unmatched by any of his Democratic predecessors in recent memory. Moreover, his White House was carefully designed to produce the most effective congressional relations of any executive staff in modern times (Friel and Young 2010). Obama's senior team of advisors possessed levels of experience and connections with Congress that previous administrations would almost certainly envy.[2] The depth and legislative know-how of his inner circle seemed to pay dividends in his first year.

In addition to Obama's presidency reflecting many unique firsts, his first-year accomplishments with Congress are historic by modern standards. His level of success in Congress (96.7 percent) was the highest of any president since *Congressional Quarterly* began tallying presidential victories in 1953 (Zeller 2010). What is more telling is how often President Obama was able to rely almost exclusively on Democrats in the House and Senate to muster winning coalitions. There were only a few instances when Democrats broke from the president. One such instance occurred on the FY 2010 defense authorization bill when House Democrats bucked a presidential veto threat by including funding for F-22 Raptor fighters and the F-35 Joint Strike Fighter.

Subsequently, the Obama Administration split the difference with Congress as the bill he signed into law dropped the F-22 but did include the F-35 authorization. A second notable intra-party fight occurred when Obama issued a signing statement on a supplemental appropriations bill declaring he would ignore congressional provisions that placed funding conditions on the World Bank and the International Monetary Fund.[3] Congressional Democrats were quick to express outrage, sending the Obama Administration a message that Congress would not tolerate the president circumventing its statutory demands when it came to the signing statement.[4]

But the few notable exceptions speak to the rule that, by and large, the Obama Administration was able to get what it needed from Democratic coalitions in Congress. The trend toward increasing party loyalty of the president's party in Congress has become an increasingly important characteristic of congressional-executive interactions. The long-term trend in the loyalty of co-partisans in Congress on votes where the president takes a clear position is evident from Figures 10.1 and 10.2. Figure 10.1 shows the average House loyalty from 1953–2009 for members of the president's party and the opposition party. The growing separation in average support between members of the president's party and the opposition party is also clearly evident. By 2009, the gap in average support of the president between the two parties is quite remarkable.

Figure 10.2 represents the average levels of Senate loyalty for the same period. The over-time pattern for the Senate reflects a growing gap, but the gap is driven more by the upward trend in the level of support from the president's party.

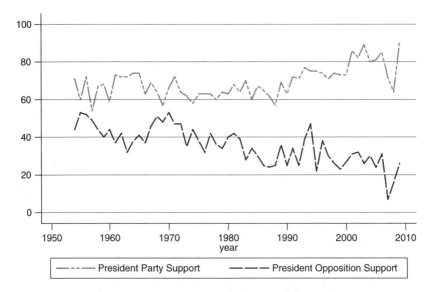

*Figure 10.1* House Average Presidential Support, 1953–2009

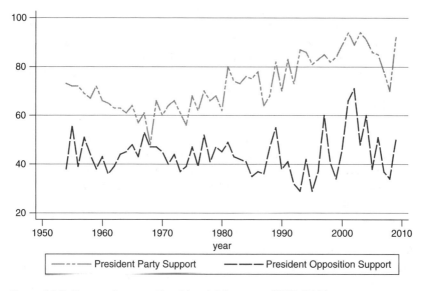

*Figure 10.2* Senate Average Presidential Support, 1953–2009

In 2009 the gap in average support between the parties in the Senate was also relatively large (42 percent), albeit not as big as in the House (64 percent). In addition, 2009 witnessed levels of party loyalty on party unity votes that were at or near all-time highs, especially in the Senate. Senator Landrieu, whose party loyalty score increased by over 20 points between 2008 and 2009, longed for the good old days when moderates could reach out to moderates from the other party saying, "I can only be a centrist if there's a center to hold on to" (Rubin 2010: 124).

Although Obama's early assertion of presidential power and leadership on Capitol Hill was impressive, indeed, this was not the only game in town. "With all due deference to separation of powers" were the unscripted words President Obama used to launch an attack against the Supreme Court during his second State of the Union Address. He went on to criticize the Court's decision in *Citizens United v. FEC*, implying that the conservative majority opinion ignored long-standing legal precedents and Congress's bipartisan attempt at campaign finance reform in order to unbridle corporate interests seeking to shape federal elections. For a few seconds during the presidential address the cameras captured Justice Alito shaking his head and mouthing silent disagreement, but it was clear the justices could do little that night to counter the president's rhetorical stage.[5] President Obama's stinging rebuke represented a preemptive strike to "trim the sails" of a conservative-leaning Court and simultaneously fed his fellow partisans in Congress an issue with populist appeal.

As the dust cleared from this rhetorical challenge to the Court and the president settled into his second year, we are reminded just how important the separation of powers context is to presidential power and the president's ability to carry out an agenda. Not only will the Supreme Court likely decide the fate of President Obama's landmark legislative achievement in health care reform, but the lower federal courts have also actively entered into the political fight, knocking down the president's executive order expanding stem-cell research and the moratorium placed on deep-water oil drilling in the Gulf (Toobin 2010). The framers placed fundamental limits on the constitutional design of separate institutions sharing powers—no one institution possesses a monopoly on power. Even without the added angst associated with separated powers, President Truman would wryly remark on the presidency, "Do this, do that, and nothing will happen" (Neustadt 1962: 9). Thus, having powers is no guarantee of exercising power.

On Capitol Hill, the president's policy fortunes during year two have changed. For one, Obama's agenda and party majorities were under siege by congressional Republicans who launched their campaign manifesto, "A Pledge to America." The pledge vows to rein in "an arrogant and out-of-touch government of self-appointed elites" and would repeal and replace Obama's prize health care reform law as well as cancel unspent funds from the "wasteful and unnecessary" stimulus bill.[6] And even within his own party, the president has had to pay a substantial cost to forge legislative victories, with party leaders having to lean heavily on both ends of the Democratic caucus to deliver the president's policy initiatives. In addition, the president's ability to persuade has eroded as his approval ratings have sunk and at this stage hover well below the 50 percent mark.[7]

The 2010 midterm elections have certainly added to the difficulty of building coalitions among nervous Democratic allies in Congress. For example, in September the Senate Democrats were unable to muster the votes necessary to bring a defense spending bill to the floor with a provision allowing the military to repeal the Don't Ask Don't Tell (DADT) policy. Unable to secure passage of this campaign promise, the Obama Administration was left with an unenviable and costly set of options. A federal Court has ruled DADT unconstitutional placing the Obama Administration's Justice Department in the position of defending a policy the president does not agree with. The president could order his Justice Department not to defend the DADT policy—thus allowing the lower Court's ruling to stand. The president could also issue an executive order. These options might or might not resonate with the broader public, but would inevitably carry significant costs by energizing an already fired up Republican base. For the moment, the president has decided to pursue a future legislative repeal of DADT—but even this will be more difficult in all likelihood given the large losses Democrats suffered from the 2010 midterm elections.

President Obama's struggles with Congress highlight a common lesson that all presidents inevitably learn—support in Congress tends to be highly uncertain, costly, and fleeting even among members of the president's party. Absent the ability to cajole Congress, presidents can win their share of policy battles with the veto or by circumventing the legislative process altogether through unilateral action (Mayer 2001; Howell 2003). But as this brief perusal shows, a president's degree of success in exercising power can change dramatically over a brief period of time. Even powers exercised through unilateral action can be subject to challenge in the separation of powers context. Presidents can't control outcomes, only the decisions they make, and each decision can affect their subsequent ability to exercise power (Neustadt 1962).

This chapter is designed to reflect upon a research agenda that might hold future insights for congressional-executive relations. The breadth and depth of work in this area is striking. In order to narrow the parameters, the focus is on the surging literature dealing with presidential unilateralism and the work on veto bargaining, which is nested within the broader bargaining and persuasion paradigm. The theme is designed to elicit greater scholarly focus on the intersection of these two literatures. All too often, quantitative analyses view presidential power as if it emanates from completely separate sources, leaving the two literatures somewhat isolated from each other. However, the view taken here suggests that future research should focus on how these areas might be interconnected and fit together to explain complementary puzzles of presidential power.

Next, the discussion offers a brief overview of this literature and sketches out a template for evaluating the relationship between Congress and the president. The argument underscores the important intersection of these two literatures by assessing the linkage between the use of presidential veto threats and the constitutional signing statement in the context of veto bargaining. The analysis illustrates temporal patterns in the use of the veto threat and constitutional signing statement, especially on appropriations legislation. Appropriations legislation has served as a major venue for perennial policy battles between Congress and the president (Kiewiet and McCubbins 1991). Moreover, the analysis from a subset of appropriations bills illustrates the efficacy of the veto threat. The findings show that Congress usually offers at least some concessions in the face of presidential veto threats. But when Congress does not concede to executive demands, the president is inclined to issue a constitutional signing statement. There is evidence that the signing statement can provide presidents with a "last mover advantage" once veto bargaining with Congress comes to an end (Kelley and Marshall 2009). In this way, the analysis shows how the president's unilateral and bargaining power could be linked to achieve the president's policy and political goals.

## Seeing the Forest through the Trees: Bargaining and Unilateralism

As the first branch, the framers made Congress the foundation of the Republic (Mann and Ornstein 2006). With the legislative branch at the forefront, it is no surprise that Congress's constitutional powers are quite formidable as compared to the other branches. Article I makes Congress the unequivocal law-making body, granting it an immense horizon over the making of all laws necessary and proper for carrying out its constitutionally prescribed powers. And among other significant powers, Congress can initiate amendments to the Constitution as well as impeach and remove from office members of the executive and judicial branches. In contrast, the powers granted to the executive and judicial branches were far less significant. Even the president's most notable legislative power—the veto—carries a notable caveat, being subject to congressional override.

Within the separation of powers system, chief executives have many advantages over their legislative counterparts, especially their adeptness at leveraging powers from constitutional ambiguity (Fatovic 2004). Moreover, the prevalence of Congress's inability to overcome collective action has left a power void that the president has effectively filled (Moe and Howell 1999; Fisher 2000; Meernik and Oldmixon 2008; Marshall and Haney 2010). Although Congress's once dominant role in exercising federal authority has largely given way to presidential government, presidents remain significantly constrained by the original constitutional formulation that placed Congress atop the separation of powers. It was the institutional limitations of the executive that marked Neustadt's seminal work five decades ago on presidential power—a central theme that gives sharp relief to the bargaining paradigm.

Neustadt (1962) significantly framed the way in which much of the literature approaches explanations of presidential power. His perspective argued that a president's power was rooted in the power to persuade and that power comes directly through bargaining with other political actors. The personal influence of the president overlaid and inherently affected all other power relationships of the presidency. Although the president's formal constitutional powers are substantial, they leave the president precariously dependent upon his personal ability to leverage the goodwill of others to achieve his ends.

In contrast to this traditional view of presidential power, there is a growing literature that emphasizes the president's reliance on unilateral action to make policy on his own. This theory of presidential power emanates from the ambiguity of Article II and the inherent institutional advantages the president enjoys over other political actors (Moe and Howell 1999). Presidential unilateralism differs from other perspectives in that it emphasizes the president's ability to act first, and act alone. In this view, presidents can employ unilateral action to establish a new policy status quo that other institutions might be unable, or because of political constraints, unwilling to change. Work in this area has shown that presidential unilateralism has taken a variety of forms such as the use of executive orders, executive agreements, proclamations, recess appointments, and signing statements (Moe and Howell 1999; Mayer 2001; Krutz and Peake 2010; Rottinghaus and Maier 2007; Black et al. 2007; Cooper 2002). As such, the president's ability to exercise unilateral tools frees him from the need of cooperation, thus the power derived from their use is largely independent of his ability to persuade others (Howell 2005).

Indeed, there is a tension that colors these two literatures. Some argue that presidential unilateralism directly challenges Neustadt's bargaining and persuasion framework, in that they are very distinct strategies, while others argue that unilateralism simply represents a different context for bargaining to take place (see, for example, Neustadt 1962; Moe and Howell 1999; Howell 2003; Dickinson 2009). The tension in the literature is, at least in part, due to how Neustadt's power by persuasion framework is viewed. For instance, some see Neustadt's personal or president-centered power as largely walled off from powers emanating from the institutional presidency (Moe 2009). For others, the personal presidency is not nearly as distinct from the institutional presidency, as Neustadt quite elegantly recognized in underlining the importance of a president's institutional "vantage points" to achieve goals (Dickinson 2009; Rudalevige 2009). Neustadt's intention seemed to be that the sources of power from the presidency and the president's personal influence were interwoven. A more nuanced view of Neustadt suggests that the many facets of power from the presidency, and thus the decisions a president makes to exercise power, are conditioned in varying degrees on his ability to bargain or persuade.

Although these different views of presidential power are often seen as incompatible, the tension is somewhat overstated. Treating bargaining and unilateralism as exclusive aspects of presidential power does have its benefits, such as sharpening analytical clarity, but at some point it potentially undermines the opportunity to study how presidential decisions in both areas may be linked and complement our broader understanding of presidential power. So, one challenge then is to develop theoretical explanations that tease out the conditions that might make the connections between bargaining and unilateral power stronger or weaker. There has already been a movement underfoot to bring areas of the presidency together that would encourage research to build a more general narrative in explaining presidential power (Waterman 2009). For example, recent work by Canes-Wrone (2009) outlines a research agenda to assess the connection between the public presidency and the administrative presidency. So, the argument here is not unique, as bringing areas of presidential power together from their disparate parts of the literature can pay dividends. The message taken from this is simply to nudge the scholarly focus to exploit the bridge(s) that may connect presidential powers to one-another—to better see the forest through the trees. Next, the discussion moves in this direction by considering the literature on veto bargaining and the president's use of the constitutional signing statement.

## Veto Bargaining and the Constitutional Signing Statement

While there have been significant strides in understanding the presidential veto, it remains a single action in a larger set of strategic behaviors that shapes veto bargaining (Deen and Arnold 2002; Conley 2003). For example, most traditional analyses of veto behavior focus exclusively on the end of the veto bargaining process—the actual veto and/or congressional overrides (see, for example, Rohde and Simon 1985; Hoff 1991; Watson 1993; Gilmour 2002). Cameron's (2000) influential work moved beyond the traditional framework by emphasizing veto chains in understanding inter-branch bargaining. In addition, his theoretical work suggested that presidential rhetoric could have a profound influence on veto bargaining despite the oft-cited principle in political science that "actions speak louder than words" (Matthews 1989; Cameron 2000). The veto threat represents one such rhetorical strategy that presidents can employ to extract concessions from an opposition majority in Congress (Sinclair 2006). Veto threats prove effective bargaining tools because of congressional uncertainty about what policy the president will accept and the anticipation that presidents will use their veto power as tough bargainers.

The game-theoretic literature has significantly added to the collective understanding of veto politics. Groseclose and McCarty (2001) add the element of audience costs to veto bargaining known as "blame-game" politics. The idea is that when the president uses a veto, his policy preferences can be viewed as more extreme to the public and his approval ratings can drop accordingly. Because presidents do not want to bear the public costs of a veto, they might be more inclined to make extensive concessions to Congress. In addition, commitment and coordination models have been utilized in the literature to extend the veto process to include veto threats. These models show how the threat can add to the president's bargaining power. Veto threats can provide valuable information to avoid confrontations across institutions. But veto threats can also impose considerable costs (constraints) when presidents do not follow through on such commitments.

The formal literature's emphasis on sequence and anticipatory behavior enhances understanding into the mechanisms of influence enjoyed by Congress and the president (Dietz 2002). For example, Cameron's work integrates the role of presidential reputation in understanding the president's veto power (2000). Cameron utilizes game-theoretic models to illustrate important sources of the veto power known as the three faces of power. In a setting of complete information, the president derives power—the first face of power—from the fact that Congress knows the president has the capability to veto any proposal (ex-post power). The second face of power stems from Congress's perfect anticipation of what policies the president will and will not accept. Cameron integrates presidential reputation to illustrate the third face of power in veto politics. In effect, the president's reputation as a tough bargainer—his willingness to veto—shapes congressional expectations and makes Congress more likely to make concessions in the bargaining game.[8]

Even more, there are different contexts in which to consider the influence of the veto threat. Conley's (2003) work emphasizes the importance of veto threats that are privately transmitted in stopping congressional policy. His findings suggest that private threats can be more effective than public threats in terms of providing the president with significant negative agenda power. Veto threats can also be used as a positive bargaining tool. From this perspective, veto threats transmit the president's intentions and preferences regarding a particular bill. This type of signaling to Congress can reduce uncertainty and make gains from cooperation with Congress possible (Matthews 1989; Cameron, Lapinski, and Riemann 2000).

The analysis conducted by Deen and Arnold develops an explanation of veto threat behavior (2002). Their argument focuses on conditions that affect the likelihood of policy conflict between Congress and the president related to such factors as the legislative environment and presidential resources. They find considerable supportive evidence for their argument. For example, their study illustrates that both legislative salience and approval levels affect the likelihood of veto threats as well as prior threat activity and the policy-type of particular bills. Certainly, this literature has been very important in both characterizing the nature of the president's power (both positive and negative) that results from threats as well as explaining veto threat behavior.

There is a growing literature on the importance of presidential unilateralism that tends to assess the use of various tools the president can use to affect policy on his own. Unlike the executive order, the signing statement does not assume the force of law but does become part of a bill's legislative history. Some signing statements are used as rhetorical opportunities to claim credit or criticize opponents of legislation. The constitutional signing statements reflect quite different purposes. The constitutional type of signing statement is designed to shape policy implementation, defend or establish precedent for presidential prerogatives, or to halt the enforcement of statutory provisions the president deems unconstitutional (Kelley and Marshall 2010). The constitutional signing statement remained largely out of the public eye until the George W. Bush Administration's aggressive use of the tool sparked considerable media attention. The most visible event occurred when President Bush issued a constitutional signing statement upon signing a FY 2006 defense appropriations bill. The bill reflected months of painstaking negotiations especially around a provision championed by Senator McCain that outlawed torture by the United States.[9] The more controversial elements of the constitutional signing statement basically declared the provisions affecting torture to be at the discretion of the unitary executive.

The signing statement has been largely overshadowed in the literature by other more prominent tools of presidential unilateralism. Cooper's work was one of a few notable exceptions (see Cooper 2002, 2005; Kelley 2003). Cooper's (2005) analysis suggested that the George W. Bush Administration employed the signing statement as a line-item veto to shape specific policy provisions and broaden the scope of presidential prerogative largely at the expense of Congress. However, the work on signing statements has recently become more visible in the literature (Berry 2009; Pfiffner 2009). Kelley and Marshall (2008) have argued that the constitutional signing statement provides the president with a "last mover advantage" in shaping policy at the end of veto bargaining.[10] The idea is that the signing statement allows the president a final opportunity to target certain provision(s) of the bill that he was unable (or unwilling) to change during prior bargaining with Congress. In this way, the constitutional signing statement could be used to move legislation closer to the president's preferred position and/or offer an interpretation on legislation that maximizes his prerogatives and discretion in implementation (Kelley and Marshall 2008).

The work on veto threats highlights its potential utility in terms of a president's *positive* power—his ability to gain concessions from Congress in legislative bargaining or as a signal to use the veto in order to protect the policy status quo (negative power). But there is a relative paucity of empirical analysis on the efficacy of the veto threat. The evidence that does exist in the legislative bargaining literature suggests that presidential veto threats do not always result in the vetoing of a bill (Cameron 2000; Conley 2004; Sinclair 2006). In fact, when Congress makes at least some concessions to presidential demands, Cameron finds that the majority of the time presidents do not follow through with a veto. Moreover, Cameron's analysis utilizes a limited sample of major legislation and found that Congress does make policy concessions (about 90 percent of the time) following a presidential veto threat (2000: 188). Nevertheless, we do not know the extent to which Congress might concede on other types of legislation.

Conley's (2004) work represents another exception focusing on the legislative outcomes resulting from President Clinton's veto behavior during the 104th–106th Congresses. His work not only illustrates the importance of the changing legislative context, but also President Clinton's success in employing the veto to thwart Republican initiatives and garner policy concessions, especially in the context of appropriations legislation (2004: 142–6). Sinclair (2006: 245–50) also looks at the rise of veto threats over time. When presidents take policy positions, she finds that Congress usually moves policy closer to the president and always does so when there is a veto threat. It has been argued here that the constitutional signing statement could play an important role in these types of situations. Although presidents tend to get what they need in legislative compromises, Congress rarely concedes completely to presidential demands. This provides presidents with an incentive to use the constitutional signing statement at the end of veto bargaining to move the policy closer to the president's preferred position—the "last mover advantage" referred to earlier.

## Descriptive Evidence

The following empirical analysis examines patterns in the use of the veto threat and the constitutional signing statement from the 99th (1985–86) to the 110th Congress (2007–08). The analysis looks at how frequently these tools are used together on the same legislative proposals. If presidents do utilize the constitutional signing statement as a mechanism to affect change in legislation at the end of bargaining, then there should be evidence of veto threats and constitutional signing statements that tend to occur together on the same legislation. Appropriations legislation has taken center-stage in the veto bargaining battles between the president and Congress in recent years (Kiewiet and McCubbins 1991). Because of the must-pass nature of the appropriations legislation, Congress often strategically places legislative riders and conflict-prone provisions that could not pass on their own as a way to force presidential acquiescence in bargaining (Conley 2004). As such, the analysis also looks at the use of these presidential tools on the subset of appropriations legislation during this period.

Additionally, the analysis offers a limited assessment on the efficacy of the veto threat in legislative bargaining. In particular, I examine the efficacy of veto threats by comparing differences in Congress's response—whether or not Congress acquiesced on appropriations bills—when the president signals a veto threat as compared to simply voicing his opposition to the legislation. As a result, the analysis is designed to assess the relationship between the veto threat and the constitutional signing statement—two very different presidential strategies in the context of veto bargaining. By doing so, the analysis seeks to illuminate how the intersection of unilateralism and bargaining might be linked and thus offer a broader understanding of how presidential decisions to use such tools can fit together in achieving the president's policy and political ends.

The data on veto threats comes from Professor Samuel Kernell's coding that lists all bills receiving veto threats for the 99th–108th Congresses.[11] The 109th and 110th Congresses were added by following Kernell's coding rules. The veto threat is a dichotomous variable that registers whether or not the president decided to issue a veto threat on a bill. The veto threat data are coded from Statements of Administration Policies (SAPs). SAPs represent written statements detailing the president's position (or that of his cabinet) on bills that are about to be debated on the floor of Congress. SAPs not only contain veto threats, but can also voice varying degrees of opposition to the bill or support of the bill.[12] SAPs are compiled by the Office of Management and Budget and usually sent to the House, House Rules Committee, or to the Senate. The early predecessor of the SAP—called budget circulars—became institutionalized after the passage of the Budget and Accounting Act of 1921 (Neustadt 1954). SAPs are now widely used and provide the president with a formal opportunity to register his views on bills before Congress. However, there has been little empirical work that employs SAPs to test theories of presidential influence or congressional-executive bargaining (see, for example, Evans and Ng 2006).

The information on the constitutional signing statements comes from signing statement data compiled by Kelley and Marshall (see for example Kelley and Marshall 2009). The constitutional signing statement variable is also a simple dichotomous indicator that captures whether or not the president issued a constitutional statement with respect to a particular bill. There are two basic types of presidential signing statements, constitutional and rhetorical. The constitutional signing statements differ from the rhetorical types in that the constitutional statements contain at least one constitutional challenge designed to protect and/or enhance presidential prerogatives. In contrast, the rhetorical statements tend to reward supporters, praise the bill, or are otherwise characterized by credit claiming.[13]

Table 10.1 shows the relative use of the presidential veto threat and constitutional signing statement on all bills that became law from 1985–2008. Column two of the table indicates the number of bills by Congress that became law. The total number of bills that became law during this period was 6,184. The third and fourth columns represent the percentage of bills becoming law that received either a veto threat or constitutional signing statement. Overall, column three suggests that presidents use the veto threat sparingly, as only a little over 3 percent of laws were passed that were threatened with the veto.[14] Column four provides a glimpse at the relative use of the constitutional signing statement. The data show that presidents attach the constitutional signing statement on over 6 percent of laws. The last column of the table allows an assessment of how frequently the veto threat and constitutional signing statement are used on the same piece of legislation. Here, the percentages are calculated from the use of veto threats and represent the percentage of veto threats that also had a constitutional signing statement attached. The patterns reflect a sizable degree of overlap between the use of veto threats and constitutional signing statements. When presidents issued a veto threat on these bills, they also quite frequently attached a constitutional signing statement—in fact, over 43 percent of the

Table 10.1 Use of Veto Threats and Constitutional Signing Statements, 99th–110th Congresses

| Congress | Bills Passed | % Bills Passed with Veto Threat | % Bills Passed with CSS | % Veto Threats with CSS |
|---|---|---|---|---|
| 99th (1985–86) Reagan | 661 | 1.2 | 4.2 | 25.0 |
| 100th (1987–88) Reagan | 710 | 5.1 | 4.2 | 22.2 |
| 101st (1989–90) Bush I | 647 | 3.9 | 8.7 | 52.0 |
| 102nd (1991–92) Bush I | 589 | 5.4 | 11.5 | 56.2 |
| 103rd (1993–94) Clinton | 463 | 0 | 2.8 | 0 |
| 104th (1995–96) Clinton | 332 | 3.3 | 4.2 | 45.5 |
| 105th (1997–98) Clinton | 393 | 8.9 | 5.1 | 22.9 |
| 106th (1999–00) Clinton | 577 | 2.8 | 5.4 | 31.3 |
| 107th (2001–02) Bush II | 376 | 2.1 | 10.4 | 75.0 |
| 108th (2003–04) Bush II | 498 | 1.4 | 9.4 | 100.0 |
| 109th (2005–06) Bush II | 481 | 3.5 | 7.1 | 94.1 |
| 110th (2007–08) Bush II | 457 | 3.5 | 1.3 | 18.8 |
| Total | 100% (N = 6,184) | 3.4% (N = 211) | 6.2% (N = 381) | 43.1% (N = 91) |

time for the entire period. This provides some initial evidence of the last mover advantage. Presidents do seem to employ veto threats and the constitutional signing statement to get what they want in veto bargaining.

Table 10.2 allows for a similar comparison in the use of veto threats and constitutional signing statements but focuses on appropriations legislation—a critical subset of bills that tend to be important for understanding veto bargaining battles between Congress and the president (Kiewiet and McCubbins 1991; Conley 2004). Like the earlier table, the second column of Table 10.2 indicates the number of spending bills that became law by Congress—a total of 595 bills for the entire period. One pattern that stands out from this table as compared to the previous one is the relatively prevalent use of the veto threat and constitutional signing statement on the subset of spending bills. Indeed, presidents issued veto threats on nearly 18 percent of the spending bills in this series—nearly six times the rate as compared to all laws from the previous table. In addition, column four shows that the spending bills attract constitutional signing statements 25 percent of the time. The last column reveals a similar pattern in the combined use of these tools—namely, when presidents issue veto

*Table 10.2* Use of Veto Threats and Constitutional Signing Statements on Appropriations Legislation, 99th–110th Congresses

| Congress | Appropriations Bills Passed | % Appropriations with Veto Threats | % Appropriations with CSS | % Veto Threats with CSS |
|---|---|---|---|---|
| 99th (1985–86) Reagan | 54 | 3.7 | 14.8 | 50 |
| 100th (1987–88) Reagan | 64 | 23.4 | 17.2 | 26.7 |
| 101st (1989–90) Bush I | 75 | 16.0 | 32.0 | 66.7 |
| 102nd (1991–92) Bush I | 81 | 20.9 | 33.3 | 58.8 |
| 103rd (1993–94) Clinton | 66 | 0 | 15.2 | 0 |
| 104th (1995–96) Clinton | 42 | 19.0 | 14.3 | 37.5 |
| 105th (1997–98) Clinton | 48 | 37.5 | 18.8 | 38.9 |
| 106th (1999–2000) Clinton | 59 | 13.6 | 18.6 | 37.5 |
| 107th (2001–02) Bush II | 31 | 16.1 | 38.7 | 80.0 |
| 108th (2003–04) Bush II | 27 | 11.1 | 44.4 | 100 |
| 109th (2005–06) Bush II | 23 | 47.8 | 60.9 | 100 |
| 110th (2007–08) Bush II | 25 | 28.0 | 20.0 | 57.1 |
| Total | 100% (N = 595) | 17.8% (N = 106) | 25.0% (N = 149) | 54.7% (N = 58) |

threats on spending bills they are followed by the constitutional signing statement a clear majority of the time (54.7 percent). Thus, Tables 10.1 and 10.2 appear to reflect a considerable degree of overlap in the use of veto threats and the constitutional signing statement. And on spending bills where congressional-executive bargaining tends to be widespread, the analysis shows that when presidents issue the veto threat, they have more frequently than not employed the constitutional signing statement as well. This suggests further support for the last mover argument and that the constitutional signing statement might be part of a broader strategy presidents use to affect legislative outcomes.

However, this raises an important question about whether or not veto threats actually yield legislative concessions in the veto bargaining process, a puzzle that has received little attention in the literature (Cameron 2000; Conley 2004; Sinclair 2006). Assessing the effects of veto threats on all legislation or even on all the spending bills would be a challenging undertaking that goes beyond the scope of this analysis. But the data in the next table probes this question for a subset of the appropriations bills from recent congresses.

Table 10.3 offers one small piece of evidence that reflects on the efficacy of the veto threat and the use of the constitutional signing statement. If the veto threat does play a significant role in the context of bargaining, then there should be evidence indicating their influence on policies passed by Congress. In particular, Congress should be more likely to make concessions on bills with explicit veto threats as compared to bills that receive less severe signals such as when the president simply voices opposition to legislation. Table 10.3 provides a limited assessment at this question using the appropriations bills from the 107th, 108th, and 109th Congresses. The table highlights two categories. One category reflects the subset of spending bills that received a presidential veto threat. As before, the threats are coded from the SAPs. In addition though, the table

Table 10.3 Presidential Veto Threats and Congress's Response on Appropriations, 107th–109th Congresses*

| Appropriations Outcome | SAP Signaled Veto Threat | SAP Signaled Opposition | Row Total |
|---|---|---|---|
| Congress Moves Bill Closer to President | 91.3% (n = 21) [CSS = 7] | 67.8% (n = 19) [CSS = 8] | 78.4% (n = 40) |
| Congress Does Not Move Bill Closer to President | 8.7% (n = 2) [CSS = 2] | 32.2% (n = 9) [CSS = 8] | 21.6% (n = 11) |
| Column Totals | 100% (n = 23) | 100% (n = 28) | 100% (n = 51) |

Note
* Data on outcomes is incomplete. There were seventeen bills in which there was not sufficient information to determine whether or not the outcome favored the president.

categorizes the subset of spending bills to which the president voiced opposition as coded from the SAP, but not an explicit veto threat. As such, the two categories reflect bills to which the president expressed varying degrees of opposition.

To establish whether or not Congress made concessions on this subset of spending bills, I searched and coded information from articles in *Congressional Quarterly* (CQ). CQ provides extensive coverage on the appropriations process and the specific spending bills. The coding captures whether or not there was any evidence that Congress made a concession(s) to any objection(s) the president raised in the SAP. If there was any evidence of a concession by Congress, the bill was coded to reflect that Congress moved the policy closer to the president's position. This is obviously a very blunt and incomplete indicator regarding the efficacy of a veto threat or the president's signaling of opposition to a bill.[15] But the table does show that Congress was more likely to make concessions on bills with a veto threat as compared to bills that receive an SAP signaling the president's milder level of opposition.

The comparison in Table 10.3 between columns two and three reflects the difference in the effects of veto threats vs. presidential opposition on spending bills. The patterns show that on over 91 percent of the appropriations bills with veto threats, there was evidence that Congress made at least one concession to the president. In contrast, evidence of concessions was much lower—occurring 68 percent of the time—on the subset of appropriations bills that received an SAP with milder signals of presidential opposition. Although very limited, this evidence suggests that the veto threat is a very effective tool in extracting legislative concessions from Congress.

The table contains one last piece of information that speaks to the possible role of the constitutional signing statement in veto bargaining. The number of spending bills is recorded in the parentheses for each category of the table. Below the parentheses there are brackets containing the number of constitutional signing statements attached to the spending bills in each category. For example, the brackets in the second column reflect that there were seven constitutional signing statements attached to spending bills with veto threats where Congress made concessions and two attached to bills with veto threats where Congress made no concessions to the president. The obvious pattern seen earlier in the analysis was that a relatively large number of spending bills provoke a constitutional signing statement. The less obvious pattern to note is to compare the rows of the table. The first row reflects categories where there was evidence of congressional concessions while the second row reflects categories where there was no evidence that Congress gave in to presidential demands. With only one exception, the second row reveals that when Congress does not acquiesce, presidents almost always respond with a constitutional signing statement. There is not enough data from the table to make systematic claims, but the limited evidence here does suggest that the constitutional signing statement might play an important role at the end of veto bargaining. In effect, the constitutional signing statement might allow the president to extract policy advantages on must-pass legislation—such as on spending bills where further concessions might have been impossible to achieve or are prohibitively costly during the bargaining process.

## Conclusion

The veto is the most widely recognized tool the president has in his arsenal of legislative powers. However, it might be that the most significant advantage of the veto is not as a weapon of last resort in stopping undesirable bills, but instead results from the veto threat bringing Congress to the bargaining table (Cronin 1975; Deen and Arnold 2002). Unfortunately, the veto threat has received considerably less systematic analysis as compared to the presidential veto.

This analysis has taken a few small steps toward describing temporal patterns in the use of veto threats and how such strategies might foster the use of the constitutional signing statement. The analysis shows that veto threats occur relatively sparingly on legislation enacted into law between the years 1985–2008. But, the veto threat is employed more frequently on appropriations bills. The comparison exemplifies the important role the appropriations process plays in the veto bargaining battles between Congress and the president (Conley 2004). The analysis from recent Congresses demonstrated the efficacy of veto threats as a bargaining tool. Indeed, Congress conceded, at least to some extent, to presidential demands on over 90 percent of the bills that evoked veto threats. When presidents signaled milder levels of opposition, the proportion of bills with evidence of congressional concessions—although still relatively high—dropped off appreciably (68 percent). Understanding and explaining these patterns in bargaining over spending also has more substantive implications for the balance of power between Congress and the president. Given the centrality of appropriations to Congress's institutional power, if it concedes to presidential demands at such high rates as those found here on spending, it likely does not bode well for congressional primacy in other areas of policy.

In the veto bargaining context presidents often get what they need to avert a veto, especially on must-pass spending legislation. *But getting what they need is not necessarily the same as getting what they want.* This analysis moves beyond the more traditional framework of veto bargaining to consider how presidents can act unilaterally to get what they want by employing the constitutional signing statement. The evidence presented here illustrates that the veto threat is often paired with the constitutional signing statement in the veto bargaining process. When presidents do not get everything they want from Congress, the signing statement provides the president with a last mover advantage to achieve additional policy gains that were not possible or were too costly during the earlier bargaining process (Kelley and Marshall 2008). The constitutional signing statement offers presidents a highly flexible strategy in that it can shape legislative agreements without sacrificing the entire bill and without the costs of issuing a veto.

Over the last twenty years, the remarkable advancements in the study of the presidency have been termed "revolutionary" (Moe 2009). Much of the spark fueling the revolution has come from analyzing how presidents get what they want through the institution and powers of the presidency. The evolving literature has focused less on the president-centered approach and more fully embraced the "New Institutionalism,"[16] which had already profoundly shaped the study of Congress and the courts (Rohde and Spaeth 1976; Shepsle and Weingast 1995). This shift in emphasis toward studying the institutional presidency has been characterized by a prevalence of rational choice-based theories that mine the richness of institutional vantage points to expose multiple factors influencing presidential choices and power (Moe 2009; Mayer 2009).

These important changes have enriched many areas in the literature. For example, the greater institutional focus has shaped the public presidency, which has significantly contributed to understanding presidential rhetoric, its structure and outputs, and its effectiveness on the public and other political actors (Tulis 1987; Kernell 2007; Edwards 2003; Canes-Wrone 2006). Similarly, these changes have spurred the expansion of the administrative presidency to assess how presidents affect the bureaucracy (Nathan 1983; Moe 1985; Waterman 1989; Durant 1992; McCarty 2004). This area has produced valuable insights into a vast array of presidential strategies that shape bureaucratic control (Aberbach and Rockman 2000) and structures within the White House (Rudalevige 2002). The emphasis on institutional structure has also allowed scholars to more fully integrate the study of the presidency into the broader separation of powers system (Krehbiel 1998; Fisher 2000; Cameron 2000; Howell 2003; Brady and Volden 2006).

A lesson to be gleaned from this literature is that the continuing expansion into the separation of powers holds a great deal of promise. More specifically, the discussion in this chapter has argued that both the bargaining and unilateral perspectives have profound implications for understanding congressional-executive relations and broader separation of powers questions (Krehbiel 1998; Cameron 2000; Mayer 2001; Howell 2003). However, there is a tension or tendency in the literature to treat presidential unilateralism and the bargaining framework as distinct spheres from which presidential power emanates. Neustadt's classic work would have us believe there is a rich overlap between the more formal powers of the presidency and bargaining. In fact, Neustadt's case studies of institutional command were notable in that they reflected responses to other failed attempts to achieve presidential ends by "softer means" (Neustadt 1962: 27). The findings from this analysis might represent a similar chain of presidential strategies whereby presidents issue the constitutional signing statement in response to the softer means of veto bargaining with Congress. Indeed, this analysis is one example that highlights the possibility that powers resulting from the unilateral and bargaining frameworks might be more complementary than contradictory.

So what direction(s) should future research take? There remains a paucity of research analyzing the impact of veto bargaining—especially veto threat behavior on legislative outcomes and the implications for the balance of power between Congress and the president (Cameron 2000; Conley 2004; Sinclair 2006). There also is a great deal of work to be done on the role(s) of the signing statement in understanding presidential power, as well as their effects on policy interpretation, bureaucratic implementation, and on the separation of powers relationships (Cooper 2005; Berry 2009; Pfiffner 2009). More work is required on how policy gridlock, political parties, and divided government shape presidential unilateralism (Howell 2003; Mayer 2009). And as the brief overview of President Obama's first two years illustrates, the policy and political fortunes of presidents are significantly shaped by partisan politics in Congress—especially during an era of high partisan polarization. However, there remains a void in the literature regarding the presidency and how it affects (or is affected by) the power of political parties in Congress (Krehbiel 1998; Cox and McCubbins 2005; Smith 2007). The argument advanced in this chapter would also encourage research to consider how presidential unilateralism intersects with congressional-executive bargaining more broadly. Much of the literature has treated presidential unilateralism as a dependent variable to be explained. But the formula offered here takes a different track, one that would emphasize how unilateral powers affect the president's agenda, the policies he chooses to pursue in the legislative realm, and how such choices affect presidential success with Congress.

## Notes

1  Unilateralism reflects the capacity of the president to "go it alone" in order to advance political and policy goals (Moe and Howell 1999).
2  For example, Phil Schiliro, the president's chief legislative liaison worked for over twenty-five years as top aide to Congressman Waxman (D-CA) (Friel and Young 2010). Schiliro has also assembled on his liaison team some of the very best leadership staffers in the business.
3  The signing statement is written presidential commentary on a bill delivered upon its signing (Kelley 2007).
4  Chairman Barney Frank of the House Financial Services Committee warned, "The notion that the administration can take the money and pick and choose what it wants to do with the conditions is unacceptable" (Zeller 2010: 114).
5  Justice Roberts retaliated soon after during a public address suggesting the president's words were "troubling," and that the Court was above the political fray when he said "To the extent the State of the Union has degenerated into a political pep rally, I'm not sure why we're there" (Toobin 2010: 8).
6  "A Pledge to America," http://pledge.gop.gov.
7  At the end of his first year, the president's public approval rating was notable at 49 percent because it tied Ronald Reagan for the lowest Gallup rating for any first-term president elected since WWII (Zeller 2010: 112).
8  The result is not unlike the logic of more general signaling games with incomplete information. For example, one equilibrium outcome in the Beer-Quiche game suggests that wimps will always drink beer for breakfast. Beer-drinking during breakfast makes the wimp look like a surly tough guy which provides the wimp cover against the troublemaker who gets more utility out of beating up wimps (Morrow 1994:

245). In essence, it is the manipulation of opponents' beliefs that illustrate the strategic advantage gained with the third face of power.

 9  Congress was compelled to address the torture issue following the public outcry resonating from abuses of detainees at Abu Ghraib and other prisons under the supervision of the U.S. military.

10  Similarly, Kelley and Marshall (2010) have found evidence that the constitutional signing statement may be used by presidents to shape legislation and achieve policy goals important to their partisans in Congress.

11  Professor Kernell's data on veto threats is publicly available through *Congressional Quarterly* (CQ).

12  It is important to note that the veto threats contained in SAPs do not constitute the entire population of threats. For example, Conley's (2003) work suggests that a significant number of veto threats are privately transmitted. Kernell (2005) has examined public veto threats from news articles, issues of *CQ Weekly*, as well as SAPs, and while he finds considerable overlap among these sources, it is not exhaustive. He does find, however, that SAPs provide greater information on the legislative provisions motivating the threat as compared to the reporting on threats from news articles. Based on this difference, veto threats contained in SAPs do seem to provide useful signals to members of Congress in the veto bargaining context.

13  See Kelley and Marshall (2008) for an extensive discussion on categorizing constitutional and rhetorical signing statements.

14  Although not shown, it is important to note that there were several hundred bills that received a veto threat that never became law. These reflect an important element of the president's negative power but will have to await future analysis.

15  The SAPs usually contain a wide variety of provisions the president opposes. The coding is certainly limited in that it does not ascertain how some provisions might be more important to the president than others. Rather, the simple method captures only when one (of potentially many) concerns raised by the president is addressed by Congress.

16  New institutionalism reflects a renewed emphasis on the formal powers and structures of institutions. The greater focus on institutional structures provided fertile ground for the growth of analytical techniques such as spatial models and game theory to study institutions.

# Chapter 11

# Congress and the Courts

## The Battle over Campaign Finance

*Sarah A. Treul*

> The judiciary ... has no influence over either the sword or the purse; no direction either of the strength or of the wealth of the society; and can take no active resolution whatever. It may truly be said to have neither *Force* nor *Will*, but merely judgment. ... It proves incontestably, that the judiciary is beyond comparison the weakest of the three departments of power; that it can never attack with success either of the other two ...
>
> *Federalist 78*

Although Alexander Hamilton describes the judiciary as the least dangerous branch in the separation of powers system in *Federalist 78*, today's federal court system plays an increasingly prominent role in the policymaking process. This chapter examines the courts' role in policymaking, and the interaction between the courts and Congress, focusing on judicial appointments and judicial review. The chapter also discusses the history of campaign finance reform, an ongoing battle between the Supreme Court and Congress. It concludes by briefly focusing on topics related to Congress and the courts in need of further research.

The Founding Fathers gave few explicit powers to the courts in Article III of the U.S. Constitution, but they were clear in Articles I and II that the other two branches of government would check the judicial branch. One of the most explicit checks on the judiciary is the manner in which vacancies on the Supreme Court (and later lower courts) are filled. According to Article II, Section 2 of the Constitution, "[The President] shall ... nominate, and by and with the Advice and Consent of the Senate, shall appoint Ambassadors, other public Ministers and Consuls, Judges of the Supreme Court. ..." While scholars debate the explicit meaning of the Senate's role of "Advice and Consent" in this process, the Founding Fathers left little doubt that both the executive and the legislative branch are to play major roles in the appointing and confirmation of federal justices (Cameron, Cover, and Segal 1990; Moraski and Shipan 1999; Binder and Maltzman 2002; Epstein and Segal 2005; Johnson and Roberts 2005). It goes without saying that the president and the Senate do not always agree on what course federal courts ought to take.

Given this consideration, battles over Supreme Court appointments (and lower court appointments) today are fierce and partisan. Although the Founding Fathers intentionally left the policymaking process somewhat ambiguous, this vagueness has allowed courts to expand their role in the legislative game. Today when the courts enter the legislative arena they frequently expand procedural rights of individuals or force executive agencies to pay greater attention to congressional intent.

Recognizing this, the Senate (especially in the face of divided government), takes its role of confirmation very seriously. The contentious confirmation battle fought over Judge Robert H. Bork in 1987 provides an excellent example of the controversy surrounding nominations to the Supreme Court today. When Justice Lewis Powell, a moderate on the Court, announced his retirement, Senate Democrats warned Republican President Ronald Reagan that they would fight any nomination that moved the Court to the right (Bork 1990). Nevertheless, Reagan nominated Bork to the Court on July 1, 1987. Bork, previously a law school professor and solicitor general, was currently serving on the U.S. Court of Appeals for the District of Columbia.

Although qualified, the nominee faced a Democratic Senate led by Senator Ted Kennedy who spoke out against Bork on the Senate floor, rallying civil rights groups and others to unite against the confirmation of Bork. Specifically, Democrats in the Senate showed great resistance to his well-published opposition to affirmative action and established rulings on abortion. The Senate voted 58 to 42 against his nomination.

Four years later, President Bush nominated Clarence Thomas to the Supreme Court. Like Bork before him, Thomas was also serving on the U.S. Court of Appeals for the District of Columbia. Having only served on the appeals court for eighteen months, Judge Thomas had relatively little experience as a judge. Given his lack of experience, the American Bar Association's review committee rated him "qualified" on their three-point scale (highly qualified, qualified, and not qualified). Two members of the committee even ranked him "not qualified," making Thomas the lowest ranked Supreme Court nominee in the ABA's history. Thomas, like Bork before him, had a history of espousing conservative views on many issues, which led to many liberal groups mobilizing against him. He also drew tough questions from the Democrats on the Judiciary Committee. The full Senate eventually confirmed Thomas by a vote of 52–48.

Confirmation battles continue to be contentious, as the Constitution implicitly grants the Supreme Court the power to declare actions of state and federal legislatures and executives unconstitutional. The Supreme Court formally exercised this power in *Marbury v. Madison* in 1803 and has ruled federal provisions unconstitutional at different rates over the course of U.S. history. In recent years, the Court has increasingly used its power of judicial review, ruling laws, and provisions unconstitutional. Growth in judicial activism since the 1970s and the reactions to judicial activism are an important part of the relationship between Congress and the courts. In addition to the Court today ruling more laws unconstitutional, it is also the case that the laws overturned today tend to be higher-profile than the more minor laws and provisions the Court used to overturn.

Of course Congress is not an innocent bystander to the decisions of the Court and its role in policymaking. As the example of campaign finance will make clear in this chapter, most important laws are the result of a back-and-forth interaction between the legislature, the president, and the courts. The legislative institutions (Congress and the president) also have several ways to indirectly influence the decisions of the Court, as Congress and the president determine the composition of the courts. The president nominates judges and the Senate confirms them, and as the examples above illustrate, this can be a contentious process. Additionally, the size of the courts, the organization of the courts, funding for the courts, and the Supreme Court's jurisdiction are all set by law and thereby by Congress (see Brisbin 2005 for an overview of Congress's checks on the Court).

Congress and the president are also able to anticipate and respond to judicial decisions. The Court's lack of enforcement authority allows Congress and the president to ignore judicial decisions. For example, in 1983 the Supreme Court ruled the use of the legislative veto unconstitutional in *Immigration and Naturalization Service v. Chadha*. The legislative veto, which was agreed upon by both Congress and the president in 1932, allows either or both chambers of Congress to pass a resolution to reject an agency's action. Although *INS v. Chadha* technically voided the legislative veto, executive departments still abide by them. This is because both Congress and the president favor a system where Congress can delegate lawmaking discretion to the executive branch without giving it complete and unchecked control. The legislative veto allows Congress to pass a resolution taking away the agency's authority if it drifts too far away from the legislature's intent.

Perhaps the most famous example of the president ignoring a Supreme Court decision was when the Court ruled in *Worcester v. Georgia* (1832) that policies to move Cherokee Indians from their land were unconstitutional. President Andrew Jackson responded to the Court's decision by saying, "They made their decision. Now, let them enforce it." Jackson followed his comments by ignoring the decision, thereby forcing the Cherokee to give up their lands and move to land west of the Mississippi River.

Recognizing the Court's ability to insert itself in the policymaking process, regardless of Congress's reaction, begs the question: what should the Court's role be? At his confirmation hearings in 2005, Chief Justice John Roberts declared himself a believer in judicial modesty, comparing the role of judges to that of umpires in a baseball game.

> Judges are like umpires. Umpires don't make the rules; they apply them. The role of an umpire and a judge is critical. They make sure everybody plays by the rules. But it is a limited role. Nobody ever went to a ball game

to see the umpire. Judges have to have the humility to recognize that they operate within a system of precedent, shaped by other judges equally striving to live up to the judicial oath.

(Chief Justice John Roberts)

While the Chief Justice's portrayal of judges as umpires might be the role intended by the Founding Fathers, courts are not simply umpires in the legislative game. Today's courts are frequently viewed as players and not just umpires. Indeed, former Supreme Court Justice Benjamin Cardozo once referred to justices as "legislators in robes." With each decision issued by the Court, the justices are influencing both current and future policy. This is all the more true today with the Court overturning more high-profile legislation than it had in the past. These laws include the Violence Against Women Act and the Religious Freedom and Restoration Act.

## The Senate and Judicial Confirmations

Recognizing the importance of the makeup of the Court for judicial decision-making and the Court's increasing role in the legislative game, the process of judicial appointment receives substantial coverage in the media. The power of judicial appointment rests with both the president and the Senate. Historically the battles in this area are fought over Supreme Court nominees, with Robert Bork in 1987 and Clarence Thomas in 1991, proving particularly controversial. While Supreme Court appointments continue to be controversial, confirmation battles today are also fought in the lower courts.

### Lower Court Nominations

Presidents typically defer a great deal of influence to same-party senators when making appointments to federal district courts and the courts of appeal. Senators typically suggest strong candidates from their home states to the president. Traditionally, the president will also consult with the home state senator(s) of his political party when a vacancy occurs within the senator's state; this unwritten custom is known as senatorial courtesy. Senatorial courtesy is institutionalized through the use of blue slips—blue sheets of paper sent out by the Chairman of the Judiciary Committee asking the senators from the nominee's home state his or her opinion. Typically a negative blue slip results in the Judiciary Committee not acting on the nominee. Even if the Committee does move forward, a negative blue slip certainly impedes confirmation. If the blue slips come back positive, the Senate Judiciary Committee studies the nominee and receives reports from the American Bar Association. The Committee then routinely recommends approval to the full Senate, which confirms the nominee.

At least this was the typical procedure prior to 1992. Beginning in 1992, however, and under the direction of the chair of the Judiciary Committee, Joseph

Biden (D-DE), the Judiciary Committee began to seriously consider some of the nominees being suggested. Rather than confirm lower court nominees put forth by the administration, the Committee decided to be more selective about which nominees would receive hearings before the 1992 election. The Committee's reluctance to hold hearings prior to this time was likely the result of the Democratic majority considering the possibility that Democrat Bill Clinton would win the presidency.

Once Bill Clinton became president, the Judiciary Committee again began to hold hearings and justices were quickly confirmed to the federal bench. However, in 1995 the Republicans took control of the Senate, drastically slowing the rate of confirmations under the Democratic administration. Since the early 1990s, it is typical for only around 50 percent of circuit court nominees to receive Senate confirmation (Rutkus and Sollenberger 2004).

This trend continued during the Bush presidency and the first years of the Obama presidency, as no recent Senate majority has held the sixty votes needed to invoke cloture, or end debate, on nominees. Many vacancies during the Bush presidency went unfulfilled for more than eighteen months, with some going up to four years between the nomination and the confirmation. Clearly the partisanship of Congress and the presidency plays a role in the appointment of lower court justices.

## Supreme Court Nominations

If partisan politics are visible in the appointment and confirmation decisions of lower court justices, they are unavoidable when it comes to nominations to the Supreme Court. Supreme Court nominations are anything but routine. When a vacancy opens on the Supreme Court, the president, senators, interest groups, and the media all carefully screen nominees. After the president puts forward a nominee, the Senate Judiciary Committee has the nominee complete a lengthy questionnaire, orders staff to do extensive background investigations, requests an evaluation from the American Bar Association, and then holds several days of hearings. Interest groups also get involved, actively lobbying senators both publicly and privately for their support or opposition of the nominee.

Whether or not the Senate decides to confirm a nominee depends on several factors. First, and perhaps most importantly, is the current partisan makeup of the Senate. Similar to lower court confirmation proceedings, when the president's party is in the majority in the Senate, the confirmation success rate is close to 90 percent. During periods of divided government, confirmation success dips to around 60 percent (Nixon and Goss 2001; Binder and Maltzman 2002; Martinek, Kemper, and Van Winkle 2002; Epstein and Segal 2005). Second, the timing of the nomination also has an effect on its success (Nixon and Goss 2001; Binder and Maltzman 2002). Typically the longer a president is in office, the less influence he is thought to have over the confirmation process since presidential capital and influence in Congress tend to decline over time.

Research also finds the more popular a president is, the more likely he is to have his nominee confirmed by the Senate.

Timing is also important for senators in connection with the confirmation process. Many argue that senators who will soon face reelection are more likely to consider public opinion when determining their confirmation vote, and opposition party senators are less likely to cooperate with the president. Of course, this consideration pales in comparison to the nominee's ideology and qualifications. The greater the ideological distance between the senator and the nominee, the less likely the senator will vote for the president's choice (Cameron et al. 1990; Ruckman 1993). The presence of just one of the factors mentioned above—increased partisanship, low presidential popularity, proximity to reelection, or the end of the presidential term—increases the likelihood of conflict in the Senate during the confirmation process (Krutz, Fleisher, and Bond 1998).

The Senate's role in the confirmation process is not to be taken lightly, though typically it does confirm the president's nominee, failing to confirm just twenty-six, or about 20 percent, of nominees to the Supreme Court. Although most nominees are confirmed, the Senate's role of "advice and consent" should be taken seriously, as it is the only check on the president's ability to appoint justices for life to the bench. According to the Constitution, judges "shall hold their offices during good behaviour," and the House can bring and vote on impeachment charges against judges. If the House impeaches a judge, the Senate then conducts a trial on the charges. In order for a judge to be convicted, two-thirds of senators present must vote to convict and remove the judge. Historically, Congress's impeachment power has not proven itself to be a source of congressional leverage over the courts. In fact, Congress is yet to remove a Supreme Court justice from office. Republicans in 1804 tried to impeach Justice Samuel Chase on several charges, but the Senate failed to get a two-thirds vote to convict. Even the threat of impeachment has only resulted in the resignation of one Supreme Court justice; Justice Abe Fortas resigned in 1969 amid revelations of questionable financial practices. Impeachment and conviction are also rare for lower federal court judges. Thirteen lower federal court judges have been impeached by the House, and only seven have been convicted by the Senate.

Given that Congress rarely asserts its authority to impeach and convict judges, that leaves the legislative branch with two primary checks on judicial behavior. The first, the Senate's ability to advise the president on appointments and its responsibility to confirm those appointments, was covered in detail above. The other power, Congress's ability to use its traditional legislative power to respond to court decisions will be discussed in greater detail below.

## Supreme Court Jurisdiction

The Constitution implicitly grants the Supreme Court the power to declare actions of state and federal legislatures and executives unconstitutional. This power of judicial review directly inserts the Court into the legislative game and the policymaking process. The Court's power of judicial review was first exercised in *Marbury v. Madison* (1803), although the Founding Fathers debated granting this power explicitly in the Constitution. Although the Court exerted its power of judicial review in the early 1800s, it initially did little in the way of strengthening the Court's power in its relations with Congress and the president. Over time, however, the Court used its broad authority to declare acts of Congress or the president unconstitutional with greater frequency.

Broadly speaking, there are two types of cases involving the interpretation of the Constitution: separation-of-powers cases, which determine whether the president or Congress has power in a particular area, and cases concerning the scope of congressional powers. In both types of cases the Court has increasingly positioned itself as a prominent player in the policymaking process. During the last forty years the Court has made decisions ranging from redistricting (e.g., *Wesberry v. Sanders* [1964]) to campaign finance (e.g., *Buckley v. Valeo* [1976]) to whether or not ballots should be recounted in Florida during the 2000 presidential election (*Bush v. Gore* [2000]). Not only can these cases directly or indirectly affect policymaking, but they also have the potential to play a role in terms of electoral accountability and representation in the United States. This section will discuss both types of judicial power, providing examples of some prominent Court cases in these areas.

### Separation-of-Powers Cases

In separation-of-powers cases, the Court must determine the constitutional powers and limitations of the other two branches of government. Depending upon the Court's decision, one branch may enjoy powers above and beyond the other in a particular area. The Court is also frequently asked to determine the extent of legislative powers generally. Separation-of-powers cases rarely came to the Court before the 1970s, as Congress tended to be more deferential to the president (Epstein et al. 2006). This changed in the 1970s when President Nixon asserted broad powers that frequently ran contrary to the wishes of a Democratically controlled Congress. Since the 1970s the Court has used these powers with increasing frequency, giving the Court a prominent role in the policymaking process.

During the Nixon presidency (1969–74), for instance, Nixon faced a Democratic-majority Congress and frequently battled with the legislative branch over federal spending. For example, Nixon claimed presidential authority to withhold funds from executive agencies even after Congress passed appropriations legislation. Nixon's impoundments frequently made their way to the courts, where Nixon typically lost. These types of separation-of-powers cases continued well into the 1980s and the presidencies of Reagan and Bush. During the 1970s and 1980s, the courts tended to follow the "doctrinal notion of separated powers"—the idea that a clear line can be drawn between the powers of the executive and legislative branches.

The case of *Immigration and Naturalization Service v. Chadha* (1983) clearly illustrates the Court's attempt to draw a clear line between the other two branches of government. In *Chadha*, the Supreme Court ruled 7 to 2 that the legislative veto was unconstitutional. A legislative veto is a process by which a congressional committee can veto an action taken by a federal agency. According to the Court, only the president has the authority to veto bills. Arguments that the legislative veto was a workable tool by which to extend authority to the executive without formally enacting the law were rejected. Despite the Court banning the legislative veto, Congress continues to use it as an oversight tool (Franklin 1986). Congress—often with the agreement of the executive branch—has used over 400 legislative vetoes since the *Chadha* decision (Fisher 1993). The Court's decision in *Chadha* and, more importantly, Congress and the executive's decision to mostly ignore it, illustrate the Court's inability to enforce its decisions and, thereby, to exert control over the two other branches of government. If the other branches agree on the distribution of authority between them, there is little the Court can do to change it.

### Congressional Power Cases

The Constitution also gives the courts the authority to decide questions of congressional power. Although the Founding Fathers specifically addressed the powers of Congress in Article I of the Constitution, the Supreme Court continues to rule on whether certain acts of Congress are permissible under the Constitution. Cases interpreting the limits of congressional power often, though by no means exclusively, focus on the commerce clause of the Constitution (Article I, Section 8). The commerce clause allows Congress to enact legislation that regulated interstate commerce. The clause is used to regulate many areas of American life that are, even if tangentially, related to interstate commerce. During the 1930s, the Court took a narrow view of the commerce clause and frequently ruled President Roosevelt's New Deal legislation unconstitutional. In *United States v. Butler* (1936) the Court ruled that the Agricultural Adjustment Act of 1933, considered the first farm bill, was unconstitutional, as the regulation of agriculture should be left up to the states.

Another area in which the courts have been active in interpreting congressional powers is in the area of campaign spending. The remainder of this chapter will focus on the relationship between the Court and Congress using campaign finance reform as an example.

## Campaign Finance Reform: Who Controls Policy?

In 1971 Congress passed the Federal Election Campaign Act (FECA), adding important amendments in 1974 and 1976. The Federal Election Campaign Act and its amendments created the Federal Election Commission (FEC) and established contribution limits to congressional campaigns and disclosure requirements. Congress's intent behind passing the legislation was to limit secret contributions and large sums of money from wealthy contributions and corporations. At this time, Congress was concerned that contributions from the wealthy and corporations were unfairly influencing elections and that these types of contributions could be harmful to the system (Corrado, Mann, and Potter 2003). More specifically, the FECA limited the size of donations that individuals, parties, and political action committees (PACs) could make to congressional candidates. Seemingly suggesting that party participation is more desirable in congressional elections than that of wealthy individuals and corporations, the FECA allowed parties to give more money directly to candidates than PACs could, and to coordinate some spending with candidates. The law also required groups and candidates to report contributions and expenditures to the FEC. The law set no limits on how much a congressional candidate could spend.

While contribution limits are adjusted each election cycle to account for changes in the consumer price index, it is always the case that PACs can contribute more to candidates than individuals can. For example, in 2010 PACs can give $5,000 to a candidate or candidate committee per election, whereas individuals can only give $2,400. Since the new law allowed PACs to contribute more money to a campaign than individuals, the number of PACs burgeoned. PACs were established in order to pad resources for campaign contributions. By collecting money from organization employees or members, PACs can give the candidate a larger sum of money than would otherwise be possible. The law led to the immediate disclosure of all contributions and expenditures by candidates, PACs, and parties. The FECA also required that all individual contributions of more than $50 must be recorded and that the name of the donor must also be recorded if the donation equals $100 or more.

### The Court's Initial Response and Congress's Reaction

Two years after the law's passage, the Court ruled in *Buckley v. Valeo* (1976) that the free speech clause of the First Amendment to the Constitution applies to campaign spending. According to the Court, Congress cannot limit individual or group expenditures to a campaign when those expenditures are not directed at a particular candidate or party. The Court held that the government's regulatory power under FECA would be construed to apply only to those funds spent on communication that "include express words of advocacy of the election or defeat" of a clearly identifiable candidate. The Court's decision was the beginning of an important distinction between "express advocacy" and "issue advocacy." According to the Court, only "express advocacy" was subject to regulation. In a footnote in the Court's opinion, the Court states that in order for communication to count as "express" it must include words like "vote for," "elect," "support," "cast your ballot for," "Smith for Congress," "vote against," "defeat," or "reject."

The Court said that limitations on campaign expenditures, similar to other limits on freedom of speech, are constitutional only if some compelling government interest exists. Of course, what constitutes a compelling government interest is left up to the Court. In *Buckley*, the Court determined that the goal of limiting electoral influence of wealthy individuals or groups did not provide a compelling government interest and ran counter to the First Amendment of the Constitution.

In response to the Court's decision in *Buckley*, Congress again amended FECA in 1979. This amendment allowed state and local parties to raise and spend money on party building, voter registration, and get-out-the-vote (GOTV) activities. Since these funds did not have to be reported to the FEC (though the law was amended in 1988 with reporting requirements) and there were no limits on contributions or expenditures, these funds were nicknamed "soft money." Soft money was money contributed by individuals and corporations to political parties (instead of directly to a candidate), to be used for party ads, party staff and office expenses, voter registration, and GOTV efforts (Sorauf 1992; Hassan 2006). The Court's decision in *Buckley*, and a later decision in *Colorado Republican Federal Campaign Committee v. Federal Election Commission* (1996), made it clear that loopholes, such as the "soft money" loophole, existed. This loophole allowed individuals and PACs who reached their contribution limit on money given directly to a candidate to continue to give to a party organization that can work on behalf of a candidate. Additionally, the federal courts interpreted "party building" in such a way that practically unlimited sums of money could be raised and spent simply by saying it was being done for this purpose. Thus, despite the legislative efforts to reform campaign finance, the Court's decisions meant that money in elections was practically as prolific as it was before the reforms began in the 1970s.

After years of partisan debate, Congress (by way of a discharge petition) decided to ban most soft money from its own campaigns with the passage of the Bipartisan Campaign Reform Act of 2002 (BCRA), which is often referred to as "McCain-Feingold" (Malbin 2003). In addition to banning soft money contributions to the parties, the BCRA increased the amount of hard money individuals could contribute to campaigns, created higher contribution limits for candidates facing self-financed candidates, and restricted "issue advocacy" by independent groups in the sixty days prior to an election (See Table 11.1 for specific congressional campaign contribution limits for the 2009–10 elections under BCRA).

Perhaps the most controversial part of BCRA was the limits it set on issue ads sixty days prior to Election Day. The sixty-day issue advocacy restriction was controversial because the *Buckley* decision seemed to suggest that this type of spending could not be regulated. Most political pundits and Supreme Court watchers were certain this provision would make its way to the Supreme Court and that when it did, it would be ruled unconstitutional. However, when the sixty-day limit did reach the Supreme Court in 2003, the Court upheld the

*Table 11.1* Congressional Campaign Contribution Limits under the Bipartisan Campaign Reform Act of 2002, for the 2009–10 Election Cycle

|  | To each candidate or candidate committee per election | To national party committee per calendar year | To state, district, and local party committee per calendar year | To any other political committee per calendar year |
|---|---|---|---|---|
| Individual may give | $2,400 | $30,400 | $10,000 (combined limit) | $5,000 |
| National Party Committee may give | $5,000 (combined limit) | No limit | No limit | $5,000 |
| State, District, & Local Party Committee may give | $5,000 | No limit | No limit | $5,000 |
| PAC (multicandidate) may give | $5,000 | $15,000 | $5,000 (combined limit) | $5,000 |
| PAC (not multicandidate) | $2,400 | $30,400 | $10,000 (combined limit) | $5,000 |
| Authorized Campaign Committee may give | $2,000 | No limit | No limit | $5,000 |

Source: Federal Election Commission, www.fec.gov.

restrictions on when groups can spend money to advocate issues in a 5 to 4 decision. In *McConnell v. FEC* (2003) the Supreme Court said that the sixty-day restriction on issue advocacy was acceptable, thereby allowing the ban on soft money. The Court said the restriction on free speech was minimal enough and justified by the government's interest in curbing corrupt practices.

Just four years later, after President George W. Bush successfully replaced Justice Sandra Day O'Connor with Justice Samuel Alito, the Court reversed itself in *FEC v. Wisconsin Right to Life* (2007). Once again the Court was bitterly divided, but this time a 5 to 4 majority, illustrating the importance of ideology and the confirmation process, held that the restriction on "issue ads" in the weeks prior to an election amounted to unconstitutional censorship. At the time of the decision, scholars and Supreme Court watchers thought that the decision would lead to an increase in the amount of corporate and union money used to indirectly campaign for or against candidates. Table 11.2 provides a brief history of campaign finance law and some of the key challenges to it in the courts.

Table 11.2 Key Dates in the Development of Campaign Finance

| Year | Branch of Government | Law/Decision | Action |
|------|----------------------|--------------|--------|
| 1971 | Congress | Federal Election Campaign Act (FECA) | Establishes disclosure requirements for federal candidates, political parties, and PACs. |
| 1974 | Congress | Amended FECA | Set limits on contributions by individuals, parties, and PACs. Established the Federal Elections Commission (FEC). |
| 1976 | Supreme Court | Buckley v. Valeo | Struck down parts of the 1974 amendments to FECA. Court said cannot limit spending by a candidate. |
| 2002 | Congress | Bipartisan Campaign Reform Act | Attempted to ban soft money in elections. |
| 2003 | Supreme Court | McConnell v. FEC | Restrictions on free speech (donations to a campaign) are minimal and thereby constitutional. |
| 2007 | Supreme Court | Wisconsin Right to Life v. FEC | Restriction on "issue advocacy" ads sixty days before an election is unconstitutional. |
| 2010 | Supreme Court | Citizens United v. FEC | Contributions by corporations and unions to political campaigns are protected under the First Amendment. |
| ? | Congress | Disclosure Act | Not passed. Attempts to prohibit foreign influence in federal elections and establish additional disclosure requirements for spending. |

## Campaign Finance Today

The scholars and Supreme Court watchers proved correct in their prediction. The debate between Congress and the Court over campaign finance did not end with *FEC v. Wisconsin Right to Life*. During the 2008 presidential election, Citizens United—a conservative, non-profit organization—produced a feature-length documentary expressing negative opinions about Hillary Clinton, which depicted her as unfit to be president. The FEC determined that the film could not be aired and Citizens United sought an injunction against the FEC in the United States District Court for the District of Columbia. In ruling that Citizens United could not broadcast the film, the District Court said the BCFA prohibited corporations from spending money to broadcast "electioneering communications" within a certain number of days before an election. The District Court said that according to *McConnell* the airing of the movie was not unconstitutional, in that the movie was *not* issue advocacy but, rather, express advocacy since it attempted to inform voters why Clinton was not fit to be president.

The Supreme Court decided to take the case and on January 21, 2010 the Court issued its ruling in *Citizens United v. FEC.* In a 5 to 4 decision the Court decided that under the First Amendment's free speech clause, corporate funding of independent broadcasts in candidate elections cannot be limited. That is, the government cannot keep corporations and unions from spending money to support (or denounce) individual candidates in an election. The majority opinion, written by Justice Anthony Kennedy (there were also three separate concurring opinions), wrote that political speech is an essential part of democracy and that this is true regardless of whether an individual or a corporation is doing the speaking (i.e., funding). The Court also ruled that BCRA's disclosure requirements are constitutional, as there is a "governmental interest" in providing the "electorate with information" about election-related funding resources. The dissent, which Justice Stevens read in part from the bench, argued that the Founding Fathers would have never viewed corporations as members of society and that the government should have an interest in regulating their ability to spend money in an attempt to influence local and national elections.

The Court's decision permits the creation of independent-expenditure only committees, so-called "super PACs," which can raise unlimited sums from corporations, unions, and other groups, as well as wealthy individuals. Super PACs can advertise for the election or defeat of federal candidates.

## What are Congress's Options?

The interaction between Congress and the Court does not have to end when the Court announces a decision. Congress can, of course, use its legislative power granted under Article I of the Constitution to respond to a Court decision. In fact, sometimes a dissenting justice will suggest in the dissent that Congress ought to write a new law to address the decision. Very occasionally, a justice will read the dissent from the bench, sending an even stronger signal that the dissenter feels very strongly that the Court got the decision wrong and that it would prefer a congressional remedy.

While it might be constitutional for Congress to reverse an unpopular Supreme Court decision, it is far from automatic. Efforts to reverse decisions can get stuck in one chamber of Congress after easily passing in the other, or remain in committee after hearings are held. Scholarship demonstrates that Congress responds to about one-third of Supreme Court decisions that overturn federal law (Ignagni and Meernik, 1994, 1997). The reason this number is so small is that both chambers and the president must agree on any response (or two-thirds of both chambers in order to override the president's veto). If the committee with jurisdiction recognizes that gaining the approval of both chambers and the president is going to be impossible, it might choose to take no action. Most commonly, members of Congress take preliminary steps to overturn the decision and speak out against it, but never take the necessary steps to actually push the legislation to the point of passage.

When Congress does decide to respond to a Court decision it considers several factors. One of these factors is public opinion. If the public is in favor of action by Congress, Congress is much more likely to respond. The issue involved can also be decisive in Congress's decision. If the issue is salient, often measured by the participation of interest groups, Congress is more likely to respond. Occasionally, as mentioned above, justices on the Court invite Congress to respond. This clearly increases the likelihood that Congress will respond. When the Court invites a congressional response, it typically is clear on which particular provisions of the law are unconstitutional, and how Congress could fix those parts by rewriting the law. The Court will sometimes even outline for Congress what changes would be considered constitutional, suggesting a role for Congress in determining the meaning of the Constitution (Fisher 1988).

## Congress's Response to *Citizens United*

Most members of Congress, including John McCain (R-AZ) and Russ Feingold (D-WI), the two senators primarily responsible for the BCRA, spoke out against the Court's decision. McCain said he was, "Disappointed by the decision of the Supreme Court" and Feingold said, "This decision was a terrible mistake. Presented with a relatively narrow legal issue, the Supreme Court chose to roll back laws that have limited the role of corporate money in federal elections since Teddy Roosevelt was president" (Hunt 2010). Former Associate Justice of the Supreme Court, Sandra Day O'Connor also shared this view, publicly stating that the ruling was likely to create "an increasing problem for maintaining an independent judiciary." She went on, "In invalidating some of the existing checks on campaign spending, the majority in *Citizens United* has signaled that the problem of campaign contributions in judicial elections might get considerably worse and quite soon" (Liptak 2010). For Justice O'Connor the Court's decision not only affects the future of congressional elections, but could also corrupt judicial elections as well.

The American public also generally disliked the Court's decision in *Citizens United*. Table 11.3 indicates that 80 percent of Americans were opposed to the Court's decision, with 65 percent saying they were strongly opposed. According to the Washington Post-ABC News Poll only 6 percent of Americans strongly supported the Court's decision in *Citizens United*. Responding to the poll, Senator Charles Schumer (D-NY), who led the legislative fight against *Citizens*

Table 11.3 Public Opinion and Citizens United

Do you support or oppose the recent ruling by the Supreme Court that says corporations and unions can spend as much money as they want to help political candidates win elections? Do you feel that way strongly or somewhat?

| | Percentage of Respondents |
|---|---|
| Strongly Support | 6 |
| Somewhat Support | 11 |
| Somewhat Oppose | 15 |
| Strongly Oppose | 65 |
| No Opinion | 2 |

Source: Washington Post-ABC News Poll conducted by telephone February 4–8, 2010, among a random national sample of 1,004 adults including users of both conventional and cellular phones. The margin of error is +/–3 percentage points.

*United*, said, "If there's one thing that Americans on the left, right, and center can all agree on, it's that they don't want more special interests in our politics" (Eggen 2010).

On January 27, 2010 during his State of the Union address, President Obama entered the legislative debate, and implored Congress to write a new law countering the Court's decision.

> Last week the Supreme Court reversed a century of law to open the floodgates for special interests—including foreign corporations—to spend without limit in our elections. Well I don't think American elections should be bankrolled by America's more powerful interests, or worse, by foreign entities. They should be decided by the American people. And I'd urge Democrats and Republicans to pass a bill that helps correct some of these problems.
>
> President Barack Obama (State of the Union 2010)

With most members of Congress sharing the president's dissatisfaction with the Court's decision, Congress took up the president's call to "pass a bill that helps correct some of these problems." The 111th Congress took up President Obama's call to respond to the Court's decision in *Citizens* with the introduction on April 24, 2010 of the Disclose Act (H.R. 5175). The bill would amend the Federal Election Campaign Act of 1971 to prohibit foreign influence in federal elections, to prohibit contributions from government contractors, and to establish additional disclosure requirements with respect to spending. The bill narrowly passed the House on June 24, 2010, but stalled in the Senate where, on September 24, 2010 it failed to gain enough votes to invoke cloture.

The failure of the Disclose Act in the Senate exemplifies how difficult it can be for Congress to respond to the Court. Even with public opinion favoring a congressional response to *Citizens* and the president promising to sign such a law, Congress was still unable to act. As discussed in Chapter 7, the procedural constraints in the Senate, such as the supermajority required to invoke cloture and end debate, make the Senate the chamber where legislation most frequently stalls.

## Campaign Finance, Elections, and Representation

The Court's decisions regarding campaign finance have had sweeping consequences for elections in the United States. As the Court rules laws regulating donations and advocacy unconstitutional, money plays an increasingly important role in elections. The latest decision in *Citizens United* looks to be no different. Scholars and pundits are concerned that, in the aftermath of *Citizens United*, organizations will be set up to accept donations of unlimited size from corporations without having to disclose who the corporations are. This concern is especially salient given Congress's inability to pass the Disclose Act.

According to campaign finance lawyers, most publicly traded companies stayed on the sidelines despite the *Citizens United* ruling, but small to medium size, privately held companies are jumping into elections now (Luo 2010). Since *Citizens United*, corporations and unions can now establish 501(c) nonprofit corporations, which allows them to engage in unlimited political activity without having to disclose their donor lists.

Whether or not this is a concern for elections and representation hinges on identifying if there is systematic bias in who these newly formed groups are giving money to. This is something that cannot be determined based on one election, but thus far all indicators point toward the decision in *Citizens United* benefiting Republicans running for Congress. According to the Center for Responsive Politics, conservative outside groups spent $184 million, and liberal outside groups spent $89 million.[1] Only time will tell if this is an advantage the Republican Party will always be able to leverage, or if the money being spent on Republican campaigns is simply the result of an electorate dissatisfied with Congress. Either way, there is little doubt that the Supreme Court's decision in *Citizens United* and Congress's inability to respond thus far affects elections, representation, and policymaking in Congress.

## Future Research on Congress and the Courts

This chapter presented a brief history of the relationship between the Supreme Court and Congress. Specifically, the chapter investigated the role the Senate plays in the confirmation of Supreme Court justices, the Court's role as policymaker, and the Court's influence in elections through its campaign finance decisions. The Supreme Court has exerted its power of judicial review in the area of campaign finance on numerous occasions. Yet Congress does not have to stand by and simply accept the Court's decision. After the Court issues its decision, Congress often goes back to the legislative drawing-board to craft new legislation that fits within the Constitutional limits as laid out by the Court. The battle over campaign finance is an excellent example of how the policymaking process plays out in Congress and the Courts.

The battle over campaign finance is far from resolved, and research on the back-and-forth between Congress and the Court is an avenue worth further exploration. The practical impact of the *Citizens United* decision was already seen in the vast change in the magnitude of political money available in the 2010 midterm election. The 2010 midterm election will go down in the history books as the most expensive midterm in the nation's history, as well as the midterm with the most anonymous money spent. Recognizing this, one avenue for future research that is particularly worth pursuing is how the Court's decision in *Citizens United* changes the role of spending in future elections. Will the Supreme Court's ruling in *Citizens United v. FEC* change how corporate executives contribute to elections? For instance, rather than spending their own money, will corporate executives spend corporate funds in support of pro-business candidates? Furthermore, now that corporations and unions are allowed to expressly advocate for the election or defeat of a candidate, will we see an increase in negative ads? Will certain types of candidates benefit more than others from the less restrictive campaign finance laws?

Of course Congress's attempt to pass the Disclose Act is unlikely to be over, although procedural hurdles make any swift legislative response unlikely. Future research analyzing the conditions under which campaign finance reform is likely to pass through both chambers of Congress could prove the key to truly understanding the role of money in elections and the conditions necessary for Congress to respond effectively to the Court.

## Note

1  http://www.opensecrets.org/outsidespending/index.php

# Chapter 12

# Congress and Interest Groups

*Anthony J. Nownes*

Textbooks will tell you that there are 535 voting members of Congress (MCs)— 100 senators and 435 representatives. These are the people charged with representing us and making public policy. But they are not alone in the legislative branch. Each member has an army of personal staffers to assist him/her, and each committee has its own staff as well. But it does not end there. There is an additional cadre of men and women involved in congressional policymaking—these are the *lobbyists*. Lobbyists are paid professionals who represent the interests of all manner of interest groups in Washington, DC. Lobbyists are an integral part of the congressional policymaking process, and they always have been. In this chapter, I discuss the role of lobbyists and the interest groups they represent in the congressional process. Specifically, I examine who lobbyists represent, what they do, and the extent to which they get what they want.

## The Interest Group Universe

No one really knows how many lobbyists there are in Washington, DC. Nonetheless, the fragmentary data that exist give us an idea of the size of the Washington lobbying community. The Center for Responsive Politics (CRP), a Washington, DC research organization that examines lobbying disclosure reports filed with Congress, concluded that 13,694 unique lobbyists registered with the federal government and actively lobbied in 2009. That's almost twenty-six lobbyists for each member of Congress (Center for Responsive Politics 2010a). In all, the CRP estimates that interest groups spent approximately $3.5 billion lobbying in Washington in 2009 (Center for Responsive Politics, 2010a).

The presence of all these lobbyists begs the following question: who do they represent? The short answer is *interest groups*—organizations that have political goals and engage in political activity to achieve them. But the longer answer is *lots of different types of organizations*. In an influential study of Washington interest groups, political scientists Frank Baumgartner and Beth Leech (2001) addressed the question of who these Washington lobbyists represent when they lobby Congress. They concluded that "businesses constitute the largest category of lobbying organizations in Washington" (Baumgartner and Leech 2001: 1196). A smaller but still substantial number of lobbyists work for trade associations—that is, organizations consisting of businesses, usually in a specific business sector. Examples of large and active trade associations include the National Association of Manufacturers and the American Petroleum Institute. "Business and trade associations," Baumgartner and Leech (2001: 1194) write, "make up more than half of the Washington lobbying community." A smaller portion still represent professional associations, which are defined broadly as groups of people engaged in the same profession (examples include the American Bar Association and the American Medical Association). Many professional associations (groups of doctors, for example) are essentially business organizations, as their members are in a sense independent businesspeople. In sum, most lobbying is done by business organizations.

Non-business organizations, however, are hardly powerless in Washington. Baumgartner and Leech find that citizen groups, which are broadly defined as membership groups that any citizen can join, also employ scores of lobbyists. Examples include the American Association of Retired Persons (AARP), the American Civil Liberties Union (ACLU), and the National Rifle Association (NRA). Though there are fewer citizen group lobbyists operating in Washington than there are business group lobbyists, political scientist Jeffrey Berry (1999) has found that citizen groups tend to get "more bang for their buck" than business groups. Berry found that though citizen groups tend to have fewer resources than the business groups with which they often tangle, they seem to exercise disproportionate influence over policy outcomes.

Labor unions such as the National Education Association (NEA) and the Service Employees International Union (SEIU) are also quite active. Total union membership in the U.S. has been declining for decades, but labor unions still are powerful political players. Finally, many Washington lobbyists represent the interests of government entities (e.g., states, cities, counties, federal government agencies, and foreign countries) when they lobby Congress. In addition to these "big five" types of interest groups (for whom the majority of lobbyists work), a handful of other types of groups also employ Washington lobbyists. Among them are coalitions (often issue-specific, temporary groups of other types of interest groups), think tanks (e.g., The American Enterprise Institute, The Heritage Foundation), colleges and universities, and charities. There are also a large number of lobbying, public relations, and consulting firms operating in Washington that offer "lobbyists for hire" to groups of all kinds.

In short, the interest group universe is a diverse place, comprising business firms, trade associations, professional associations, citizen groups, labor unions, and other types of groups. Business interests are particularly well represented before Congress. Citizen groups, however, are also quite active, and there is some evidence that they are disproportionately influential.

## What Do All These Groups and Lobbyists Want? And Why Do MCs Listen to Them?

No organization *has* to lobby. For example, corporate powerhouses such as AT&T, ExxonMobil, General Electric, and Microsoft could simply sell what they sell and ignore politics altogether. Similarly, labor unions could avoid political action and devote all their resources to collective bargaining, professional associations could eschew lobbying and focus on all the other things they do (such as licensing and keeping members up to date on new professional practices), and citizen groups could limit themselves to servicing their members (i.e., providing them with benefits such as magazines and t-shirts).

### Why Do Interest Groups Lobby?

But organizations of all kinds *do* choose to lobby. Why? The answer is: *because what the government does affects them.* Corporations are governed by numerous laws, rules, and regulations that affect their ability to turn a profit. The federal government regulates numerous facets of their operations. Moreover, many companies lobby Congress because they can (and do) receive lucrative government contracts. Similarly, labor unions, professional associations, and citizen groups lobby because what the government does affects their members. Because the federal government does so many things that affect so many people and so many institutions, government decisions affect interest groups. This is why interest groups try to affect government decisions.

### Why Do MCs Listen to Lobbyists?

It is not difficult to understand why interest groups lobby Congress; they want to influence congressional decisions that affect them. But why do MCs choose to listen to lobbyists? The most convincing answer to this question comes from political scientist John R. Wright (1996), a leading interest group scholar who formulated "the communications theory of lobbying."[1] Wright starts with the premise that a lobbyist's basic "stock in trade" is information. Lobbyists use the information they have to attempt to affect MCs' decisions. From here, Wright (1996: 82) posits that members of Congress have three interdependent goals: (1) reelection; (2) good public policy; and (3) influence within Congress (see also Fenno 1973). First and foremost, sitting MCs want to win reelection. They cannot accomplish anything if they are not in office. Second, MCs want to make good public policy. Despite what many citizens think of them, MCs really do care about making good policy. Third, MCs want to be influential in Congress. Without the power to introduce bills and get other MCs to go along with them, MCs cannot achieve their second goal of making good policy.

Wright notes that achieving these three goals is not easy for MCs. It is not easy because Congress is a perilously uncertain environment. "The attainment of these goals," Wright (1996: 82) says, "is complicated by the fact that legislators cannot be certain about how voters will react to their policy decisions, how policies will actually work once implemented, or what kinds of political complications might arise during the legislative process." In short, while MCs have clear-cut goals, they are unsure of precisely how to achieve them—which is why lobbyists enter the picture. Lobbyists are useful to MCs because they provide information to them—information that the lobbyists hope will affect MCs' decisions. MCs accept and often welcome this information because it reduces MCs' uncertainty and helps them attain their goals. Wright (1996: 75) concludes that lobbyists "achieve influence in the legislative process by strategically providing information to change or reinforce legislators' beliefs about legislative outcomes, the operational effects of policies, and the electoral ramifications of their actions."

To summarize, Wright argues that lobbyists try to exert influence by providing information to MCs—information that helps MCs achieve their goals. According to Wright (1996: 88), the information lobbyists provide fits into three basic categories: (1) political information "about the status and prospect of bills;" (2) electoral information "about the electoral implications of legislators' support for or opposition" to a bill; and (3) policy information about "the likely economic, social, or environmental consequences of proposed policies." These three types of information correspond roughly with MCs' goals. Political information speaks to MCs' influence within Congress, electoral information speaks to MCs' reelection goals, and policy information speaks to MCs' desire to make good public policy.

So which of these three types of information do lobbyists typically provide to MCs when they lobby? In their recent multi-year study of congressional lobbying, Baumgartner et al. (2009) addressed this. And while they used a more complex typology of information than Wright, their results are easily translatable. In sum, lobbyists tend to focus primarily upon *policy information* when they lobby (Baumgartner et al. 2009: Ch. 7; see also Kersh 2006). They find that feasibility arguments—that is, arguments "that raise concerns or offer reassurance about the feasibility of policy opinions"—are the most common types of lobbying arguments (Baumgartner et al. 2009: 133). Two other types of arguments are also very common. First are "argument[s] that the policy at hand promoted a widely shared goal or, alternatively, stood in the way of achieving some broad, appealing goal (e.g., public safety, improving the economy, improving rural health care)." Second are arguments involving "imposing or reducing costs on nongovernmental actors" (Baumgartner et. al. 2009: 133). All three arguments entail the provision of policy information. While the provision of political or electoral information is not unheard of, it is relatively uncommon.

## How Do Lobbyists Try to Get What They Want?

In short, lobbying is primarily about providing information. But how and where do lobbyists provide information? Numerous studies have addressed this question, and their findings are remarkably uniform. Before I summarize these studies, however, I must make the following general point about lobbying: lobbying seldom involves *only* the legislature. This chapter and this book are about Congress, so I will not discuss either executive branch lobbying or judicial branch lobbying, but it is important to keep in mind that for most lobbyists, legislative lobbying is but one part of a larger lobbying strategy that might include executive branch lobbying, grassroots lobbying, and perhaps even judicial lobbying. While political scientists often separate legislative lobbying from other types of lobbying, lobbyists themselves tend to view lobbying holistically as a multifarious activity.

### Lobbying Tactics

Political scientists and journalists alike have studied congressional lobbying for well over a century (early works include Herring 1929; Schriftgiesser 1951; Milbrath 1963). Yet not until Schlozman and Tierney's (1983) landmark study, did we have a good sense of precisely what tactics lobbyists who lobbied MCs used. Schlozman and Tierney's findings, which have been confirmed many times over (see, for example, Walker 1991; Kollman 1998; Baumgartner et al. 2009), suggest that one tactic in particular forms the cornerstone of most legislative lobbying campaigns—*meeting personally with MCs and/or their staffers.* Meeting personally is, Baumgartner et al. (2009: 154) report, "the quintessential lobbying tactic." It is also considered the most effective lobbying technique in a lobbyist's arsenal. Personal meetings afford lobbyists the opportunity to present information of all kinds to legislators and their aides.

The thing that is perhaps most striking about contemporary legislative lobbying is that it looks a lot like legislative lobbying has always looked—it entails face-to-face contact, often in the halls of government. This is not to say that legislative lobbying always entails face-to-face contact. Surveys have shown that a number of other legislative lobbying techniques are often widely and regularly utilized. For example, surveys show that majorities of Washington lobbyists do favors for legislators who need assistance, help to draft legislation, and inspire citizens to contact legislators (see Baumgartner and Leech 1998: Ch. 8).

One lobbying technique of particular interest to scholars, the media, and citizens alike, is contributing money to legislators' campaigns. This common technique is very controversial because it is often viewed as little more than legal bribery. To understand how lobbyists and interest groups engage in this type of lobbying, it is necessary to know a few things about campaign finance law. The most important thing to know is this: *All interest groups are forbidden by law to contribute money to candidates for federal office.* How then do interest groups make monetary contributions to candidates? The answer is somewhat complicated. To summarize, the law says that some types of interest groups, including some business corporations, trade associations, professional associations, labor unions, and citizen groups, are allowed to form political action committees (PACs) that *can* contribute money to candidates.

The rules and regulations that govern how PACs operate are complex. But the basics are as follows. If an interest group wants to contribute money to a candidate for federal office, the group must form a separate but affiliated organization called a PAC. The PAC can then collect money from individuals affiliated with the parent organization (that is, the interest group that started the PAC). Then the PAC can take this money and contribute it to candidates for federal office. Currently, federal law says that an individual can contribute $5,000 per year to each PAC he/she supports, and the PAC can contribute $5,000 per candidate, per election. It is a little more complicated than this, but these are the basics.

An example can help illustrate how a real-life PAC operates. Let us say that communications giant AT&T wants to contribute money to some congressional candidates. To do this, the company would form a PAC—say, the AT&T PAC. The PAC would then solicit money from certain people affiliated with AT&T—specifically, people who are part of the company's "restricted class" including executives, administrative personnel, and shareholders. Then the PAC would turn around and contribute money to congressional candidates it supports. I did not make this example up. AT&T's PAC, officially known as AT&T Federal Political Action Committee, is a large and very active PAC. During the 2008 election cycle the PAC gave more than $4,000,000 in federal contributions (Center for Responsive Politics 2010b).

In mid-2009 the Federal Election Commission (which regulates PAC giving and maintains disclosure reports) reported that there were 4,611 registered federal PACs. Of these 4,611, a little over one-third were affiliated with business corporations, approximately 6 percent were affiliated with labor unions, and approximately 35 percent were unaffiliated with any parent group (unaffiliated PACs often focus on electoral politics). The other approximately 30 percent of PACs were affiliated with other types of groups including professional associations, trade associations, and citizen groups. During the 2007–08 election cycle PACs donated $379.97 million to House and Senate candidates (Federal Election Commission 2009b). In sum, one way that an interest group can try to influence legislation is to form a PAC and contribute money to candidates for Congress. Not all interest groups are allowed to form PACs, but many are.

### Monitoring and Other Non-lobbying Activities

While meeting with legislators and giving money to legislators are the activities that come to mind when most people think of lobbying, the reality of lobbying is a bit different. Specifically, the reality of lobbying involves a lot of waiting and watching. Qualitative studies show that most lobbyists spend considerable time working in their offices rather than actively lobbying. What precisely are they doing? Interest group scholar Robert Salisbury (1990: 224) answers:

The tasks that are both the most time consuming and the most important are concerned not so much with persuading government officials to act one way or another as with keeping track of what is happening in the policy process, alerting the client organizations to developments relevant to their interests, and developing appropriate strategies of response or adaptation.

Arguably the most important non-lobbying activity is monitoring (see Heinz et al. 1993: especially Ch. 4; Kersh 2006). Monitoring is broadly defined as keeping track of what government and other interest groups and lobbyists are up to. Monitoring government is important for a number of reasons. First, monitoring government enables lobbyists to identify policy proposals that affect the interest(s) they represent. Second, monitoring government gives lobbyists crucial information about the political prospects of the policy proposals that might affect them. As Wright (1996) notes, one of the types of information that lobbyists provide to government officials is political information. Only by monitoring government can lobbyists acquire such information. Third, for many types of lobbyists—especially those representing business firms—monitoring government is crucial for keeping the organized interests they represent out of trouble. Harris (1989) has noted that to comply with complex and manifold government policies, interest groups must be aware of, and understand, them. For highly regulated organizations such as business firms, monitoring government is essential.

Monitoring other interest groups and lobbyists also is important. Lobbyists make decisions every day about which branches of government to lobby, which individuals to lobby, and the types of strategies and tactics to use. Austen-Smith and Wright (1992) show that under certain conditions lobbyists decide which legislators to lobby partially based upon what their opponents are doing (or at least their expectations about what their opponents *will* do). Similarly, Holyoke (2003) concludes that an interest group's choice of which venue(s) to lobby is profoundly affected by the choices of its opponents. Holyoke also finds that a group's choice of tactics is affected by what its opponents do.

A closely related activity is researching—that is, gathering and generating policy information to be used in a lobbying campaign. Interestingly, while lobbyists are clearly vital sources of policy information for government officials, there is some evidence that lobbyists themselves are not always the primary sources of this information (Kersh 2006). Although lobbyists frequently pass policy information along to government officials, the information itself is often produced by non-lobbyists (e.g., academics and organization staff members). Nevertheless, Kersh notes that lobbyists themselves, often by dint of their considerable expertise and knowledge, are frequently the originators as well as the purveyors of policy information (401).

Lobbyists also spend considerable time interacting with their clients (Kersh 2006). For contract lobbyists, or lobbyists for hire, clients are the people to whom they report within the organization(s) they represent. For an in-house lobbyist, the client is the person or group of people to whom she reports within the single organization she represents. Kersh (2002) argues that client interaction takes many forms. For example, when they interact with their clients, lobbyists: (1) explain issues (i.e., engage in "educating and instructing clients" (237)); (2) discuss strategy (i.e., the proper course of subsequent action); (3) broker meetings (i.e., arrange or attend "meetings between client and public official" (237)); (4) solicit business; (5) receive directions; and (6) prepare clients for meetings with public officials. Of these activities, explaining issues and discussing strategy take up the most time. Other scholars highlight the importance of client interaction as well. Ainsworth and Sened (1993), for example, note that a lobbyist's role often extends to informing clients about government activity. Indeed, one of the reasons that lobbyists monitor government and other organized interests and lobbyists is to gather information they can then pass on to their clients.

### Who Do Lobbyists Lobby?

The question of which legislators are lobbied has received a surprisingly large amount of attention over the years. Many people assume that lobbying is about arm-twisting and threats; that is, lobbyists try to get what they want by convincing public officials who disagree with them to change their minds. Early studies of lobbying, however, cast doubt upon this assumption. For example, Bauer, Pool, and Dexter (1963) concluded that lobbyists focus their efforts on MCs who already agree with them, working not to change people's minds but, rather, to bolster the efforts of those already on their side. Other studies conducted around the same time reported similar findings (see, e.g., Matthews 1960). The logic here is hard to argue with. First, getting people to change their mind is difficult (see Milbrath 1963). Second, lobbying allies is important because it makes allies grateful and can even affect the level of effort they exert on a group's behalf (Hall and Wayman 1990). More recently, Hall and Deardorff (2006) argue that lobbyists focus their efforts on allies, essentially subsidizing their legislative activities. The lobbyist's "proximate objective," they argue, "is *not* to change legislators' minds but to assist natural allies in achieving their own, coincident objectives" (Hall and Deardorff 2006: 69, italics in original). Legislators have a powerful incentive to listen to interest groups because legislating is a long and arduous process, and MCs and their staffers have limited resources. In short, MCs need help and allied lobbyists are happy to provide it.

This basic view of lobbyists as subsidizers and information-providers to their friends is somewhat counterintuitive, as it suggests that lobbyists are more or less powerless to convert their opponents and do not even try. Moreover, this view implies that lobbyists are rather minor players in the policy process, as they help MCs get what they already want rather than affecting the direction of policy per se. Empirically this view of lobbyists has received only mixed support. For example, Austen-Smith and Wright (1994) show that lobbyists spend considerable time lobbying legislators who oppose them and often try to counteract lobbying conducted by opposing groups. Hojnacki and Kimball (1998) show that lobbyists often lobby their legislative allies when a bill they support is in committee, then expand their lobbying efforts and lobby undecideds and opponents if the bill reaches the floor. Finally, in his textured study of Common Cause, Rothenberg (1992) shows that lobbyists often expend a great deal of time lobbying undecided legislators.

Though there is some lingering disagreement among political scientists about this, the empirical literature appears to contradict any strong version of the argument that lobbyists never lobby legislators who disagree with them or undecideds. In all, there is considerable evidence that lobbyists lobby their friends, their enemies, and undecideds in Congress.

### Is Lobbying Sleazy?

Citizens and scholars alike often raise one additional question: Is lobbying sleazy? While many believe the answer to this question is "yes," the actual evidence on lobbying suggests otherwise. One reason for this is that Congress has rules that limit what lobbyists can do. In 2007, Congress passed the Honest Leadership and Open Government Act. The Act forbids members of Congress and their staffers from accepting almost any gifts or travel from lobbyists. The Act also tightened lobbyist registration rules. As for money, federal law limits how much PACs and lobbyists can give to candidates for office. Today, individuals (including lobbyists) can give only $2,400 per candidate per election. The corresponding limit for PACs is $5,000. These are not insignificant amounts of money, but it is not the case that PACs and lobbyists can contribute billions to the candidates they support; they cannot. In short, federal law prohibits many of the sleazy activities that some citizens take for granted as lobbying staples. Moreover, there is evidence that lobbyists take these laws very seriously, especially since Republican uber-lobbyist Jack Abramoff was sent to federal prison.

## Interest Group Influence in Congress

In the previous section I noted that many Americans believe that lobbyists are sleazy. They feel much the same about Congress. In short, people do not like Congress very much (see, e.g., Hibbing and Larimer 2008). Why is this the case? There are several answers to this question, but one is that many citizens believe that many MCs do the bidding of powerful "special interests" and regularly ignore the wishes of their constituents. Is this true? Are interest groups and lobbyists powerful forces in congressional politics? To what extent do lobbyists get what they want from Congress? It is to these important questions that I turn next.

## The Question of Interest Group Influence: It's Hard to Answer

So how much influence *do* interest groups and lobbyists exert over congressional decisions? Unfortunately for scholars and students, the answer to this question has proven elusive. Why? First, it is impossible to know for certain why members of Congress behave the way they do. If a senator, for example, votes "No" on a piece of gun control legislation, did she do it because the National Rifle Association's PAC gave her campaign committee $5,000 last year? Or did she do it because she received thousands of letters from her constituents saying that she should vote "No?" Or could it be that the senator has always been ideologically predisposed to oppose gun control? The fact is that we can never really know why MCs do the things they do, because we cannot get inside their heads. This is simply another way of saying that many factors affect the way MCs behave. Among the most important influences on congressional behavior are constituency preferences, ideology, and party. Other factors affect MCs' behavior as well, including pressure from party leaders, the president, ranking committee members, and other MCs (Kingdon 1989). In short, because so many factors affect how MCs behave, it is impossible to know for certain where lobbying fits in.

A second reason that assessing interest group influence is difficult is that measuring influence accurately is impossible. It turns out that what looks like *influence* is often simply *agreement*. Going back to our senator and gun control legislation, let us assume that we studied her legislative behavior and found that she had received thousands of dollars in contributions from the NRA's PAC over the years, had met repeatedly with NRA lobbyists in the weeks before a roll-call vote on gun control legislation, and then voted the way the NRA wanted her to. Does all this mean that the NRA influenced her vote? No. Just because an MC behaves the way a lobbyist wants her to, does not mean that the lobbyist affected her. It might simply mean that the MC agreed with the lobbyist all along.

Finally, it is difficult to determine how much power interest groups exert over congressional decisions because the legislative process is a multi-stage one. First, there is the *agenda-setting* stage, in which issues reach the congressional agenda. Second, there is the *committee stage*, during which bills are marked up. Third, there is the *floor stage*, in which legislation is actually voted upon by MCs. The fact that the legislative process has three stages makes it very difficult to determine precisely where interest groups and lobbying fit in. Why? Consider, for example, a study of roll-call votes. Let's say that we definitively show that interest groups and their lobbyists do not affect the way MCs vote on legislation. Can we conclude that interest groups and their lobbyists do not exercise influence? No. It might be that interest groups do not influence MCs' voting decisions, but do affect the way MCs behave in committees or which issues reach the legislative agenda.

## PAC Contributions

In short, figuring out how much influence interest groups and lobbyists exercise in the legislative process is very difficult. This has not stopped scholars from trying, however. The last stage of the legislative process—the roll-call stage— arguably has attracted more scholarly attention than the other two stages. This is the case because roll-call behavior is easy to observe, and thus good data on roll-call votes are available.

*PACs and roll-call votes.* Many studies of roll-call votes address the question of interest group influence by asking, do PAC contributions affect how MCs vote on legislation? The results have been mixed. Some studies show that PAC contributions do indeed affect floor voting (see, e.g., Evans 1986; Saltzman 1987; Langbein 1993), while others show they do not (Grenzke 1989; Rothenberg 1992; Wawro 2001). In all, the evidence suggests that PAC contributions sometimes affect the way MCs vote and sometimes do not. It appears that PACs are most likely to affect congressional voting on issues that are non-salient and non-ideological (see Wright 1985; Magleby and Nelson 1990; Neustadtl 1990; Davis 1993, Witko 2006). These issues are ripe for PAC influence, the argument goes, because other factors that affect MCs' voting behavior are less relevant than they are on high-profile issues.

*PAC money and committees.* Some scholars point out that PAC money is probably more influential at the committee stage than at the vote stage. They base this assertion on the fact that MCs might be more receptive to PACs in committees rather than on the floor because committee proceedings are generally shielded from public scrutiny. Along these lines, Hall and Wayman (1990) argue that PAC money might not buy votes, but might buy effort. Their analyses show that PAC money given to sympathetic legislators can act to increase these legislators' efforts. In a follow-up study, Witko (2006) shows that PAC money does indeed affect legislative effort within committees, but only on issues that are visible and ideological.

*PAC money and access.* While there is some debate about how PAC money affects MCs' behavior within committees and on the floor, there is widespread agreement that PAC money can buy access to legislators. The argument is simple—PACs contribute money to legislators so the parent group's lobbyists can get their "foot in the door." In her large-scale study of PAC contributions in the House, Langbein (1986) shows that money can indeed buy access to House members. Grenzke (1989) and others reach a similar conclusion, and the idea that "money buys access" has been elevated more or less to the status of conventional wisdom (see, e.g., Herndon 1982; Wright 1990; Birnbaum 2000; Lowery and Brasher 2004: Ch. 5). The data on PAC behavior supports the view that PAC money buys access, or at the very least is designed to do so. Specifically, studies demonstrate that all else being equal, more PAC money goes to committee chairs, members of the majority party, and incumbents (for a summary, see Rozell, Wilcox, and Madland 2006: Ch. 3). All of this suggests that PACs contribute money so their lobbyists can have access to whoever happens to be in charge.

And yet there is some reason to suspect that the conventional wisdom is flawed. First, there is some evidence (see Chin, Bond, and Geva 2000; Chin 2005) suggesting that money offers little access to legislators. Instead, access is reserved for those with direct constituent ties and district interests. Additionally, there is considerable evidence that many PACs give for electoral reasons rather than to gain access. In other words, many PACs do not give to affect roll-call votes or committee effort, but give to affect who wins. This point of view is supported by studies showing that many PACs are either unaffiliated PACs or are affiliated with organizations that do not have lobbyists (see, e.g., Wright 1989; Gais and Walker 1991; Gais 1996). However, more recent work by Tripathi, Ansolabehere, and Snyder (2002) shows that while many groups—especially labor unions—follow an "electoral strategy" and give money to ideological allies, most PAC money comes from groups that follow an "access strategy" and thus use PAC money to get their proverbial "foot in the door."

So does PAC money buy access? Unfortunately, there is no definitive answer to this question. A careful reading of the literature suggests that "Yes, sometimes" is a reasonable answer. I am most convinced by studies showing that PAC money can indeed affect how much attention MCs pay to interest groups and their lobbyists. Other factors may be more important than PAC money in determining to whom MCs decide to grant an audience, but money is still important.

### Lobbying and Policy Outcomes

Does lobbying affect congressional policy decisions? Rather than review the extensive literature in an attempt to address this question, I will summarize what I consider the two dominant threads of theorizing about interest group influence: *subgovernment theory*, and *neopluralism*. While subgovernment theory has grown unfashionable of late, neopluralism continues to attract and hold scholarly adherents. To understand what interest group scholars think about the influence of lobbyists on congressional policymaking, it is necessary to understand these two strands of theory.

*Subgovernments.* As interest groups proliferated in mid-twentieth-century America, political scientists began to take note of their role in policymaking. For example, Truman (1951) argued in *The Governmental Process*, that interest groups were influential players in the political process. In the policy battles he investigated, Truman found interest group influence everywhere. In case after case, he saw MCs interacting extensively with interest groups before reaching their final decisions. Truman stopped short of concluding that interest groups dominated policymaking, but he implied that MCs and other government officials were quite responsive to interest groups.

Truman and other early interest group scholars (see, e.g., Latham 1952; Golembiewski 1960) demonstrated that studying Congress in isolation was silly; interest groups and their lobbyists simply had to be considered to understand how congressional decisions were really made. It is interesting to note that many of the early studies of interest groups did not see them as particularly threatening. Several empirical studies essentially argued that interest groups were legitimate linkage institutions, and provided a useful and benign service to MCs by providing them with information to help them make decisions (Bauer et al. 1963; Milbrath 1963).

All this attention to interest groups eventually led to the formulation of a new theory of interest group influence—subgovernment theory.[2] Essentially, subgovernment theorists argued that individual policy areas had their own subgovernments (or "iron triangles"), each of which consisted of a severely limited number of interest groups, MCs, and program administrators, who interacted on a stable and ongoing basis to make policy (Berry 1989: 172–4). Wright (1996: 168–9) describes how the veterans' affairs subgovernment worked: "House and Senate Veterans' Affairs Committees in Congress, the Veterans Administration, and organizations such as the American Legion and the Veterans of Foreign Wars (VFW) work[ed] together in developing policies on education, health care, and housing for veterans." The defense subgovernment was similarly configured, as House and Senate committees that dealt with defense issues, defense contractors, and bureaucrats from the U.S. interacted regularly to make defense policy.

Subgovernment theorists argued that the congressional decisions that came out of these iron triangles were self-serving in that they provided benefits for the participants in the subgovernment but none for the public as a whole. The interest groups portrayed by subgovernment theorists were extremely influential. Their lobbyists were more or less on equal footing with the MCs with whom they interacted regularly. Moreover, most active and important groups had a subgovernment of their own (i.e., farm groups worked in the agriculture subgovernment, labor unions worked in the labor subgovernment, defense contractors worked in the defense subgovernment, etc.). Interest groups engaged in extensive logrolling in which they minded their own business, stuck to their own subgovernments, and continued to make policy.

Is subgovernment theory accurate? On the one hand, it seems to have gotten a lot of things right. For example, it correctly noted that policy decisions are not made merely by one institution of government (e.g., Congress), but are a function of ongoing relationships between lobbyists and government officials from both the legislative and executive branches. Second, it recognized that most interest groups have fairly narrow policy concerns. Finally, it drew attention to the fact that interest groups often work together with other like-minded groups to get what they want. On the other hand, subgovernment theory was deeply flawed.[3] First, it completely ignores the president. Presidents are extremely important in the policymaking process (see, e.g., Baumgartner et al. 2009: Ch. 11). Second, it portrays the policymaking process as consensual and stable, which is not the case. Third, subgovernment theory implies that groups do not fight with each other but, rather, accommodate each other. We know this is not true. Since the explosion of citizen groups in the 1960s and 1970s (Walker 1991), few large and important policy areas are home to consensual policymaking, and conflict is commonplace as sets of groups square up to each other (see, e.g., Heinz et al. 1993; Baumgartner et al. 2009). Finally, subgovernment theory implies that interest groups that can work themselves into iron triangles tend to get what they want. But this is not the case. In the real world, policies create winners *and* losers.

*Neopluralism.* The weaknesses of subgovernment theory led a new generation of interest group scholars to reexamine the question of interest group influence. And though research conducted over the past twenty-five years on group influence is broad and varied, it is safe to say that most interest group scholars accept some version of the neopluralist view of interest group influence, which resulted from this attention. This view is far too complex to fully present here; but at its core is the idea that interest group influence is contingent and situational (Heinz et al. 1993; Kollman 1998). In the congressional context, the ability of interest groups to get what they want is severely constrained by legislators' preferences, the byzantine nature of the lawmaking process, the presence of opposing groups, the ability of the president to offer new policy proposals that demand legislative attention, the unpredictable nature of electoral politics, and the effects of external events (such as 9/11) that can scramble the legislative agenda.

And there are three other things that severely hamper interest groups' ability to get what they want. First, there is the power of the status quo. Baumgartner et al. (2009) conclude that interest groups have a very hard time affecting policy because policy is stubbornly resistant to change. In particular, they conclude that (2009: 241–2):

> In spite of millions of dollars often spent on all the latest lobbying techniques and the involvement of some of the nation's most powerful corporations, consultants, and political leaders, most lobbying campaigns end in a stand-off, the status quo policy remaining in place.

"The sources of the bias in favor of the status quo," they continue, "are numerous." One of the most important sources of this bias is interest groups' and lobbyists' inability to get anyone's attention. There are lots of things going on in Congress and, as a lobbyist, getting an MC to pay attention to you is not easy.

The second thing that hampers interest groups' ability to get what they want is their own behavior. A lot of interest group and lobbyist activity is not really designed to affect policy at all. As noted earlier, many lobbyists spend most of their time doing things other than lobbying (Wright 1996; Hojnacki 1997; Carpenter, Esterling, and Lazer 1998).

The third and final thing that inhibits interest groups' ability to get what they want is the ubiquity of information in Washington. Information is the primary weapon in the lobbyist's arsenal. But Washington in general, and Congress in particular, are awash with information. In most policy areas, Baumgartner et al. (2009: 250) argue, players are "commonly aware, as a group, of the facts and figures associated with the justification for the current policy, various proposals to change it, and research or experiences in states, communities, or foreign countries suggesting how any policy changes might be implemented." This makes the lobbyist's job difficult. First, it reduces the probability that any one lobbyist can bring new information to bear on any subject. Second, it means that even if a lobbyist is capable of bringing new and potentially persuasive information to bear on a policy issue, she is likely to be met swiftly by opponents who can counter her argument. Baumgartner et al. (2009: 250) argue:

> But when a new argument is introduced to the policy community, it is assessed by others who are equally expert on the background and technical details of the policy as the one making the proposal. Elements of the debate that the advocate promoting the new argument chooses to ignore can be quickly brought to the attention of others.

In short, the neopluralist view suggests that interest groups do not have their run of Washington, and true power resides just where our system puts it—in the hands of government officials. Neopluralists, whose views are backed by extensive empirical research, portray groups as far from dominant. As Richard A. Smith (1995: 106) argues, "the impact of lobbying is conditional on the value of other variables." But this statement is vaguely unsatisfying because it begs the question: When and under what conditions can and do interest groups affect policy outcomes? Even the most die-hard neopluralist understands that although interest groups face obstacles when they attempt to affect policy, they do sometimes get what they want from government. So the question is, when?

The first and most obvious answer is that interest groups that *oppose* change are more likely to be successful than are interest groups that *propose* change. Again, the status quo is difficult to change, and playing defense is easier than playing offense. Of course, if *only* interest groups oppose change—that is, if all other important actors desire change—they are not likely to prevail; such is the nature of policymaking. But the likelihood of success in any case is higher when interest groups are lobbying in favor of the status quo.

Second, there is evidence that interest groups that operate in narrow "issue niches" and thus do not ask for much from policymakers, are more likely to exert influence than groups that ask for major change. Browne (1990) argues that in the crowded and chaotic policymaking environment of Washington, the best way for a group to survive and affect policy is to pick a narrow and unique issue identity that makes it "marketable" to policymakers. Focusing narrowly bestows two great advantages upon an interest group. First, it allows the group to develop a reputation for expertise that it need not share with other groups. Second, it allows a group to avoid opposition from other groups. According to this "niche theory" of representation, interest groups affect policy, but only on small, relatively invisible policy issues. Thus, almost by definition, niche-seeking groups tend to ask for less than they really want because their primary goal is to find comfortable spots where they face no opposition. Smith (2000) provides indirect evidence in support of niche theory by showing that on big overarching "non-niche" issues of interest to the business community, business interest groups are more or less powerless. This is the case because they almost invariably face strong opposition from the other side on such issues. Moreover, big issues tend to be partisan and ideological, and thus MCs and other government decision-makers tend to already have strong opinions about them. "Niche theory" is logically appealing. In addition, it is compelling because empirical studies (see especially Baumgartner and Leech 2001) show that many issues before Congress receive the attention of only a small handful of interest groups. Nonetheless, the notion that groups that focus narrowly tend to get what they want from government more than groups that do not has not been widely tested, and at this point we have only suggestive evidence that it is true.

Baumgartner et al. (2009) also show that interest groups have a relatively higher chance of success when they have lots of government officials on their side. Interest groups are not particularly influential when they ask for things that lots of people in government do not want. This finding provides a corrective to any naive notion that interest groups regularly foist their demands on reluctant MCs.

Finally, there is evidence that, *ceteris paribus*, interest groups with more resources tend to get more from Congress than interest groups with fewer resources. Baumgartner et al. (2009: 237) provide the most definitive word on the subject, finding that "resources are a predictor of policy success" (see also Heinz et al. 1993: Ch. 11). Resources help interest groups and coalitions of interest groups attract scarce attention, and allow interest groups and coalitions of groups to get the best and most persuasive information. But resources are the proverbial double-edged sword. While it is nice to have lots of resources, lots of resources tend to mobilize opposition, thus blunting their effects.

In the end, neopluralists offer unsatisfying (but accurate) answers to the question of how much influence interest groups exert over congressional decisions. For example, Baumgartner et al. (2009: 237), after considering the effects of lobbying on policy change, conclude: "it is difficult to find reliable predictors of policy change." Similarly, after conducting numerous painstaking analyses to determine which lobbyists and interest groups are successful and which are not and why, Heinz et al. (1993: 351) conclude: "The most important point, however, is that so much of the variance in success is not explained by these analyses. This suggests that the determinants of success are usually situation specific." In the end, we are left to conclude that when MCs make decisions, interest groups will always be around. And there is plenty of evidence that MCs listen to them. But they are seldom determinative.

## Conclusion

Tens of thousands of interest groups spend billions of dollars each year trying to affect decisions. These groups target Congress in particular. Interest groups lobby Congress because what Congress does affects them. MCs listen to interest groups and lobbyists because they represent citizens and powerful economic interests active in their districts. Moreover, interest groups and their lobbyists help MCs fulfill their goals.

Interest groups and lobbyists perform many functions. But in the end, most lobbying activity comes down to *providing information*. In short, information, rather than money or a bribe or a threat, is the primary weapon in the lobbyist's arsenal. The main type of information that lobbyists provide is policy information—information about the effects of a proposed or existing policy. Lobbyists provide information to MCs in a variety of ways, but one lobbying technique in particular is very common and effective—meeting personally with MCs or congressional staff. Many interest groups also testify before legislative hearings, and contribute money to candidates. There is some debate among scholars about who within Congress interest groups and their lobbyists lobby, but the bulk of the evidence suggests that lobbyists at one time or another lobby their friends, their enemies, and undecideds.

Just how powerful are interest groups? This is an exceedingly difficult question to answer. Those who have addressed it have come up with the following answer: *It depends*. In other words, sometimes interest groups exercise a great deal of influence and sometimes they do not. Certainly the available evidence suggests that interest groups are far from dominant players in congressional politics. The policymaking process simply is too chaotic, and MCs themselves too autonomous and powerful, for us to conclude that interest groups and lobbyists call the shots in Washington. However, careful empirical studies show that interest groups do tend to be powerful players in Washington, largely by dint of their positions in networks of decision-makers.

Perhaps the most important thing that interest group scholars can tell students and scholars of Congress is that to understand Congress we must also understand interest groups. They are integral parts of the congressional policymaking process, and they work closely with MCs and congressional staff. Still, we have much to learn about precisely what role they play in the congressional decision-making process, and hopefully we can come up a few more answers in the years to come.

## Notes

1 See also Nownes (2006) for a related discussion.
2 Prominent subgovernment theorists include Cater (1964), Freeman (1955), and Maass (1951). For a related discussion on subgovernment theory, see Nownes (2000: 198–202).
3 For empirical studies that cast doubt on subgovernment theory, see Bosso (1987), Cook (1998), and Hansen (1991).

# Chapter 13

# Congressional Spending
## The Special Case of Earmarks

*Michael H. Crespin and Charles J. Finocchiaro*

Since the time of the Founding, spending politics in the U.S. Congress has developed from a relatively simple process to a very complex series of procedures. In early congresses, the separate chambers would simply create ad-hoc committees to write bills that would appropriate (or designate) money for various projects. The bills would then be debated in the Committee of the Whole before the respective chambers would hold a vote. For example, when then-Representative John C. Calhoun wanted to advance legislation to fund internal improvements such as roads and canals across the United States—what would become the Bonus Bill of 1817—he simply formed a committee to write the bill and then introduced it in the House. The House took up the bill a few months later and after some debate, it passed the House and then the Senate. Although President Madison vetoed the bill on constitutional grounds, the process tracks reasonably well with the standard textbook description of how a bill becomes a law.

Today, an in-depth treatment of the spending process could fill an entire textbook. Budgeting now involves multiple committees, various bureaucratic agencies, and complicated parliamentary maneuvers. Although the process has evolved from straightforward to intricate, there has been one constant: disagreements over how much money to spend and where to send it. Before moving on to a discussion of the politics of federal spending with a specific focus on legislative earmarks, we begin by providing a sketch of the current budgetary process.

## The Congressional Budget Process

After the passage of the Congressional and Budget Impoundment Control Act of 1974, the congressional budget process became much more routinized. In short, this act set up a number of steps with specific deadlines that the Congress is supposed to meet in order to pass a budget for the upcoming fiscal year. In addition, the act called for the creation of the House and Senate Budget Committees and the Congressional Budget Office (CBO). The main goal was to streamline the process and create a budget blueprint, the Budget Resolution.

The resolution would set overall spending limits before the appropriations committees would determine levels for the specific governmental accounts. Table 13.1 lists the steps and dates. While Congress rarely meets this schedule, the steps can act as a guide to understanding the general process.[1]

Before Congress begins to allocate money to the various governmental programs and agencies, the president submits his budget to the House and Senate. Well before the deadline, the president usually works with the heads of executive agencies and the Office of Management and Budget (OMB) to determine spending levels. The president's budget generally includes estimates for money coming into the government (revenues), money going out (expenditures), and differences between the two (either debt or surplus). In addition, the president's budget also includes projections for the next five years. Although the president's budget cannot bind Congress, it often acts as a starting point for any negotiations between parties, committees, or chambers. When the president is popular, especially under unified government, Congress is more likely to respond to his requests. When presidential popularity is low, or during divided government, Congress often sets overall budget lines that are different from what the president recommends (Oleszek 2007).

After the president submits his proposed budget in early February, the House and Senate budget committees hold hearings while the CBO prepares a report on the economic and budgetary outlook. The hearings allow authoriz-

Table 13.1 The Congressional Budget Process Timetable

| Deadline | Action |
| --- | --- |
| First Monday in February | President submits budget to Congress |
| February 15 | CBO submits report on economic and budget outlook to budget committees |
| Six weeks after President's budget is submitted | Committees submit reports on views and estimates to respective budget committees |
| April 1 | Senate Budget Committee reports budget resolution |
| April 15 | Congress completes action on budget resolution |
| June 10 | House Appropriations Committee reports last regular appropriations bill |
| June 30 | House completes action on regular appropriations bills and any required reconciliation legislation |
| July 15 | President submits mid-session review of his budget to Congress |
| October 1 | Fiscal Year begins |

Source: Introduction to the Federal Budget Process CRS Report (98–721)

ing committees to provide their views on the budget within their specific areas of jurisdiction. Although the CBO is a creation of the Congress, it is generally considered a non-partisan and independent agency. The CBO's report includes budget baseline projections for revenue and expenditures and also reestimates the president's budget. The report allows Congress to compare different spending proposals to the level of spending proposed by the president.

Once the CBO issues its reports and the budget committees hold their hearings, each budget committee issues a separate budget resolution for consideration on the floor of their respective chambers. It is important to note that these documents are concurrent resolutions, which means that they do not go to the president for his approval and do not carry the force of law. In the House, the resolution goes to the floor under normal procedure, typically with a special rule that governs how it will be considered. In some years, the rule allows members to offer amendments in the nature of a substitute that replaces the entire resolution with a completely different budget proposal. Usually, the alternative proposals are offered by groups such as the Congressional Black Caucus or the fiscally conservative Blue Dog Coalition and the leadership is careful to make sure they do not pass. The alternative proposals are a form of position taking, and members use them to boost their reelection chances (Mayhew 1974a).

In the Senate, the resolution is considered privileged so it cannot be filibustered, although the rules still allow for fifty hours of debate. Once the two chambers pass their respective resolutions, they reconcile any differences via a conference committee. When the conference completes its work and both chambers pass the compromise resolution, Congress moves on from setting overall levels in the budget to setting levels for specific programs and agencies through the appropriations process.

According to Oleszek (2007), it is important to understand the difference between authorizing and appropriating. When Congress uses its authorizing powers, it creates (or continues) a particular agency or program. This work is traditionally done in authorizing committees such as the Agriculture Committee or Transportation Committee.[2] Authorization alone, however, does not allow a program to operate since some sort of funding is usually required. If funding is necessary, Congress uses the appropriations process to allocate money for the agency or program. According to the "textbook" view of the legislative process, the twelve appropriations subcommittees in the House and Senate each write a bill that funds the authorized programs and agencies for the upcoming fiscal year. Each of the twelve bills covers a defined area of jurisdiction (or set of issues). The bills then go to the floor of the respective chambers where they are voted on separately. Any differences between the chambers are then either worked out in conference or through a process of passing the bills back and forth until agreement is reached. If both chambers can agree on the changes, the final bills receive a vote and then make their way to the president's desk for his signature or veto.

Table 13.2 lists the names of the appropriations subcommittees for the House and Senate as well as their respective chairs for the 111th Congress (2009–11). In order to facilitate passing the appropriations bills in a timely manner, Congress reorganized the subcommittees in 2007 so that each subcommittee in the House would have the same jurisdiction as its counterpart in the Senate. Daniel Inouye (D-HI) and David Obey (D-WI) are the chairs of the full appropriations committees in the Senate and House, respectively. Since the Democrats had a majority in each chamber during this Congress, their members served as chairs of the twelve subcommittees as well. These subcommittee chairs are often referred to as the "Cardinals" due to the large budgets they effectively control. As the subcommittees work on their separate bills, they decide how much funding, if any, to give to the programs that fall under their jurisdictions. Although the authorizing committees can offer recommended funding levels, the appropriators are under no obligation to follow those guidelines. If the committees fail to provide money for a program, it might exist on paper but will not be able to operate effectively.

Because unforeseen circumstances can arise and because Congress has a habit of not always following standard procedure, the appropriations committees are sometimes called upon to pass supplemental or continuing funding bills. Supplemental appropriations might be used to provide funding for disaster relief or other emergencies. For example, after Hurricane Katrina hit the Gulf Coast in 2005, Congress quickly passed a measure to provide $10.5 billion for food, shelter, and other relief efforts (Lake and Chite 2005). If Congress does not pass the annual appropriations bills on time, a "continuing resolution" (or CR) is used to provide funding until a regular bill is passed. While the number of bills passed on time each year has varied (in 2010, not a single appropriations

*Table 13.2* House and Senate Appropriations Subcommittees, 111th Congress

| Subcommittee | Senate Chair | House Chair |
| --- | --- | --- |
| Agriculture | Herb Kohl (WI) | Rosa DeLauro (CT) |
| Commerce, Justice, Science | Barbara Mikulski (MD) | Alan Mollohan (WV) |
| Defense | Daniel Inouye (HI) | Norman Dicks (WA) |
| Energy and Water | Bryon Dorgan (ND) | Peter Visclosky (IN) |
| Financial Services | Richard Durbin (IL) | José Serrano (NY) |
| Homeland Security | Frank Lautenberg* (NJ) | David Price (NC) |
| Interior and Environment | Dianne Feinstein (CA) | James Moran (VA) |
| Labor, HHS, Education | Tom Harkin (IA) | David Obey (WI) |
| Legislative Branch | Ben Nelson (NE) | Debbie Wasserman Schultz (FL) |
| Military Construction, VA | Tim Johnson (SD) | Chet Edward (TX) |
| State, Foreign Operations | Patrick Leahy (VT) | Nita Lowery (NY) |
| Transportation, HUD | Patty Murray (WA) | John Olver (MA) |

* Interim Chair

bill had passed both chambers by the start of the 2011 fiscal year in October), continuing resolutions have been required every year for at least a decade. For the 2001 fiscal year, twenty-one continuing resolutions were enacted prior to Congress and the president finally settling on appropriations just days before the Christmas holiday.

To obtain a clearer picture of overall government spending, it is necessary to differentiate between *discretionary spending*, which Congress can change from year to year, and *mandatory spending* (or direct spending) for interest payments on the national debt and entitlement programs such as Medicare, Medicaid, and Social Security. The latter group encompasses programs that must be funded by the government each year based on existing law. Discretionary spending amounts for programs such as defense, transportation, and agriculture, on the other hand, are set each year. Figure 13.1 provides a breakdown over time of different budget categories as a percentage of total spending.[3] According to the figure, the government has been spending a smaller share of the budget on defense since the 1960s and devoting more of the total budget to items such as Social Security, Medicaid, and Medicare. As the population ages, and health care costs rise, budget projections indicate even more money will go to these categories and less will remain for discretionary spending. In addition, the government will need to spend a larger share of the budget on servicing the growing national debt. In the future, a major challenge facing policymakers will be the need to find a way to bring spending down, increase the amount of money flowing to the federal treasury, or some combination of the two.

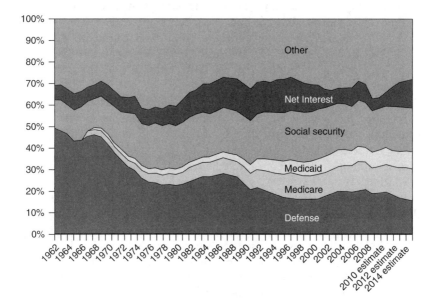

*Figure 13.1* Federal Budget Categories as Percentage of Total

## Political Science Research on the Politics of Spending

Previous scholarship on Congress's role in federal spending has typically been grounded in one of two broader theoretical approaches to studying legislative organization: distributive theories of lawmaking or the more recently emergent group of theories that posit a consequential role for political parties in determining legislative outcomes. Here we will briefly review each school of thought.

Distributive theories grew out of the influential work of David Mayhew (1974a), and were developed by a group of scholars including Fiorina (1977), Weingast (1979), Ferejohn (1986), Shepsle and Weingast (1987) and Weingast and Marshall (1988). To briefly summarize, they advance the argument that much of what we see in Congress's internal organization and operation is a function of members' inherent interest in promoting the sorts of policies that allow them to distribute benefits to their constituents to further their reelection goal. One key example is the committee system. Distributive scholars believe committees exist in large part to help legislators build "logrolls," which are coalitions across sets of issues that enable the legislature as a whole to get things done (see also Arnold 1990). This sort of mutually beneficial, "if you scratch my back, I'll scratch yours" sort of arrangement is facilitated by the ability of members to choose committee seats that are of interest to their constituents (a process known as "self-selection"), with committees then deferring to one another to promote the unique interests of the membership of the House as a whole. This arrangement is solidified, according to Weingast and Marshall (1988), by the power of committees to control issues that fall within their jurisdiction and members' ability to hold onto their committee seats through the seniority rule. The ramifications of the distributive arrangement of interests within Congress is a system characterized by inefficient spending promoted by members with a high demand for the federal benefits controlled by their respective committees.

Starting in the early 1990s, and corresponding to the increasing levels of polarization in Congress, a number of influential arguments have been made promoting the view that lawmaking is, at least to a significant degree, shaped by the interests of legislative parties. For instance, Cox (2001) and Cox and McCubbins (1993, 2002, 2005) advance a "cartel" model of legislative politics, in which the majority party takes control of the procedural aspects of the legislative process and exercises a veto over what will be considered on the floor of the House of Representatives. Thus, the key to party success is maintaining control of the agenda—and the majority party acts to ensure that legislation that would divide its members never sees the light of day. The conditional party government theory of Rohde (1991) and Aldrich and Rohde (1998, 2000a, 2001) suggests that the ability of parties and their leaders to extract gains and advance their position in the legislative process depends critically on the degree to which the parties represent two cohesive groups that are at odds with one another on the key issues of the day. When polarization is high, leaders are endowed by the rank and file with the resources necessary to actively promote the party's agenda.[4] Although most studies of parties have dealt with various aspects of the leadership and agenda setting, some scholarship has applied party-based models specifically to the appropriations process (Kiewiet and McCubbins 1985, 1991; Aldrich and Rohde 2000b). Assuming that sending money to states and districts improves an incumbent's reelection chances, the majority party has a compelling reason to seek to advantage its members by steering more distributive benefits to them as opposed to the minority.

One fairly recent study by Balla et al. (2002) bridges the two literatures just described. The authors find that while House majority-party members are not more or less likely to receive a pork-barrel project than those from the minority (the study examined academic earmarks), the majority party does receive more dollars of pork. They find this pattern to be consistent with a rationale in pork-barreling of "blame avoidance"—that by cutting the minority in on the benefits (albeit at a lesser rate), the majority party insulates itself from charges of fiscal irresponsibility. In important ways, this perspective helps to reconcile what had been inconsistencies between the theoretical claims of universalistic distributive theories and the empirical results of majoritarian-based perspectives (Levitt and Snyder 1995; Carsey and Rundquist 1999; Lee and Oppenheimer 1999; Lee 2000). While Balla et al. (2002) uncovered a majority-party advantage in the House, this result did not extend to the Senate (see also Evans (2004), who analyzed Senate appropriations earmarks from three fiscal years), which they argue is in line with the comparatively weak partisan structure in that body (Huitt 1961; Ripley 1969; Sinclair 1989). Crespin and Finocchiaro (2008a), however, show that the same dynamic does indeed exist in the upper chamber, with the majority party taking about 60 percent of earmark dollars. The finding is based on the logic that the majority party in the Senate, while enjoying less procedural advantages than the House majority party, still benefits from the "must-pass" nature of appropriations legislation, control of the agenda within committees by virtue of holding all committee chairs, and through less-visible yet important procedural tools such as the motion to table, which allows senators to bypass consideration of amendments via a simple majority vote.

## Electoral Returns to Federal Spending

An underlying assumption of prior research on distributive politics and particularism, which is the steering of benefits to targeted constituencies, is that members engage in such practices with electoral considerations in mind. Moreover, members who face uncertainty over their reelection should be even more likely to seek pork (Stein and Bickers 1994). Despite the conventional wisdom, however, previous research has not found a consistent relationship between the amount of pork delivered to constituents and legislators' electoral performance. For instance, Feldman and Jondrow (1984)—who examine federal construction money and employment—do not observe a relationship between federal benefits and the vote shares of incumbent representatives. The same is true of Frisch's (1998) study of earmarks from the 103rd Congress and Stein and Bickers' (1994) analysis of the total number of projects. The latter, however, do uncover a link at the individual level: when aware of a new project, a voter is more likely to cast a vote for the incumbent. In other work, they also find that members who are successful in channeling resources to their districts are less likely to draw a strong challenger in the subsequent election (Bickers and Stein 1996). In sum, this body of research suggests that while pork might not have a direct relationship with incumbents' vote shares, it could well generate indirect returns via other factors that affect elections.

The absence of strong empirical support for a direct link between pork and elections prodded scholars to begin looking for a more nuanced connection. Sellers (1997) suggests that the benefits of federal money will be felt differentially depending on the context. He finds, for instance, that liberal legislators are rewarded while fiscal conservatives are not. Alvarez and Saving (1997) arrive at a similar conclusion—finding that Democrats benefit while Republicans do not. Most recently, in their analysis of House elections, Lazarus and Reilly (2010) determine that Democrats gain traction in the realm of traditional distributive spending (direct transfers) while Republicans in conservative districts benefit from distributive benefits of the contingent liability nature (e.g., small business loans). Taken as a whole, research on the connection between federal spending and electoral politics suggests that pork can be translated into votes, however its impact is often conditional.

## Conference Committees and Strategic Considerations in Budgetary Politics

The focus of members of Congress on getting reelected shapes in significant ways the choices they make and the actions they undertake while in office. In an attempt to demonstrate their political effectiveness, legislators have always sought to steer federal benefits back to their constituents. Just as members of Congress throughout the nineteenth century paid a great deal of attention to tariff rates that would affect local businesses and consumers (O'Halloran 1994), their modern counterparts are often consumed with finding ways to fund local projects, thereby raising their profile and producing opportunities to claim credit. As former House Speaker Thomas P. "Tip" O'Neill of Massachusetts was fond of saying, "All politics is local." With this in mind, many legislators find it very attractive to carve out a reputation at least partially built on prowess at the "pork barrel." Targeted projects—often inserted via "earmarks," which direct a specific amount of money to a particular activity or entity in a state or district—bring favorable coverage. And they have very little downside, unlike casting a vote on a controversial issue, which is likely to make both friends and enemies. Not surprisingly, they have grown in both frequency and cost over time, as shown in Figure 13.2.[5]

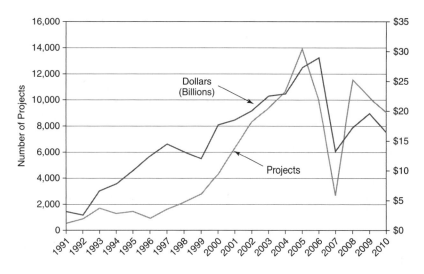

*Figure 13.2* Earmarks over Time

Of course, engaging in locally oriented pork-barrel politics is not without controversy of its own. In recent years, a growing number of "porkbusters" have emerged in Congress (Bovitz 2002). These mostly Republican members—the ranks of which include Representative Jeff Flake and Senator John McCain of Arizona, Senator Jim DeMint of South Carolina, and Senator Tom Coburn of Oklahoma—have built their reputations in part on their criticism of earmarks and federal spending more generally. Arguing that such projects are self-serving, deficit-growing, and best left to the determination of disinterested individuals and agencies, they have at times stemmed the tide of earmarks and been able to bog down the appropriations process in Congress. Others, such as Representative Jim Clyburn, also of South Carolina and the Democratic Whip in the House, argue that legislators know their districts best and can aid groups that do not have the clout of a Washington lobbyist (Behre 2007). Furthermore, Congress is the branch the framers endowed with the "power of the purse."

As the controversy surrounding earmarks has grown in recent years—due in part to greater public scrutiny and the efforts of groups such as Citizens Against Government Waste (CAGW) and Taxpayers for Common Sense—they have increasingly come under fire and many have advocated reform of the process if not an outright cessation of earmarking. One particular area that has received a considerable amount of attention is the practice of "airdropping"—which refers to adding earmarks at the conference committee stage of the legislative process, after the House and Senate have completed their work on a spending bill and often far-removed from the public's eye. Because conference committees are among the more archaic features of congressional politics, critics charge that they serve perfectly the interests of party and committee leaders in stacking the deck in their favor. For instance, a member facing a tough bid for reelection might be able to secure funding for some additional projects, and committee chairs might take an extra helping of pork before the final details of the bill are worked out.

Although the procedures for a conference committee appear to be straightforward, they can actually be quite complicated.[6] Here we describe some of these procedures using the Fiscal Year 2008 Defense Appropriations bill as an example. We also detail the revised earmark rules each chamber adopted during the 110th Congress (2007–08) and discuss how the electoral goals of members of Congress contributed to their strategic sidestepping of the "reforms" they implemented.[7] In the next section, we consider the implications of this bicameral feature of the budgetary process more broadly and explore who wins and who loses.

Generally, the House will consider the regular appropriations bills before the Senate, although this is by convention, not rule. The Constitution simply mandates that the House must move first on legislation that raises revenue and does not grant one chamber the prerogative to move first on spending bills. Late in the day on August 4, 2007, and stretching into the early hours of the 5th, the House began debating and amending the Department of Defense Appropriations bill, H.R. 3222, with subcommittee chair Representative John Murtha (D-PA) acting as the bill's manager on the floor. After taking roll-call votes on several amendments, including four by porkbuster Jeff Flake (R-AZ), the House passed the bill 395–13.

After returning from recess on September 4, the House sent a message to the Senate requesting the concurrence (agreement) of the Senate on H.R. 3222. On September 14, the Senate Appropriations Committee reported (recommended) the House bill with the addition of an amendment in the nature of a substitute. The amendment struck the language after the enacting clause—essentially all the content—from the House bill and replaced it with language from the Senate version. So, while the number for the bill to be debated in the Senate was H.R. 3222, the text of the bill was not identical to that passed by the House. This is a frequent means by which the House and Senate reconcile competing versions of legislation. In the simplest case, one chamber might consider a bill from another chamber and pass it with no changes. If one chamber passes the other's bill without amendments, it can then proceed to the president. Alternatively, the second-moving chamber can amend the other chamber's bill, as occurred in this instance.

Soon after the amended version of H.R. 3222 was reported, the Senate took it up for consideration. On October 3, after some debate and immediately before passage, the bill's manager, Senator Daniel Inouye (D-HI), asked for "unanimous consent that the Senate proceed to vote on passage of the bill, that upon passage, the Senate insist on its amendment, request a conference with the House on the disagreeing votes of the two Houses, and the Chair be authorized to appoint conferees on the part of the Senate with the subcommittee appointed as conferees" (*Congressional Record* [hereafter, *CR*] 10/03/07 pg. S12523). The Senate then passed the bill using a voice vote, insisted on its amendment, and named all the members of the Appropriations Defense subcommittee as conferees.[8]

On October 4, the Senate sent a message to the House informing them of the results of the previous day and asking for concurrence with the Senate amendments. Just over a month later, on November 5, Rep. Murtha made a motion to disagree with the Senate amendment and agree to the conference requested by the Senate.[9] If the House was to agree (or concur) with the Senate amendment, then it would be accepting the Senate version of the bill and a conference would not be necessary. The House agreed to Rep. Murtha's motion via a voice vote and the Speaker pro tempore appointed the members of the House Defense Appropriations subcommittee, along with the full committee chair and ranking member, to the conference committee.[10] Although the Speaker has the right to appoint House members to the conference committee, generally the chair and ranking member of the committee or subcommittee produce the list of conferees. In the Senate, the body can elect conferees but it usually allows the presiding officer to appoint them based on a list from the committee or subcommittee of jurisdiction. According to Lazarus and Monroe (2007), the Speaker of the House can pack the committee with additional members if she feels it will help produce outcomes closer to the majority-party position.

For 2007, the Appropriations Committee and the eventual conference committee were working under new earmark rules adopted in the House as part of the package of rules for the 110th Congress (H. Res. 6) as well as H. Res. 491, which was adopted in June. Rule XXI requires a listing of earmarks and their sponsors while H. Res 491, which was only in effect for the 110th Congress, dealt specifically with earmarks added in conference.[11] If a list of earmarks and sponsors is not available, then a member can raise a point of order against consideration of the legislation or conference report. Further, special rules—the vehicles used to bring bills to the floor for consideration in the House—are not supposed to waive points of order (or objections) dealing with the new conference provisions, as shown in Section 2 of H. Res. 491 (see Table 13.3). If a member raises a point of order (objection) on the special rule, then it is resolved with a vote on the question of consideration, not a ruling from the chair. If the majority votes in favor of considering the special rule, then the legislative process moves forward, even if the special rule does violate House rules. In this way, a majority of the House can, at any time, decide to set aside its standing rules. As we will discuss later, the special rule for the conference report did in fact contain language that waived all points of order.

In terms of conference committees, the new H. Res. 491 also required a listing of any new earmarks added in conference to the conference report *and* the joint explanatory statement. Technically, the *conference report* contains the text that will reconcile the differences between the legislation that passed the House

Table 13.3 Text of H. Res. 491, 110th Congress

---

## H. Res. 491

### In the House of Representatives, U.S.,
June 18, 2007.

Resolved, That during the remainder of the 110th Congress it shall not be in order to consider a conference report to accompany a regular general appropriation bill unless the joint explanatory statement prepared by the managers on the part of the House and the managers on the part of the Senate includes a list of congressional earmarks (as that term is used in clause 9(d) of rule XXI) in the conference report or joint statement (and the name of any Member, Delegate, Resident Commissioner, or Senator who submitted a request to the respective House or Senate committee for each respective item included on such list) that were not committed to the conference committee by either House, not in a report on such bill, and not in a report of a committee of the Senate on a companion measure.

SEC. 2. It shall not be in order to consider a rule or order that waives the application of the first section of this resolution.

SEC. 3. A point of order under this resolution shall be disposed of by the question of consideration under the same terms as specified in clause 9(b) of rule XXI.

Attest:

Clerk.

---

and the Senate, while the *explanatory statement* explains the conference report. The respective chambers vote on the conference report, but not the explanatory statement. The difference between the two reports allowed the Senate to avoid a new rule that chamber had adopted. If the list is not included, then a member can raise a point of order and the House must vote on the question of consideration.

The Senate passed similar legislation dealing with the disclosure of earmarks but with a few differences—most minor and one major. The Senate rule regarding earmarks was part of S. 1, the Honest Leadership and Open Government Act of 2007. Since the Senate does not use special rules to consider legislation, the new Senate rule did not allow the chamber to vote on a motion to proceed with legislation unless the committee chair (or majority leader) declared a list of earmarks and sponsors to be available on the Internet forty-eight hours before the vote. If the list was unavailable, a Senator could raise a point of order that must be dealt with before moving forward. Waiving these rules or points of order would require sixty votes to uphold the motion.

The major difference between the two chambers had to do with "airdrops" in conference. In short, the Senate rules did not allow its members to add earmarks to the conference report. However, they do not say anything about including new earmarks in the joint explanatory statement. Although previous Senate rules prohibited adding anything new to a bill in conference (such as an earmark) because it was beyond the scope of the differences between the chambers, the old rule was easy to skirt, especially if the Senate was using the House bill with their text inserted as an amendment in the nature of a substitute (Longley and Oleszek 1989: 234).[12] The new rules allowed a Senator to voice objection to an "airdropped" earmark by using the procedural motion known as "raising a point of order." This move makes it possible for the Senate to strike (or remove) the earmark in question from the report without rejecting the entire committee recommendation. If the Senate chooses this course, the House must then agree to the modified conference report.[13] The Senate can move to waive the points of order, however, if three-fifths of the chamber agrees to it.

Returning to the Defense bill, the conference committee met and quickly filed their report—which included twenty-four new earmarks totaling $59 million—on November 6, the day after the House agreed to conference with the Senate (CR 11/08/2007 pg. H13312). However, rather than listing the new projects in the conference report itself, the conferees relegated the details to the joint explanatory statement. When on November 7 the Rules Committee drafted its special rule (H. Res. 806) to provide for consideration of the conference report, it waived all points of order, a decision which clearly violated clause 9 of new House Rule XXI, not to mention the routinely waived three-day rule (requiring bills to be available seventy-two hours prior to their consideration). A day later, as the House began consideration of H. Res 806, Rep. Flake (R-AZ) raised a point of order against the rule because of the blanket waiver it contained, while Rep. Louise Slaughter (D-NY) defended the work of the Rules Committee, arguing that the conference report met the disclosure requirements relating to earmarks. After some debate, the House voted along party lines in favor of considering the matter by a count of 220–191 (CR H13311–13314), and then voted to end debate and adopt the rule by a similar margin. Finally, the House agreed to the conference report with a sweeping 400–15 vote.

Later in the day, the Senate began its consideration of the conference report. After some debate, Senator McCaskill (D-MO) voiced objection to the conference report but realized that there were no parliamentary options available to stop it from moving forward. She stated:

> Unfortunately, I have since discovered there are still some gaps in the ethics bill that need to be filled. One of which has to do with the difficulty of raising a 60-vote point of order on earmarks added during appropriations conference negotiations. S.1 says that we can do that. But in reality, we really can't. Most of these added funding earmarks are contained in the Joint Explanatory Statement of Managers, which, technically, isn't part of the conference report bill text. What that means is we can't raise a point of order against those earmarks to strike them out of the bill.
>
> (CR 11/08/2007 S14147)

After hearing McCaskill's objection, the Senate adopted the conference report by a simple voice vote and sent it on to the president for his signature. In this case, the Senate acted as one would predict of a body motivated by electoral considerations—a rule change was put in place that had little effect in limiting the "problem" of airdrops. While senators could claim success by enacting reform, they could also achieve their electoral goals since the reform had little consequence on their ability to generate pork. This pattern is in line with a body of work by congressional scholars that finds that congressional reforms are rarely successful and, when enacted, often bring with them unintended consequences. For instance, Adler (2002) demonstrates that members of Congress are very hesitant to change the "rules of the game" because doing so alters the certainty that members desire in building a career. In the present case, the only significant change to the earmarking process was the production of a list of names corresponding to the member requesting the earmark. While this is surely an advance in transparency, it is also a beneficial one for most legislators, who for years have trumpeted their success in bringing projects back to their states and districts. If anything, their claims are only that much more credible to voters.

## Bicameralism and Earmarks

The preceding section highlighted the complexity of the legislative process in Congress when it comes to determining budgetary matters. Each chamber is unique and presents its own variety of procedural nuances. Thus, when the chambers deal with one another, it is no surprise to find that they do so with strategic considerations in mind. This raises a number of interesting questions about who wins and who loses when competing House and Senate bills enter the fray of being reconciled with one another. One thing that makes appropriations bills unique is that they are "must-pass" legislation. If not passed, some government activities (if not entire agencies) will shut down, as was the case with the government shutdowns of late 1995 and early 1996. This makes appropriations bills attractive vehicles for other things.

Interestingly, compared to the House or Senate, scholars have paid less attention to the conference committee process. Much of the earlier work on this topic focused on the question of which chamber wins, or is more likely to win. Some came to the conclusion that the Senate dominates conference (Fenno 1966; Vogler 1970; Kanter 1972) while others found the House wins more often (Steiner 1951). Ferejohn (1974 and 1975) concludes that it depends on how "winning" is measured and the answer may be unclear since the House strategically lowers its budget requests knowing the Senate would restore them to the higher levels in conference. Finally, Strom and Rundquist (1977) argue that the winner is generally the chamber that moves second. Previous work was more likely to conclude that the Senate did better because scholars often focused on appropriations and tax bills, measures where the House was the first mover.

Van Beek (1995) focused on how conference committees have changed now that committee chairs are no longer strong and many important bills have overlapping jurisdiction due to their omnibus nature. One consequence, Van Beek argues, is that the role of party leaders has increased at the expense of commit-tee members. This idea stands in contrast to Shepsle and Weingast (1987) who argued that the views of committee chairs dominate conference committees and give the committee a veto after the floor moves. Although we do not go into much detail here, this point is worth more investigation with respect to the appropriations process since appropriations subcommittee chairs are quite powerful.

In his important study of the appropriations process, Fenno (1966) provides an in-depth exploration of conference proceedings. He says that conferees must balance the goals of the parent chamber while trying to reach a compromise with the other (p. 616). Conferees must fight to win for their chamber but at the same time know it is imperative to produce a bill that can pass both chambers. With these goals in mind, conferees express the idea that there will be give-and-take in conference and neither chamber will win on all of the disagreements. According to Fenno, however, the Senate appears to get the better of the House during conference negotiations. Although Fenno wrote *The Power of the Purse* over forty years ago, members likely approach conference proceedings today with similar mindsets. However, at least one item has changed. It is unlikely that House members can still claim to be the guardians of the treasury and blame the Senate for adding personal projects to appropriations bills.

Van Beek (1995: 6) implicitly argues that conference committees for appro-priations bills do not take on the importance of more substantive legislation because most of the changes at this stage are quantitative in nature and involve splitting differences rather than adding or dropping whole programs. Although new programs are not generally added or dropped at the conference stage for appropriations bills, as we will show below, conferees add many new items to spending packages after they have passed the respective chambers.

We examine earmarks in conference committees using data on "pork" com-piled by the nonprofit, nonpartisan organization Citizens Against Government Waste (CAGW). Since 1991, CAGW has released an annual report identifying the pork-barrel projects contained in the annual appropriations bills that fund the various activities of the federal government. According to this organiza-tion, "a 'pork' project is a line-item in an appropriations bill that designates tax dollars for a specific purpose in circumvention of established budgetary proce-dures."[14] Recent reports by the Congressional Research Service document simi-lar trends in earmarks and a database produced by the Office of Management and Budget corroborates the CAGW definition and measurement of pork.

Numerous observers have noted a sizeable increase in both the number and value of pork-barrel projects since the 1990s. While explaining that trend is not our aim here (though we will describe it further in the final section of this chapter), the pattern is clearly borne out in the data compiled by CAGW (see also Crespin and Finocchiaro 2008a; Crespin, Finocchiaro, and Wanless 2009). Most importantly for the task at hand, we observe a similar increase in confer-ence committee projects as well. Figure 13.3 displays the proportion of pork

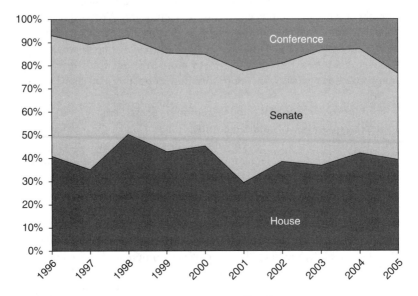

*Figure 13.3* Source of Pork as Percentage of Total

dollars as a function of the stage of the legislative process in which they were added to the bill: whether in the House, the Senate, or in conference. As the figure shows, most pork is tacked on to a bill prior to its referral to conference. On average, a little more than 45 percent of pork is added in the Senate, slightly less than 40 percent in the House, and about 16 percent in conference. That said, even though the percentage is small, it could be that certain members are targeted at this stage of the process.

We begin our analysis with a consideration of the distribution of conference committee pork across the individual appropriations bills and across years. The size of the circles in Figure 13.4 represents the total amount of pork in $10,000s added in conference for each subcommittee or omnibus bill during fiscal years 1996–2005. The data range from missing, meaning there was no conference report for a particular bill that year, to no pork added in conference (a dot) to the almost $4.7 billion added in conference to the 2005 omnibus appropriations bill. Shaded circles mean there was a significant difference in the amount of pork received by states with conference committee members and all other states. There were an average of 20.8 states represented in each subcommittee conference and 21.9 on the omnibus bills. For nearly all of these cases, the conferees were members of the respective appropriations subcommittee. These results indicate that when conference committee members add more than a token amount of pork, most of it goes to states with a conferee. This suggests to us a strong institutional component to the distribution of pork dollars. These results also demonstrate that some subcommittees, such as Veterans

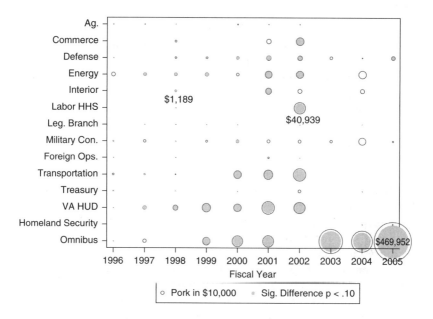

*Figure 13.4* Amount of Pork and Conferee vs. Non-Conferee Difference by Subcommittee

Administration—Housing & Urban Development and Transportation, tend to add significant amounts of pork in conference while other committees, such as Agriculture, Legislative Branch and Foreign Operations, add almost no pork at this final stage. Finally, the figure indicates a relative trend toward more pork each year in nearly all of the bills, which reflects the overall growth in the number and cumulative dollar value of earmarks over this time period.

There also appears to be a large amount of pork added to the omnibus bills (vehicles that serve as a catch-all for the individuals spending bills that did not pass on their own), although this could be a function of which bills were rolled into the larger package. For example, in fiscal years 2003–05, conferees added quite a bit of pork into the omnibus bills. However, most of the bills that usually add pork at the conference stage were put in the omnibus packages. If we compare the pork added to regular bills in 2002 with the omnibus package in 2003 (minus the two bills passed separately in 2003) we see a difference of only about $65 million in favor of the omnibus bill. One interesting avenue of future research involves differentiating the individual bill components from each omnibus package. This will allow researchers to better determine whether omnibus bills are loaded with earmarks because of the nature of an omnibus bill or simply because many traditionally pork-laden bills are often rolled into one larger bill.

## Conclusion and Future Directions

When the House and Senate produce their separate versions of the annual spending bills, a number of factors enter into the distributive calculus. As we have shown elsewhere, partisan, institutional, and at times even electoral considerations exert a substantial impact on the division of earmarks. The conference stage seems to operate a bit differently. What matters the most is who is seated at the conference table (for greater detail on this point, see Crespin and Finocchiaro 2008b). States represented in the conference committee typically do better when there is pork to be distributed. Beyond that, we find little evidence that other factors consistently enter into the decision-making of appropriators. Of course, as our analysis also describes, there is simply less money distributed at the conference stage—so this could make it more difficult to draw firm conclusions.

A number of fruitful avenues exist for further analysis. Recent rule changes identifying who requested each earmark provide a rich opportunity to draw important information from the most recent appropriations cycle, thereby taking advantage of the implications of members being able to even more directly claim credit for trafficking in earmarks. It also provides a clearer window into House decision-making, since in the past, scholars would typically have to assume that an earmark for a particular project was requested by the member representing that district. These rich new data will allow scholars to describe more explicitly the individual-level dynamics at work in the conference committee, as well as more systematically study the new process for earmarking in Congress.

Additionally, more nuanced analyses of the earmark process are necessary to round out our understanding of how congressional spending changes. Research on the geographic basis of pork has the potential to fundamentally alter our view of pork-barrel politics. Might it be the case that certain regions of the country benefit more than others when it comes to particular types of pork? Intuitively, this makes sense. States and districts in the Midwest and Sun Belt have a higher demand for agricultural projects (and pork) than do their counterparts in urban areas. Thus, accounting for the electoral benefits of pork across regions might well demonstrate key variation in its impact on members and districts. Similarly, the appropriations process is one that plays primarily at the level of the subcommittee. With this in mind, researchers need to be sensitive to variation across these smaller units and account for differences at this level. Preliminary research indicates that some factors (such as the vulnerability of the incumbent) matter more on some subcommittees than others. Accounting for and explaining these different processes—which Fenno (1966) noted more than a generation ago—is a key part of the puzzle of earmarks that has largely escaped attention to date.

As we look ahead to the future of earmarks in Congress, it seems likely that they will remain a contentious part of the broader debate over budgets. While critics and advocates will continue to disagree over their broader impact—whether they are symptomatic of a larger problem or a drop in the proverbial ocean—it is clear that policymakers face momentous decisions in the years ahead. Those of all political stripes agree that the federal budget cannot be sustained indefinitely on its present course. Yet dealing with deep deficits and structural commitments that are expensive in the long run is not politically attractive to members concerned about reelection. Budgetary politics is and has been at the heart of debate between the parties. The adoption of President Reagan's budgets in the early 1980s and President Clinton's budgets in the mid-1990s exhibited a great deal of conflict and at times brought the government to a grinding halt—as with the temporary government shutdowns of 1995–96. In 2011, for the first time since passage of the Congressional Budget Act in 1974, the House of Representatives failed to pass a budget resolution, which is simply the starting point of the months-long budget process in Congress (Allen 2010). Also, none of the regular appropriations bills were passed by the October 1 start of the federal fiscal year. Such setbacks are not terribly unusual for a contentious election year, but they do indicate the challenges Congress faces—as well as the hesitancy of its members—when difficult choices are required.

## Notes

1 For a more detailed look at the process, please see Keith (2008).
2 See Chapter 5 for a discussion of congressional committees.
3 The data for this figure come from the Budget of the United States Government, Historical Tables Fiscal Year 2011, http://www.gpoaccess.gov/usbudget/fy11/hist.html (accessed September 30, 2010).
4 We would refer the reader to Cox and McCubbins (2005) for a more thorough review of the congressional organization literature. For criticism of partisan theories, see e.g., Krehbiel (1993, 1999, 2000).
5 The data for this figure come from Citizens Against Government Waste, Pork Trends, 1991–2010. http://www.cagw.org/reports/pig-book/#trends (accessed September 30, 2010).
6 Refer back to Chapter 9 for a more extensive discussion of bicameral resolution via conference committees.
7 Our description of the process draws heavily from floor debates and information from the *Congressional Record*. Bach (2001), Rybicki (2007), and Streeter (2008) provide greater detail on the intricacies of the conference report process and the new earmark rules.
8 By insisting on their amendment and calling for a conference committee, the Senate sent a signal that they wished to by-pass the alternative procedure for reconciling differences between the two chambers. If the House and Senate do not pass identical bills, then they must either (a) resolve the differences by passing the bill back and forth, amending the bill until one chamber concurs with the other's amendments, or (b) call for a conference committee. Exchanging and amending a bill between the chambers cannot go on indefinitely because amendments beyond the second degree (an amendment to an amendment) are not in order. If a chamber refuses to accept the other's changes during this process, it can also call for a conference report.
9 Even if both chambers wish to go to conference, they cannot act at the same time

because a chamber can only move on a bill if they have the so-called "papers" in their possession. These papers include the official copy of the bill and messages between the two chambers.

10  The House also took a roll call to agree to close portions of the conference meeting to the public if they contained classified information.

11  The list of earmarks now contained in the appropriation bills is sometimes referred to as earmark "requests." This is something of a misnomer since the list only contains requests that were granted. In reality, members do not receive funding for all their requests. The House has institutionalized the process for requesting pork to the point that there are web-based forms to be filled out. House members request a limited number of projects and are asked to rank those projects. There is no limit to the number of projects a senator can request. Unfortunately for researchers, these requests are not publicly available, and senators have indicated their desire to keep the requests private.

12  The House has similar rules regarding out of scope material added in conference but routinely includes waivers of points of order in special rules.

13  The Senate can successfully appeal the ruling of the chair with three-fifths of the chamber voting in the affirmative.

14  In order to be included in the annual report, a project must meet at least two of the following criteria: requested by only one chamber of Congress; not specifically authorized; not competitively awarded; not requested by the president; greatly exceed the president's budget request or the previous year's funding; not the subject of congressional hearings; or serve only a local or special interest. In practice, every project identified by CAGW meets the last criterion, so that what distinguishes the various projects is the way in which they were added outside of the conventional appropriations process. CAGW is careful to note that theirs is not a comprehensive list of earmarks, in that earmarks, which designate funds for a specific beneficiary or locality, might or might not be included via established budgetary procedures. As such, only those earmarks inserted outside the established rules are categorized as pork.

# Bibliography

Aberbach, Joel D., and Bert A. Rockman. 2000. *In the Web of Politics: Three Decades of the U.S. Federal Executive.* Washington, DC: Brookings Institution Press.

Abney, Glen, and John D. Hutcheson. 1981. "Race, Representation, and Trust: Changes in Attitudes after the Election of a Black Mayor." *Public Opinion Quarterly* 45(1): 91–101.

Abramson, Paul R., John H. Aldrich, and David W. Rohde. 1987. "Progressive Ambition among United States Senators." *Journal of Politics* 49(1): 3–35.

Adams, Charles Francis, ed. 1876. *Memoirs of John Quincy Adams.* Volume X. Philadelphia: J. B. Lippincott and Company.

Adams, James, and Samuel Merrill. 2008. "Candidate and Party Strategies in Two-Stage Elections Beginning with a Primary." *American Journal of Political Science* 52(2): 344–59.

Adler, E. Scott. 2002. *Why Congressional Reforms Fail: Reelection and the House Committee System.* Chicago, IL: University of Chicago Press.

Ainsworth, Scott, and Itai Sened. 1993. "The Role of Lobbyists: Entrepreneurs with Two Audiences." *American Journal of Political Science* 37(3): 834–66.

Ainsworth, Scott, and Marcus Flathman. 1995. "Unanimous Consent Agreements as Leadership Tools." *Legislative Studies Quarterly* 20(1): 177–95.

Aldrich, John H. 1995. *Why Parties? The Origin and Transformation of Political Parties in America.* Chicago, IL: University of Chicago Press.

Aldrich, John H., and David W. Rohde. 1997. "Balance of Power: Republican Party Leadership and the Committee System in the 104th House." Paper presented at the Annual Meeting of the Midwest Political Science Association, Chicago, IL.

Aldrich, John H., and David W. Rohde. 1998. "The Transition to Republican Rule in the House: Implications for Theories of Congressional Politics." *Political Science Quarterly* 112: 541–67.

Aldrich, John H., and David W. Rohde. 2000a. "The Consequences of Party Organization in the House: The Role of the Majority and Minority Parties in Conditional Party Government." In J. R. Bond and R. Fleisher (eds) *Polarized Politics: Congress and the President in a Partisan Era.* Washington, DC: CQ Press.

Aldrich, John H., and David W. Rohde. 2000b. "The Republican Revolution and the House Appropriations Committee." *Journal of Politics* 62(1): 1–33.

Aldrich, John H., and David W. Rohde. 2001. "The Logic of Conditional Party Government: Revisiting the Electoral Connection." In Lawrence Dodd and Bruce Oppenheimer (eds) *Congress Reconsidered,* 7th ed. Washington, DC: CQ Press, pp. 269–92.

Aldrich, John H., and David W. Rohde. 2009. "Congressional Committees in a Continuing Partisan Era." In Lawrence Dodd and Bruce Oppenheimer (eds) *Congress Reconsidered*, 9th ed. Washington, DC: CQ Press, pp. 217–40.

Aldrich, John H., Mark M. Berger, and David W. Rohde. 2002. "The Historical Variability of Conditional Party Government, 1877–1994." In David W. Brady and Mathew D. McCubbins (eds) *Party, Process, and Political Change in Congress: New Perspectives on the History of Congress*. Stanford, CA: Stanford University Press.

Alexander, DeAlva Stanwood. 1916. *History and Procedure of the House of Representatives*. Houghton Mifflin Company.

Allen, Jonathan. 2010. "Congress Sees No Budget Rush." *Politico*. http://www.politico.com/news/stories/0410/35647.html (accessed November 1, 2010).

Alvarez, R. Michael, and Jason L. Saving. 1997. "Deficits, Democrats, and Distributive Benefits: Congressional Elections and the Pork Barrel in the 1980s." *Political Research Quarterly* 50: 809–31.

Amar, Vik D. 1988. "The Senate and the Constitution." *The Yale Law Journal* 97(6): 1111–30.

Ansolabehere, Stephen, and Alan Gerber. 1996. "The Effects of Filing Fees and Petition Requirements on U.S. House Elections," *Legislative Studies Quarterly* 22(2): 249–64.

Ansolabehere, Stephen, and Philip Edward Jones. 2010. "Constituents' Responses to Congressional Roll-Call Voting." *American Journal of Political Science* 54(3): 583–97.

Ansolabehere, Stephen, James. M. Snyder, Jr., and Charles Stewart III. 2001. "The Effects of Party and Preferences on Congressional Roll-Call Voting." *Legislative Studies Quarterly* 26: 533–72.

Ansolabehere, Stephen, John Mark Hansen, Shigeo Hirano, and James M. Snyder, Jr. 2006. "The Decline of Competition in U.S. Primary Elections, 1908–2004." In Michael P. McDonald and John Samples (eds) *The Marketplace of Democracy*. Washington, DC: Brookings Institution Press, pp. 74–101.

Ansolabehere, Stephen, John Mark Hansen, Shigeo Hirano, and James M. Snyder, Jr. 2010. "More Democracy: The Direct Primary and Competition in U.S. Elections." *Studies in American Political Development* 24(1): 190–205.

Arnold, R. Douglas. 1990. *The Logic of Congressional Action*. New Haven, CT: Yale University Press.

Arrow, Kenneth J. 1950. "A Difficulty in the Concept of Social Welfare." *The Journal of Political Economy* 58(4): 328–46.

Austen-Smith, D., and J. R. Wright. 1992. "Competitive Lobbying for a Legislator's Vote." *Social Choice and Welfare* 9(3): 229–57.

Austen-Smith, D., and J. R. Wright. 1994. "Counteractive Lobbying." *American Journal of Political Science* 38(1): 25–44.

Bach, Stanley. 1990. "From Special Orders to Special Rules: Pictures of House Procedures in Transition." Presented at the 1990 annual meeting of the American Political Science Association.

Bach, Stanley. 2000. "Legislative Procedures and the Legislative Agenda in the House of Representatives." CRS Report for Congress, pp. 96–708.

Bach, Stanley. 2001. "Conference Reports and Joint Explanatory Statements." CRS Report for Congress, pp. 98–382.

Bach, Stanley, and Steven Smith. 1988. *Managing Uncertainty in the House of Representatives: Adaptation and Innovation in Special Rules*. Washington, DC: Brookings Institution.

Bailey, Michael, and David W. Brady. 1998. "Heterogeneity and Representation: The Senate and Free Trade." *American Journal of Political Science* 42: 524–44.

Balla, Steven J., Eric D. Lawrence, Forrest Maltzman, and Lee Sigelman. 2002. "Partisanship, Blame Avoidance, and the Distribution of Legislative Pork." *American Journal of Political Science* 46: 515–25.

Banks, Jeffrey S., and D. Roderick Kiewiet. 1989. "Explaining Patterns of Candidate Competition in Congressional Elections." *American Journal of Political Science* 33(4): 997–1015.

Barilleaux, Ryan J., and Christopher S. Kelley. 2010. *The Unitary Executive and the Modern Presidency.* College Station: Texas A&M Press.

Barrett, Andrew, and Matthew Eshbaugh-Soha. 2007. "Presidential Success on the Substance of Legislation." *Political Research Quarterly* 60: 100–12.

Bartels, Larry M. 2000. "Partisanship and Voting Behavior, 1952–1996." *American Journal of Political Science* 44(1): 35–50.

Bartels, Larry M. 2008. *Unequal Democracy: The Political Economy of the New Gilded Age.* Princeton, NJ: Princeton University Press.

Bauer, R. A., I. D. Pool, and L. A. Dexter. 1963. *American Business and Public Policy: The Politics of Foreign Trade.* New York: Atherton Press.

Baum, Lawrence A. 2006. *The Supreme Court,* 9th ed. Washington, DC: CQ Press.

Baumgartner, F. R., and B. L. Leech. 1998. *Basic Interests: The Importance of Groups in Politics and in Political Science.* Princeton, NJ: Princeton University Press.

Baumgartner, F. R., and B. L. Leech. 2001. "Interest Niches and Policy Bandwagons: Patterns of Interest Group Involvement in National Politics." *Journal of Politics* 63(4): 1191–213.

Baumgartner, F. R., J. M. Berry, M. Hojnacki, D. C. Kimball, and B. L. Leech. 2009. *Lobbying and Policy Change: Who Wins, Who Loses, and Why.* Chicago, IL: The University of Chicago Press.

Beckmann, Matthew N. 2008. "The President's Playbook: White House Strategies for Lobbying Congress." *Journal of Politics* 70: 407–19.

Behre, Robert. 2007. "Clyburn Defends Budget Earmarks." *The Post and Courier* (Charleston, SC), 21 February: B1.

Bensel, Richard. 1984. *Sectionalism and American Political Development, 1880–1980.* Madison: University of Wisconsin Press.

Bensel, Richard. 1990. *Yankee Leviathan: The Origins of Central State Authority in America, 1859–1877.* Cambridge, MA: Cambridge University Press.

Bensel, Richard. 2000. *The Political Economy of American Industrialization, 1877–1900.* New York: Cambridge University Press.

Bensel, Richard. 2004. *The American Ballot Box in the Mid-Nineteenth Century.* New York: Cambridge University Press.

Berkman, Michael. 1993. "Former State Legislators in the House of Representatives: Policy and Institutional Mastery." *Legislative Studies Quarterly* 18(1): 77–104.

Berkman, Michael, and James Eisenstein. 1999. "State Legislators as Congressional Candidates: The Effects of Prior Experience on Legislative Recruitment and Fundraising." *Political Research Quarterly* 52: 481–98.

Bernhard, William, and Brian R. Sala. 2006. "The Remaking of an American Senate: The 17th Amendment and Ideological Responsiveness." *Journal of Politics* 68: 345–57.

Berry, J. M. 1989. *The Interest Group Society,* 2nd ed. Glenview, IL: Scott, Foresman/ Little Brown.

Berry, J. M. 1999. *The New Liberalism: The Rising Power of Citizen Groups*. Washington, DC: The Brookings Institution Press.

Berry, Michael J. 2009. "Controversially Executing the Law: George W. Bush and the Constitutional Signing Statement." *Congress & the Presidency* 36: 244–71.

Bianco, William T. 1984. "Strategic Decisions on Candidacy in U.S. Congressional Districts." *Legislative Studies Quarterly* 9(2): 351–64.

Bianco, William T. 1994. *Trust: Representatives and Constituents*. Michigan: University of Michigan Press.

Bianco, William T., David B. Spence, and John D. Wilkerson. 1996. "The Electoral Connection in the Early Congress: The Case of the Compensation Act of 1816." *American Journal of Political Science* 40: 145–71.

Bickers, Kenneth N., and Robert M. Stein. 1996. "The Electoral Dynamics of the Federal Pork Barrel." *American Journal of Political Science* 40: 1300–26.

Biglaiser, Glen, David J. Jackson, and Jeffrey S. Peake. 2004. "Back on Track: Support for Presidential Trade Authority in the House of Representatives." *American Politics Research* 32: 679–97.

Binder, Sarah A. 1995. "Partisanship and Procedural Choice: Institutional Change in the Early Congress, 1789–1823." *Journal of Politics* 57: 1093–118.

Binder, Sarah A. 1997. *Minority Rights, Majority Rules: Partisanship and the Development of Congress*. New York: Cambridge University Press.

Binder, Sarah A. 2006. "Parties and Institutional Choice Revisited." *Legislative Studies Quarterly* 31: 413–52.

Binder, Sarah A. 2007. "Where do Institutions Come From? Exploring the Origins of the Senate Blue Slip." *Studies in American Politics Development* 21(Spring): 1–15.

Binder, Sarah A., and Forrest Maltzman. 2002. "Senatorial Delay in Confirming Federal Judges." *American Journal of Political Science* 46(1):190–9.

Binder, Sarah A., and Forrest Maltzman. 2004. "The Limits of Senatorial Courtesy." *Legislative Studies Quarterly* 29(1): 5–22.

Binder, Sarah A., and Steven S. Smith. 1997. *Politics or Principle? Filibustering in the United States Senate*. Washington, DC: Brookings Institution Press.

Binder, Sarah A., Anthony J. Madonna, and Steven S. Smith. 2007. "Going Nuclear, Senate Style." *Perspectives on Politics* 4: 729–40.

Birnbaum, J. H. 2000. *The Money Men: The Real Story of Fund-raising's Influence on Political Power in America*. New York: Crown Publishers.

Bishin, Benjamin G. 2000. "Constituency Influence in Congress: Do Subconstituencies Matter?" *Legislative Studies Quarterly* 25: 389–415.

Bishop, Bill. 2008. *The Big Sort: Why the Clustering of Like-Minded America is Tearing Us Apart*. Boston, MA: Houghton, Mifflin.

Black, Duncan. 1948. "On the Rationale of Group Decision-Making." *Journal of Political Economy* 56: 23–34.

Black, Duncan. 1958. *The Theory of Committees and Elections*. New York: Cambridge University Press.

Black, Earl, and Merle Black. 1987. *Politics and Society in the South*. Cambridge, MA: Harvard University Press.

Black, Gordon S. 1972. "A Theory of Political Ambition: Career Choices and the Role of Structural Incentives." *American Political Science Review* 66(1): 144–55.

Black, Ryan C., Anthony J. Madonna, Ryan J. Owens, and Michael S. Lynch. 2007.

"Adding Recess Appointments to the President's Tool Chest of Unilateral Powers." *Political Research Quarterly* 60(4): 645–54.

Boehmke, Frederick J. 2006. "The Influence of Unobserved Factors on Position Timing and Content in the NAFTA Vote." *Political Analysis* 14: 421–38.

Boehmke, Frederick J., Sean Gailmard, and John W. Patty. 2006. "Whose Ear to Bend? Information Sources and Venue Choice in Policy-Making." *Quarterly Journal of Political Science* 1: 139–69.

Bond, Jon R., and Richard Fleisher. 2000. *Polarized Politics: Congress and the President in a Partisan Era.* Washington, DC: CQ Press.

Bond, Jon R., Cary Covington, and Richard Fleisher. 1985. "Explaining Challenger Quality in Congressional Elections." Journal of Politics 47: 510–29.

Bond, Jon R., Richard Fleischer, and Jeffery Talbert. 1997. "Partisan Differences in Candidate Quality in Open Seat House Races, 1976–1994." *Political Research Quarterly* 50(2): 281–99.

Bork, Robert H. 1990. *The Tempting of America: The Political Seduction of the Law.* New York: Touchstone Press.

Bosso, C. J. 1987. *Pesticides and Politics: The Life Cycle of a Public Issue.* Pittsburgh, PA: University of Pittsburgh Press.

Bovitz, Gregory L. 2002. "Electoral Consequences of Porkbusting in the U. S. House of Representatives." *Political Science Quarterly* 117: 455–77.

Box-Steffensmeier, Janet M. 1996. "A Dynamic Analysis of the Role of War Chests in Campaign Strategy." *American Journal of Political Science* 40(2): 352–71.

Brace, Paul. 1984. "Progressive Ambition in the House: A Probabilistic Approach." *Journal of Politics* 46(2): 556–71.

Brady, David W. 1973. *Congressional Voting in a Partisan Era: A Study of the McKinley Houses and a Comparison to the Modern House of Representatives.* Lawrence: University of Kansas Press.

Brady, David W. 1991. *Critical Elections and Congressional Policy Making.* Palo Alto, CA: Stanford University Press.

Brady, David W., and Craig Volden. 2006. *Revolving Gridlock: Politics and Policy from Jimmy Carter to George W. Bush.* Boulder, CO: Westview Press.

Brady, David, Kara Buckley, and Douglas Rivers. 1999. "The Roots of Careerism in the U.S. House of Representatives." *Legislative Studies Quarterly* 24(4): 489–510.

Brady, Michael C. 2008. "A Party in the Conference Room: Partisan theories of Congress and Conference Committee Bargaining 1981–2008." Doctoral Dissertation.

Branton, Regina P. 2009. "The Importance of Race and Ethnicity in Congressional Primary Elections." *Political Research Quarterly* 62(3): 459–73.

Brewer, Paul, and Christopher J. Deering. 2005. "Musical Chairs: Interest Groups, Campaign Fund-Raising, and Selection of House Committee Chairs." In P. S. Herrnson, R. G. Shaiko, and C. Wilcox (eds) *The Interest Group Connection: Electioneering, Lobbying, and Policymaking in Washington.* Washington, DC: CQ Press.

Brisbin, Richard A., Jr. 2005. "The Judiciary and the Separation of Powers." In Kermit L. Hall and Kevin T. McGuire (eds) *The Judicial Branch.* New York: Oxford University Press, pp. 89–115.

Browne, W. P. 1990. "Organized Interests and Their Issue Niches: A Search for Pluralism in a Policy Domain." *Journal of Politics* 52(2): 477–509.

Brunell, Thomas L. 2008. *Redistricting and Representation: Why Competitive Elections are Bad for America.* New York: Routledge.

Buchler, Justin. 2005. "Competition, Representation, and Redistricting." *Journal of Theoretical Politics* 17(4): 431–63.

Burden, Barry C. 2007. *The Personal Roots of Representation*. Princeton, NJ: Princeton University Press.

Burden, Barry C., and Tammy M. Frisby. 2004. "Preferences, Partisanship, and Whip Activity in the House of Representatives." *Legislative Studies Quarterly* 29: 569–90.

Burdette, Franklin. 1940. *Filibustering in the Senate*. Princeton, NJ: Princeton University Press.

Burns, Nancy, Kay Lehman Schlozman, and Sidney Verba. 2001. *The Private Roots of Public Action: Gender, Equality, and Political Participation*. Cambridge, MA: Harvard University.

Cain, Bruce E., John A. Ferejohn, and Morris P. Fiorina. 1987. *The Personal Vote: Constituency Service and Electoral Independence*. Cambridge, MA: Harvard University Press.

Calvert, Randall L. 1985. "The Value of Biased Information: A Rational Choice Model of Political Advice." *The Journal of Politics* 47(2): 530–55.

Cameron, Charles M. 2000. *Veto Bargaining: Presidents and the Politics of Negative Power*. New York: Cambridge University Press.

Cameron, Charles, Albert Cover, and Jeffrey Segal. 1990. "Senate Voting on Supreme Court Nominees: A Neoinstitutional Model." *American Political Science Review* 84(2): 525–34.

Cameron, Charles, David Epstein, and Sharyn O'Halloran. 1996. "Do Majority-Minority Districts Maximize Black Substantive Representation in Congress?" *American Political Science Review* 90: 794–812.

Cameron, Charles M., John S. Lapinski, and Charles R. Riemann. 2000. "Testing Formal Theories of Political Rhetoric." *Journal of Politics* 62: 187–205.

Campbell, Angus. 1960. "Surge and Decline: A Study of Electoral Change." *Public Opinion Quarterly* 24(3): 397–418.

Campbell, James E. 1997. *The Presidential Pulse of Congressional Elections*. Lexington: University of Kentucky Press.

Canes-Wrone, Brandice. 2001. "The President's Legislative Influence from Public Appeals." *American Journal of Political Science* 45: 313–29.

Canes-Wrone, Brandice. 2006. *Who Leads Whom? Presidents, Policy, and the Public*. Chicago, IL: The University of Chicago Press.

Canes-Wrone, Brandice. 2009. "Administrative Politics and the Public Presidency." *Presidential Studies Quarterly* 39(1): 25–37.

Canes-Wrone, Brandice, and Scott DeMarchi. 2002. "Presidential Approval and Legislative Success." *Journal of Politics* 64: 491–509.

Canes-Wrone, Brandice, David W. Brady, and John F. Cogan. 2002. "Out of Step, Out of Office: Electoral Accountability and House Members' Voting." *American Political Science Review* 96(1): 127–40.

Canes-Wrone, Brandice, Julia Rabinovich, and Craig Volden. 2007. "Who Parties? Floor Voting, District Ideology, and Electoral Margins." In David W. Brady and Mathew D. McCubbins (eds) *Party, Process, and Political Change in Congress: New Perspectives on the History of Congress*. Stanford, CA: Stanford University Press.

Canes-Wrone, Brandice, William Howell and David E. Lewis. 2008. "Toward a Broader Understanding of Presidential Power: A Reevaluation of the Two Presidencies Thesis." *Journal of Politics* 70(1): 1–16.

Canon, David T. 1990. *Actors, Athletes, and Astronauts: Political Amateurs in the United States Congress*. Chicago, IL: University of Chicago Press.

Canon, David T. 1993. "Sacrificial Lambs or Strategic Politicians? Political Amateurs in U.S. House Elections." *American Journal of Political Science* 37(4): 1119–41.

Canon, David, and Charles Stewart III. 2001. "The Evolution of the Committee System in Congress." In Lawrence C. Dodd and Bruce I. Oppenheimer (eds) *Congress Reconsidered*, 7th ed. Washington: CQ Press.

Canon, David, and Charles Stewart III. 2002. "Parties and Hierarchies in Senate Committees, 1789–1946." In Bruce I. Oppenheimer (ed.) *U.S. Senate Exceptionalism*. Columbus: Ohio State University Press.

Carpenter, D. P., K. M. Esterling, and D. M. J. Lazer. 1998. "The Strength of Weak Ties in Lobbying Networks: Evidence from Health-Care Politics in the United States." *Journal of Theoretical Politics* 10(4): 417–44.

Carpenter, Daniel, Kevin Esterling and David Lazer. 2004. "Friends, Brokers and Transitivity: Who Informs Whom in Washington Politics?" *Journal of Politics* 66: 224–46.

Carroll, Royce, and Henry A. Kim. 2010. "Party Government and 'The Cohesive Power of Public Plunder'." *American Journal of Political Science* 54: 34–44.

Carsey, Thomas M., and Barry Rundquist. 1999. "Party and Committee in Distributive Politics: Evidence from Defense Spending." *Journal of Politics* 61: 1156–69.

Carson, Jamie L. 2003. "Strategic Interaction and Candidate Competition in U.S. House Elections: Empirical Applications of Probit and Strategic Probit Models." *Political Analysis* 11(4): 368–80.

Carson, Jamie L. 2005. "Strategy, Selection, and Candidate Competition in U.S. House and Senate Elections." *Journal of Politics* 67(1): 1–28.

Carson, Jamie L., and Michael H. Crespin. 2004. "The Effect of State Redistricting Methods on Electoral Competition in United States House of Representatives Races." *State Politics and Policy Quarterly* 4(Winter): 455–69.

Carson, Jamie L., and Erik J. Engstrom. 2005. "Assessing the Electoral Connection: Evidence from the Early United States." *American Journal of Political Science* 49: 746–57.

Carson, Jamie L., and Jeffery A. Jenkins. 2011. "Examining the Electoral Connection across Time." *Annual Review of Political Science* 14: 25–46.

Carson, Jamie L., and Jason M. Roberts. 2005. "Strategic Politicians and U.S. House Elections, 1874–1914." *Journal of Politics* 67: 474–96.

Carson, Jamie L., and Jason M. Roberts. N.d. *Ambition, Competition, and Electoral Reform: The Politics of Congressional Elections Across Time*. Book Manuscript.

Carson, Jamie L., and Ryan Vander Wielen. 2002. "Partisan and Strategic Considerations in Conferee Selection in Congress." Paper presented at the annual meeting of the Midwest Political Science Association. Chicago, IL, April 25–28.

Carson, Jamie L., Jeffery A. Jenkins, David W. Rohde, and Mark A. Souva. 2001. "The Impact of National Tides and District-Level Effects on Electoral Outcomes: The Congressional Elections of 1862–63." *American Journal of Political Science* 45: 887–98.

Carson, Jamie L., Erik J. Engstrom, and Jason M. Roberts. 2006. "Redistricting, Candidate Entry, and the Politics of Nineteenth-Century U.S. House Elections." *American Journal of Political Science* 50(2): 283–93.

Carson, Jamie L., Erik J. Engstrom, and Jason M. Roberts. 2007. "Candidate Quality, the Personal Vote, and the Incumbency Advantage in Congress." *American Political Science Review* 101(2): 289–301.

Carson, Jamie L., Michael H. Crespin, Charles J. Finocchiaro, and David W. Rohde. 2007. "Redistricting and Party Polarization in the U.S. House of Representatives." *American Politics Research* 35: 878–904.

Carson, Jamie L., Gregory Koger, Matthew Lebo, and Everett Young. 2010. "The Electoral Costs of Party Loyalty in Congress." *American Journal of Political Science* 54(3): 598–616.

Cater, D. 1964. *Power in Washington: A Critical Look at Today's Struggle to Govern in the Nation's Capital.* New York: Random House.

Center for American Women and Politics (CAWP). 2010. "Women in Elective Office 2010, CAWP Fact Sheet." *National Information Bank on Women in Public Office,* Eagleton Institute of Politics. Rutgers, NJ: Rutgers University.

Center for Responsive Politics. 2010a. *Lobbying Database.* Washington, DC: Center for Responsive Politics. Online document accessed at http://www.opensecrets.org/lobbyists/ on September 8, 2010.

Center for Responsive Politics. 2010b. *AT&T Inc. Expenditures.* Washington, DC: Center for Responsive Politics. Online document accessed at http://www.opensecrets.org/pacs/expenditures.php?cmte=C00109017&cycle=2008 on September 24, 2010.

Chambers, William Nisbet. 1956. *Old Bullion Benton: Senator from the New West.* Boston, MA: Little, Brown and Company.

Chin, M. L. 2005. "Constituents Versus Fat Cats: Testing Assumptions About Congressional Access Decisions." *American Politics Research* 33(6): 751–86.

Chin, M. L., J. R. Bond, and N. Geva. 2000. "A Foot in the Door: An Experimental Study of PAC and Constituency Effects on Access." *Journal of Politics* 62(2): 534–49.

Chiou, Fang-Yi, and Lawrence S. Rothenberg. 2003. "When Pivotal Politics Meets Partisan Politics." *American Journal of Political Science* 47 (July): 503–22.

Chiou, Fang-Yi, and Lawrence S. Rothenberg. 2009. "A Unified Theory of U.S. Lawmaking: Preferences, Institutions, and Party Discipline," *Journal of Politics* 71: 1257–72.

Clausen, Aage, and Clyde Wilcox. 1987. "Policy Partisanship in Legislative Recruitment and Behavior." *Legislative Studies Quarterly* 12: 243–63.

Clinton, Joshua D. 2006. "Representation in Congress: Constituents and Roll Calls in the 106th House." *Journal of Politics* 68: 397–409.

Clinton, Joshua D., and John Lapinski. 2008. "Laws and Roll Calls in the U.S. Congress, 1889–1994." *Legislative Studies Quarterly* 33: 511–42.

Clinton, Joshua D., and Adam Meirowitz. 2004. "Testing Theories of Strategic Voting in Legislatures: A Reexamination of the Compromise of 1790." *American Journal of Political Science* 48: 675–89.

Clinton, Joshua D., Simon Jackman, and Douglas Rivers. 2004. "The Statistical Analysis of Roll-Call Voting: A Unified Approach." *American Political Science Review* 98: 355–70.

Coleman, John J., and Paul F. Manna. 2000. "Congressional Campaign Spending and the Quality of Democracy." *Journal of Politics* 62(3): 757–89.

Coleman, Mrs. Chapman, ed. 1871. *The Life of John J. Crittenden.* 2 volumes. Philadelphia, PA: J.B. Lippincott and Company.

Collie, Melissa P. 1988. "Universalism and the Parties in the U.S. House of Representatives, 1921–1980." *American Journal of Political Science* 32(4): 865–83.

Colton, Calvin, ed. 1904. *The Works of Henry Clay, Comprising His Life, Correspondence, and Speeches.* 10 volumes. New York: G.P. Putnam's Sons.

Conley, Richard S. 1999. "Derailing Presidential Fast-Track Authority: The Impact of

Constituency Pressure and Political Ideology on Trade Policy in Congress." *Political Research Quarterly* 54: 785–99.

Conley, Richard S. 2003. "George Bush and the 102nd Congress: The Impact of Public and Private Veto Threats on Policy Outcomes." *Presidential Studies Quarterly* 33(4): 730–50.

Conley, Richard S. 2004. "President Clinton and the Republican Congress, 1995–2000: Political and Policy Dimensions of Veto Politics in Divided Government." *Congress & the Presidency* 31(2): 133–60.

Cook, C. E. 1998. *Lobbying for Higher Education: How Colleges and Universities Influence Federal Policy.* Nashville, TN: Vanderbilt University Press.

Cooper, Joseph. 1970. *The Origins of the Standing Committees and the Development of the Modern House.* Houston, TX: Rice University Publications.

Cooper, Joseph, and David W. Brady. 1981. "Institutional Context and Leadership Style: The House from Cannon to Rayburn." *American Political Science Review* 75: 411–25.

Cooper, Phillip J. 2002. *By Order of the President: The Use and Abuse of Executive Direct Action.* Lawrence: University of Kansas Press.

Cooper, Phillip J. 2005. "George W. Bush: Edgar Allan Poe, and the Use and Abuse of Presidential Signing Statements." *Presidential Studies Quarterly* 35(3): 515–32.

Corrado, Anthony, Thomas E. Mann, and Trevor Potter. 2003. *Inside the Campaign Finance Battle: Court Testimony on the New Reforms.* Washington, DC: Brookings Institution Press.

Cox, Gary W. 1987. *The Efficient Secret: The Cabinet and the Development of Political Parties in Victorian England.* New York: Cambridge University Press.

Cox, Gary W. 2001. "Agenda Setting in the U.S. House: A Majority-Party Monopoly?" *Legislative Studies Quarterly* 26: 185–210.

Cox, Gary W., and Jonathan Katz. 1996. "Why Did the Incumbency Advantage in U.S. House Elections Grow?" *American Journal of Political Science* 40(2): 478–97.

Cox, Gary W., and Mathew D. McCubbins. 1993. *Legislative Leviathan: Party Government in the House.* Berkeley: University of California Press.

Cox, Gary W., and Mathew D. McCubbins. 2002. "Agenda Power in the U.S. House of Representatives." In David W. Brady and Mathew D. McCubbins (eds) *Party, Process, and Political Change in Congress: New Perspectives on the History of Congress.* Stanford, CA: Stanford University Press.

Cox, Gary W., and Mathew D. McCubbins. 2005. *Setting the Agenda: Responsible Party Government in the U.S. House of Representatives.* New York: Cambridge University Press.

Cox, Gary W., and Keith T. Poole. 2002. "On Measuring Partisanship in Roll Call Voting: The U.S. House of Representatives, 1877–1999." *American Journal of Political Science*, 46(3):477–89.

CQ Almanac Online. 2003. "Energy Bill Falls Short." *CQ Almanac Online,* accessed November 30, 2010.

Crespin, Michael H., and Charles J. Finocchiaro. 2008a. "Distributive and Partisan Politics in the U.S. Senate: An Exploration of Earmarks." In Nathan W. Monroe, Jason M. Roberts, and David W. Rohde (eds) *Why Not Parties? Party Effects in the United States Senate.* Chicago, IL: University of Chicago Press, pp. 229–51.

Crespin, Michael H., and Charles J. Finocchiaro. 2008b. "The Politics of Earmarks in Conference Committees." Paper presented at the annual meeting of the American Political Science Association, Boston, MA.

Crespin, Michael H., and David W. Rohde. 2010. "Dimensions, Issues, and Bills: Appropriations Voting on the House Floor." *Journal of Politics* 72: 976–89.

Crespin, Michael H., Charles J. Finocchiaro, and Emily Wanless. 2009. "Perception and Reality in Congressional Earmarks." *The Forum: A Journal of Applied Research in Contemporary Politics* 7(2): Article 1.

Cronin, Thomas E. 1975. *The State of the Presidency.* Boston, MA: Little, Brown and Company.

Crook, Sara Brandes, and John R. Hibbing. 1985. "Congressional Reform and Party Discipline: The Effects of Changes in the Seniority System on Party Loyalty in the US House of Representatives." *British Journal of Political Science* 15(2): 207–26.

Crook, Sara Brandes, and John R. Hibbing. 1997. "A Not-So-Distant Mirror: The 17th Amendment and Congressional Change." *American Political Science Review.* 845–53.

Cutler, Wayne, Earl J. Smith, and Carese M. Parker, eds. 1979. *Correspondence of James K. Polk.* Volume V. Nashville, TN: Vanderbilt University Press.

Davidson, Roger H. 1981. "Subcommittee Government: New Channels for Policymaking." In T. E. Mann and N. J. Ornstein (eds) *The New Congress.* Washington, DC: American Enterprise Institute.

Davis, Christopher. 2003. "The Speaker of the House and the Committee on Rules." Printed in the proceedings of *The Cannon Centenary Conference.* House Document 108–204.

Davis, F. L. 1993. "Balancing the Perspective on PAC Contributions: In Search of an Impact on Roll Calls." *American Politics Quarterly* 21(2): 205–22.

Deen, Rebecca E., and Laura W. Arnold. 2002. "Veto Threats as a Policy Tool: When to Threaten?" *Presidential Studies Quarterly* 32: 30–45.

Deering, Christopher, and Steven S. Smith. 1997. *Committees in Congress.* 3rd ed. Washington, DC: CQ Press.

Den Hartog, Chris, and Nathan Monroe. 2008. "Agenda Influence and Tabling Motions in the U.S. Senate." In Nathan W. Monroe, Jason M. Roberts, and David W. Rohde (eds) *Why Not Parties: Party Effects in the United States Senate.* Chicago, IL: University of Chicago Press.

Den Hartog, Chris, and Nathan W. Monroe. 2011. *Agenda Setting in the U.S. Senate: Costly Consideration and Majority Party Advantage.* New York: Cambridge University Press.

Dennis, Steven T. 2010. "No Clear-Cut Successors for Defeated 'Old Bulls'." *Roll Call,* November 4.

Denzau, Arthur T., William Riker, and Kenneth Shepsle. 1985. "Farquharson and Fenno: Sophisticated Voting and Home Style." *American Political Science Review* 79: 1117–34.

Dexter, L. A. 1969. *How Organizations are Represented in Washington.* Indianapolis: Bobbs-Merrill.

Dickinson, Matthew J. 2009. "We All Want a Revolution: Neustadt, New Institutionalism, and the Future of Presidency Research." *Presidential Studies Quarterly* 39(4): 736–70.

Dietz, Nathan. 2002. "Presidential Influence on Congress." In James A. Thurber (ed.) *Rivals for Power: Presidential-Congressional Relations.* New York: Rowman & Littlefield Publishers, Inc.

Dion, Douglas. 1997. *Turning the Legislative Thumbscrew: Minority Rights and Procedural Change in Legislative Politics.* Ann Arbor: University of Michigan Press.

Dodd, Lawrence C., and Bruce I. Oppenheimer. 1977. "The House in Transition." In L. C. Dodd and B. I. Oppenheimer (eds) *Congress Reconsidered*. Washington, DC: CQ Press.

Dodd, Lawrence C., and Bruce I. Oppenheimer. 1985. "The House in Transition: Partisanship and Opposition." In In L. C. Dodd and B. I. Oppenheimer (eds) *Congress Reconsidered*. Washington, DC: CQ Press.

Downs, Anthony. 1957. *An Economic Theory of Democracy*. New York: Harper Collins.

Dubin, Michael J. 1998. *United States Congressional Elections, 1788–1997: The Official Results of the Elections of the 1st Through 105th Congresses*. Jefferson, NC: McFarland & Company.

Durant, Robert F. 1992. *The Administrative Presidency Revisited: Public Lands, the BLM, and the Reagan Revolution*. Albany: State University of New York Press.

Edwards III, George C. 2003. *On Deaf Ears: The Limits of the Bully Pulpit*. New Haven, CT: Yale University Press.

Edwards III, George C., and Andrew Barrett. 2000. "Presidential Agenda Setting in Congress." In Jon R. Bond and Richard Fleisher (eds) *Polarized Politics: Congress and the President in a Partisan Era*. Washington, DC: CQ Press.

Eggen, Dan. 2010. "Poll: Large Majority Opposes Supreme Court Decision on Campaign Financing." *Washington Post*, February 17.

Engstrom, Erik J. 2006. "Stacking the States, Stacking the House: The Politics of Congressional Redistricting in the 19th Century." *American Political Science Review* 100: 419–28.

Engstrom, Erik J., and Samuel Kernell. 2005. "Manufactured Responsiveness: The Impact of State Electoral Laws on Unified Party Control of the Presidency and U.S. House of Representatives, 1840–1940." *American Journal of Political Science* 49(3): 547–65.

Engstrom, Erik J., and Samuel Kernell. 2007. "The Effects of Presidential Elections on Party Control of the Senate under Indirect and Direct Elections." In David Brady and Mathew D. McCubbins (eds) *Party, Process, and Political Change in Congress*, Volume 2. Palo Alto, CA: Stanford University Press, pp. 37–52.

Epstein, David, David Brady, Sadafumi Kawato, and Sharyn O'Halloran. 1997. "A Comparative Approach to Legislative Organization: Careerism and Seniority in the United States and Japan." *American Journal of Political Science* 41(3): 965–98.

Epstein, Lee, and Jeffrey A. Segal. 2005. *Advice and Consent: The Politics of Judicial Appointments*. New York: Oxford University Press.

Epstein, Lee, Jeffrey A. Segal, Harold J. Spaeth, and Thomas G. Walker. 2006. *The Supreme Court Compendium*. 4th ed. CQ Press.

Erikson, Robert S. 1988. "The Puzzle of Midterm Loss." *Journal of Politics* 50(4): 1011–29.

Erikson, Robert S., Michael MacKuen, and James A. Stimson. 2002. *The Macro Polity*. New York: Cambridge University Press.

Espino Rodolfo, and David T. Canon. 2009. "Vote Switching in the U.S. House." *Journal of Politics* 71: 324–38.

Evans, C. Lawrence. 2010. *The Whip Systems of Congress*. Unpublished manuscript, The College of William and Mary.

Evans, C. Lawrence, and Claire E. Grandy. 2009. "The Whip Systems of Congress." In Lawrence C. Dodd and Bruce I. Oppenheimer (eds) *Congress Reconsidered*. 9th ed. Washington, DC: CQ Press, pp. 189–216.

Evans, C. Lawrence, and Stephen Ng. 2006. "The Institutional Context of Veto Bargaining." In James A. Thurber (ed.) *Rivals for Power: Presidential-Congressional Relations.* 3rd ed. New York: Rowman & Littlefield Publishers, pp. 183–208.

Evans, C. Lawrence, and Walter J. Oleszek. 1997. *Congress Under Fire: Reform Politics and the Republican Majority.* Boston, MA: Houghton, Mifflin.

Evans, C. Lawrence, and Walter J. Oleszek. 2000. "The Procedural Context of Senate Deliberation," in Burdett A. Loomis (ed.) *Esteemed Colleagues: Civility and Deliberation in the U.S. Senate.* Washington, DC: Brookings Institution Press.

Evans, D. M. 1986. "PAC Contributions and Roll-call Voting: Conditional Power." In A. J. Cigler and B. A. Loomis (eds.) *Interest Group Politics.* 2nd ed. Washington, DC: CQ Press, pp. 114–32.

Evans, Diana. 2004. *Greasing the Wheels: Using Pork Barrel Projects to Build Majority Coalitions in Congress.* New York: Cambridge University Press.

Fair, Ray C. 2009. "Presidential and Congressional Vote-Share Equations." *American Journal of Political Science* 53(1): 55–72.

Fatovic, Clement. 2004. "Constitutionalism and Presidential Prerogative: Jeffersonian and Hamiltonian Perspectives." *American Journal of Political Science* 48(3): 429–44.

Federal Election Commission. 2009a. *Number of Federal PACs Increases.* Washington, DC: Federal Election Commission. Online document accessed at http://www.fec.gov/press/press2009/20090309PACcount.shtml on September 25, 2010.

Federal Election Commission. 2009b. *Congressional Candidates Raised $1.42 Billion in 2007–2008.* Washington, DC: Federal Election Commission. Online document accessed at http://www.fec.gov/press/press2009/2009Dec29Cong/2009Dec29Cong.shtml, on September 24, 2010.

Feldman, Paul, and James Jondrow. 1984. "Congressional Elections and Local Federal Spending." *American Journal of Political Science* 28: 147–63.

Fenno, Richard F., Jr. 1962. "The House Appropriations Committee as a Political System: The Problem of Integration." *The American Political Science Review* 56(2): 310–24.

Fenno, Richard F., Jr. 1965. *The Power of the Purse.* Boston, MA: Little, Brown and Co.

Fenno, Richard F., Jr. 1966. *The Power of the Purse: Appropriations Politics in Congress.* Boston, MA: Little, Brown and Co.

Fenno, Richard F., Jr. 1973. *Congressmen in Committees.* Boston, MA: Little, Brown and Co.

Fenno, Richard F., Jr. 1978. *Home Style: House Members in Their Districts.* Boston, MA: Little, Brown.

Ferejohn, John A. 1974. *Pork Barrel Politics: Rivers and Harbors Legislation, 1947–1968.* Stanford, CA: Stanford University Press.

Ferejohn, John A. 1975. "Who Wins in Conference Committee?" *Journal of Politics* 37(4): 1033–46.

Ferejohn, John A. 1986. "Logrolling in an Institutional Context." In G. C. Wright, L. N. Rieselbach, and L. C. Dodd (eds) *Congress and Policy Change.* New York: Agathon Press, pp. 223–53.

Fink, Evelyn C. 1995. "Institutional Change as a Sophisticated Strategy: The Bill of Rights as a Political Solution," *Journal of Theoretical Politics* 7: 477–510.

Fink, Evelyn C. 2000. "Representation by Deliberation: Changes in the Rules of Deliberation in the U.S. House of Representatives, 1789–1844." *Journal of Politics* 62: 1109–25.

Finocchiaro, Charles J., and Jeffery A. Jenkins. 2008. "In Search of Killer Amendments in the Modern U.S. House." *Legislative Studies Quarterly* 33: 263–94.

Finocchiaro, Charles J., and David W. Rohde. 2008. "War for the Floor: Partisan Theory and Agenda Setting in the U.S. House of Representatives." *Legislative Studies Quarterly* 33: 35–62.

Fiorina, Morris P. 1977. *Congress: Keystone of the Washington Establishment*. New Haven, CT: Yale University Press.

Fiorina, Morris P. 1992. *Divided Government*. New York: Macmillan.

Fiorina, Morris P. 1994. "Divided Government in the American States: A Byproduct of Legislative Professionalism?" *American Political Science Review* 88: 304–16.

Fiorina, Morris P. 2005. "Keystone Reconsidered." In Lawrence C. Dodd and Bruce I. Oppenheimer (eds) *Congress Reconsidered*. 8th ed. Washington, DC: CQ Press, pp. 159–80.

Fiorina, Morris P. 2009. *Disconnect: The Breakdown of Representation in American Politics*. Norman: University of Oklahoma Press.

Fisher, Louis. 1988. *Constitutional Dialogues*. Princeton, NJ: Princeton University Press.

Fisher, Louis. 1993. "The Legislative Veto: Invalidated, It Survives." *Law and Contemporary Problems* 56: 288.

Fisher, Louis. 2000. *Congressional Abdication on War and Spending*. College Station: Texas A&M University Press.

Fordham, Benjamin O. 2008. "Economic Interests and Congressional Voting on Security Issues." *Journal of Conflict Resolution* 52: 623–40.

Forgette, Richard G. 2004. "Congressional Party Caucuses and Coordination: Assessing Caucus Activity and Party Effects." *Legislative Studies Quarterly* 29: 407–30.

Fox, Richard L., and Jennifer L. Lawless. 2003. "Family Structure, Sex-Role Socialization, and the Decision to Run for Office," *Women & Politics* 24(4): 19–48.

Fox, Richard L., and Jennifer L. Lawless. 2004. "Entering the Arena? Gender and the Decision to Run for Office." *American Journal of Political Science* 48(2): 264–80.

Fox, Richard L., and Jennifer L. Lawless. 2005. "To Run or Not to Run for Office: Explaining Nascent Political Ambition." *American Journal of Political Science* 49(3): 642–59.

Fox, Richard L., and Jennifer L. Lawless. 2010. "If Only They'd Ask: Gender, Recruitment, and Political Ambition." *Journal of Politics* 72(2): 310–26.

Fox, Richard L., and Jennifer L. Lawless. 2011. "Gaining and Losing Interest in Running for Office: The Concept of Nascent Ambition. *Journal of Politics*, forthcoming.

Fox, Richard L., Jennifer L. Lawless, and Courtney Feeley. 2001. "Gender and the Decision to Run for Office. *Legislative Studies Quarterly* 26(3): 411–35.

Francis, Wayne L. and Lawrence Kenny. 1996. "Position Shifting in Pursuit of Higher Office." *American Journal of Political Science* 40(3): 768–86.

Francis, Wayne L., and Lawrence Kenny. 2000. *Up the Political Ladder: Career Paths in U.S. Politics*. Thousand Oaks, CA: Sage Publications.

Franklin, Daniel Paul. 1986. "Why the Legislative Veto Isn't Dead." *Presidential Studies Quarterly* 16(3): 491–502.

Freeman, J. L. 1955. *The Political Process: Executive Bureau-Legislative Committee Relations*. Garden City, New York: Doubleday.

Freeman, Jo. 1986. "The Political Culture of the Democratic and Republican Parties." *Political Science Quarterly* 101(3): 327–56.

Friedman, John N., and Richard T. Holden. 2009. "The Rising Incumbent Reelection Rate: What's Gerrymandering Got to Do With It?" *Journal of Politics* 71(2): 593–611.

Friel, Brian, and Kerry Young. 2010. "A Trying Relationship." *CQ Weekly*, September 13, pp. 2076–84.

Frisch, Scott A. 1998. *The Politics of Pork: A Study of Congressional Appropriation Earmarks.* New York: Garland Publishing.

Frisch, Scott A., and Sean Q. Kelly. 2006. *Committee Assignment Politics in the U.S. House of Representatives.* Norman: University of Oklahoma Press.

Fulton, Sarah A., Cherie D. Maestas, L. Sandy Maisel, and Walter J. Stone. 2006. "The Sense of a Woman: Gender, Ambition and the Decision to Run for Congress." *Political Research Quarterly* 59(2): 235–48.

Gaddie, Ronald Keith. 2004. *Born to Run: Origins of the Political Career.* Lanham, MD: Rowman & Littlefield.

Gaddie, Keith, and Charles Bullock III. 2000. *Elections to Open Seats in the U.S. House: Where the Action Is.* Lanham, MD: Rowman & Littlefield.

Gailmard, Sean, and Thomas Hammond. N.d. "Intercameral Bargaining and Intracameral Organization in Legislatures." *Journal of Politics*, forthcoming.

Gailmard, Sean, and Jeffery A. Jenkins. 2007. "Negative Agenda Control in the Senate and House: Fingerprints of Majority Party Power." *Journal of Politics* 69: 689–700.

Gailmard, Sean, and Jeffery A. Jenkins. 2009. "Agency Problems, the 17th Amendment, and Representation in the Senate." *American Journal of Political Science* 53: 324–42.

Gais, Thomas. 1996. *Improper Influence: Campaign Finance Law, Political Interest Groups, and the Problem of Equality.* Ann Arbor: The University of Michigan Press.

Gais, Thomas, and Jack Walker, Jr. 1991. "Pathways to Influence in American Politics." In Jack Walker, Jr. (ed.) *Mobilizing Interest Groups in America.* Ann Arbor: University of Michigan Press, pp. 103–21.

Gamm, Gerald, and Kenneth Shepsle. 1989. "Emergence of Legislative Institutions: Standing Committees in the House and Senate, 1810–1825." *Legislative Studies Quarterly* 14: 39–66.

Gamm, Gerald, and Steven S. Smith. 2000. "Last Among Equals: The Presiding Officer of the Senate." In Burdett A. Loomis, (ed.) *Esteemed Colleagues: Civility and Deliberation in the United States Senate.* Washington, DC: Brookings Institution Press.

Gilens, Martin. 2009. "Preference Gaps and Inequality in Representation." *PS: Political Science and Politics* 42: 335–41.

Gilmour, John B. 2002. "Institutional and Individual Influences on the President's Veto." *The Journal of Politics* 64: 198–218.

Gimpel, James G., Frances E. Lee, and Joshua Kaminski. 2006. "The Political Geography of Campaign Contributions in American Politics." *Journal of Politics* 68: 626–39.

Gimpel, James G., Frances E. Lee, and Shanna Pearson-Merkowitz. 2008. "The Check is in the Mail: Interdistrict Funding Flows in Congressional Elections." *American Journal of Political Science* 52: 373–94.

Gold, Martin, and Dimple Gupta. 2005. "The Constitutional Option to Change Senate Rules and Procedures: A Majoritarian Means to Overcome the Filibuster." *Harvard Journal of Law and Public Policy* 28: 205–72.

Golembiewski, R. T. 1960. "'The Group Basis of Politics': Notes on Analysis and Development." *American Political Science Review* 54(4): 962–71.

Goodman, Craig, and Timothy Nokken. 2004. "Lame Duck Legislators and Consideration of the Ship Subsidy Bill of 1922." *American Politics Research* 32: 465–89.

Gordon, Sanford C., and Catherine Hafer. 2007. "Corporate Influence and the Regulatory Mandate." *Journal of Politics* 69: 300–19.

Gordon, Sanford C., and Dimitri Landa. 2009. "Do the Advantages of Incumbency Advantage Incumbents?" *Journal of Politics* 71(4): 1481–98.

Gordon, Sanford C., Gregory A. Huber, and Dimitri Landa. 2007. "Challenger Entry and Voter Learning." *American Political Science Review* 2(May): 303–20.

Gould, Lewis. L. 2005. *The Most Exclusive Club: A History of the Modern United States Senate.* New York: Basic Books.

Grenzke, J. M. 1989. "PACs and the Congressional Supermarket: The Currency is Complex." *American Journal of Political Science* 33(1): 1–24.

Griffin, John D. 2008. "Measuring Legislator Ideology." *Social Science Quarterly* 89: 337–50.

Griffin, John D., and Brian Newman. 2007. "The Unequal Representation of Latinos and Whites." *The Journal of Politics* 69(4): 1032–46.

Griffith, E. S. 1939. *The Impasse of Democracy: A Study of the Modern Government in Action.* New York: Harrison Hilton Books.

Grofman, Bernard, Robert Griffin, and Gregory Berry. 1995. "House Members who Become Senators: Learning from a 'Natural' Experiment." *Legislative Studies Quarterly* 20: 513–29.

Grofman, Bernard, William Koetzle, and Anthony J. McGann. 2002. "Congressional Leadership 1965–96: A New Look at the Extremism versus Centrality Debate." *Legislative Studies Quarterly* 27: 87–105.

Grose, Christian. 2005. "Disentangling Constituency and Legislator Effects in Legislative Representation." *Social Science Quarterly* 86: 427–43.

Grose, Christian R., and Bruce I. Oppenheimer. 2007. "The Iraq War, Partisanship, and Candidate Attributes: Explaining Variation in Partisan Swing in the 2006 House Elections." *Legislative Studies Quarterly* 32: 531–57.

Groseclose, Tim, and Nolan McCarty. 2001. "The Politics of Blame: Bargaining Before an Audience." *American Journal of Political Science* 1: 100–19.

Groseclose, Tim, and Jeffrey Milyo. 2010. "Sincere Versus Sophisticated Voting in Congress: Theory and Evidence," *Journal of Politics* 72: 60–73.

Groseclose, Tim, Steven D. Levitt, and James M. Snyder, Jr. 1999. "Comparing Interest Group Scores across Time and Chambers: Adjusted ADA Scores for the U. S. Congress," *American Political Science Review* 93: 33–50.

Haeberle, Steven H. 1978. "The Institutionalization of the Subcommittee in the United States House of Representatives." *The Journal of Politics* 40(4): 1054–65.

Hager, Gregory L., and Jeffery C. Talbert. 2000. "Look for the Party Label: Party Influences on Voting in the U.S. House." *Legislative Studies Quarterly* 25: 75–99.

Hall, Richard L., and A. V. Deardorff. 2006. "Lobbying as Legislative Subsidy." *American Political Science Review* 100(1): 69–84.

Hall, Richard L., and C. Lawrence Evans. 1990. "The Power of Subcommittees." *The Journal of Politics* 52(2): 335–55.

Hall, Richard L., and Robert Van Houweling. 1994. "Avarice and Ambition: Representatives' Decisions to Run for or Retire from the U.S. House." *American Political Science Review* 89(1): 121–36.

Hall, Richard L., and F. W. Wayman. 1990. "Buying Time: Moneyed Interests and the Mobilization of Bias in Congressional Committees." *American Political Science Review* 84(3): 797–820.

Hansen, J. M. 1991. *Gaining Access: Congress and the Farm Lobby, 1919–1981*. Chicago, IL: The University of Chicago Press.

Harding, Garrett. 1968. "The Tragedy of the Commons." *Science* 162(3859): 1243–8.

Harlow, Ralph Volney. 1917. *The History of Legislative Methods in the Period Before 1825*. New Haven, CT: Yale University Press.

Harris, Ruth. A. 1989. "Politicized Management: The Changing Face of Business in American Politics." In R. A Harris and S. M. Milkis (eds) *Remaking American Politics*. Boulder, CO: Westview Press, pp. 261–86.

Hassan, Ruth A. 2006. "BCRA and the 527 Groups." In Michael Malbin (ed.) *The Election after Reform: Money, Politics, and the Bipartisan Campaign Reform Act*. Lanham, MD: Rowman and Littlefield.

Hatfield, Mark O. 1997. *Vice Presidents of the United States, 1789–1993*. Washington, DC: United States Government Printing Office.

Hayes, M. T. 1981. *Lobbyists and Legislators: A Theory of Political Markets*. New Brunswick, NJ: Rutgers University Press.

Hayes, Matthew, Matthew V. Hibbing, and Tracy Sulkin. 2010. "Redistricting, Responsiveness, and Issue Attention." *Legislative Studies Quarterly* 35: 91–116.

Heaney, M. T. 2004. "Outside the Issue Niche: The Multidimensionality of Interest Group Identity." *American Politics Research* 32(6): 611–51.

Heberlig, Eric S., and Bruce A. Larson. 2007. "Party Fundraising, Descriptive Representation, and the Battle for Majority Control: Shifting Leadership Appointment Strategies in the U.S. House of Representatives, 1990–2002." *Social Science Quarterly* 88(2): 404–21.

Heckman, James J., and James Snyder. 1997. "Linear Probability Models of the Demand for Attributes with an Empirical Application to Estimating the Preferences of Legislators." *Rand Journal of Economics* 28(SI): S142–S189.

Heinz, J. P., E. O. Laumann, R. L. Nelson, and R. H. Salisbury. 1993. *The Hollow Core: Private Interests in National Policy Making*. Cambridge, MA: Harvard University Press.

Hennig, Robert Alan. 1997. "Between the Margins: Party Politics and Committee Power in Conference Committees of the United States House of Representatives." Unpublished doctoral dissertation.

Herndon, J. F. 1982. "Access, Record, and Competition as Influences on Interest Group Contributions to Congressional Campaigns." *Journal of Politics* 44(4): 996–1019.

Hero, Rodney E., and Robert R. Preuhs. 2010. "Black-Latino Political Relationships: Policy Voting in the U.S. House of Representatives." *American Politics Research* 38: 531–62.

Herrick, Rebekah, and Michael K. Moore. 1993. "Political Ambition's Effect on Legislative Behavior: Schlesinger's Typology Reconsidered and Revisited." *Journal of Politics* 55(3): 765–76.

Herring, E. P. 1929. *Group Representation Before Congress*. Baltimore, MD: The Johns Hopkins University Press.

Herrnson, Paul. 1988. *Party Campaigning in the 1980s*. Cambridge, MA: Harvard University Press.

Hersch, Philip L., and Gerald S. McDougall. 1994. "Campaign War Chests as a Barrier to Entry in Congressional Races." *Economic Inquiry* 32(4): 630–41.

Hetherington, Marc J. 1998. "The Political Relevance of Political Trust." *American Political Science Review* 92: 791–808.

Hetherington, Marc J. 1999. "The Effect of Political Trust on the Presidential Vote, 1968–96." *American Political Science Review* 93: 311–26.

Hetherington, Marc J., Bruce Larson, and Suzanne Globetti. 2003. "The Redistricting Cycle and Strategic Candidate Decisions in U.S. House Races." *Journal of Politics* 65(4): 1221–34.

Hibbing, J. R., and C. W. Larimer. 2008. "The American Public's View of Congress." *The Forum* 6(3): Article 6.

Hibbing, John R., and Elizabeth Theiss-Morse. 1995. *Congress as Public Enemy: Public Attitudes Toward American Political Institutions.* New York: Cambridge University Press.

Hinckley, Barbara. 1971. *The Seniority System in Congress.* Bloomington: Indiana University Press.

Hinckley, Barbara. 1976. "Seniority 1975: Old Theories Confront New Facts." *British Journal of Political Science* 6(4): 383–99.

Hinds, Asher. 1907. *Hinds' Precedents of the House of Representatives of the United States.* U.S. Government Printing Office.

Hines, Eric H., and Andrew J. Civettini. 2004. "Strategic Choices and Conference Committee Appointments in the U.S. House, 194th–106th Congresses." Presented at the annual meeting of the Midwest Political Science Association: Chicago, IL April 15–18, 2004.

Hixon, William, and Bryan W. Marshall. 2002. "Examining Claims of Procedural Choice: The Use of Floor Waivers in the U.S. House. *Political Research Quarterly* 55: 923–38.

Hoadley, John F. 1980. "The Emergence of Political Parties in Congress." *American Political Science Review* 74: 757–79.

Hoadley, John F. 1986. *Origins of American Political Parties, 1789–1803.* Lexington: University of Kentucky Press.

Hoff, Samuel B. 1991. "Presidential Support and Veto Use, 1889–1989." *American Politics Quarterly* 19: 310–23.

Hojnacki, M. 1997. "Interest Groups' Decisions to Join Alliances or Work Alone." *American Journal of Political Science* 41(1): 61–87.

Hojnacki, M., and D. C. Kimball. 1998. "Organized Interests and the Decision of Whom to Lobby in Congress." *American Political Science Review* 92(4): 775–90.

Holt, Michael F. 1992. *Political Parties and American Political Development from the Age of Jackson to the Age of Lincoln.* Baton Rouge: Louisiana State University Press.

Holt, Michael F. 1999. *The Rise and Fall of the American Whig Party.* Oxford: Oxford University Press.

Holyoke, T. T. 2003. "Choosing Battlegrounds: Interest Group Lobbying Across Multiple Venues." *Political Research Quarterly* 56(3): 325–36.

Homans, George. 1950. *The Human Group.* New York: Harcourt Brace.

Howell, William G. 2003. *Power Without Persuasion: The Politics of Direct Presidential Action.* Princeton, NJ: Princeton University Press.

Howell, William G. 2005. "Unilateral Powers: A Brief Overview." *Presidential Studies Quarterly* 35(3): 417–39.

Huitt, Ralph. 1961. "Democratic Leadership in the Senate." *American Political Science Review* 55: 331–44.

Hulse, Carl, and Robert Pear. 2009. "Sweeping Health Care Plan Passes House." *New York Times*, November 8.

Hunt, Kasie. 2010. "John McCain, Russ Feingold diverge on Court ruling" *Politico.* January 21.

Ignagni, Joseph, and James Meernik. 1994. "Explaining Congressional Attempts to Reverse Supreme Court Decisions." *Political Research Quarterly* 47(2): 353–71.

Ignagni, Joseph, and James Meernik. 1997. "Judicial Review and Coordinate Construction of the Constitution." *American Journal of Political Science* 41(2): 447–67.

Jackson, Robert A. 1996. "The Mobilization of Congressional Electorates." *Legislative Studies Quarterly* 21: 425–45.

Jacobs, Lawrence R., and Theda Skocpol. 2010. *Health Care Reform and American Politics: What Everyone Needs to Know.* New York: Oxford University Press.

Jacobson, Gary C. 1980. *Money in Congressional Elections.* New Haven, CT: Yale University Press.

Jacobson, Gary C. 1989. "Strategic Politicians and the Dynamics of U.S. House Elections, 1946–86." *American Political Science Review* 83(3): 773–93.

Jacobson, Gary C. 2009. *The Politics of Congressional Elections.* 7th ed. New York: Longman.

Jacobson, Gary C., and Samuel Kernell. 1981. *Strategy and Choice in Congressional Elections.* New Haven, CT: Yale University Press.

Jacobson, Gary C., and Samuel Kernell. 1983. *Strategy and Choice in Congressional Elections.* 2nd ed. New Haven, CT: Yale University Press.

James, Scott C. 2007. "Timing and Sequence in Congressional Elections: Interstate Contagion and America's Nineteenth-Century Scheduling Regime." *Studies in American Political Development* 21: 181–202.

Jameson, J. Franklin, ed. 1900. "'Correspondence of John C. Calhoun,' Annual Report of the American Historical Association for 1899, Volume II." Washington, DC: Government Printing Office.

Jenkins, Jeffery A. 1998. "Property Rights and the Emergence of Standing Committee Dominance in the Nineteenth Century House of Representatives." *Legislative Studies Quarterly* 23: 493–519.

Jenkins, Jeffery A. 1999. "Examining the Bonding Effects of Party: A Comparative Analysis of Roll-Call Voting in the U.S. and Confederate Houses." *American Journal of Political Science* 43: 1144–65.

Jenkins, Jeffery A. 2011. "The Evolution of Party Leadership." In Eric Schickler and Frances E. Lee (eds) *The Oxford Handbook of the American Congress.* Oxford: Oxford University Press.

Jenkins, Jeffery A., and Michael C. Munger. 2003. "Investigating the Incidence of Killer Amendments in Congress." *Journal of Politics* 65: 498–517.

Jenkins, Jeffery A., and Timothy P. Nokken. 2008. "Legislative Shirking in the Pre-Twentieth Amendment Era: Presidential Influence, Party Power, and Lame-Duck Sessions of Congress, 1877–1933." *Studies in American Political Development* 22: 111–40.

Jenkins, Jeffery A., and Brian R. Sala. 1998. "The Spatial Theory of Voting and the Presidential Election of 1824." *American Journal of Political Science* 42: 1157–79.

Jenkins, Jeffery A., and Charles Stewart III. 1997. "Order from Chaos: The Transformation of the Committee System in the House, 1816–1822." Paper presented at the annual meeting of the American Political Science Association, Washington, DC.

Jenkins, Jeffery A., and Charles Stewart III. 2002. "Order from Chaos: The Transformation of the Committee System in the House, 1816–1822." In David W. Brady and

Mathew D. McCubbins (eds) *Party, Process, and Political Change in Congress: New Perspectives on the History of Congress.* Stanford, CA: Stanford University Press.

Jenkins, Jeffery A., and Charles Stewart III. 2003. "Out in the Open: The Emergence of *Viva Voce* Voting in House Speakership Elections." *Legislative Studies Quarterly* 28: 481–508.

Jenkins, Jeffery A., Justin Peck, and Vesla M. Weaver. 2010. "Between Reconstructions: Congressional Action on Civil Rights, 1891–1940." *Studies in American Political Development* 24: 57–89.

Jessee, Stephen, and Neil Malhotra. 2010. "Are Congressional Leaders Middle Persons or Extremists? Yes." *Legislative Studies Quarterly* 35: 361–92.

Johnson, Ronald N., and Gary D. Libecap. 1994. *The Federal Civil Service System and the Problem of Bureaucracy: The Economics and Politics of Institutional Change.* Chicago, IL: University of Chicago Press.

Johnson, Timothy R., and Jason M. Roberts. 2005. "Pivotal Politics, Presidential Capital, and Supreme Court Nominations." *Congress and the Presidency* 32(Spring): 31–48.

Jones, David R. 2003. "Position Taking and Position Avoidance in the U.S.Senate." *Journal of Politics* 65(3): 851–63.

Jones, David R., and Monika L. McDermott. 2004. "The Responsible Party Government Model in House and Senate Elections." *American Journal of Political Science* 48: 1–12.

Jones, David R., and Monika L. McDermott. 2009. *Americans, Congress, and Democratic Responsiveness: Public Evaluations of Congress and Electoral Consequences.* Ann Arbor: The University of Michigan Press.

Kahane, Leo H. 1996. "Senate Voting Patterns on the 1991 Extension of the Fast-Track Trade Procedures: Prelude to NAFTA." *Public Choice* 87: 35–53.

Kanter, Arnold. 1972. "Congress and the Defense Budget: 1960–1970." *American Political Science Review* 66(1): 129–43.

Kanthak, Kristin, and Rebecca B. Morton. 2001. "The Effects of Primary Systems on Congressional Elections." In Peter Galderisi and Mike Lyons (eds) *Congressional Primaries and the Politics of Representation.* Lanham, MD: Rowman and Littlefield.

Katznelson, Ira, and John S. Lapinksi. 2006. "At the Crossroads: Congress and American Political Development." *Perspectives on Politics* 4: 243–60.

Kazee, Thomas A. 1980. "The Decision to Run for the U.S. Congress: Challenger Attitudes in the 1970s." *Legislative Studies Quarterly* 5(1): 79–100.

Kazee, Thomas A., and Mary C. Thornberry. 1990. "Where's the Party? Congressional Candidate Recruitment and American Party Organization." *Western Political Quarterly* 43: 61–80.

Keith, Robert. 2008. "Introduction to the Federal Budget Process." CRS Report for Congress 98–721.

Kelley, Christopher S. 2003. "The Unitary Executive and the Presidential Signing Statement." Unpublished dissertation. Miami University. http://www.ohiolink.edu/etd/view.cgi?acc_num=miami1057716977.

Kelley, Christopher S. 2007. "Contextualizing the Signing Statement." *Presidential Studies Quarterly* 37(4): 737–48.

Kelley, Christopher S., and Bryan W. Marshall. 2008. "The Last Word: Presidential Power and the Role of Signing Statements." *Presidential Studies Quarterly* 38: 248–67.

Kelley, Christopher S., and Bryan W. Marshall. 2009. "Assessing Presidential Power:

Veto Politics and Signing Statements as Coordinated Strategies." *American Politics Research* 37(May): 508–33.

Kelley, Christopher S., and Bryan W. Marshall. 2010. "Going it Alone: The Politics of Signing Statements from Reagan to Bush II." *Social Science Quarterly* 91(1): 168–87.

Kernell, Samuel. 1977a. "Toward Understanding 19th Century Congressional Careers: Ambition, Competition, and Rotation." *American Journal of Political Science* 21: 669–93.

Kernell, Samuel. 1977b. "Presidential Popularity and Negative Voting: An Alternative Explanation of the Midterm Congressional Decline of the President's Party." *American Political Science Review* 71(1): 44–66.

Kernell, Samuel. 1986. *Going Public: New Strategies of Presidential Leadership.* Washington, DC: CQ Press.

Kernell, Samuel, ed. 2005. *Statements of Administration Policy, 99th–108th Congresses.* Washington, DC: CQ Press.

Kernell, Samuel. 2007. *Going Public: New Strategies of Presidential Leadership.* 4th ed. Washington, DC: CQ Press.

Kersh, Rogan. 2002. "Corporate Lobbyists as Political Actors: A View from the Field." In A. J. Cigler and B. A. Loomis (eds) *Interest Group Politics.* 6th ed. Washington, DC: CQ Press, pp. 225–48.

Kersh, Rogan. 2006. "Lobbyists and the Provision of Political Information." In Burdett Loomis and Allan Cigler (eds) *Interest Group Politics.* 7th ed. Washington, DC: CQ Press.

Key, V. O. 1949. *Southern Politics in State and Nation.* New York: Vintage Books.

Kiewiet, D. Roderick, and Langche Zeng. 1993. "An Analysis of Congressional Career Decisions, 1947–86." *American Political Science Review* 87: 928–41.

Kiewiet, D. Roderick, and Mathew D. McCubbins. 1985. "Congressional Appropriations and the Electoral Connection." *Journal of Politics* 47: 59–82.

Kiewiet, D. Roderick, and Mathew D. McCubbins. 1991. *The Logic of Delegation: Congressional Parties and the Appropriations Process.* Chicago, IL: University of Chicago Press.

King, David C., and Richard J. Zeckhauser. 2003. "Congressional Vote Options." *Legislative Studies Quarterly* 28: 387–411.

Kingdon, John W. 1989. *Congressmen's Voting Decisions.* Ann Arbor: University of Michigan Press.

Koger, Gregory. 2010. *Filibustering: A Political History of Obstruction in the House and Senate.* Chicago, IL: University of Chicago Press.

Kollman, K. 1998. *Outside Lobbying: Public Opinion and Interest Group Strategies.* Princeton, NJ: Princeton University Press.

Kolodny, Robin. 1998. *Pursuing Majorities: Congressional Campaign Committees in American Politics.* Norman: University of Oklahoma Press.

Kousser, Thad. 2005. *Term Limits and the Dismantling of State Legislative Professionalism.* Cambridge: Cambridge University Press.

Krasno, Jonathan N., and Donald Phillip Green. 1988. "Preempting Quality Challengers in House Elections." *Journal of Politics* 50(4): 920–36.

Krehbiel, Keith. 1988. "Spatial Models of Legislative Choice." *Legislative Studies Quarterly* 13: 259–319.

Krehbiel, Keith. 1990. "Are Congressional Committees Composed of Preference Outliers?" *American Political Science Review* 84(1): 149–63.

Krehbiel, Keith. 1991. *Information and Legislative Organization*. Ann Arbor: The University of Michigan Press.

Krehbiel, Keith. 1993. "Where's the Party?" *British Journal of Political Science* 23: 235–66.

Krehbiel, Keith. 1998. *Pivotal Politics: A Theory of U.S. Lawmaking*. Chicago, IL: Chicago University Press.

Krehbiel, Keith. 1999. "Paradoxes of Parties in Congress." *Legislative Studies Quarterly* 24: 31–64.

Krehbiel, Keith. 2000. "Party Discipline and Measures of Partisanship." *American Journal of Political Science* 44: 212–27.

Krehbiel, Keith. 2006. "Macropolitics and Micromodels: Cartels and Pivots Reconsidered." In E. S. Adler and J.S. Lapinski (eds) *The Macropolitics of Congress*. Princeton, NJ: Princeton University Press.

Krehbiel, Keith, and Adam Meirowitz. 2002. "Minority Rights and Majority Power: Theoretical Consequences of the Motion to Recommit." *Legislative Studies Quarterly* 27(2): 191–218.

Krehbiel, Keith, and Alan Wiseman. 2001. "Joseph G. Cannon: Majoritarian from Illinois." *Legislative Studies Quarterly* 26: 357–89.

Krehbiel, Keith, Kenneth A. Shepsle, and Barry R. Weingast. 1987. "Why Are Congressional Committees Powerful?" *The American Political Science Review* 81(3): 929–45.

Krutz, Glen S. and Jeffrey Peake. 2010. *Treaty Politics and the Rise of Executive Agreements*. Ann Arbor, MI: University of Michigan Press.

Krutz, Glen S., Richard Fleisher, and Jon R. Bond. 1998. "From Abe Fortas to Zoe Baird: Why Some Presidential Nominations Fail in the Senate." *American Political Science Review* 92(4): 871–81.

Ladewig, Jeffrey. 2010. "Ideological Polarization and the Vanishing Marginals: Retrospective Roll-Call Voting in the U.S. Congress." *Journal of Politics* 72: 499–512.

Lake, Jennifer, and Ralph Chite. 2005. "Emergency Supplemental Appropriations for Hurricane Katrina Relief." CRS Report for Congress RS22239.

Langbein, L. I. 1986. "Money and Access: Some Empirical Evidence." *Journal of Politics* 48(4): 1052–62.

Langbein, L. I. 1993. "PACs, Lobbies and Political Conflict: The Case of Gun Control." *Public Choice* 77(3): 551–72.

Lapinski, John S. 2008. "Policy Substance and Performance in American Lawmaking, 1877–1894." *American Journal of Political Science* 52: 235–51.

Latham, E. 1952. *The Group Basis of Politics: A Study in Basing-Point Legislation*. Ithaca, NY: Cornell University Press.

Lawless, Jennifer L., and Richard L. Fox. 2005. *It Takes a Candidate: Why Women Don't Run for Office*. Cambridge: Cambridge University Press.

Lawless, Jennifer L., and Richard L. Fox. 2010. *It Still Takes a Candidate: Why Women Don't Run for Office*. Cambridge: Cambridge University Press.

Lawrence, Eric D., Forrest Maltzman, and Steven S. Smith. 2006. "Who Wins? Party Effects in Legislative Voting." *Legislative Studies Quarterly* 31: 33–69.

Lawrence, Eric D., Forrest Maltzman, and Paul J. Wahlbeck. 2001. "The Politics of Speaker Cannon's Committee Assignments." *American Journal of Political Science* 45: 551–62.

Lazarus, Jeffrey. 2006. "The Multiple Effects of Term Limits on State Legislators' Career Decisions." *State Politics and Policy Quarterly* 6: 357–83.

Lazarus, Jeffrey. 2008. "Buying In: Testing the Rational Model of Candidate Entry." *Journal of Politics* 70: 837–50.

Lazarus, Jeffrey, and Nathan Monroe. 2007. "The Speaker's Discretion: Conference Committee Appointments in the 97th through 106th Congresses." *Political Research Quarterly* 60(4): 593–606.

Lazarus, Jeffrey, and Shauna Reilly. 2010. "The Electoral Benefits of Distributive Spending." *Political Research Quarterly* 63: 343–55.

Lee, David S., Enrico Moretti, and Matthew Butler. 2004. "Do Voters Affect or Elect Policies? Evidence from the U.S. House." *Quarterly Journal of Economics* 119(3): 807–59.

Lee, Francis E. 2000. "Senate Representation and Coalition Building in Distributive Politics." *American Political Science Review* 94: 59–72.

Lee, Frances E. 2009. *Beyond Ideology: Politics, Principles, and Partisanship in the U.S. Senate*. Chicago, IL: University of Chicago Press.

Lee, Francis E., and Bruce I. Oppenheimer. 1999. *Sizing Up the Senate: The Unequal Consequences of Equal Representation*. Chicago, IL: University of Chicago Press.

Leighton, Wayne A., and Edward J. Lopez. 2002. "Committee Assignments and the Cost of Party Loyalty." *Political Research Quarterly* 55: 59–90.

Levendusky, Matthew. 2009. *The Partisan Sort: How Liberals Became Democrats and Conservatives Became Republicans*. Chicago, IL: University of Chicago Press.

Levitt, Steven. 1996. "How Do Senators Vote? Disentangling the Role of Voter Preferences, Party Affiliation, and Senator Ideology." *The American Economic Review* 86: 425–41.

Levitt, Steven D., and James M. Snyder, Jr. 1995. "Political Parties and the Distribution of Federal Outlays." *American Journal of Political Science* 39: 958–80.

Levmore, Saul. 1992. "Bicameralism: When Are Two Decisions Better Than One?" *International Review of Law and Economics* 12: 145–62.

Levy, Dena, and Peverill Squire. 2000. "Television Markets and the Competitiveness of House Elections." *Legislative Studies Quarterly* 45(2): 313–25.

Liptak, Adam. 2010. "Former Justice O'Connor Sees Ill in Election Finance Ruling." *The New York Times*, January 26.

Longley, Lawrence D., and Walter J. Oleszek. 1989. *Bicameral Politics: Conference Committees in Congress*. New Haven, CT: Yale University Press.

Lowery, D., and H. Brasher. 2004. *Organized Interests and American Government*. New York: McGraw-Hill.

Lowi, Theodore J. 1969. *The End of Liberalism: Ideology, Policy, and the Crisis of Public Authority*. 1st ed. New York: Norton.

Lublin, David. 1994. "Quality, Not Quantity: Strategic Politicians in U.S. Senate Elections, 1952–1990," *Journal of Politics* 56: 228–41.

Luo, Michael. 2010. "Spending by Interest Groups Drives G.O.P. Lead in Ads." *The New York Times*, September 13.

Lupia, Arthur, and Gisela Sin. 2007. "How the President and Senate Affect the Balance of Power in the House: A Constitutional Theory of Legislative Bargaining." Manuscript.

Lynch, Michael, and Anthony J. Madonna. 2008. "Viva Voce: Implications of the Disappearing Voice Vote." Paper presented to the annual meeting of the Midwest Political Science Association.

Lynch, Michael S., and Anthony Madonna. 2009. "The Vice President in the U.S. Senate:

Examining the Consequences of Institutional Design." Paper presented at the University of Georgia American Political Development Working Group.

Lynch, Michael S., Anthony J. Madonna, and Jason M. Roberts. 2010. "The Majority Party and the Rules Committee: Bargaining over Chamber Procedure." Paper presented at the Annual Meeting of the Southern Political Science Association, Atlanta GA.

Maass, A. 1951. *Muddy Waters: The Army Engineers and the Nation's Rivers.* Cambridge, MA: Harvard University Press.

Maddox, H. W. J. 2004. "Opportunity Costs and Outside Careers in US State Legislatures." *Legislative Studies Quarterly* 29(4): 517–44.

Madonna, Anthony J. 2011. "Winning Coalition Formation in the U.S. Senate: The Effects of Legislative Decision Rules and Agenda Change." *American Journal of Political Science* 55(2): 276–288.

Maestas, Cherie. 2000. "Professional Legislatures and Ambitious Politicians: Policy Responsiveness of Individuals and Institutions." *Legislative Studies Quarterly* 25(4): 663–90.

Maestas, Cherie. 2003. "The Incentive to Listen: Progressive Ambition, Resources and Opinion Monitoring among State Legislators." *Journal of Politics* 65(2): 439–56.

Maestas, Cherie D., and Cynthia Rugeley. 2008. "Reassessing the Experience Bonus: Candidate Quality and Campaign Receipts in U.S. House Elections." *American Journal of Political Science* 52(3): 520–35.

Maestas, Cherie D., L. Sandy Maisel, and Walter J. Stone. 2005. "National Party Efforts to Recruit State Legislators to Run for the U.S. House." *Legislative Studies Quarterly* 2: 277–300.

Maestas, Cherie, Sarah A. Fulton, L. Sandy Maisel, and Walter J. Stone. 2006. "When to Risk It? Institutions, Ambitions, and the Decision to Run for the U.S. House." *American Political Science Review* 100(2): 195–208.

Magleby, Daniel B. 2008. "Pretended Legislation: Explaining the Frequency and Impact of Congressional Conference Committees." Paper presented at the Conference on Bicameralism, Vanderbilt University.

Magleby, D. B., and C. J. Nelson. 1990. *The Money Chase: Congressional Campaign Finance Reform.* Washington, DC: Brookings Institution Press.

Maisel, L. Sandy. 2001. *Parties and Elections in America: The Electoral Process.* Lanham, MD: Rowman and Littlefield.

Maisel, L. Sandy, and Walter J. Stone. 1997. "Determinants of Candidate Emergence in U.S. House Elections: An Explanatory Study." *Legislative Studies Quarterly* 22(1): 79–96.

Maisel, L. Sandy, Cherie Maestas, and Walter J. Stone. 2002. "The Party Role in Congressional Competition." In L. Sandy Maisel (ed.) *The Parties Respond,* 4th ed. Boulder, CO: Westview.

Malbin, Michael. 2003. *Life After Reform: When the Bipartisan Campaign Reform Act Meets Politics.* Lanham, MD: Rowman and Littlefield.

Manley, John F. 1965. "The House Committee on Ways and Means: Conflict Management in a Congressional Committee." *The American Political Science Review* 59(4): 927–39.

Manley, John F. 1969. "Wilbur D. Mills: A Study in Congressional Influence." *The American Political Science Review* 63(2):442–64.

Manley, John F. 1970. *The Politics of Finance: The House Committee on Ways and Means.* Boston, MA: Little, Brown.

Mann, Thomas E., and Norman J. Ornstein. 2006. *The Broken Branch: How Congress is Failing America and How to Get it Back on Track*. New York: Oxford University Press.

Mann, Thomas E., and Raymond E. Wolfinger. 1980. "Candidates and Parties in Congressional Elections." *American Political Science Review* 74: 617–32.

Marshall, Bryan W. 2002. "Explaining the Role of Restrictive Rules in the Postreform House." *Legislative Studies Quarterly* 27: 61–85.

Marshall, Bryan W. 2005. *Rules for War: Procedural Choice in the U.S. House of Representatives*. Burlington, VT: Ashgate Publishing.

Marshall, Bryan W., and Patrick J. Haney. 2010. "Aiding and Abetting: Congressional Complicity in the Rise of the Unitary Executive." In Ryan J. Barilleaux and Christopher S. Kelley (eds) *The Unitary Executive and the Modern Presidency*. College Station: Texas A&M University Press, pp. 188–216.

Marshall, Bryan W., and Brandon C. Prins. 2007. "Strategic Position Taking and Presidential Influence in Congress." *Legislative Studies Quarterly* 32: 257–84.

Martin, Andrew D., and Kevin M. Quinn. 2002. "Dynamic Ideal Point Estimation via Markov Chain Monte Carlo for the U.S. Supreme Court, 1953–1999." *Political Analysis* 10: 134–53.

Martin, Lisa L. 2005. "The President and International Commitments: Treaties as Signaling Devices." *Presidential Studies Quarterly* 35: 440–65.

Martinek, Wendy, Mark Kemper, and Steve Van Winkle. 2002. "To Advise and Consent: The Senate and Lower Federal Court Nominations, 1977–1998." *Journal of Politics* 64: 337–61.

Martis, Kenneth C. 1982. *The Historical Atlas of United States Congressional Districts, 1789–1983*. New York: Free Press.

Martis, Kenneth C. 1989. *Historical Atlas of Political Parties in the United States Congress, 1789–1989*. New York: Macmillan.

Masters, Nicholas A. 1961. Committee Assignments in the House of Representatives. *The American Political Science Review* 55(2): 345–57.

Matthews, Donald R. 1959. The Folkways of the United States Senate: Conformity to Group Norms and Legislative Effectiveness. *The American Political Science Review* 53(4): 1064–89.

Matthews, Donald R. 1960. *U.S. Senators and Their World*. Chapel Hill: University of North Carolina Press.

Matthews, Steven A. 1989. "Veto Threats: Rhetoric in a Bargaining Game." *Quarterly Journal of Economics* 104: 347–69.

Mayer, Kenneth R. 2001. *With the Stroke of a Pen: Executive Orders and Presidential Power*. Princeton, NJ: Princeton University Press.

Mayer, Kenneth R. 2009. "Thoughts on the Revolution in Presidential Studies." *Presidential Studies Quarterly* 39(4): 781–5.

Mayhew, David R. 1974a. *Congress: The Electoral Connection*. New Haven, CT: Yale University Press.

Mayhew, David R. 1974b. "Congressional Elections: The Case of the Vanishing Marginals." *Polity* 6(3): 295–317.

Mayhew, David R. 2005. *Divided We Govern: Party Control, Lawmaking and Investigations, 1946–2002*. 2nd ed. New Haven, CT: Yale University Press.

McCarty, Nolan. 2004. "The Appointments Dilemma." *American Journal of Political Science*, 48(3): 413–28.

McCarty, Nolan, and Lawrence Rothenberg. 1996. "Commitment and the Campaign Contribution Contract." *American Journal of Political Science* 40: 872–904.

McCarty, Nolan, Keith T. Poole, and Howard Rosenthal. 1997. *Income Redistribution and the Realignment of American Politics.* Washington, DC: AEI Press.

McCarty, Nolan, Keith T. Poole, and Howard Rosenthal. 2001. "The Hunt for Party Discipline in Congress." *American Political Science Review* 95: 673–88.

McCarty, Nolan, Keith T. Poole and Howard Rosenthal. 2006. *Polarized America: The Dance of Ideology and Unequal Riches.* Cambridge, MA: The MIT Press.

McCown, Ada C. 1927. *The Congressional Conference Committee.* New York: Columbia University Press.

McDermott, Monika L., and David R. Jones. 2005. "Congressional Performance, Incumbent Behavior, and Voting in Senate Elections." *Legislative Studies Quarterly* 30: 235–57.

McQuillan, Lawrence J., and Lydia D. Ortega. 1992. "Conference Committee Participation and Party Loyalty." *Public Choice* 64(4): 485–94.

Meernik, James, and Elizabeth Oldmixon. 2008. "The President, Senate, and the Costs of Internationalism." *Foreign Policy Analysis* 4: 187–206.

Meinke, Scott R. 2005. "Long-term Change and Stability in House Voting Decisions: The Case of the Minimum Wage." *Legislative Studies Quarterly* 30: 103–26.

Meinke, Scott R. 2007. "Slavery, Partisanship, and Procedure: The Gag Rule, 1836–1845." *Legislative Studies Quarterly* 32: 33–57.

Meinke, Scott R. 2008a. "Who Whips? Party Government and the Expansion of House Whip Networks." *American Politics Research* 36: 639–68.

Meinke, Scott R. 2008b. "Institutional Change and the Electoral Connection in the Senate: Revisiting the Effects of Direct Election." *Political Research Quarterly* 61: 445–57.

Meirowitz, Adam, and Keith Krehbiel. 2002. "Power and the Motion to Recommit." *Legislative Studies Quarterly* 27: 191–218.

Milbrath, L. W. 1963. *The Washington Lobbyists.* Chicago, IL: Rand McNally.

Miller, Susan M., and L. Marvin Overby. 2010. "Parties, Preferences, and Petitions: Discharge Behavior in the Modern House." *Legislative Studies Quarterly* 35: 187–210.

Miller, Warren E., and Donald E. Stokes. 1963. "Constituency Influence in Congress." *American Political Science Review* 57: 45–57.

Moe, Terry M. 1985. "The Politicized Presidency." In John E. Chubb and Paul E. Peterson (eds) *The New Direction in American Politics.* Washington, DC: Brookings Institution Press.

Moe, Terry M. 2009. "The Revolution in Presidential Studies." *Presidential Studies Quarterly* 39(4): 701–24.

Moe, Terry M., and William G. Howell. 1999. "Unilateral Action and Presidential Power: A Theory." *Presidential Studies Quarterly* 29(4): 850–73.

Moncrief, Gary F. 1999. "Recruitment and Retention in U.S. Legislatures." *Legislative Studies Quarterly* 24: 173–208.

Moncrief, Gary F., Peverill Squire, and Malcolm E. Jewell. 2001. *Who Runs for the Legislature?* Upper Saddle River, NJ: Prentice Hall.

Mondak, Jeffrey J. 1995. "Competence, Integrity, and the Electoral Success of Congressional Incumbents." *Journal of Politics* 57: 1043–69.

Monroe, Nathan W., and Gregory Robinson. 2008. "Do Restrictive Rules Produce Non-Median Outcomes? A Theory with Evidence from the 101st–108th Congresses." *Journal of Politics* 70: 217–31.

Monroe, Nathan W., Jason M. Roberts, and David W. Rohde, eds. 2008. *Why Not Parties? Party Effects in the United States Senate*. Chicago, IL: University of Chicago Press.

Moraski, Byron J., and Charles R. Shipan. 1999. "The Politics of Supreme Court Nominations: A Theory of Institutional Constraints and Choices." *American Journal of Political Science* 43(4): 1069–95.

Morrow, James D. 1994. *Game Theory for Political Scientists*. Princeton, NJ: Princeton University Press.

Murphy, Chad, and Antoine Yoshinaka. 2009. "Are Mapmakers Able to Target and Protect Congressional Incumbents? The Institutional Dynamics of Electoral Competition." *American Politics Research* 37(6): 955–82.

Nagler, Jonathan. 1989. "Strategic Implications of Conferee Selection in the House of Representatives." *American Politics Quarterly* 17: 54–79.

Nathan, Richard P. 1983. *The Administrative Presidency*. New York: Wiley.

Nelson, Garrison, and Charles Stewart III. 2010. *Committees in the U.S. Congress, 1993–2010*. Washington, DC: CQ Press.

Neustadt, Richard E. 1954. "Presidency and Legislation: The Growth of Central Clearance." *American Political Science Review* 4: 641–71.

Neustadt, Richard E. 1962. *Presidential Power: The Politics of Leadership*. New York: John Wiley & Sons, Inc.

Neustadtl, A. 1990. "Interest-Group PACsmanship: An Analysis of Campaign Contributions, Issue Visibility, and Legislative Impact." *Social Forces* 69(2): 549–64.

Niskanen, William A. 1971. *Bureaucracy and Representative Government*. Chicago, IL: Aldine, Atherton.

Nixon, David, and David Goss. 2001. "Confirmation Delay for Vacancies on the Circuit Courts of Appeals." *American Politics Research* 29: 246–74.

Nokken, Timothy. 2000. "Dynamics of Congressional Loyalty: Party Defection and Roll Call Behavior, 1947–1997." *Legislative Studies Quarterly* 25: 417–44.

Nownes, A. J. 2000. *Pressure and Power: Organized Interests in American Politics*. Boston, MA: Houghton Mifflin.

Nownes, A. J. 2006. *Total Lobbying: What Lobbyists Want (and How They Try to Get It)*. New York: Cambridge University Press.

O'Connor, Patrick. 2009. "GOP Protests Term Limit Change." *Politico*. January 5. Available at: http://www.politico.com/news/stories/0109/17043.html. Last accessed November 18, 2010.

O'Halloran, Sharyn. 1994. *Politics, Process, and American Trade Policy*. Ann Arbor: University of Michigan Press.

Oleszek, Walter J. 2007. *Congressional Procedures and the Policy Process*. 7th ed. Washington, DC: CQ Press.

Oleszek, Walter J. 2008. "Whither the Role of Conference Committees: An Analysis", edited by Congressional Research Service. Washington, DC: CQ Press.

Oppenheimer, Bruce I. 2005. "Deep Red and Blue Congressional Districts: The Causes and Consequences of Declining Party Competitiveness." In Lawrence C. Dodd and Bruce I. Oppenheimer (eds) *Congress Reconsidered*. Washington, DC: CQ Press, pp. 135–58.

Oppenheimer, Bruce I., James A. Stimson, and Richard W. Waterman. 1986. "Interpreting U.S. Congressional Elections: The Exposure Thesis." *Legislative Studies Quarterly* 11(2): 227–47.

Ornstein, Norman J. 1975. "Causes and Consequences of Congressional Change: Sub-committee Reforms in the House of Representatives, 1970–73." In N. J. Ornstein (ed.) *Congress in Change: Evolution in reform.* New York: Praeger Publishers.

Ornstein, Norman J., Thomas E. Mann, and Michael J. Malbin. 2008. *Vital Statistics on Congress, 2008.* Washington, DC: Brookings Institution Press.

Orren, Karen, and Stephen Skowronek. 2004. *The Search for American Political Development.* Cambridge: Cambridge University Press.

Ortega, Lydia D., and Lawrence J. McQuillan. 1992. "Conference Committee Participation and Party Loyalty." *Public Choice* 74(4): 485–94.

Ortega, Lydia D., and Lawrence J. McQuillan. 1996. "Why Does the Senate 'Win' in Conference Committee?: A Stability Explanation." *Public Choice* 87: 101–16.

Owens, John E. 1997. "The Return of Party Government in the U.S. House of Representatives: Central Leadership-Committee Relations in the 104th Congress." *British Journal of Political Science* 27(2): 247–72.

Paddock, Joel. 1992. "Inter-Party Ideological Differences in Eleven State Parties: 1956–1980." *The Western Political Quarterly* 45(3): 751–60.

Palmer, Anna. 2010. "Neal, Levin Still Vying for Top Slot on Ways and Means." *Roll Call,* November 9.

Palmer, Anna, and Tory Newmyer. 2010. "Race for Ways and Means Gavel Heats Up on K Street." *Roll Call,* April 28.

Parsons, Stanley B., William W. Beach, and Michael J. Dubin. 1986. *United States Congressional Districts and Data, 1843–1883.* New York: Greenwood.

Parsons, Stanley B., Michael J. Dubin, and Karen Toombs Parsons. 1990. *United States Congressional Districts and Data, 1883–1913.* New York: Greenwood.

Parsons, Talcott, and Edward Shils. 1951. *Toward a General Theory of Action.* Cambridge, MA: Harvard University Press.

Patty, John W. 2010. "Dilatory or Anticipatory? Voting on the Journal in the House of Representatives." *Public Choice* 143: 121–33.

Peabody, Robert L. 1963. "The Enlarged Rules Committee." In R. L. Peabody and N. W. Polsby (eds) *New Perspectives on the House of Representatives.* Chicago, IL: Rand-McNally.

Peabody, Robert L. 1976. *Leadership in Congress: Stability, Succession, and Change.* Boston, MA: Little, Brown.

Pfiffner, James P. 2009. "Presidential Signing Statements and Their Implications for Public Administration." *Public Administration Review,* March/April: 249–55.

Pitkin, Hannah Fenichel. 1967. *The Concept of Representation.* Berkeley: University of California Press.

Poage, George Rawlings. 1936. *Henry Clay and the Whig Party.* Chapel Hill: University of North Carolina Press.

Polsby, Nelson W. 1968. "The Institutionalization of the U.S. House of Representatives." *The American Political Science Review* 62(1): 144–68.

Polsby, Nelson W. 1975. "Legislatures." In F. I. Greenstein and N. W. Polsby (eds) *The Handbook of Political Science.* Reading, MA: Addison-Wesley.

Polsby, Nelson W., and Eric Schickler. 2002. "Landmarks in the Study of Congress since 1945." *Annual Review of Political Science* 5: 333–67.

Polsby, Nelson W., Miriam Gallaher, and Barry Spencer Rundquist. 1969. "The Growth of the Seniority System in the U.S. House of Representatives." *American Political Science Review* 63(3): 787–807.

Poole, Keith T., and Howard Rosenthal. 1997. *Congress: A Political-Economic History of Roll Call Voting.* Oxford: Oxford University Press.

Powell, Richard J. 2000. "The Impact of Term Limits on the Candidacy Decisions of State Legislators in U.S. House Elections." *Legislative Studies Quarterly* 25(4): 645–61.

Pressman, Jeffrey L. 1966. *House vs. Senate: Conflict in the Appropriations Process.* New Haven, CT: Yale University Press.

Ragusa, Jordan M. 2009. "Coordination and Partisanship in Modern Conference Committees." Paper presented at the Bicameralism Conference at Duke University, Durham, NC.

Ramirez, Mark D. 2009. "The Dynamics of Partisan Conflict on Congressional Approval." *American Journal of Political Science* 53(3): 681–94.

Remini, Robert V. 1991. *Henry Clay: Statesman for the Union.* New York: W.W. Norton & Company, Inc.

Reynolds, John Francis. 2006. *The Demise of the American Convention System, 1880–1911.* New York: Cambridge University Press.

Riker, William H. 1980. Implications from the Disequilibrium of Majority Rule for the Study of Institutions. *The American Political Science Review* 74(2):432–46.

Ripley, Randall. 1969. *Power in the Senate.* New York: St. Martin's Press.

Roberts, Jason M. 2005. "Minority Rights and Majority Power: Conditional Party Government and the Motion to Recommit in the House, 1909–2000." *Legislative Studies Quarterly* 30: 219–34.

Roberts, Jason M. 2007. "The Statistical Analysis of Roll-Call Data: A Cautionary Tale." *Legislative Studies Quarterly* 32: 341–60.

Roberts, Jason M. 2010. "The Development of Special Orders and Special Rules in the U.S. House, 1881–1937." *Legislative Studies Quarterly* 35: 307–36.

Roberts, Jason M., and Lauren Cohen Bell. 2008. "Scoring the Senate: Scorecards, Parties, and Roll-Call Votes." In Nathan W. Monroe, Jason M. Roberts, and David W. Rohde (eds) *Why Not Parties? Party Effects in the United States Senate.* Chicago, IL: University of Chicago Press.

Roberts, Jason M., and Steven S. Smith. 2003. "Procedural Contexts, Party Strategy, and Conditional Party Voting in the U.S. House of Representatives, 1971–2000." *American Journal of Political Science* 47(2): 305–17.

Roberts, Jason M., and Steven S. Smith. 2007. "The Evolution of Agenda-Setting Institutions in Congress: Path Dependency in the House and Senate Institutional Development." In David W. Brady, and Mathew D. McCubbins (eds) *Party, Process, and Political Change in Congress: Further New Perspectives on the History of Congress, Volume II.* Stanford, CA: Stanford University Press, pp. 182–204.

Roberts, Jason M., Steven S. Smith, and Stephen R. Haptonstahl. 2008. "The Dimensionality of Congressional Voting Reconsidered." Paper presented at the annual meeting of the American Political Science Association, Boston, MA.

Robinson, James A. 1963. *The House Rules Committee.* Indianapolis, IN: Bobbs-Merrill.

Rohde, David W. 1974. "Committee Reform in the House of Representatives and the Subcommittee Bill of Rights." *Annals of the American Academy of Political and Social Science* 411: 39–47.

Rohde, David, W. 1979. "Risk Bearing and Progressive Ambition: The Case of Members of the United States House of Representatives." *American Journal of Political Science* 23(1): 1–26.

Rohde, David W. 1991. *Parties and Leaders in the Postreform House.* Chicago, IL: University of Chicago Press.

Rohde, David W. 1994. "Parties and Committees in the House: Member Motivations, Issues, and Institutional Arrangements." *Legislative Studies Quarterly* 19: 341–61.

Rohde, David W., and Kenneth A. Shepsle. 1978. "Thinking About Legislative Reform." In Leroy N. Rieselbach (ed.) *Legislative Reform: The Policy Impact.* Lexington, MA: Lexington Books.

Rohde, David W., and Dennis M. Simon. 1985. "Presidential Vetoes and Congressional Response: A Study of Institutional Conflict." *American Journal of Political Science* 29: 397–427.

Rohde, David W., and Harold J. Spaeth. 1976. *Supreme Court Decision Making.* San Francisco, CA: Freeman.

Rothenberg, Lawrence S. 1992. *Linking Citizens to Government: Interest Group Politics at Common Cause.* New York: Cambridge University Press.

Rothenberg, Lawrence S., and Mitchell Sanders. 1999. "Rational Abstention and the Congressional Vote Choice." *Economics and Politics* 11: 311–40.

Rottinghaus, Brandon, and Jason Maier. 2007. "The Power of Decree: Presidential Use of Executive Proclamations, 1977–2005." *Political Research Quarterly* 60(2): 338–43.

Rozell, M. J., C. Wilcox, and D. Madland. 2006. *Interest Groups in American Campaigns: The New Face of Electioneering.* 2nd ed. Washington, DC: CQ Press.

Rubin, Richard. 2010. "An Ever Thicker Dividing Line." *CQ Weekly*, January 11, pp. 122–5.

Ruckman, P. S., Jr. 1993. "The Supreme Court, Critical Nominations, and the Senate Confirmation Process." *Journal of Politics* 55: 793–805.

Rudalevige, Andrew. 2002. *Managing the President's Program: Presidential Leadership and Legislative Policy Formulation.* Princeton, NJ: Princeton University Press.

Rudalevige, Andrew. 2009. "The Administrative Presidency and Bureaucratic Control: Implementing a Research Agenda." *Presidential Studies Quarterly* 39(1): 10–24.

Rusk, Jerrold G. 1970. "The Effect of the Australian Ballot Reform on Split Ticket Voting: 1876–1908." *American Political Science Review* 64(Dec.): 1220–38.

Rutkus, Denis S., and Mitchel A. Sollenberger. 2004. "Judicial Nomination Statistics: U.S. District and Circuit Courts, 1977–2003." *CRS Report for Congress.*

Ryan, Josh M. 2011. "The Disappearing Conference Committee: The Use of Procedures by Minority Coalitions to Prevent Conferencing." *Congress & the Presidency* 38(1): 101–25.

Rybicki, Elizabeth. 2003. "Unresolved Differences: Bicameral Negotiations in Congress, 1877–2002." Paper prepared for the History of Congress Conference, University of California San Diego, December 5–6, 2003.

Rybicki, Elizabeth. 2005. "Conference Committee and Related Procedures: An Introduction." *CRS Report for Congress* RS22239.

Rybicki, Elizabeth. 2007. "Senate Rules Changes in the 110th Congress Affecting Restrictions on the Content of Conference Reports." *CRS Report for Congress* RS22733.

Rybicki, Elizabeth. 2008. "Resolving Legislative Differences in Congress: Conference Committees and Amendments Between the Houses." *CRS Report*, Order Code 98-696 GOV.

Salisbury, R. H. 1990. "The Paradox of Interest Groups in Washington—More Groups, Less Clout." In A. King (ed.) *The New American Political System*, 2nd version. Washington, DC: The AEI Press, pp. 203–29.

Saltzman, G. M. 1987. "Congressional Voting on Labor Issues: The Role of PACs." *Industrial and Labor Relations Review* 40(2): 163–79.

Sanbonmatsu, Kira. 2002. "Political Parties and the Recruitment of Women to State Legislatures." *Journal of Politics* 64(3): 791–809.

Sanders, Elizabeth. 1999. *Roots of Reform: Farmers, Workers and the American State.* Chicago, IL: University of Chicago Press.

Schickler, Eric. 2000. "Institutional Change in the House of Representatives: A Test of Partisan and Ideological Power Balance Models." *American Political Science Review* 94: 269–88.

Schickler, Eric. 2001. *Disjointed Pluralism: Institutional Innovation and the Development of the U.S. Congress.* Princeton, NJ: Princeton University Press.

Schickler, Eric, and Kathryn Pearson. 2009. "Agenda Control, Majority Party Power, and the House Committee on Rules, 1937–1952." *Legislative Studies Quarterly* 34: 455–92.

Schickler, Eric, John M. Sides, and Eric McGhee. 2003. "Remaking the House and Senate: Personal Power, Ideology, and the 1970s Reforms." *Legislative Studies Quarterly* 28: 297–333.

Schickler, Eric, Kathryn Pearson, and Brian D. Feinstein. 2010. "Congressional Parties and Civil Rights Politics from 1933 to 1972." *Journal of Politics* 72: 672–89.

Schiller, Wendy J. 2006. "Building Careers and Courting Constituents: U.S. Senate Representation 1889–1924." *Studies in American Political Development* 20: 185–97.

Schiller, Wendy, and Charles Stewart III. 2004. "U.S. Senate Elections before 1914." Paper presented at the annual meeting of the Midwest Political Science Association, Chicago, IL.

Schiller, Wendy, and Charles Stewart III. 2006. "Challenging the Myths of 19th Century Party Dominance: Evidence from Indirect Senate Elections 1871–1913." Paper presented at the annual meeting of the Congress and History Conference, Yale University.

Schiller, Wendy, and Charles Stewart III. 2008. "Party Loyalty and the Election of U.S. Senators, 1871–1913." Paper presented at the annual meeting of the Midwest Political Science Association, Chicago, IL.

Schlesinger, Joseph A. 1966. *Ambition and Politics: Political Careers in the United States.* Chicago, IL: Rand McNally and Co.

Schlozman, K. L., and J. T. Tierney. 1983. "More of the Same: Washington Pressure Group Activity in a Decade of Change." *Journal of Politics* 45(2): 351–77.

Schriftgiesser, K. 1951. *The Lobbyists: The Art and Business of Influencing Lawmakers.* Boston, MA: Little, Brown.

Seager, Robert, and Melba Porter Hay, eds. 1988. *The Papers of Henry Clay.* Volume IX. Lexington: University Press of Kentucky.

Sellers, Patrick J. 1997. "Fiscal Consistency and Federal District Spending in Congressional Elections." *American Journal of Political Science* 41: 1024–41.

Shanks, Henry Thomas, ed. 1953. *The Papers of Willie Person Mangum.* Volume III. Raleigh, NC: State Department of Archives and History.

Shepsle, Kenneth A. 1979. "Institutional Arrangements and Equilibrium in Multidimensional Voting." *American Journal of Political Science* 23: 27–60.

Shepsle, Kenneth A. 1989. "Studying Institutions: Some Lessons from the Rational Choice Approach." *Journal of Theoretical Politics* 1: 131–47.

Shepsle, Kenneth A., and Barry R. Weingast. 1981. "Structure-induced Equilibrium and Legislative Choice." *Public Choice* 37(3): 503–19.

Shepsle, Kenneth A., and Barry R. Weingast. 1987. "The Institutional Foundations of Committee Power." *American Political Science Review* 81(1): 85–104.

Shepsle, Kenneth A., and Barry R. Weingast. 1995. *Theories of Congressional Institutions.* Ann Arbor: University of Michigan Press.

Silbey, Joel H. 1985. The Partisan Imperative: The Dynamics of American Politics before the Civil War. New York: Oxford University Press.

Sinclair, Barbara. 1983. *Majority Leadership in the U.S. House.* Baltimore, MD: Johns Hopkins University Press.

Sinclair, Barbara. 1989. *The Transformation of the U.S. Senate.* Baltimore, MD: Johns Hopkins University Press.

Sinclair, Barbara. 1995. *Legislators, Leaders, and Lawmaking: The U.S. House of Representatives in the Postreform Era.* Baltimore, MD: Johns Hopkins University Press.

Sinclair, Barbara. 2000. "Hostile Partners: The President, Congress, and Lawmaking in the Partisan 1990s." In Jon R. Bond, and Richard Fleisher (eds) *Polarized Politics: Congress and the President in a Partisan Era.* Washington, DC: CQ Press.

Sinclair, Barbara. 2006. *Party Wars: Polarization and the Politics of National Policy Making.* Norman: University of Oklahoma Press.

Sinclair, Barbara. 2007. *Unorthodox Lawmaking: New Legislative Processes in the U.S. Congress.* 3rd ed. Washington, DC: CQ Press.

Skinner, Richard M. 2007. *More than Money. Interest Group Action in Congressional Elections.* Lanham, MD: Rowman Littlefield.

Skowronek, Stephen. 1982. *Building a New American State: The Expansion of National Administrative Capacities, 1877–1920.* Cambridge: Cambridge University Press.

Smith, Lauren Edwards, Laura R. Olson, and Jeffrey A. Fine. 2010. "Substantive Religious Representation in the U.S. Senate: Voting Alignment with the Family Research Council." *Political Research Quarterly* 63: 68–82.

Smith, M. A. 2000. *American Business and Political Power: Public Opinion, Elections, and Democracy.* Chicago, IL: The University of Chicago Press.

Smith, R. A. 1995. "Interest Group Influence in the U.S. Congress." *Legislative Studies Quarterly* 20(1): 89–139.

Smith, Steven S. 1989. *Call to Order: Floor Politics in the House and Senate.* Washington, DC: Brookings Institution Press.

Smith, Steven S. 2007. *Party Influence in Congress.* Cambridge: Cambridge University Press.

Smith, Steven S., and Marcus Flathman. 1989. "Managing the Senate Floor: Complex Unanimous Consent Agreements Since the 1950s." *Legislative Studies Quarterly* 14: 349–74.

Smith, Steven S., and Eric D. Lawrence. 1997. "Party Control of Committees in the Republican Congress." In L. C. Dodd and B. I. Oppenheimer (eds) *Congress Reconsidered.* Washington, DC: CQ Press.

Smith, Steven S., Jason M. Roberts, and Ryan J. Vander Wielen. 2009. *The American Congress.* 6th ed. New York: Cambridge University Press.

Snyder, James M., Jr., and Tim Groseclose. 2000. "Estimating Party Influence in Congressional Roll Call Voting." *American Journal of Political Science* 44: 193–211.

Sorauf, Frank J. 1992. *Inside Campaign Finance.* New Haven, CT: Yale University Press.

Squire, Peverill. 1989. "Competition and Uncontested Seats in U.S. House Elections." *Legislative Studies Quarterly* 14(2): 281–95.

Squire, Peverill. 1992. "Challenger Quality and Voting Behavior in U.S. Senate Elections." *Legislative Studies Quarterly* 17: 247–64.

Squire, Peverill, and John R. Wright. 1990. "Fundraising by Non-incumbent Candidates for the U.S. House of Representatives." *Legislative Studies Quarterly* 15: 89–98.

Steen, Jennifer A. 2006. *Self-Financed Candidates in Congressional Elections.* Ann Arbor: University of Michigan Press.

Stein, Robert M., and Kenneth Bickers. 1994. "Universalism and the Electoral Connection: A Test and Some Doubts." *Political Research Quarterly* 47: 295–317.

Steiner, Gilbert Yale. 1951. *The Congressional Conference Committee: Seventieth to Eightieth Congresses.* Urbana: University of Illinois Press.

Stewart III, Charles. 1989. *Budget Reform Politics: The Design of the Appropriations Process in the House of Representatives, 1865–1921.* Cambridge: Cambridge University Press.

Stimson, James A., Michael B. MacKuen, and Robert S. Erikson. 1995. "Dynamic Representation." *American Political Science Review* 89: 543–65.

Stokes, Donald. 1967. "Parties and the Nationalization of Electoral Forces." In William Nisbet Chambers and Walter Dean Burnham (eds) *The American Party System: Stages of Political Development.* New York: Oxford University Press.

Stone, Walter J., and L. Sandy Maisel. 2003. "The Not-So-Simple Calculus of Winning: Potential U.S. House Candidates' Nomination and General Election Prospects." *Journal of Politics* 65(4): 951–77.

Stone, Walter J., and Elizabeth N. Simas. 2010. "Candidate Valence and Ideological Positions in U.S. House Elections." *American Journal of Political Science* 54(2): 371–88.

Stone, Walter J., L. Sandy Maisel, and Cherie Maestas. 2004. "Quality Counts: Extending the Strategic Politician Model of Incumbent Deterrence." *American Journal of Political Science* 48(3): 479–95.

Stone, Walter J., Sarah A. Fulton, Cherie Maestas, and L. Sandy Maisel. 2010. "Incumbency Reconsidered: Prospects, Strategic Retirement, and Incumbent Quality in U.S. House Elections." *Journal of Politics* 72(1): 178–90.

Story, Joseph. 1833. *Commentaries on the Constitution of the United States.* Boston, MA: Hilliard, Gray and Company.

Streeter, Sandy. 2008. "Earmark Reform: Comparison of New House and Senate." CRS Report for Congress RL34462.

Strom, G.S., and B.S. Rundquist. 1977. "A Revised Theory of Winning in House Senate Conferences." *American Political Science Review* 71(June): 448–53.

Sulkin, Tracy. 2009. "Campaign Appeals and Legislative Action." *Journal of Politics.* 71: 1093–1108.

Summers, Mark W. 2004. *Party Games: Getting, Keeping, and Using Power in Gilded Age Politics.* Chapel Hill: University of North Carolina Press.

Swift, Elaine K. 1996. *The Making of an American Senate: Reconstitutive Change in Congress, 1787–1841.* Ann Arbor: University of Michigan Press.

Taylor, Andrew J. 2008. "Strategic Intercameral Behavior and the Sequence of Congressional Lawmaking." *American Politics Research* 36: 451–74.

Theriault, Sean M. 1998. "Moving Up or Moving Out: Career Ceilings and Congressional Retirement." *Legislative Studies Quarterly* 23(3): 419–33.

Theriault, Sean M. 2003. "Patronage, the Pendleton Act, and the Power of the People." *Journal of Politics* 65: 50–68.

Theriault, Sean M. 2006. "Party Polarization in the U.S. Congress: Member Replacement and Member Adaptation." *Party Politics* 12(4): 483–503.

Theriault, Sean M. 2008. *Party Polarization in Congress*. New York: Cambridge University Press.

Tiefer, Charles. 1989. *Congressional Practice and Procedure*. New York: Greenwood Press.

Toobin, Jeffrey. 2010. "Without a Paddle: Can Stephen Breyer save the Obama Agenda in the Supreme Court?" *The New Yorker*, September 27, pp. 34–41.

Tripathi, M., S. Ansolabehere, and J. M. Snyder, Jr. 2002. "Are PAC Contributions and Lobbying Linked? New Evidence from the 1995 Lobby Disclosure Act." *Business and Politics* 4(2): Article 2.

Truman, D. B. 1951. *The Governmental Process: Political Interests and Public Opinion*. New York: Knopf.

Truman, D. B. 1959. *The Congressional Party: A Case Study*. New York: Wiley.

Tufte, Edward R. 1973. "The Relationship Between Seats and Votes in Two-Party Systems." *American Political Science Review* 67(2): 540–54.

Tulis, Jeffrey K. 1987. *The Rhetorical Presidency*. Princeton, NJ: Princeton University Press.

Tullock, Gordon. 1981. "Why So Much Stability?" *Public Choice* 37(2): 189–204.

Uslaner, Eric M. 1998. "Let the Chits Fall Where They May? Executive and Constituency Influences on Congressional Voting on NAFTA." *Legislative Studies Quarterly* 23: 347–71.

Van Beek, Stephen D. 1995. *Post Passage Politics: Bicameral Resolution in Congress*. Pittsburgh: University of Pittsburgh Press.

Van Houweling, Robert P. 2007. "An Evolving End Game: The Partisan Use of Conference Committees, 1953–2003." In David Brady and Mathew McCubbins (eds) *Process, Party and Policy Making: Further New Perspectives on the History of Congress*. Stanford, CA: Stanford University Press.

Vander Wielen, Ryan J. 2010a. "Why Conference Committees?: A Policy Explanation for the Use of Conference." Unpublished Paper.

Vander Wielen, Ryan J. 2010b. "The Influence of Conference Committees on Policy Outcomes." *Legislative Studies Quarterly* 35(4): 487–518.

Vander Wielen, Ryan J., and Steven S. Smith. n.d. "Majority Party Bias in U.S. Congressional Conference Committees." Unpublished Manuscript.

Verba, Sidney. 2003. "Would the Dream of Political Equality Turn Out to be a Nightmare?" *Perspectives on Politics* 1663–79.

Vogler, David J. 1970. "Patterns of One House Dominance in Congressional Conference Committees." *Midwest Journal of Political Science* 14(2): 303–20.

Vogler, David J. 1971. *The Third House: Conference Committees in the United States Congress*. Chicago, IL: Northwestern University Press.

Volden, Craig, and Elizabeth Bergman. 2006. "How Strong Should Our Party Be? Party Member Preferences over Party Cohesion." *Legislative Studies Quarterly* 31: 71–104.

Walker, J. L., Jr. 1991. *Mobilizing Interest Groups in America: Patrons, Professions, and Social Movements*. Ann Arbor: The University of Michigan Press.

Wand, Jonathan N., Kenneth W. Shotts, Jasjeet S. Sekhon, Walter R. Mebane, Jr., Michael C. Herron, and Henry E. Brady. 2001. "The Butterfly Did It: The Aberrant Vote for Buchanan in Palm Beach County, Florida." *American Political Science Review* 95(4): 793–810.

Ware, Alan. 2000. "Anti-Partyism and Party Control of Political Reform in the United States: The Case of the Australian Ballot." *British Journal of Political Science* 30(1): 1–29.

Ware, Alan. 2002. *The American Direct Primary: Party Institutionalization and Transformation in the North*. New York: Cambridge University Press.

Waterman, Richard W. 1989. *Presidential Influence and the Administrative State*. Knoxville: University of Tennessee Press.

Waterman, Richard W. 2009. "The Administrative Presidency, Unilateral Power, and the Unitary Executive Theory." *Presidential Studies Quarterly* 39(1): 5–9.

Watson, Richard A. 1993. *Presidential Vetoes and Public Policy*. Lawrence: University Press of Kansas.

Wawro, Gregory. G. 2001. "A Panel Probit Analysis of Campaign Contributions and Roll-Call Votes." *American Journal of Political Science* 45(31): 563–79.

Wawro, Gregory, and Eric Schickler. 2004. "Where's the Pivot? Obstruction and Law-making in the Pre-cloture Senate." *American Journal of Political Science* 48(4): 758–74.

Wawro, Gregory, and Eric Schickler. 2006. *Filibuster: Obstruction and Lawmaking in the U.S. Senate*. Princeton, NJ: Princeton University Press.

Wawro, Gregory, and Eric Schickler. 2010. "Legislative Obstructionism." *Annual Review of Political Science* 13: 297–319.

Weingast, Barry R. 1979. "A Rational Choice Perspective on Congressional Norms." *American Journal of Political Science* 23: 245–63.

Weingast, Barry R., and William Marshall. 1988. "The Industrial Organization of Congress." *Journal of Political Economy* 91: 132–63.

Welch, Susan, and John R. Hibbing. 1997. "The Effects of Charges of Corruption on Voting Behavior in Congressional Elections, 1982–1990." *Journal of Politics* 59: 226–39.

Wilkerson, John D. 1999. "'Killer Amendments' in Congress." *American Political Science Review* 93: 535–52.

Wilson, Woodrow. 1936[1885]. *Congressional Government: A Study in American Politics*. New York: Riverside Press.

Wiltse, Charles M., and Harold D. Moser, eds. 1982. *The Papers of Daniel Webster*. Volume V. London: University Press of New England.

Wiseman, Alan E. 2004. "Tests of Vote-Buyer Theories of Coalition Formation in Legislatures." *Political Research Quarterly* 57: 441–50.

Witko, C. 2006. "PACs, Issue Context, and Congressional Decisionmaking." *Political Research Quarterly* 59(2): 283–95.

Wolak, Jennifer. 2007. "Strategic Retirements: The Influence of Public Preferences on Voluntary Departures from Congress." *Legislative Studies Quarterly* 32(2): 285–308.

Wolfensberger, Donald. 2007. "The Motion to Recommit in the House: The Creation, Evisceration, and Restoration of a Minority Right." In David W. Brady, and Mathew D. McCubbins (eds) *Party, Process, and Political Change: Further New Perspectives on the History of Congress*. Volume 2. Stanford, CA: Stanford University Press, pp. 271–95.

Wright, J. R. 1985. "PACs, Contributions, and Roll Calls: An Organizational Perspective." *American Political Science Review* 79(2): 400–14.

Wright, J. R. 1989. "PAC Contributions, Lobbying, and Representation." *Journal of Politics* 51(3): 713–29.

Wright, J. R. 1990. "Contributions, Lobbying, and Committee Voting in the U.S. House of Representatives." *American Political Science Review* 84(2): 417–38.

Wright, J. R. 1996. *Interest Groups and Congress: Lobbying, Contributions, and Influence.* Boston, MA: Allyn and Bacon.

Xie, Tao. 2006. "Congressional Roll-Call Voting on China Trade Policy." *American Politics Research* 34: 732–58.

Yearley, Clifton K. 1970. *The Money Machines: The Breakdown and Reform of Governmental and Party Finance in the North, 1860–1920.* Albany: State University of New York Press.

Young, Garry, and Vicky Wilkins. 2007. "Vote Switchers and Party Influence in the U.S. House," *Legislative Studies Quarterly* 32: 59–77.

Young, James Sterling. 1966. *The Washington Community, 1800–1828.* New York: Columbia University Press.

Zaller, John. 1998. "Politicians as Prize Fighters: Electoral Selection and the Incumbency Advantage." In John G. Geer (ed.) *Politicians and Party Politic.* New York: Palgrave Macmillan, pp. 125–85.

Zeller, Shawn. 2010. "Historic Success, At No Small Cost." *CQ Weekly*, January 11, pp. 112–15.

# Index